Critical Issues in Teaching Social Studies
K–12

Critical Issues
in Teaching Social Studies
K–12

BYRON G. MASSIALAS   **RODNEY F. ALLEN**

Florida State University

Wadsworth Publishing Company

I(T)P® An International Thomson Publishing Company

Belmont • Albany • Bonn • Boston • Cincinnati • Detroit • London • Madrid • Melbourne •
Mexico City • New York • Paris • San Francisco • Singapore • Tokyo • Toronto • Washington

Education Editor: Sabra Horne
Assistant Editor: Claire Masson
Editorial Assistant: Louise Mendelson
Production Services Coordinator: Debby Kramer
Production: Robin Gold/Forbes Mill Press
Print Buyer: Karen Hunt
Permission Editor: Jeanne Bosschart
Copy Editor: Robin Gold
Illustrator: Rachel Allen
Text Designer: Robin Gold
Cover Designer: Cassandra Chu
Compositor: Wolf Creek Press
Printer: Malloy Lithographing, Inc.

Printed in the United States of America
1 2 3 4 5 6 7 8 9 10

For more information, contact Wadsworth Publishing Company:

Wadsworth Publishing Company
10 Davis Drive
Belmont, California 94002, USA

International Thomson Publishing Europe
Berkshire House 168-173
High Holborn
London, WC1V 7AA, England

Thomas Nelson Australia
102 Dodds Street
South Melbourne 3205
Victoria, Australia

Nelson Canada
1120 Birchmount Road
Scarborough, Ontario
Canada M1K 5G4

International Thomson Editores
Campos Eliseos 385, Piso 7
Col. Polanco
11560 México D.F. México

International Thomson Publishing GmbH
Königswinterer Strasse 418
53227 Bonn, Germany

International Thomson Publishing Asia
221 Henderson Road
#05-10 Henderson Building
Singapore 0315

International Thomson Publishing Japan
Hirakawacho Kyowa Building, 3F
2-2-1 Hirakawacho
Chiyoda-ku, Tokyo 102, Japan

Library of Congress Cataloging-in-Publication Data
Critical issues in teaching social studies, K to 12 / [edited by]
  Byron G. Massialas, Rodney F. Allen.
       p.   cm.
    New ed. of: Crucial issues in the teaching of social studies.
  1964.
    Includes bibliographical references (p.).
    ISBN: 0-534-19752-3
    1. Social sciences—Study and teaching—United States.
  I. Massialas, Byron G.   II. Allen, Rodney F.
  III. Massialas, Byron G.   Crucial issues in the teaching
  social studies.
LB1584.C716   1996   95-41210
300'.71--dc20

CONTENTS

 # PREFACE

IN LATE SUMMER, 1964, Byron G. Massialas' and Andreas M. Kazamias' *Crucial Issues in the Teaching of Social Studies: A Book of Readings* was published. Today that volume is an interesting historic document—interesting for what it reveals about the constant, enduring issues of social studies teaching and learning and for what form those issues took three decades earlier. Professors and teachers grappled over the reasons for teaching social studies and the goals to be achieved. Curriculum leaders and their colleagues debated the most appropriate organization of the social-studies curriculum, a debate mainly cast in terms of teaching separate academic disciplines or providing integrated, thematic courses in grades K to 12. Was the purpose of social studies to have learners master "content" as an end in itself, or should teachers use questions to engage learners in reflective inquiry with an emphasis upon challenging their conventional thinking and upon developing decision-making skills? The controversial issues that some educators thought should have been studied in classrooms included religion, sex education, and Communism. To safeguard the rights of everyone, the authors made the case for needing a written school policy on the study of such issues.

After three decades, the context of social studies in schooling has changed and the societal occasion for debate on particular issues has also changed, but fundamental issues about social education and social studies for citizenship education have endured. In this book the arguments continue about just what social studies is and how it should be defined. What are its goals? Why not history and geography courses instead of "social studies?" If we are educating students for life in a democratic society, what should this mean for the context of such education—the classroom, its organization, decision making, and authority structure? Is there a "hidden curriculum" in schooling that needs to be uncovered, revealed, and made explicit for reflective analysis by teachers and learners in social studies?

Although Communism no longer seems a threat in our time, student achievement does. Issues endure over motivation for achievement, especially regarding appropriate definitions of "achievement" in our society, and social education, as well as over the nature of the democratic classroom and appropriate motivational strategies. Are our students mainly to master content from teachers and texts, or should they be engaged in critical thinking? If the latter, which methods are effective and democratically appropriate? Additional societal steam is generated over the place of values and value development in social studies curricula and classrooms. Should social studies teachers stand for anything other than ethical neutrality? Should the curriculum overtly seek to change or direct students' value commitments? In the global village, should teachers, texts, and curricula set out to provide other perspectives on events and issues than those considered the standard, conventional perceptions of mainline American society? What is the proper place of the global community and multiculturalism in American social studies?

Today, school testing and accountability are far greater concerns to authorities than in the 1960s. Is the evaluation of student performance simply to yield formative data for students, so they might learn and improve their performance, or is such "testing" for grading, sorting, and comparison? Beyond issues of testing and standards for assessment, new issues have arisen as society has changed. What is the place of multicultural education within the social education of children and youth? Should learners with disabilities be mainstreamed into the social studies classrooms, and should their needs and concerns be integrated into the courses of study in social studies? How should social studies curriculum and teaching respond to our understanding of gender issues and concern for gender equity in a pluralistic, democratic society?

The technology of "computers" raises equity issues of another sort, as well as a plethora of educational questions about their incorporation into democratic citizen education within social studies. Do new technologies tend to make private and individual an enterprise that must be group-oriented and social? Do these technologies foster drill and mastery of mandated content or offer endless opportunities for data collection and analysis, including simulations of socio-political behaviors and historical and cultural archives? But, alas, even with new peoples amongst us and with new technologies to assist us, we have the enduring issue of academic freedom. What can social studies, and its teachers and texts, do in challenging convention, in raising questions about social assumptions, and in fostering issues-oriented social participation?

The chapters in this volume provide beginning and experienced teachers of social studies the means to think systematically and reflectively on these questions and others that are fundamental to our profession. Each chapter identifies critical issues in an important social studies topic and raises more questions than it provides answers. The intent of the contributing authors is to engage the readers into productive discussions of these issues as they go about their jobs of providing the classroom conditions under which children and youth learn how the socio-political system operates and the role of citizens in it. If eventually the issues raised in this book reach the classroom, the main purpose of the book will have been accomplished.

It should be noted that the selection of issues to be analyzed goes hand in hand with the *Curriculum Standards for the Social Studies: Expectation for Excellence* (1994) released by a Task force of The National Council for the Social Studies. The contributing authors explicitly or implicitly are in agreement with the NCSS's statement that "the primary purpose of social studies is to help young people develop the ability to make informed and reasoned decisions for the public good as citizens of a culturally diverse, democratic society in an interdependent world" (Standards, p. vii). The ten themes proposed by the NCSS Task Force—which include cultural diversity, global concerns, technology, student development and identity, and civic ideals and practices—coincide with many topics and issues analyzed by the contributing authors. Hopefully both of these books will generate the needed incentive for the profession to go beyond rhetoric and engage in an open dialogue about professional challenges and priorities for the social studies.

Today we have many indications of a revival of social studies as an instructional field. The very nature of persistent, complex issues makes inevitable the demand for social studies educators at all levels of schooling to address these issues and provide, in community with others, an appropriate civic education for all children and youth. In this manner, we will not only fulfill our professional obligations, we will better profess the intellectual values and community commitments inherent in our calling—the vocation of the social studies educator.

We thank those who reviewed the manuscript and provided helpful suggestions to make this a better book: Mohammed Farouk, Florida International University; Terry Whealon, Northern Illinois University; Virginia S. Wilson, Duke University; Randall R. Butler, Northern Arizona University; and Keith Barton, Northern Kentucky University.

Byron G. Massialas
Rodney F. Allen
Tallahassee, Florida

A Note to Reflective Readers

With each of the following chapters, the authors provide a text with complete academic citations to document their treatment of the issues. In addition to these sources, the authors offer an annotated bibliography for additional reading and reflection. Each author provides a few reflective questions about the issues in his or her chapter, so that you will have one more tool to assess your own grasp of the issues and your progress in thinking about these issues. A glossary at the end of each chapter provides the authors' definitions of key terms, as they were used.

CONTRIBUTORS

Rodney F. Allen is Professor of Social Science Education in the Department of Educational Theory and Practice at Florida State University, Tallahassee. A former teacher in the public schools of the State of Delaware, he has been active in the education and continuing development of classroom teachers in the United States and abroad. His specialities include classroom practice and curriculum development in social studies education, with emphasis upon the role of history and geography in the civic education of children, youth, and adults.

Argy Araboglou holds degrees from Northeastern University in Chicago and from Florida State University. She has served as a bilingual teacher and science instructor in the Illinois and Florida public schools. Currently she is serving as a teacher in the Broward County (FL) public schools where she has the opportunity to apply theories of learning and instruction to the multicultural classroom. She has conducted in-service training workshops on basic skills in the United States and abroad. She is interested in interdisciplinary curriculum development and in hands-on instruction focusing on concepts and activities that connect science, social studies, and the humanities.

Leslie Rebecca Bloom is an Associate Professor of Curriculum and Instruction at Iowa State University in Ames, Iowa. She received her doctorate in Curriculum Studies in Indiana University. She teaches courses in curriculum theory, qualitative research methodologies, and secondary education. Her research focuses on multiculturalism and on feminist methodology and interpretive practices for understanding narrative data.

Charles K. Curtis is Associate Professor of Social and Educational Studies and Coordinator of the Social Studies Program in the Teacher Education Program, The University of British Columbia. He received the doctorate in Special Education from Utah State University. Before accepting a position in the Faculty of Education, he taught special education classes in high schools in the Greater Vancouver area. He has developed programs for teaching civil rights to persons with mental handicaps, as well as serving as an advisor to local and provincial advocacy groups of mentally handicapped adults.

Anna M. Evans is Assistant Professor of Social Studies and Global Education, Florida International University. She received her doctorate from Iowa State University in international/global education policy development. She taught at the State University of New York, Fredonia, before joining the faculty at Florida International in 1991. Her specialties are cultural geography and intercultural education.

James Leming is currently professor of education at Southern Illinois University where he is, among other things, the coordinator of the graduate program in social studies education. He holds degrees from the University of Illinois and the University of Wisconsin. Over the past 30 years he has been active as either a teacher of social studies or as a researcher and author in the fields of moral education and social studies education. His primary research interests are the contribution of schools to the moral, social, and political development of youth.

Wilma S. Longstreet is Professor of Curriculum and Instruction at the University of New Orleans. She has been Dean of Education at DePaul University and at the University of New Orleans. Dr. Longstreet has a long list of publications including *Curriculum for a New Millennium* (co-authored with

Dr. Harold G. Shane), *Aspects of Ethnicity,* and *A Design for Social Education in the Open Classroom* (co-authored with Dr. Shirley H. Engle). Since 1985, she has been editor of the *Louisiana Journal for the Social Studies.* She has served on numerous publications boards including *Educational Forum, International Journal for the Social Studies,* and *Educational Leadership.* Her current research interests include issues-oriented social education for democratic citizenship and for equal opportunity. She continues to stress participant research with her doctoral students and is currently working on a handbook for action research.

Byron G. Massialas is Professor of Education at Florida State University in Tallahassee. He served as high-school instructor in Indiana and Illinois and was on the faculties of the University of Chicago and the University of Michigan before his appointment at FSU. He has conducted research and written extensively on inquiry teaching and reflective thinking, on social issues instruction, and on international education. His most recent publications as author or co-author include *Florida City and County Government: A Teacher Handbook for the High School Level* (1991); *Arab Education in Transition* (1991); and *Core Skills for Training Teachers in Jordan: A Handbook* (1992). He is currently involved with projects on multicultural/multilingual education.

Frances E. Monteverde received her bachelor's degree from Indiana University of Pennsylvania and her master's degree from the Overseas Graduate Program of the University of Alabama, Tuscaloosa. She studied Latin American History at the University of New Mexico and taught social studies at an Albuquerque public high school. For more than twenty years, she lived in Mexico City where she served as teacher, department chairperson, and administrator at the American School Foundation, A.C. Ms. Monteverde conducted study-tour courses to the People's Republic of China in 1984 and 1987. Ms. Monteverde is a doctoral candidate and teaching assistant in Curriculum and Instruction at The University of Texas, Austin. Her research focuses on the rhetoric of critical thinking during World War II and the treatment of foreign cultures in U.S. schoolbooks. She is interested in the promotion of global education and intercultural understanding.

Jack L. Nelson is Professor II (University equivalent of Distinguished Professor) at Rutgers University, where he has taught since 1968. His academic background includes a B.A. from the University of Denver, M.A. from California State University at Los Angeles, and Ed.D. from the University of

Southern California. He taught in the public schools of Riverside, California, and on the faculties of California State University, Los Angeles, State University of New York at Buffalo, and San Jose State University. In addition, he has been a visiting scholar at Cambridge University, Curtin University in Australia, University of Colorado, University of California at Berkeley, and Stanford University. He served as book editor for *Social Education,* founding editor of *Social Science Record,* editor of *Theory and Research in Social Education,* and was the founding chair of the College and University Faculty Assembly of the National Council for Social Studies. As a scholar, Professor Nelson has published 16 books and about 150 articles and reviews in a variety of journals, among his recent books is *Critical Issues in Education* with K. Carlson and S. Palonsky (1993, McGraw-Hill), and *Secondary Social Studies* with J. Michaelis (1980, Prentice-Hall).

Anna S. Ochoa is a Professor of Education at Indiana University in Bloomington, Indiana. She has taught social studies at the elementary, junior high, and secondary levels for thirteen years. She received the bachelor's degree at Wayne State University, the master's degree in history at the University of Michigan, and the Ph.D. in Curriculum (Social Studies) at the University of Washington. She is a past president of the National Council for the Social Studies.

Ron H. Pahl is currently the Coordinator of Secondary Social Studies Teacher Education at the California State University, Fullerton. He is a veteran of 15 years of secondary-school teaching and administration in Botswana, Africa, and the United States. He coordinated the early stages of development for the K to 12 Botswana Social Studies Programme and co-authored the Social Studies Framework for the State of Maryland. He is currently an Executive Editor of *The Social Studies* and has won national awards for his work in computer education and social studies.

James P. Shaver is Professor of Secondary Education, and Dean of the School of Graduate Studies, Utah State University, Logan. He has taught at the junior high and high school levels. In 1976, he was President of the National Council for the Social Studies. His numerous books and articles include materials for students, research reports, and discussions of research philosophy, rationale-building, and rationales for social studies.

Jo Ann Cutler Sweeney received her bachelor's, master's, and Ph.D. degrees from the University of Michigan. Her Ph.D. is in social-science research and social-studies education, K to 12. She is currently the chairwoman of the

Department of Curriculum and Instruction and professor at The University of Texas at Austin. She has published numerous articles and contributed to books in the area of social studies education and economic education. She currently serves as Director of the Advancement of Economic Education Project, affiliated with Economics America. Dr. Sweeney has cross-cultural curriculum development experience in several foreign nations, and her research interests include economic education, cross-cultural and comparative education, and social studies education.

Jan L. Tucker is Professor of Social Studies Education and Director of the Global Awareness Program, Florida International University. He taught social studies in the secondary schools of Indiana for 10 years and has been a member of the faculties of Indiana University, Stanford University, and Florida International University. He is a former president of the National Council for the Social Studies and has written extensively on social studies, global education, and teacher education.

Ronald L. VanSickle is Professor of Social Science Education at The University of Georgia where he works with preservice and inservice social studies teachers. He currently is Associate Director of the University of Georgia Center for Economic Education. He earned degrees in social studies education at Ball State University and Indiana University, Bloomington, and taught high-school social studies in Indiana. His research and publications focus on cooperative learning, problem solving, teaching for higher-order thought in social studies, and economic education.

William W. Wilen is Professor of Education in the Department of Teacher Development and Curriculum Studies at Kent State University where he teaches secondary social studies education and instruction. He has taught at the high-school level in Maryland and, as summer visiting faculty, has taught at several other colleges and universities. Involvement in professional organizations includes governance responsibilities and presentations at the annual conferences of the National Council for the Social Studies. His latest book is *Dynamics of Effective Teaching* (2nd edition, 1992), and his articles on questioning and interaction, and instructional improvement have appeared in numerous journals. He also co-authored a chapter in the recent *Handbook of Research on Social Studies Teaching and Learning* (1991).

Chapter One

INTRODUCTION: WHAT SHOULD WE TEACH IN SOCIAL STUDIES? AND WHY?

Rodney F. Allen
Florida State University

IN HIS FOREWORD to a National Council for the Social Studies Bulletin on *Defining the Social Studies* (1977), then president of the NCSS Howard Mehlinger wrote

> The field of social studies is so caught up in ambiguity, inconsistency, and contradiction that it represents a complex educational enigma (p. 1).

Mehlinger proceeded to point out that social studies continued to "defy any final definition acceptable to all factions of the field." For a century, those engaged in social studies have seemed unable to define it, to bring order and a system from chaos. Definitions of social studies have been marked more by the conflict that they raise, than by the order and conceptual clarity that they offer. The definitions create conflict, not consensus. Such conflicts moved one interested educator to ask whether it is time to abandon the mythology that a discipline of "social studies" exists and whether it would not be harmonious and pragmatic to rename the NCSS to The National Council for Teachers of History and Social Science (Keller, 1991).

Following Mehlinger and Clair W. Keller, readers might reflect upon the following scenarios—asking which activities might be "social studies" and which are not.

1. On her third-grade walking tour of High Street, Shannon takes notes and draws accompanying maps while the leader points to examples of continuity and change, building by building. This activity is a part of her school and community program of Heritage Education.

2. Having studied the arguments and passions involved in changing the school logo and mascot to what many argue is more culturally sensitive options, Carlos presents his government class' position and supporting reasons. School board members ask questions, and Carlos responds concisely with answers from class deliberations.

3. Following a review day on Thursday, TaShana and her classmates arrive in history class to take a test on 20 vocabulary words, 10 heroes and heroines, and a plethora of factual details from Chapter 14 on the War of 1812.

4. Continuing their study of water quality in Lake Lafayette, Mr. Lopez-Morgan's class collects water samples, analyzes them, and begins to prepare a report on a year-long study for neighborhood groups and the state environmental protection agency.

5. Students and faculty at Osceola Middle School are proud that three students from seventh-grade geography won honors in the state geography bee. They were masters of locations, places, and movements, recalling information from their course.

6. Today Melvin's economics class has a guest speaker who will discuss supply, demand, and pricing at her seafood markets in the city. The speaker will share her computer-generated records on supply, sales, and prices for a variety of seafoods over the past decade.

7. Melissa is looking forward to her second-grade unit on the theme of responsibility. Her teacher will use art, stories, and writing to engage the class in identification of responsibilities, including the treatment of private property.

Most Americans will think of each of these scenarios as belonging within "social studies." Their conceptions of "social studies" include the mastery of history lessons, the memory of geographic terms and information, and the opportunity to perform in the arenas of civic dialogue and participation. But for teachers and educators concerned with curriculum development, definitional concerns about social studies or *the* social studies are important to deciding what to teach, where to teach it, and how connections are constructed across lessons and grade levels. Definitions suggest what is *in* and what is *outside* the purview of this subject in the curriculum. A definition, skillfully crafted, provides a systematic framework and allows for more reasonable curriculum decisions.

A social studies curriculum guide prepared for Missouri schools offers a pragmatic definition: "Social studies in this guide is defined as an area within the school curriculum that draws ideas from a variety of areas, including history, the social sciences, and the humanities, for purposes of citizenship education" (Missouri, 1980, p. 11). An early definition that endured for a long time was "The social studies are the social sciences simplified for pedagogical purposes" (Wesley and Wronski, 1958, p. 3). But many educators saw this as too vague, on the one hand, and too narrow, on the other.

A competing definition offered by Shirley Engle (1960) was based on the premise that the tasks of social scientists are drastically different from the tasks of social studies educators—the former being interested in the production of new knowledge, the latter in the education of citizens. Engle argued that students in social studies should examine problems and issues for the purpose of decision making, which may draw upon social science and historical knowledge, but rely also on the values, attitudes, and experiences of all the participants.

In 1992, the National Council for the Social Studies took yet another step to define itself and our curriculum field with this definition:

> Social studies is the integrated study of the social sciences and humanities to promote civic competence. Within the school program, social studies provides coordinated, systematic study drawing upon such disciplines as anthropology, archeology, economics, geography, history, law, philosophy, political science, psychology, religion, and sociology, as well as appropriate content from the humanities, mathematics, and natural sciences. The primary purpose of social studies is to help young people develop the ability to make informed and reasoned decisions for the public good as citizens of a culturally diverse, democratic society in an interdependent world (NCSS, 1993).

Has the definition issue been settled? One suspects not. The NCSS definition focuses heavily upon the knowledge to be employed from many sources, but is silent upon intellectual and political skills beyond "decision making." Participation and action are ignored or implied, depending upon each reader's interpretation. While the NCSS was writing its definition, James Barth (1991) offered a view that social studies might well be

> The interdisciplinary integration of social science and humanities concepts for the purpose of practicing citizenship skills on critical social issues (Barth, 1991, p. 19).

Barth continues to reason that educators who consider themselves social studies educators generally hold to the following four beliefs: first, that social studies in grades K to 12 is preparation for citizenship; second, content to be studied should be concepts and themes focused upon personal and social issues; third, the content should be integrated and interdisciplinary; and fourth, the process of decision making is the guide to classroom instruction (Barth, 1991, p. 19). But Professor Barth does not tell us how many teachers and curriculum leaders doing "social studies" think of themselves as "social studies educators" rather than as history teachers, geographic educators, elementary school teachers, or economic educators. To many, social studies is a school subject in which diverse interests (that is, interest groups) seek a place to contribute. The presence of the school subject and the many contributors is a sign that there is no integration of their contributions into a meaningful whole or any commonality in their goals.

Definitional tensions seem to play out along a continuum. At one end are the advocates of teaching academic disciplines, paralleling college course subjects such as history and geography, political science and economics, while decrying "social studies" as a mishmash lacking intellectual traditions and integrity. At the other end of the continuum are those advocates of a unified social studies wherein knowledge and skills are borrowed from disciplines, ignoring disciplinary boundaries, and fused to permit the systematic study of the needs of students and society, especially the civic needs. Barth's, Engle's, and the NCSS definitions envision social studies as a unified field, grades K to 12; later in this chapter with the national standards movement, we shall clearly see definitions firmly rooted in the academic disciplines.

The many voices with different definitions make the task of deciding what to teach in social studies and how to teach it a more confusing enterprise at every grade level, K to 12.

FROM DEFINITIONS TO RATIONALE: HOW DO WE JUSTIFY OUR TEACHING OF SOCIAL STUDIES?

For social studies educators, definitional confusion can be an educational opportunity. When a democratic nation requires its children and youth to devote so much time to schooling and when it allocates so many resources to education, the policies and curriculum of schooling should be a matter of professional and public debate. Students, parents, and other participants in social studies school policies and curriculum decisions may rightfully expect a reasoned justification for curriculum decisions. What are the goals of social studies curriculum and teaching? Upon what assumptions are decisions made? Are these assumptions valid? Are our choices reasonable?

Any deliberation about the rationale for social studies, grades K to 12, must clarify the realities constructed by the persons involved. The historian Charles A. Beard (1934) reminded social studies educators at all grade levels that

> Every human brought up in a society inevitably has in mind a frame of social knowledge, ideas and ideals—a more or less definite pattern of things deemed *necessary,* things deemed *possible* and things deemed *desirable;* and to this frame or pattern, his thought and action will be more or less consciously referred (p. 181).

Carl Kaestle (1982) labeled this frame or pattern using the term *social outlook*, which he defined as

> A set of compatible propositions about human nature and society that help an individual to interpret complex human problems and take action that the individual believes is in his or her best interests and the best interest of society as a whole (p. 125).

When teachers, parents, and academics engage in discussions about what the goals of social studies should be and what should be taught, the *social outlook* that each has constructed over time is always an implicit influence in those discussions. Any reasonable discussion must seek first to make the social outlooks (and assumptions) more explicit. This is especially important because much debate on the nature of social studies seem dialectic—contensions between bi-polar positions, such as historians to social scientists, geographers to social studies advocates, academic traditionalists in disciplines to those favoring a more relevant, integrated content centered on issues or problems (Lybarger, 1991).

James Shaver and Harold Berlak (1968) argued that any curriculum decision in social studies involves a large number of assumptions. These assumptions fall into four broad categories: (1) conceptions of the social world, including ideals and purposes; (2) conceptions of the nature of knowledge upon which education is to be based; (3) conceptions of the nature of thinking; and (4) conceptions of the ways of learning and teaching. For example, if social studies is for citizenship education, then what construction of "citizen" will educators use? What are the alternative conceptions and visions of "citizens"? What is the conception of "society" into which this "citizen" will be educated? How pluralistic is our vision? How global is our perspective? How pluralistic and global should they be?

Debate over goals and their justification provides an opportunity for social studies educators to model public policy dialogue for parents and other community members. The inclusiveness of participation reflects commitments to democratic participation. And then, the justified goals provide a basis for judging the consistency between those goals and the social studies programs that follow (Newmann, 1977).

In a study of elementary school social studies programs, Jere W. Brophy and Janet Alleman (1993) reported no shortage of lofty goal statements in school policy documents. Unfortunately, these goals were not analyzed as expressions of a social outlook and then used to guide curriculum design, instructional planning, and assessment. Far too often the lofty goals, left unexamined, were lost in the process of implementation. Losing focus on clear goals, the curriculum in elementary social studies frequently provided long lists of skills and disconnected bits of information.

HOW SHOULD WE ARGUE FOR OUR VIEW OF THE PURPOSE OF SOCIAL STUDIES?

The continuing arguments over the most appropriate goals, content, and rationale for social studies in grades K to 12 would be less intense if social studies were more like other school subjects. Mathematics education has a single academic discipline counterpart, mathematics. It is so with English education, art education, and music education. Even science education, with academic input from multiple disciplines, most often shares an orientation toward knowing and inquiring among its academic disciplines. Social studies does not have a clean disciplinary focus.

The debates concerning the nature of social studies might be sorted out in a model suggested by Barth and S. Samuel Shermis (1970). They suggest that three traditions or *orientations* toward the goals and purposes of social studies as a school subject have dominated that debate for a century. The three orientations are the following:

1. Social studies as *citizenship transmission*, in which the central contention is that patriotism, cultural heritage, cardinal values of the political tradition, and agreed upon perspectives should be transferred to new generations by the schools.
2. Social studies as *social science*, in which students are to be engaged in the mastery of concepts, generalizations theories, and inquiry processes from these academic disciplines that will promote improved citizenship and social enhancement.
3. Social studies as *reflective inquiry*, in which it is believed that citizens are best educated by engaging in in-depth examination of enduring social issues and through that public inquiry develop the habits of mind to free themselves and public policy from unexamined conventions and develop the habits of the heart to have democratic regard for others and for the institutions that promote the common good.

Any consumer of newspapers, talk-radio, or television journals can see conflicts about school reform cast in terms of Barth and Shermis's three competing traditions. Freedom to learn in social studies is frequently challenged by complaining parents, interest group leaders, or concerned citizens. These complaints illustrate the differing conceptions of the goals and purposes of social studies. On the one hand, people express concerns that reflect a vision that education is a vehicle for ensuring ideological conformity to ancestral values and beliefs or for perpetuating valued conventions. Students should be protected from social realities and from ideas that can be considered "controversial" or too mature. These advocates capture the essence of the "cultural transmission" orientation.

On the other hand, the marketplace of ideas offers advocates who argue for challenging children and youth intellectually and for learning directed toward critical thinking on real world problems. These people expect children to examine pollution in the second grade as a theme in integrated units. They envision middle-school students debating term limits for elected officials and alternative public policy positions in response to issues of criminal violence in their communities. They cannot conceive of a high-school social studies program devoid of controversial public issues for student study and debate as the basis for developing mature judgment, intellectual imagination, and civic commitment. In these expectations the reflective inquiry tradition stands in marked contrast to the "cultural transmission" point-of-view.

Although Barth and Shermis provide a construction that helps educators sort out arguments over matters of rationale and policy, Alan Tom (1969) developed an innovative construct for viewing these same debates. Behind each argument about goals and purposes were one of three types of people—ideal types—as the ultimate outcomes of social education:

1. *Personal Man*, who "is a wise consumer of the products of our economy, is satisfied with the vocation he has selected, has a rewarding home life, and has a meaningful relationship with other people."
2. *Scholarly Man*, who "attempts among other things to examine a human problem or situation objectively…, tries to develop an increasingly accurate understanding of his own behavior, is familiar with social science concepts, and strives to keep informed."
3. *Public Man*, who "is characterized by such activities as regular voting, volunteer work in social service agencies, participation in groups concerned with issues."

Although Tom's Scholarly Man with the focus on inquiry and understanding parallels Barth and Shermis' social-science tradition, and though Tom's Public Man, centered on issues and participation, parallels Barth and Shermis' reflective-inquiry tradition, Tom's Personal Man is no analogue for Barth and Shermis' citizenship-transmissions tradition. Personal Man is self-absorbed, an individual, competent in matters of living, but private. Personal Man can balance his checkbook, safely drive his car, cast a ballot to protect his interests, read Great Books, speak in public, and read maps and globes. These competencies are advocated by people engaged in school improvement, including social studies.

But Tom's archetypes of social studies outcomes are too narrowly cast to cover the diverse nature of the arguments about the kinds of "persons" the best social studies should seek to produce. Using Tom's construct of "persons" as outcomes, debates over social studies suggest a five or seven "person" characterization of the visions people have and argue for when making curriculum decisions and planning programs. These are the following:

1. *The Conforming Person*, who has learned uncritically the social conventions and accepted those conventions, their basis in values and authority, and seeks to live in harmony with them and with others of similar commitments and understandings; this conforming person knows, accepts, and lives in obedience to the given standards.

2. *The Personal Person*, who comes up in educational debate in two characters:
   a. The Personal Person who is *personally competent* in the affairs and tasks of living, similar to Tom's Personal Man who could balance his checkbook, drive his car, figure his taxes, and sail two points off the wind.
   b. The Personal Person who is accomplished in social relations, understands his or her commitments and feels self-actualized and in control and has his or her "act" together.

3. *The Scholarly Person*, who also comes up in educational debate in two forms:
   a. The Scholarly Person who has mastery over known facts, concepts, theories, and constructs in an academic discipline, but whose knowledge is rote, *passive*, inert in its learning and its use.
   b. The Scholarly Person who has mastered the processes of inquiry of an academic discipline, can raise questions appropriate to that discipline, and can apply what was learned through *active* investigation.

4. *The Public Person*, who is a participant in the civic culture, is committed to a public philosophy that balances interests and ideals and recreates those value commitments through reflective inquiry and action on public issues in concern with a community of others.

5. *The Radical Person*, who is a social critic, a nonconformist (in the Anglican or Puritan sense), a dissenter with a vision or ideology to view social reality and perceive problems and possibilities—some are in the streets and others do policy studies, in both places they are active.

If you think of the many curriculum or instructional proposals that make the daily media, you will see that some fit neatly into one or more "person" characterizations. For example, suggestions that the social studies include volunteer service for children and youth could fit the Conforming Person, Private Person Type B, Public Person, or Radical Person characterizations. Proposals for critical thinking on real-world issues might, depending upon the details, fit the outcomes inherent in the Radical Person, Public Person, or perhaps the Scholarly Person Type B.

The Radical Person is the direct antithesis of Barth and Shermis' (1970) citizenship or cultural transmission tradition or the Private Man as delineated by Tom (1969). The Radical Person's commitments are centered on change and improvement in the quality of life in communities, local to global. Engle and Anna Ochoa (1988) call for a social studies program in schools that is directed to this "resocialization" of youth. George Harrison Wood (1984) calls this "democratic transformation," where students develop their commitments to equality and justice as democratic values by the analysis of their lives and the life situations of others. Education is linked directly and constantly with students' life experiences. Such civic education is often a hallmark of small communities having independent schools, often with a religious orientation. Rarely are public schools considered to have curriculum or instruction so focused upon social transformation (Stanley and Nelson, 1986).

Democratic transformation education is more often associated with the work of NGOs (nongovernmental organizations) working in developing nations among the rural or urban poor or with the work of community organizers amidst poverty pockets in the United States. George W. Chilcoat and Jerry A. Ligon (1994) examined the work of the Mississippi Freedom Schools, founded in 1963 by the Student Nonviolent Coordinating Committee (SNCC) as a part of the civil rights liberation movement. Students examined their own experience and perspectives as initiating moves in transformation. The academic knowledge employed was useful knowledge for this transformation, stressing social, economic, and political thought that provided diverse perspectives for reflection. Words were linked to actions. As understanding developed, students sought to change themselves and their communities.

This characterization of "persons" as the outcomes or "products" of teaching and learning social studies is a tool for teachers and others to use to question advocates of various curriculum proposals. Advocates of law education in social studies might be asked about their vision of law study: Is it to be critical, raising questions about the nature and function of current law and legal practice set against conceptions of justice? Is it to be inert, centering on legal vocabulary and memorized noun-names for "rights"? To those who advocate the mastery of certain information and themes called "basic," social educators might ask to what purpose. *Basic* to what activity or goal?

Ultimately, the interrogative use of this characterization of "persons" as the outcomes of social education reveals advocates' conceptions of the society for which students are being educated. What is this Good Society? Some ideal or vision? Some reality that advocates perceive? Some past glory to which advocates wish to return? Are students as educated persons expected to prepare for a return, fit into some current reality, or reconstruct the social order?

In the real world of curriculum design, of course, no social studies program would focus singularly upon one type of "person" as an end product of social education. Amalgams would be expected, but being clear about goals for social studies in school and classrooms—similar to mission statements or vision statements in planning—focus our attention and give us categories and commitments with which to judge the plethora of movements seeking a place in the social studies curriculum: values education, law education, geographic education, history education, heritage education, values clarification, cognitive moral education, issues-centered education, integrated learning, critical thinking, community participation, and multicultural education, to name a few of the more meritorious movements (Kaltsounis, 1994).

For our purposes in this chapter, it is important to keep in mind that teachers of social studies and their curriculum development colleagues must respond to the interests and ideas of advocates from each of these movements. In addition, the many traditions and "persons" outlined here have their supporters in various intensities and with varying degrees of influence, but they each in turn are due a place in an open, democratic forum to press their cases for curriculum inclusion.

HOW SHOULD WE ORGANIZE OUR SCOPE AND SEQUENCE IN SOCIAL STUDIES?

By the end of the 1980s, the tradition curriculum pattern in the United States was remarkably akin to the 1916 recommendations of the Committee on Social Studies of the National Education Association (Hertzberg, 1981). The main changes are demise of "community civics" courses and the absence of the innovative Problems of Democracy course from the 1916 suggestions and their replacement with social science discipline courses. Otherwise, subject matter knowledge was organized and delivered in textbooks to teachers and their students following an "expanding horizons" model, beginning with the student and moving "outward in concentric circles" to family, neighborhood, community, state, nation, and world or western hemisphere. The middle school pattern anticipated the high school—world studies of some sort, followed by American history, followed by the study of government. Students received three years of American history, geography in the upper elementary and middle school years, and only world cultures remained as an integrated subject.

Table 1–1   Traditional Curriculum Patterns

Grade	Topic	Grade	Topic
K	Self, School, Community, Home	7	World Cultures or Eastern Hemisphere
1	Families and the Home	8	American History
2	Neighborhoods	9	"Civics" or Geography
3	Communities	10	World History
4	State History and Geographic Regions	11	United States
5	American History	12	American Government or Economics or Sociology or Psychology
6	World Cultures or Western Hemisphere		

Table 1–2   California History—Social Science Framework

Grade	Topics or Subjects	Grade	Topics or Subjects
K	Working and Learning Now and Long Ago	9	Elective Courses in History: Social Science (chosen from modern state history, physical or world-regional geography, comparative world religions, the humanities, area studies, women's studies, ethnic studies, law-related education, anthropology, sociology, and psychology)
1	A Child's Place in Time and Space		
2	People Who Make a Difference		
3	Continuity and Change		
4	California: A Changing State		
5	United States History and Geography: Making a New Nation	10	World History, Culture, and Geography: The Modern World
6	World History and Geography: Ancient Civilizations	11	United States History and Geography: Continuity and Change in the Twentieth Century
7	World History and Geography: Medieval and Early Modern Times		
8	United States History and Geography: Growth and Conflict	12	Principles of American Democracy and Economics

In the 1980s some states responded to public dissatisfaction with schooling and to reports of historic and geographic "illiteracy" with curriculum reforms. In social studies, the State of California was the first to rewrite its curriculum scope and sequence of subject matter content, blending an emphasis on history with geography (California State Board of Education, 1988). (See Tables 1–1 and 1–2.) The expanding horizons model was replaced. Great emphasis was placed upon literature study and the use of sources rather than textbook narratives.

In the early grades the emphasis in California on biography, mythology, and children's literature harked back to a pre-expanding horizons era. The curriculum advocates in 1899 urged the study of literature and legends along

Table 1–3   Florida Curriculum Framework

Grade	Course of Study	Grade	Course of Study
K	My Family and Others	6	Geography: Asia, Oceania, and Africa
1	Families Near and Far		
2	Our Cultures, Past and Present: Unity and Diversity in the United States	7	Geography: Europe and the Americas
		8	Florida: Challenges and Choices
3	Beginnings: People, Places, and Events: Studies of Turning Points in World History	9	Eastern and Western Heritage: World History to 1750
		10	United States History to 1920
4	United States and Florida History and Geography to 1880	11	U.S. History in the Context of World History, 1848 to the Present
5	United States and Florida History and Geography since 1880	12	American Political System and American Economic System

with the biographies of historical characters. In 1909 it was suggested that grades one and two examine "Indian life" and Thanksgiving, along with Washington's birthday and local events.

In 1990, the State of Florida released its new curriculum model Connections, Challenges, Choices (Florida Department of Education, 1990). (See Table 1–3.) Again, history and geography were selected as the mainstream disciplines to use as curriculum organizers. Both disciplines were in the forefront of national educational standards movement, which is discussed later. The middle school curriculum was devoted almost entirely to geography, with courses in government and economics reserved for the final year of high school.

The Florida plan departs from the expanding environments pattern, as did California's curriculum. The curriculum in the early grades diverges from a simple chronological approach to history teaching and learning. In addition, the Florida plan identifies linkages to curriculum content and themes in other subjects, such as science, English, fine arts, and foreign languages.

But with these examples of curriculum innovation, little change occurred relative to the continuities in arranging subject matter over grade levels. The constance is still more striking than the change.

For most social studies students in elementary schools within the United States the curriculum is organized on the basis of "expanding horizons." This basis is an expression of the pedagogical viewpoint that children learn best when beginning with familiar objects and places, such as families and homes, and move gradually to the exploration of the children's state, nation, and global communities. This point of view is thought to be based upon psychological principles wherein children's learning capabilities emerged from the concrete to the abstract, from the familiar to the unfamiliar (Massialas, 1994). But there are contrary positions taken by many social studies educators. Some argue for a social studies curriculum based upon themes or problems. For example, teachers and students might examine gift-giving using historical examples in their communities, followed by a study of gift-giving in the context of Korean society, its traditional and contemporary life styles, and then use personal narratives and interviews with parents and other community neighbors about their giving of gifts, and the meanings of those behaviors. The pattern followed is "then, there, and here" (past, geographic, and now—the students' lived experience), and the goals and materials are most often multidisciplinary. Students study integrated units or themes with reading, writing, science, and social studies merged together.

Other educators in both secondary and elementary schools argue for social studies curriculum organized on the basis of separate subjects, such as geography, history, and political science. These educators point to what they see as the fundamental integrity of academic disciplines with their questions, points of view, concepts, and structures. The social studies curriculum, in their judgment, should communicate this substantive structure of knowledge in particular disciplines. Advocates of national curriculum standards in history, geography, civics and government (see below) support the vision of a curriculum centered on separate academic disciplines. Those advocates of social studies standards are more open about curriculum organization, but *tend to* support a thematic organization in K to 6 social studies with secondary school curricula focused upon subjects, including chronologically centered history courses. (National Council for the Social Studies, 1994.)

Criticism of the expanding horizon approach ranges from its basis in the logic of adults, not children, to its age-grade orientation and its omission of issues of immediate concern to children (Joyce, Little, and Wronski, 1991). Criticism of the conventional discipline-oriented curriculum focuses upon its unresponsiveness to current social problems and issues facing learners and other citizens. Critics question whether a discipline-oriented social studies can educate an increasingly diverse population to be civic minded and active participants.

Not satisfied with these organizing schemes, social studies educators had sought other theories. The NCSS Task Force on Scope and Sequence (Jarolimek, 1984) used what it called a "holistic-interactive approach" (p. 253) to recommend the following:

Kindergarten: Awareness of Self in a Social Setting
Grade One: The Individual in Primary Groups
Grade Two: Meeting Basic Needs in Nearby Social Groups
Grade Three: Sharing Earth-Space with Others
Grade Four: Human Life in Varied Environments
Grade Five: The People of the Americas (plural)

Grade Six: People and Culture

Grade Seven: A Changing World of Many Nations

Grade Eight: Building a Strong and Free Nation

Grade Nine: Systems That Make a Democratic Society Work

Grade Ten: Origins of Major Cultures

Grade Eleven: The Maturing America (singular)

Grade Twelve: An array of choices, some of which are discipline based and others which are problem- or issues-oriented.

The Board of the National Council elected not to endorse one scope and sequence as an official position, especially because this task force plan was controversial. The continuing debate over scope and sequence illustrated the diversity of opinion within the profession. Issues continue on the best definition of our field, the most important conception of the educational outcome from studying social studies, and the best and most appropriate scope and sequence for teaching and learning (Patrick, 1992).

TWO ISSUES ON CONTROVERSIAL INNOVATIONS

R. Freeman Butts (1977) once observed that the urge to promote civic education in the public schools accelerates in times of crisis or rapid social change. When liberal social reformers need social cohesion to mobilize groups behind their endeavor, such as during the American Revolution, Progressive Era, New Deal, or Great Society, civic education takes on an urgency. Also, civic education comes to the fore when

> conservative forces see the need for social cohesion to rally around their version of the American way of life and to stave off threats from alien sources... (p. 26).

The two issues that follow illustrate these continuing debates in social studies education, grades K to 12. The two issues involve E.D. Hirsch, Jr.'s ideas of Cultural literacy as a means to preserve cultural unity with a shared body of learning information, and the continuing attempt to raise standards in schools through the imposition of world class standards for school subjects by academic discipline.

⇌ *Issue #1 Should "Cultural Literacy" Be an Organizing Vision Directing Social Studies Education?*

In 1987, E.D. Hirsch, Jr., a professor of English at the University of Virginia, created waves in the educational community with the publication of his book *Cultural Literacy: What Every American Needs to Know.* He argued that one of the main functions of schooling was to teach core knowledge—the literate national vocabulary. According to his position, a common body of information that constitutes cultural literacy in our society. If you are going to be a working member of society, then you have to have the same background knowledge that others have. This knowledge includes history, literature, geography, the arts, and religion. His book includes a 63-page list of some 5,000 elements for basic cultural literacy. He calls this list the *extensive curriculum* that should be included in every child's education. But the *intensive curriculum* deals in themes and rigorous study in-depth. This study would integrate history, literature, and the arts.

Professor Hirsch plans a series of school books with themes and an articulated scope and sequence to develop students' understanding. His first volume is "What Your First Grader Needs to Know." History study, for example, commences with simple stories about George Washington, Ben Franklin, and the Liberty Bell, moving to narratives on the suffragist movement by the fourth grade. Students read the life of Frederick Douglass, Lincoln's Gettysburg Address, and a host of perennials in the American tradition. Hirsch also encourages lessons on the students' local communities and their concerns.

Apparently the extensive curriculum gets more attention than the intensive. Critics of Hirsch's program question the Eurocentric bias that they see in his list of 5,000 items, which is continually under review. Critics claim that the extensive curriculum is inert, fixed, and leads to passive learning, where "facts" will be ladled out to children for memorization to pass multiple-choice tests. Hirsch plans to test for cultural literacy at grades 3, 6, 9, and 12.

These same critics are concerned that educators might rush to include lists of cultural literacy items as trivia for memorization in textbooks and teacher guides. Rather than improve social education, such behavior will retard it. Teachers will be under greater pressure to teach more and more information without time to develop meaning or memorable instructional encounters with history and literature.

Though concurring with Hirsch's concern for cultural literacy, Fred M. Newmann (1988) argued that the only way to achieve this is to immerse students from the earlier grades in the in-depth study of a limited number of themes that are culturally significant and can integrate history, geography, the arts, and literature.

Cultural literacy as a movement comes to the social studies without significant pedagogical insights and without any depth to the rationale for its extensive curriculum, which has drawn the most attention. Even with curriculum ladders and grade-level books, critics see it as fragmented and aloof from so much of teachers' and society's worries about children and youth.

For teachers, the "cultural literacy" emphasis raises the enduring curriculum issue in social studies between the stress upon the mastery of "basics" and the desire for an open exploration of ideas, ideals, and issues of concern to learners and their communities.

⇄ Issue #2 *Should National Standards Be Imposed Upon Social Education in Diverse School Communities?*

In the fall of 1989, at Charlottesville, Virginia, President George Bush, the Secretary of Education, and 50 state governors met to exert their combined effort to prepare national goals for American schools. In April 1991, President Bush unveiled the report, *America 2000*, and declared an educational revolution. Six national goals were proclaimed that would lead to world-class schools, with national tests (now voluntary) at grades 4, 8, and 12. Goal Three was of particular interest. It dealt with student achievement:

> American students will leave grades four, eight, and twelve having demonstrated competency in challenging subject matter including English, mathematics, science, history, and geography; and every school in America will ensure that all students learn to use their minds well so that they may be prepared for responsible citizenship, further learning, and productive employment in our modern economy (U.S. Department of Education, 1991).

No mention was made of civics, government, or other social sciences in this initial plan. No mention was made of a unified social studies; history and geography were core disciplines.

Immediately, teams began writing standards for history and geography. Standards were key to letting students know what to strive for, letting teachers know what to teach for, and letting the public have the means to assess the schools' instructional performance.

In 1994, Walter Parker wrote that four sets of standards in our field were in the final stages of production. History standards were produced by the National Center for History in the Schools, Los Angeles, with $1.6 million from the Federal government. The Geography Standards were produced by a consortium, including the National Geographic Society and the National Council for Geographic Education, for $700,000. The Center for Civic Education, Calabasas, California, produced the Civics standards for $780,000 from the Federal government and the Pew Charitable Trusts. And, finally, the social studies standards were produced by the National Council for the Social Studies with $70,000 of its own funds.

The history standards treat American history and world history, with attention to the elementary grades. The Geography for Life (1994) has standards for grades K to 4, 5 to 8, and 9 to 12. Social studies standards center upon 10 major themes, such as culture, time, continuity and change, civic ideals, and global connections. For each category and at several grade levels, the social studies standards provide teaching ideas in vignettes of classroom

Ten Thematic Strands

Ten themes serve as organizing strands for the social studies curriculum at every school level (early, middle and high school); they are interrelated and draw from all of the social science disciplines and other related disciplines and fields of scholarly study to build a framework for social studies curriculum design.

I Culture

Human beings create, learn, and adapt culture. Human cultures are dynamic systems of beliefs, values, and traditions that exhibit both commonalities and differences. Understanding culture helps us understand ourselves and others.

II Time, continuity, and change

Human beings seek to understand their historic roots and to locate themselves in time. Such understanding involves knowing what things were like in the past and how things change and develop—allowing us to develop historic perspective and answer important questions about our current condition.

III People, places, and environment

Technological advancements have insured that students are aware of the world beyond their personal locations. As students study content related to this theme, they create their spatial views and geographic perspectives of the world; social, cultural, economic, and civic demands mean that students will need such knowledge, skills, and understandings to make informed and critical decisions about the relationship between human beings and their environments.

IV Individual development and identity

Personal identity is shaped by one's culture, by groups and by institutional influences. Examination of various forms of human behavior enhances understanding of the relationships between social norms and emerging personal identities, the social processes which influence identity formation, and the ethical principles underlying individual action.

V Individuals, groups, and institutions

Institutions exert enormous influence over us. Institutions are organizational embodiments to further the core social values of those who compose them. It is important for students to know how institutions are formed, what controls and influences them, how they control and influence individuals and culture, and how institutions can be maintained or changed.

VI Power, authority, and governance

Understanding of the historic development of structures of power, authority, and governance and their evolving functions in contemporary society is essential for the emergence of civic competence.

VII Production, distribution, and consumption

Decisions about exchange, trade, and economic policy and well-being are global in scope, and the role of government in policy making varies over time and from place to place. The systematic study of an interdependent world economy and the role of technology in economic decision making is essential.

VIII Science, technology, and society

Technology is as old as the first crude tool invented by prehistoric humans, and modern life as we know it would be impossible without technology and the science which supports it. Today's technology forms the basis for some of our most difficult social choices.

(continued)

Ten Thematic Strands (continued)

IX   Global connections

The realities of global interdependence require understanding of the increasingly important and diverse global connections among world societies before there can be analysis leading to the development of possible solutions to persisting and emerging global issues.

X   Civic ideals and practices

All people have a stake in examining civic ideals and practices across time, in diverse societies, as well as in determining how to close the gap between present practices and the ideals upon which our democratic republic is based. An understanding of civic ideals and practices of citizenship is critical to full participation in society.

*Expectations of Excellence: Curriculum Standards for Social Studies (1994). Washington, DC: National Council for the Social Studies.

---

encounters and then show sample assessments to illuminate the theme and performance-based assessment (Parker, 1994).

The National Standards come to social studies in four packages. History advocates want their own curriculum, as do advocates for geography. Both sets of educators see their disciplines as integrative, as do the civics-standards writers. The social studies standards are integrative, but, it is asserted, with "too little regard" for history and geography at each grade level. Thus, teachers and curriculum personnel in social studies are left with four separate horses to ride. Certainly the four will not be taught separately in schools.

Critics of the national standards movement fear more loss of local educational control and a national curriculum. Educators fear the loss of flexibility in curriculum and teaching and the spector of a mandated curriculum with high-stakes testing of students at several grade levels in multiple subjects. John O'Neil (1993) identified three equity concerns about standards: (1) Is it really possible to create standards that apply equally to all students? (2) What will be done to build schools' capacity to help all students attain these higher standards? and (3) What kind of tests will be used to measure whether students have attained the new standards? And, equally important, is the question: Are uniform standards appropriate for a nation as diverse as the United States?

John Goodlad (1992) raises the most fundamental challenges to the use of national standards to yield better educational attainment. Will success on these standards turn around the erosion in America's global competitiveness? Will tests as surrogates for real-world incentives provide the motivation to reengage students in learning? Will we drive more students to drop out? Will standards and student performance testing function to widen the socio-economic schism in our society?

In the literature of social studies, why do we read more about standards and testing, Goal Three, than about Goal One on aiding all children in America to be ready to learn when they start school? Or about Goal Two, which expects to raise the high school graduation rate to 90 percent, at least. Given the many pathologies of society, what should the priorities of social studies curriculum and instruction be? Suicide prevention, conflict mediation, programs for working youth, assistance for limited English proficient learners, or world-class standards on the War of 1812?

Where once educated persons feared the loss of wisdom and knowledge in a blizzard of information, so now social studies can ponder what it has lost in voluminous sets of national, world-class standards. We are left once more with what seems an eternal question: What shall we teach? And why?

CONCLUSION

For beginning teachers and experienced educators, these are exciting times for social studies curriculum and instruction. Our communities and nation are opening to new challenges and opportunities; the continuing transitions in the global community test our old understandings and raise new questions. Not only can these transformations engage us as educators and learners, they also are the vehicles to engage our students in new ideas to master, new conceptions of community to which to commit ourselves, and new, much broader visions of citizenship and responsibility to guide our behavior.

But these possibilities will remain mere potential unless social studies educators at all levels can define the field with ideas appropriate to the new reality and can construct a more collective vision of the goals of social studies to which we should all teach and learn. When we asked in this chapter what should we teach in social studies?, the answer was always *students.* Our students. When it comes to what should we teach them, building a rationale and a scope and sequence, the answers will not come from textbooks or remote gurus, but must be argued and decided by people like you—new and experienced teachers together in community with one another. This is not always a satisfying answer, but it is the best answer we have in a democratic society, where citizens must have the power to make these decisions.

Reflective Questions

1. *Why should classroom teachers, K to 5, 6 to 8, or 9 to 12 be concerned about understanding the definitions of social studies? What can an adequate definition of social studies do for teachers and curriculum personnel in social studies?*

2. *As society and students have changed over the years, has the social studies program in schools (as you understand it or remember it) kept pace? Has it kept pace and changed? Should it have kept pace by changing?*

3. *How do you account for the popularity of history and geography as the principal (and most popular) disciplines taught within the social studies?*

4. *The "expanding horizons" approach to social studies in the elementary school scope and sequence has had great staying power. How do you explain this? Is it based in principle or psychology on today's realities? Why? Why not?*

5. *What is the proper role of such social sciences as anthropology, economics, political science, and human geography in the social studies at grades K to 5, 6 to 8, and 9 to 12?*

6. *Why are national curriculum standards so very controversial in American education? And in social studies?*

7. *Which types of social studies advocates, given the systems or typologies in this chapter, would be most accepting of "cultural literacy" approaches to our field? Why?*

8. *How would you test the following assertion: "Problems-oriented social studies educators have greater influence in times of crisis, such as Depressions and economic transitions; cultural transmission advocates in times of war or external threats, real or imagined?"*

9. *Why is the design and implementation of a social studies program an open, public policy question, where citizens have a place in the forum as much as professional educators?*

10. *Given the divisions in social studies and different positions being advocated, what positions are you ready to take on matters of definition, the purpose and intended outcomes of social studies, scope and sequence, national standards, and cultural literacy?*

GLOSSARY

cultural literacy   The view that curriculum can be built upon and should reflect an agreed-upon list of information and ideas that "educated persons in our society" should know to communicate in the context of our national culture.

national standards   A plan for improving education, K–12, by setting standards and getting popular consensus on those higher standards as a route to national civic and economic excellence.

rationale   Reason for being; a justification for a policy or a position on a definition, a statement of purpose or goals, or a curriculum plan (scope and sequence).

scope   Refers to the range of content, attitudes, values, intellectual skills, and other learner experiences to be included in the social studies curriculum; what is to be "covered."

sequence   Refers to the order in which these items of content, values, skills, and other learner experiences occur in the curriculum; the plan for teaching elements within the scope of social studies over time within a grade level and across grade levels in a step-by-step progression.

social studies   A singular, unified and integrated view of the field in contrast with "the social studies," a plural statement, indicating an amalgam or loose confederation of disciplines.

ANNOTATED BIBLIOGRAPHY

Barr, R.D., J.L. Barth, and S.S. Shermis (1977). *Defining the Social Studies.* Washington, DC: National Council for the Social Studies.

Although not without its critics, this volume reports and expands upon the discussion of the "three traditions" in social studies. In the appendix, Shirley H. Engle offers another, emerging "tradition" based upon critical theory.

Engle, Shirley H. (1960). "Decision-Making: The Heart of the Social Studies." *Social Education* 24(7):301–306.

The most important single statement of the case for social studies as a unified discipline of its own, centered upon the study of issues to educate citizens for a democratic society (see Leming on citizenship as the goal of social studies).

Expanding Children's World in Time and Space: National Standards for History for Grades K–4 (1994). Los Angeles: National Center for History in the Schools.

A discipline-based discussion of historical understanding, of historical thinking, and of the purpose of high standards. Interestingly, the content standards are sequenced in "expanding horizon" fashion—from family, to neighborhood, to state, to nation, and to other peoples in many cultures. Expanded Edition.

Geography for Life: National Geography Standards (1994). Washington, DC: Geography Education Standards Project.

Copyrighted by National Geographic Research and Exploration, the text defines geographic education, outlines skills and content, and proceeds to develop 18 standards at the K to 4, 5 to 8, and 9 to 12 grade levels.

Leming, James S. (1989). "The Two Cultures of Social Studies Education." *Social Education* 53(5):404–408.

Drawing upon the two cultures themes of C.P. Snow, Professor Leming develops a view of social studies divided into a culture of theorists (professors) and a culture of teachers who have differing beliefs, values, and behaviors that separate not only them, but also the field of social studies education. Leming offers three issues that need a "cross-cultural" dialogue to bring ourselves together.

National Council for the Social Studies (1994). *Expectations of Excellence: Curriculum Standards for Social Studies.* Washington, DC: The National Council for the Social Studies. Bulletin 89.

This document offers a unified view of social studies based upon 10 thematic strands to be taught at each school level (elementary, middle, and high school). Also included are illustrative curriculum standards, student performance expectations, and examples of classroom examples of the standards in action.

National Standards for Civics and Government (1994). Calabasas, CA: Center for Civic Education.

This volume contains standards in civics and government study clustered for Grades K to 4, 5 to 8, and 9 to 12. Each individual standard is preceded by a question, a content summary, and a statement of the standard with statements indicating student behavior to achievement of the standard.

National Standards for United States History: Exploring the American Experience (1994). Los Angeles: National Center for History in the Schools.

A discipline-based discussion of standards in historical thinking and in historical content over 10 eras from "The Meeting of Three Worlds" to the present, with examples of student achievement, Grades 5 to 12. Expanded Edition.

National Standards for World History: Exploring Paths to the Present (1994). Los Angeles: National Center for History in the Schools.

A discipline-based discussion of standards in historical thinking and in historical content over 10 eras from the beginnings to the twentieth century, with examples of student achievement, Grades 5 to 12. Expanded Edition.

Ravitch, Diane (1993). "Launching a Revolution in Standards and Assessments." *Phi Delta Kappan* 74(10):767–772.

A visiting fellow at the Brookings Institution, Washington, D.C., Diane Ravitch outlines her view on the need for national curriculum standards with teacher development, classroom support, and various assessments in keeping with those standards.

REFERENCES

Barth, James L. (1991). "Beliefs that Discipline the Social Studies." *International Journal of Social Education* 6(2):19–26.

Barth, James L. and S. Samuel Shermis (1970). "Defining the Social Studies: An Exploration of Three Traditions." *Social Education* 34(2):743–751.

Beard, Charles A. (1934). *The Nature of the Social Sciences in Relation to Objectives of Instruction.* New York: Charles Scribner's.

Brophy, Jere E. and Janet Alleman (1993). "Elementary Social Studies Should Be Driven by Major Social Education Goals." *Social Education* 56(1):27–32.

Butts, R. Freeman (1977). "Historical Perspective on Civic Education in the United States," in National Task Force on Citizenship Education, *Education for Responsible Citizenship.* New York: McGraw-Hill.

California State Board of Education (1988). *History–Social Science Framework for California Public Schools.* Sacramento: California Department of Education.

Chilcoat, George W. and Jerry A. Ligon (1994). "Developing Democratic Citizens: The Mississippi Freedom Schools as a Model for Social Studies Instruction." *Theory and Research in Social Education* 22(2):128–174.

Engle, Shirley H. and Anna S. Ochoa (1988). *Education for Democratic Citizenship: Decision-Making in the Social Studies.* New York: Teachers College Press.

Engle, Shirley H. (1960). "Decision-Making: The Heart of Social Studies Instruction." *Social Education* 24(7):301–306.

Goodlad, John I. (1992). "On Taking Reform Seriously." *Phi Delta Kappan* 74(3):232–238.

Florida Department of Education (1990). *Connections, Challenges, Choices: Social Studies Curriculum Framework.* Tallahassee: The Florida Department of Education.

Hertzberg, H.W. (1981). *Social Studies Reform, 1880–1980.* Boulder, CO: Social Science Education Consortium.

Hirsch, E.D., Jr. (1987). *Cultural Literacy: What Every American Needs to Know.* Boston: Houghton Mifflin.

Jarolimek, J. (1984). "In Search of a Scope and Sequence: Report of the NCSS Task Force on Scope and Sequence." *Social Education* 48(4):249–262.

Joyce, W.W., T.H. Little, and S.P. Wronski (1991). "Scope and Sequence, Goals, and Objectives: Effects of Social Studies." Pp. 321–331 in *Handbook of Research on Social Studies Teaching and Learning,* edited by James P. Shaver. New York: Macmillan.

Kaestle, Carl (1982). "Ideology and American Education History." *History of Education Quarterly* 22(1):123–137.

Kaltsounis, T. (1994). "Democracy's Challenge as the Foundation of the Social Studies." *Theory and Research in Social Education* 22(2): 176–193.

Keller, C.W. (1991). "It Is Time to Abolish the Mythology That the Social Studies Constitute a Discipline." *International Journal of Social Education* 6(2):69–75.

Lybarger, M.B. (1991). "The Historiography of Social Studies: Retrospect, Circumspect, and Prospect." Pp. 3–15 in *Handbook of Research on Social Studies Teaching and Learning,* edited by James P. Shaver. New York: Macmillan.

Massialas, Byron G. (1994). "Social Studies: Secondary Programs." *International Encyclopedia of Education.* London: Pergamon, pp. 5578–5582.

Mehlinger, Howard Q. (1977). "Foreword," in Barr, R.D., J.L. Barth, and S. Shermis, *Defining the Social Studies.* Washington, DC: The National Council for the Social Studies.

Missouri Department of Elementary and Secondary Education (1980). *A Guide to Social Studies Curriculum Development for Missouri Educators.* Columbia, MO: The Missouri Department of Elementary and Secondary Education.

National Council for the Social Studies (1993). "Definition Approved." *The Social Studies Professional,* January–February, p. 1.

National Council for the Social Studies (1994). *Expectations of Excellence: Curriculum Standards for Social Studies,* Bulletin 89. Washington, DC: The National Council for the Social Studies.

Newmann, F.M. (1977). "Building a Rationale for Civic Education." *Building Rationales for Citizenship Education,* edited by James P. Shaver. Washington, DC: National Council for the Social Studies.

Newmann, F.M. (1988). "Another View of Cultural Literacy: Go for Depth." *Social Education* 52(6):432–438.

O'Neil, John (1993). "The Challenge of Higher Standards: Can National Standards Make a Difference?" *Educational Leadership* 50(5):4–8.

Parker, Walter C. (1994). "The Standards are Coming," *Educational Leadership* 51(5):84–85.

Patrick, J.J. (1992). "Topics in the Social Studies Curriculum, Grades K–12." Pp. 65–82, in *Social Studies Curriculum Resource Handbook.* Millwood, NY: Kraus International.

Shaver, James P. and Harold Berlak, editors (1968). *Democracy, Pluralism, and the Social Studies: Readings and Commentary.* Boston: Houghton Mifflin.

Stanley, W.B. and T. Nelson (1986). "Social Education for Social Transformation." *Social Education* 50(6):528–533.

Tom, Alan (1969). "An Approach to Selecting Among Social Studies Curriculum: An Occasional Paper." St. Louis: The Metropolitan St. Louis Social Studies Center, Washington University, mimeographed.

U.S. Department of Education (1991). *America 2000: An Education Strategy.* Washington, DC.

Wesley, E.B. and S.P. Wronski (1958). *Teaching Social Studies in High School.* Boston: D.C. Heath, p. 3.

Wood, George Harrison (1984). "Schooling in a Democracy: Transformation or Reproduction?" *Educational Theory* 34(3):219–239.

Chapter Two

Creating A Civic Culture: Questioning Classroom Assumptions

Jo Ann C. Sweeney and Frances E. Monteverde
University of Texas, Austin

BEFORE YOU BEGIN THIS CHAPTER, close your eyes and visualize a typical classroom. What are the students doing? Where are you in the room? Describe the physical features of the room. How would you characterize the noise level of the students? What do you judge to be the emotional tone of the environment? Can you think of one or two experiences that helped you draw these mental images? Is your mental image the kind of classroom in which you would want to be a student?

We all want easy answers and formulas to deal with classroom life. Upon reflection, we sometimes discover that the "canned plan" actually interferes with our real experiences and intuitions about what works. Many texts suggest a separation between classroom management and instructional activities. This chapter asks you to reflect upon the connection between "effective teaching practices" and the "instructional program." If you approach this chapter with an open mind, you may conclude that, although there are no easy formulas, you are capable of constructing a learning environment in which you and your students thrive—intellectually, emotionally, socially, aesthetically.

To develop a classroom culture for authentic teaching and learning, today's educators confront a bewildering array of guidelines, mandates, policies, and rules. Prescriptions range from teacher-structured behavior modification to student-negotiated charters and social contracts. Additionally, teachers feel an obligation to satisfy diverse and sometimes conflicting expectations, as well as their personal professional standards.

Print and electronic media paint a *Clockwork Orange* image of social pathology upon the murals of the public school. Unfortunately, in some large urban districts, the sketches of vandalism, violence, insubordination, drugs, gang warfare, sexual promiscuity, apathy, and declining achievement are all too real. Understandably concerned for their youngsters' safety and discipline, parents perceive major school problems to be misbehavior, students' lack of interest, and substance abuse (Goodlad, 1984).

Besides media and parental complaints, public officials and corporate leaders clamor for stricter controls, more rigorous curricula, or, as a minimum, mastery of the "basics." In February 1990, then President Bush and the 50 state governors established six major goals for education, the *America 2000* proposal. They targeted the creation of disciplined schools, free from drugs and violence, and classroom environments conducive to learning by the year 2000.

"Truths" from Theory and Research: Information Processing and Effective Practices

Canons of educational theory and research affect teachers' decision making. The information processing model, which draws on social-cognitive and behaviorist learning research, influenced classroom instruction in the 1980s. According to this theory, humans acquire, store, and retrieve knowledge similarly to the mechanical functions of a computer (Marshall, 1995; Bruner, 1990). Teachers guide chunks of information through short-term memory to long-term memory, the "data bank" that can be accessed by "executive control." The model prescribes carefully sequenced instruction that includes these steps: gain attention, state objectives, stimulate recall of prior knowledge, present stimulus, provide guidance, elicit performance, provide feedback, assess performance, and enhance retention and transfer (Gagne, 1985).

Early information-processing theory defined learning as the connection of bits of information to the storage bin of "prior knowledge." Later theories stress the idea that learning is the unique, constant construction of meaning influenced not only by prior knowledge, but also by emotional and sociocultural factors (Alexander, Schallert, and Hare, 1991). Despite recent efforts of cognitive specialists to refine and "humanize" a more flexible learning model (Beers, 1987; Johnson-Laird, 1991; Kintsch, 1988; Sadoski, Paivio, and Goetz, 1991) many school administrators still expect teachers to follow the older, mechanical, step-by-step format.

Furthermore, the information-processing theory assumed that the more data stored in long-term memory, the easier the acquisition of new information and the greater the capacity for higher-order thinking. Gary McKenzie suggested the need to identify and teach specific skills and information before engaging students in complex problem solving (cited in Stanley, 1991). Jere E. Brophy and Thomas L. Good (1986, p. 341) reported that students of high socioeconomic status (SES), who presumably have greater stores of facts and knowledge, seemed to require intellectual stimulation and "interesting things to do" when they finished assignments. Low SES students, on the other hand, needed close supervision, small assignments, and more drill-and-practice exercises. Following these precepts, the thoughtful teacher might well wonder when students possess sufficient information to discuss current social issues, and if underclass or working class youngsters will ever possess the prerequisite competence to participate in decisions about public affairs.

To explain task motivation in this structured approach, Robert M. Gagne (1985, p. 307) cites David P. Ausubel (1968):

> Motivation is *not* an indispensable condition for learning….Ignore the unmotivated student's state for the time being and concentrate on teaching him as effectively as possible. Some degree of learning will ensue…and from the initial satisfaction of learning he will, *hopefully*, develop the motivation to learn more….The most appropriate way of arousing motivation to learn is to focus on the cognitive rather than on the motivational aspects of learning, and to rely on the motivation that is developed from successful educational achievement to energize further learning….(emphasis added).

Thus, by leading students to the fountain of knowledge and force-feeding small successful acquisitions, the teacher hopefully whets the thirst for further study and a desire for competence. Ausubel's suggestions tacitly accept behaviorist concepts such as shaping, stimulus, response, reward, and reinforcement, instead of assuming innate human curiosity.

Effective-teaching research, a related body of work of the 1970s and 1980s, also affected instruction in the past decade. Investigators claimed that specific teacher behaviors (process) correlated with high student achievement (product) as measured by standardized tests (Stanley, 1991; Doyle, 1986). This "process-product" research advised educators to teach, enforce, and reinforce "going-to-school" skills, that is, the rules and procedures for a smooth-running, brisk-paced workplace.

During the first weeks of school, "effective" teachers focus attention on the rules, obedience, and orderly behavior. Quickly moving about the classroom, "withit" instructors continuously monitor students to prevent "off-task" or disruptive behavior. They deliver rewards to obedient pupils and issue penalties for noncompliance. As do the managers of scientifically efficient factories, teachers reduce complex learning tasks to essential steps. They direct whole-class instruction and minimize distractions that compete with the teacher for attention. As a means of quality control, they regularly and consistently check seatwork and homework, the production of their student-workers. The system requires constant vigilance from the first day to the last. Following a century-old industrial model, the teacher-manager retains control through a "planned prevention and maintenance system" (Evertson, 1987).

In 1986, Walter P. Doyle cautioned, "Teachers often appear to subordinate instruction to management concerns" (p. 394). Because schools and classrooms are unique, order is not absolute silence and rigid conformity. It is defined partly by teacher's actions, but also by contexts, curriculum, and class activities. Teachers who use academic work to maintain control may actually undermine curricular purposes. In the social studies, for example, Shirley Engle and Anna S. Ochoa declared,

> The persistent study of social problems is at the very heart of the social studies endeavor....In a democracy the socializing process must be balanced by *countersocialization*, which emphasizes independent thinking and responsible social criticism. These abilities are fundamental to improving the quality of democratic life in a changing pluralistic nation (cited in Leming, 1989, p. 404).

Do one-word, fill-in-the-blank worksheets in history and geography direct students' attention to current political and socioeconomic topics? How well do teachers' lectures foster a youngster's interest in contentious civic concerns? Are notetaking and seatwork exercises adequate as preparation for active participation in community decisions? Simplified, concrete assignments, which students seem to prefer, do not threaten order. In a small South Texas high school, Douglas E. Foley (1990) observed "making out practices," that is, unspoken agreements between teachers and students to "make it through" the impersonal, compulsory education system. Teachers traded passing grades for minimum paperwork "production" while students agreed to cooperate in exchange for easily earned academic credits. Such "making out games" side-tracked instruction from projects that challenge students to think for themselves and to understand social issuess that affected their lives.

Doyle (1986) noted that focusing on order and rules at the outset of the year, the teacher immediately assumes an authoritarian image, one who is obliged to catch "culprits" and police conduct as demonstrations of competence. "The teacher's management task," he counters, "is primarily one of establishing and maintaining work systems for classroom groups rather than spotting and punishing misbehavior." (p. 423). Order is "fragile, a permanent pressure on classroom life" that teachers constantly need to protect. Earlier cautions notwithstanding, Doyle concludes, "Indeed, the use of...recitations and seatwork and the practice of routinizing most classroom procedures and activities appear to be reasonable strategies" (p. 424).

Similarly to Doyle, Brophy and Good (1986) pointed to the limits of effective teaching research:

> Data linking teacher behavior to achievement should not be used for teacher evaluation or accountability.... It would be inappropriate to penalize teachers for failing to follow overly rigid behavioral prescriptions....

> Teachers vary not only in their success in producing achievement, but in their success in fostering positive attitudes, personal development, and good group relations.... Success in one dimension does not necessarily imply success on others. It is possible to optimize progress along several dimensions...but beyond some point, further progress toward one objective will come at the expense of progress in another...

> Too much of even a generally good thing is still too much (p. 366).

Nevertheless, in their final recommendations, Brophy and Good (1986) repeated Gagne's sequenced steps and reiterated McKenzie's point: A great deal of drill and practice of basic skills and knowledge is essential, "just as essential to complex and creative intellectual performance as they are to the performance of a virtuoso violinist" (p. 367).

Despite warnings from various researchers (cited in Stanley, 1991), the resounding litany in the 1980s emphasized drill and practice, fragmented information and skills, recitation and seatwork, teacher-imposed order and control. (See Merlin C. Wittrock, *Handbook of Research on Teaching*, 3rd edition, 1986.) The approach fit not only traditional teacher practices (Cuban, 1984), but also the politically conservative, "back to the basics" agenda. Local, state, and federal officials zealously pounced on the canon, a seemingly inexpensive solution to the nation's economic and educational woes.

Instead of dealing with structural weaknesses in the economy, politicians preferred to blame education for the country's recessionary distress. Writing as a Harvard economist before he became Secretary of Labor, Robert Reich (1991) reported that during the 1980s the United States as a nation had cut back on investment in education. Just when "intellectual capital had become a uniquely important national asset" (p. 46), per-pupil expenditures fell below eight other industrial countries. Teachers' wages in constant dollars remained near the levels of the early 1970s. Ironically, "the schools facing the biggest social problems [in the poorest jurisdictions] have [gotten] the least help" (p. 47). Reich contrasted the United States with Germany, France, and Japan, nations that invested significantly in education, research, and training to create skilled manpower for high-wage jobs.

In the United States on the other hand, education agencies mandated accountability systems and staff development programs based upon the correlations in "effective-practices" research and "information-processing" theories. Teacher education courses disseminated the findings as prescriptive guides, the Competency Based Teacher Education programs. William B. Stanley (1991) asserted that these "simplistic applications" probably appalled teacher-effectiveness investigators (p. 252). The communities of educators and political decision-makers probably need to acknowledge the limitations of the early canon, and to consider later refinements of the theory, as well as other conceptions of learning and teaching. Social studies professionals need to consider the incongruency between civic competency goals and the teaching-learning models advocated in the 1980s.

Effects of the Canon

John Goodlad's (1984) report of 38 schools in 13 diverse American communities perhaps illustrates the consequences of process-product, information-prcessing ideology. He cast the school image in drab, dull grays, devoid of flair and excitement. The emotional tone was flat, with little joy, anger, or enthusiasm. Teachers retained control in authoritarian classrooms where whole-group instruction rather than activities or projects predominated. Teachers professed to aim for higher-thinking goals, but used repetitive seatwork and simple, one-answer test items for recall of information. Students held social studies in low esteem.

As the decade unfolded, other critics observed that reform efforts had not improved public education (McCaslin and Good, 1992). Despite the emphasis on acquisition of basic skills and information, American students' scores on tests of mathematics, general information, and vocabulary compared unfavorably with those in other industrial nations (Finn, 1987). Research by L. McNeil and N. Johnson (cited in Cusick, 1991) suggested that bureaucratic control, obedience to authority, and compliance with orders had become the major goals. Teachers reduced "academic content to work sheets, lists, and short-answer tests" (p. 284). Critical theorists Michael W. Apple and Henry A. Giroux (cited in Stanley, 1991) condemned the teaching effectiveness model, claiming that the prescriptive lessons transformed teachers into deskilled technicians. Conformist students were unprepared to deal with community and moral problems. Renate Nummela Caine and Geoffrey Caine (1991), who base their explanations of learning on physiological, brain-based research, questioned both the factory metaphor of schooling and process-product research. They charged that American students cannot think, given a decade of behavior modification, narrow learning outcomes, and threatening school experiences (p. 72). Defiantly, they recommended that teachers "get out of the memorization business" (pp. 21–22).

Critics concerned with the nation's economic sector identified needs that education should meet. Reich's (1991) analysis of "the real economy" declared: "Our nation's future economic success depends...on our unique attributes—the skills and insights of our workforce, and how well we link those skills and insights to the world economy" (p. 36). To enhance our advantage in the global marketplace, he targeted three core skills: problem identification, problem solving, and the innovative ability to link new technologies with products, services, and human resources.

With consultants from The Hudson Institute and The American Society for Training and Development, the U.S. Labor Department published *Demographics as Destiny: The U.S. Work Force in the Year 2000* (Johnson, 1989) and *Work Place Basics: The Skills Employers Want* (American Society for Training and Development, 1989). These documents stressed the need to cultivate in all youth the attitudes and abilities for flexible decision making, creativity, and adaptive interpersonal relationships. Population projections and labor market trends suggest a coming shortfall of human resources, a condition that favors all intellectually sophisticated employees, regardless of their socio economic status or cultural backgrounds.

In a similar vein, David P. Snyder and Gregg Edwards (1992) outlined future corporate needs. Although they foresaw an interim of painful economic adjustment extending to the year 2010, they predicted an "info-tech world" where key skills will be communication, reasoning, computation, and analysis. Both the public- and private-sector institutions strongly recommended experiential, on-the-job training to supplement formal instruction. Both groups suggest that highly structured classrooms, which stress memory-recall, regulations, and obedience, have not met the vocational needs of the current generation.

Signs of an Ideological Shift

Rhetoric in the professional literature indicates movement away from the information processing, process-product ideology. Throughout this century, reformers, but especially social studies educators (Evans, 1991), have opposed factory-like rituals and seatwork simulations of learning and teaching. In 1991, O.L. House claimed that demands for more school work, accountability, and strict discipline originated with conservative political thought. Accordingly, compliant researchers acquiesced to that political agenda rather than work to inform genuine school reform (cited in McCaslin and Good, 1992). After more than a decade, key political and business leaders, as well as conservative and liberal institutions, have called for a shift in educational emphases. Recent publications in education reflect this shift.

From the core of the process-product research community, Good and Brophy (1991) announced a *"newer* kind of research" about "teaching for understanding and higher-order applications," areas neglected by the *"process-effects"* research (emphasis added, pp. 442, 448). In their fifth edition of *Looking in Classrooms,* more than half the revised chapter on instruction deals with methods to promote decision making, problem solving, creativity, and critical thinking. The authors proclaimed, "Increasingly, research is pointing to thoughtful discussion, and not just teacher lecturing or student recitation, as characteristic of the classroom discourse involved in teaching for understanding" (p. 449). They identified nine components of "good subject matter teaching" (p. 450).

Although Good and Brophy (1991) declared such research "is still in its infancy" (p. 450), their list bears remarkable similarity to the kinds of objectives and practices undertaken in the Eight-Year Study more than 50 years ago. Sponsored by the Progressive Education Association, the study dealt with 22 public schools and 26 private schools from 1932 to 1940 (Aiken, 1942). Among other findings, the study pointed to "many avenues of study to acquire skills and achievement, including the present interests of students" (p. 22–23). Acting in a period of economic stress and transformation similar to today, participants in the eight-year experiment identified problem solving and reflective thinking as major goals linked to the schools' central purpose, the promotion of democracy. This brief comparison highlights the need to critically examine "new" theory, research, and remedies through the lens of historical narratives.

In the April 1992 *Educational Researcher*, McCaslin and Good reported a growing consensus that curriculum focuses too heavily on drill of facts and low-level concepts. In the 1980s, students gained recognition by obeying rules, paying attention, and taking few academic risks. The authors criticized teachers' failure to relate instruction to students' prior knowledge and the reliance on behavior modification to control classroom behavior. In fact, they argued persuasively that such practices are incompatible with programs that profess to teach self control, autonomous problem solving, and critical thought. Thinking noiselessly, "without peer communication and social exchange," students "get by" (p. 12). Such a management system coupled with a curriculum for creativity is a contradiction in terms, an oxymoron (p. 12). Departing from the Brophy and Good report in the 1986 *Handbook of Research on Teaching*, this article denounced the channeling of low SES students into facile curricula devoid of opportunities to study critical issues.

An unmistakable sign of the ideological shift occurred in the June 1992 *ASCD Curriculum Update*, a publication of the prestigious Association for Supervision and Curriculum and Development. Entitled "Teaching Thinking: Educators Shift from Recall to Reasoning," the pamphlet discussed several process-product assumptions (Willis, 1992). It questioned the "overproceduralization" or mechanization of thinking strategies, and stressed the social construction of knowledge rather than the storage and retrieval of memorized information. Instead of standardized testing and short-answer quizzing, the ASCD paper urged teachers to assess thinking skills by observing class discussions and portfolios of student work. The text ended on an optimistic note: "Teachers [will be] 'rejuvenated' by the change from dispenser of knowledge to sparker of ideas" (p. 8).

But will most teachers relish the opportunity to "rejuvenate," to shift to a student-centered mode and more complex, provocative activities? Failed plans for reform litter the history of American education as teachers often have clung to familiar, comfortable, lecture-recitation formats (Cuban, 1984). For example, the "New Social Studies" of the 1960s gained narrow acceptance partly because many perceived inquiry as a methodology imposed by elite scholars with little exposure to school realities (Hertzberg, 1981). Will teachers now relinquish the mantle of power-holder for the role of power-sharer with students? How much experimentation, creativity, and "disorder" will school administrators and local communities tolerate?

If teachers themselves have not learned through Socratic dialogue and inquiry projects, will they have the confidence and conviction to initiate such activities? Given the tendencies and assumptions of the previous decade, it is not surprising that prospective young teachers vaguely remember their precollegiate social studies classes. Informal surveys revealed few who could name the disciplines in the field and the variety of activities or materials that can be used. Most described social studies as "boring" and associated the subject with worksheets and the recall of information. (In addition to the two authors' observations, R. Wilhelm [1991] reported similar responses from students in social studies methods classes.)

Perhaps those concerned with the preparation of future social studies teachers need to counteract some effects of the 1980s "reforms." Leadership within the field seems to support the idea. Repeating the civic message of the Eight-Year Study, as well as the Engle and Ochoa declaration, the National Council for the Social Studies proclaimed:

> The primary purpose of social studies is to help young people develop the ability to make informed and reasoned decisions for the public good as citizens of a culturally diverse, democratic society in an interdependent world (Preface, 1992 Statement of Standards).

In October 1994, the National Board for Professional Teaching Standards (NBPTS) (Hunt, 1994) released a draft outlining the knowledge, skills, and dispositions or commitments that prospective social studies and history teachers should attain. The document revived critical thinking as a central goal, the concept of teaching as a complex process, and the development of civic competence as a major purpose. The NBPTS document distinguishes between the acquisition of surface information and the deep coverage of topics. Thus, two key professional groups in the field have joined the call to shift away from the dominant paradigm of the 1980s.

We return to the dichotomy expressed by McCaslin and Good (1992). It is a salient point for social studies teachers. Anyone who has experienced on-line mass production has engaged in mindless, monotonous, tedious work. What meaning will students make of an instructional program that advocates independent reflection, informed decision making, and civic activity, yet simultaneously prohibits discussion, social interaction, self expression, and challenges to the "brisk-paced" production system? Can teachers credibly compartmentalize higher-level learning from factory-like socialization?

To develop the problem-solving skills that Reich and others have targeted as crucial, professors and their student teachers can begin with healthy skepticism about prescriptive memorization, "devoid of significance and purpose" (Schallert, 1987, p. 74). Classes might focus on the construction of multiple meanings, fundamental principles, dissonances, and topics that generate curiosity and interest. In a class discussion of social studies methods for elementary teachers at the University of Texas, Austin, only one student of 22, Kelly, remembered social studies as a valuable experience. She related features of a unit that took place in the early 1970s at her Des Moines, Iowa, elementary school.

> In an "open-classroom" setting, six teachers of the fourth and fifth grades collaborated on two-weeks of instruction about World War II. After large-group explanations by teachers in a resource center, the children met in small groups to discuss their impressions, reactions, and opinions.

> They consulted a variety of reading materials, analyzed photos from the period, studied the clothing styles, and learned songs related to the war effort. As the work progressed, they kept journals and created timelines with drawings to portray their understandings. As "junior historians," they conducted interviews with adults who had lived through that era.

> Kelly did not remember taking tests nor drill-and-practice sessions covering the content. She did recall, "Even those who didn't like school loved that unit. World War II came alive for all of us." More than 20 years later, she traced her continuing interest and avid reading about the subject to those elementary school experiences.

Recovering her own past as a legitimate point of reference, the beginning teacher had an opportunity to "unpack" her assumptions about "positivist cognitive science." Teachers often ignore or seldom focus on the meanings that students create, assuming that the pupils' cultural backgrounds are not valuable. The student is, in the teacher's mind, not an "expert." According to Jerome Bruner (1990), "the willingness to construe knowledge and values from multiple perspectives without the loss of commitment to one's own values" is the keystone of democratic culture (p. 30). Through such personal historical narratives, future professionals create the sort of "folk psychology" that signals a shift away from the reductionist pedagogy of the 1980s (Bruner 1990, Chapter 1).

Besides the academic program, educators might question prescriptions for classroom management and discipline. Theona McQueen (1992) suggests several principles that a reflective teacher might ponder:

1. "[Self-discipline] is controlling one's own behavior without constant and continuous reminders from teachers, parents, supervisors, police officers or 'whoever is in charge'" (p. 145).

2. "[T]he importance and power of modeling cannot be overemphasized" (p. 145).

3. "Effective classroom managers accept responsibility for student learning" (p. 32).

4. "[Teachers] do not compromise by letting students determine goals and standards" (p. 33).

5. "After self-discipline is taught, anything can be taught; and until self-discipline is learned, anything learned is worthless" (p. 144).

Is self-discipline defined in terms of external factors, "those in charge"? Do these statements imply obedience to authority, even if it conflicts with one's internal, ethical standards? Is this definition congruent with the principles of outstanding moral leaders who defied authority? Would Mohandas K. Gandhi, Jesus of Nazareth, and Martin Luther King, Jr. have met the criteria for self-discipline? Is there somewhat of a discrepancy between teachers' setting the standards and assuming responsibility for student learning, and the students' developing self-discipline? To this question, McCaslin and Good (1992) reply,

> As long as the teacher controls the management system (e.g., does the alerting and maintains the accountability), students cannot learn self-regulation, problem solving, and self-control....[Authoritative management] requires that rules and structures—the scaffolding—be adjusted so that students progressively assume more responsibility for self-control (p.13).

In her discussion of classroom management, McQueen (1992) repeats the last premise with modification: "...after you have taught discipline, you can teach anything; and until you have taught discipline, nothing is learned" (p. 168). Does she assume that pupils must first become obedient subjects, before they are capable of learning? Do human beings learn continuously, with or without structures and deliberate effort? Brain-based theories suggest they do.

Brain-Based Education: Another Consideration

Our mental constructs about learning shape the ways we go about schooling. Undoubtedly, the information-processing theory has produced valuable insights about the learning; however, the computer conception of learning inadequately explains complex human mental functions (Nummela Caine and

Caine, 1991; Beers, 1987). If teachers believe that a great store of knowledge is a prerequisite for higher-order thinking, teachers may limit classroom activities to a series of mechanized "inputs" of arbitrary information and "outputs" of correctly recalled responses. They may ignore the kinds of activities that foster multiple meanings, or connections, between seemingly isolated pieces of information. An alternative explanation of learning bases its precepts upon the way the human brain is believed to function physiologically. The next section of this chapter reviews key issues of the brain-based theory and research

Instead of a linear memory system, brain-based theory assumes at least two types of memory: (1) the *taxon* system (from "taxonomies" or lists) which is described in the information-processing theory, and (2) the *locale* system (Nummela Caine and Caine, 1991, Chapter 4). The latter develops "naturally," with or without deliberate rehearsal or memorization. The locale system monitors and organizes a "thematic map" of all accumulated knowledge—declarative, emotional, conditional, sociocultural, procedural—the "prior knowledge" defined by Patricia A. Alexander, Diane L. Schallert, and Victoria Hare (1991). Because the locale, or spatial memory system "drives the search for meaning," Nummela Caine and Caine find an affinity between brain-based theory and the whole-language theory of comprehension (p. 85). The locale system accounts for the greatest store of memories, most of which are tacit, unrehearsed, and unreinforced by rewards.

For example, the initial discussion of this chapter triggered the memory of a conversation with a mentor professor thirty years before. A legal scholar and political scientist, the professor had fled from a Latin American dictatorship and eventually became a U.S. citizen. He related his son's first experiences in an American public school system:

> After his first day in elementary school, the boy told his parents about the committees he would work on, and the projects he and his classmates would carry out. Through his son's stories, the professor came to appreciate more fully the role of education in democracy, and to understand partially why imitations of the U.S. Constitution had failed in Latin America. In contrast with the schools in his country of origin, he claimed the schools in the United States taught children to discuss, organize, and take responsibility for their learning. The concept of participation in school activities was taken for granted in the culture.

What caused the recall of this seemingly forgotten vignette? Certainly not drill and practice rehearsals over the years. The human brain, unlike the mechanical computer model, has the innate and autonomous capacity to create unique meanings among diverse sets of information. According to the theory, socially interactive situations, like the discussions about this chapter, enhance the locale system's capacity to draw connections between significant experiences. The former professor's lesson about participatory democracy in

U.S. classrooms seemed most appropriate for inclusion in a chapter about social studies and classroom cultures today.

Although the taxon and locale systems interact in a dynamic, ongoing fashion, the taxon memory tends to shut down the locale system. Nummela Caine and Caine (1991) advise teachers to focus sparingly on the taxon system and instead design lessons that encourage students to organize personally meaningful "thematic maps." Consider this narrative.

> Following the "effective practices" model, a student teacher of eighth grade U.S. history designed a lesson about the judicial branch of government. She presented a list of random "facts" about the federal court system, including such points as the number of circuit courts; the steps in the appointment process; the kinds of decisions rendered; the names of the current Supreme Court justices, their salaries, ages, genders, and ethnic or racial backgrounds. The student teacher guided the students in drill and practice to learn the information, then gave an independent practice exercise, a short-answer test over the material. The students dutifully took notes, memorized the data, and, for the most part, earned a passing grade on the quiz for that day.

Later, the student teacher expressed concern about pupil apathy and lack of enthusiasm. They did not ask questions, nor show interest in knowing how the court system affected them personally. They did not discuss the implications of lifetime appointments, nor the momentous court cases under consideration. The pupils seemed not to recognize the significance of the presidential elections for the composition of the court. Did the students need to memorize information before they considered major problems facing the judicial branch or the relationship between the court system and the larger picture of current affairs? How could the student teacher have arranged the lesson to elicit more independent thought and less memory-recall?

To explain motivation in the information-processing theory, Good and Brophy (1991, pp. 298–299) distinguish between "intrinsic motivation" from "motivation to learn." The former is "an affective, emotional response" linked to fun or recreation.* Motivation to learn is "primarily a cognitive or intellectual response....an enduring disposition to value learning...to take pride in acquiring knowledge and skills" (p. 299).

Nummela Caine and Caine (1991) argue that to separate the affective from cognitive creates a false dichotomy. Emotions act as critical energizers or constraints in learning, and students absorb and store the entire experience. Paul MacLean reports, "Emotions give a sense of reality to what we do and

---

* Webster's definition says nothing about emotion. Intrinsic...1. belonging to the real nature of a thing; not dependent on external circumstances; essential; inherent 2. *Anat.* located within, or exclusively of, a part.

think" (cited in Nummela Caine and Caine, 1991, p. 57). For example, a student may cognitively learn a list (taxon) of countries and capitals to earn a passing grade, but affectively learn to dislike geography. The cognitive "input" may be forgotten, unless it is used or rehearsed regularly, whereas the negative attitude may be retained as tacit knowledge for many years. The following vignette illustrates the strength of emotional or affective perceptions over cognitive learning.

> In Spring 1992, a white, middle-class student teacher was covering a social studies unit on the 1960s civil rights movement when the "Rodney King verdict" was announced. Believing that the jury had not rendered a just decision as punishment for police brutality, African-American citizens rioted in protest in the city of Los angeles.
>
> Seizing the "teachable moment" to relate the academic program to current events, the student teacher initiated a discussion about the case. She wanted the students, who were low SES African-Americans and Hispanic-Americans, to understand how the jury had arrived at its decision and to consider alternative responses that the rioters in Los Angeles could have made. In retrospect, she mused that her hidden agenda was probably to persuade the pupils that the U.S. system of justice could work, and that the rioters were not justified.
>
> If that group of eleventh graders had been exposed to the prescribed curriculum, they had studied the U.S. Constitution, the Bill of Rights, checks and balances, separation of powers, federalism, the judicial branch and its system of appeals. They were in the process of learning about Martin Luther King's nonviolent civil disobedience movement when the verdict came down. Cognitively, they probably knew, at least vaguely, how the system is supposed to work.
>
> Their socio-emotional experiences and observations of the videotaped police beatings of Rodney King outweighed the cognitive content of their schooling. They drew meanings quite different from those of the student teacher. "The system," they believed, "is rigged against minorities." Options such as court appeals, passive disobedience, peaceful demonstrations, and the power of the ballot, had not really changed the treatment of nonwhite minorities in the United States. The violence had been justified, most students in the class concluded. Although they may have demonstrated knowledge of U.S. government on tests and assignments, their attitude toward it was one of cynicism. It did not live up to its promises.

In that open discussion, the student teacher learned about the meanings her pupils had constructed. The cognitive elements she had hoped to teach proved less durable than the affective connections the students drew of their own free will. Of one thing she became convinced: Unlike lecture-recitation-seatwork, discussion of topics that had meaning for students elicited almost total, active participation.

Good and Brophy (1991) argue that the colloquial use of the term "intrinsic motivation" is misleading: "We study or do something not for its sake but for *our* sake—because it brings us pleasure, meets our needs, or in some other way provides enjoyable stimulation or satisfaction" (pp. 298–299). Nummela Caine and Caine (1991) explain that intrinsic motivation is conducive to creativity, whereas extrinsic motivation actually demotivates when students focus on the reward or avoidance of punishment rather than the challenge of exciting assignments. To counter the "psychological egoist" explanation of motivation (Rachels, 1986, Chapter 5), brain-based theory claims that the prefrontal cortex created the human capacity to abstract, to transcend personal concerns, and to act compassionately (Nummela Caine and Caine, 1991).

The massive efforts of secondary and university students who volunteered for grueling, dangerous relief work after Mexico City's earthquake in 1985 suggested that young people *can* be moved by more than rewards and punishments. Their original impetus to action came from the need to help suffering, needy people. To imply that the students risked safety and comfort for personal satisfaction grossly denies their higher moral purposes. When classes resumed after the crisis subsided, students who had not been very scholarly before returned to school with changed attitudes. Some, who worked directly with doctors during the disaster, chose careers in medicine. Doctors in Mexico do not uniformly earn high salaries as doctors in the United States do.

MacLean's triune brain theory (cited in Nummela Caine and Caine, 1991, Chapter 5) contributes important concepts for understanding classroom cultures that promote creativity, problem solving, and critical thinking. Physiologically and functionally, the brain divides into three evolutionary layers:

1. *The R-complex,* or reptilian part, is located in the brain stem and is concerned with survival and body maintenance. It accounts for such behaviors as the establishment of territory, the formation of hierarchies, preening, nesting, mating rites, and flocking tendencies. Under perceived threat or stress, this region tends to dominate. The responses are automatic, reactive, ritualistic, unimaginative. "Flight or fight" responses are typical. The R-complex is resistant to change and less adaptive.

2. *The limbic system* (amygdala and hippocampus) monitors emotions and organizes new information in the locale memory system. Located in the center of the brain, it mediates between the R-complex and the neocortex. It can inhibit or redirect the R-complex; however, under stress, cortisol inhibits this area and the cortex, and the ability to think or respond imaginatively. Under conditions of challenge, adrenalin and noradrenalin strengthen this area's functions, if there are breaks between the challenges.

3. *The neocortex,* the newer area comprises five-sixths of the total brain and is believed to be the site of higher levels of thought, creativity, and adaptive problem solving. Under stress or threat, it "shuts down" and the organism "down shifts" to the reptilian complex.

Although the three regions interact and influence each other, certain conditions and chemical reactions can inhibit or strengthen various functions of the brain. Leslie Hart (cited in Nummela Caine and Caine, 1991) insists, "Cerebral learning and threat conflict directly and completely" (p.76). On the other hand, the neocortex does function best in state of "relaxed alertness" and challenge. In that state, students feel safe to take academic risks.

A teacher's major task, then, is to transform perceived threats or sense of helplessness to challenges. The constant barrage of test-like events, work sheets, and rapid fire recitation does not reduce threat. Deemphasizing letter and numerical grades, loosening rigid rules, and eliminating the nonstop regimen of work would reduce stress. Interspersing periods of work with relaxation, introducing a variety of activities, and scheduling time to take stock would produce an atmosphere of "relaxed alertness" and challenge. By the same token, too much unpredictability or disorder produce stress and threat. Brain-based theory does not advocate *laissez faire* education. To encourage higher levels of thinking, teachers and administrators must ensure that the classroom and school are safe from physical danger and psychological stress, such as fighting, bigotry, and drug-related gang warfare. Students need a predictable classroom culture. Educators, but especially social studies teachers, need to balance freedom and control.

Except for its discussion of attitude formation, the information-processing model focuses more on academic performances and acquisition of knowledge than on learning social interaction. Neurophysiological research claims that rich social experiences and environments create more highly developed brains, and an increased capacity to learn. Early childhood, a critical period for brain growth, requires "safe, consistent environments that provide…a variety of rich emotional, social, and cognitive interaction" (Nummela Caine and Caine, 1991, p. 30). They assume that the human species is biologically driven to belong to a group, to relate, and interact with others.

As mentioned earlier, in a threatening or repressive atmosphere, the reasoning part of the brain shuts down, and the R-complex summons "reptilian responses" to deal with the perceived helplessness (pp. 67–68). In schools where order and obedience take precedence over the curriculum, students prefer ritualistic, unambiguous, unimaginative, minimal academic tasks. Peer-group affiliation, which is less adaptive, becomes the reason for going to school (Cusick, 1991). Teachers who perceive students as threatening revert to R-complex behavior by imposing rigid, inflexible rules and consequences. Students resort to flight; teachers resort to fight. Rather than repress the drive for affiliation, brain-based theory suggests the redirection of R-complex preferences (Nummela Caine and Caine, 1991).

Phillip A. Cusick (1991) discusses adolescents' universal tendency to form cliques, or tightly bonded peer groups. As Foley (1990) also noted, they reflect the class hierarchy of the greater society. Students give fierce loyalty to the group rather than enter into the total school community, and except for a talented minority, most prefer not to enter the competition for grades and honors. Some lower SES groups become antagonistic to school norms and defiantly resist authorities (Cusick, 1991; Foley, 1990). They prefer to stay in the clique where status is secure and norms are predictably, but rigidly maintained.

By emphasizing "corrosive individualism" (Grant, 1980, cited in Cusick, 1991), and discouraging peer interactions, the school culture militates against participation in the larger community. Schooling today contradicts Horace Mann's rationale for the common school, the vehicle to transcend socioeconomic differences and learn the principles of a republican form of government (Spring, 1989). Brain-based theory would argue that schools also militate against the neocortical, higher-level functions and encourage R-complex, lower-level functions. Both philosophical and physiological reasons support the case for social interaction in educational activities.

To correct this deeply entrenched pattern, Cusick would replace "the minimalist contractural model, lodged in a bureaucratic hierarchy" with a "moral learning community" (p. 287). He recommends building-based control and the restoration of teacher autonomy to build classroom norms, as well as to initiate self-evaluation. Nummela Caine and Caine (1991) echo Cusick's proposal with the stipulation that general principles guide the setting of standards and norms. Some of their guidelines are shown in Box 2–1.

Box 2–1   Considerations for Brain-Based School Culture
Adapted From Nummela Caine and Caine (1991)

1. The design and administration of the total school sends messages to students that shape what is learned (p. 84).

2. Socially constructed knowledge from the community and environment influences students' learning and the meanings they create (p. 87).

3. "Everyone a teacher and everyone a learner" (p. 118). Teachers can redirect the R-complex drive for affiliation by creating supportive classroom cultures. Teachers retain respect by demonstrating continuous learning and interest in the subject matter. Students retain dignity and self-worth in an environment where their meanings and knowledge are sought and valued (p. 128).

4. Each classroom and school can develop protocols, customs, courtesies, elements of playfulness, and mutually respectful attitudes within the contexts of the communities they serve (p. 123–124).

The brain-based explanation of learning has implications for the ways teachers conduct instruction and create classroom cultures for authentic learning and teaching. It can provide another basis for thinking about schooling. Although "behaviorally stated objectives reduce wasted time in temporary diversions, ephemeral entertainment, or other irrelevancies" (Popham, 1968, cited in Nummela Caine and Caine, 1991, p. 105), precisely those spontaneous or open-ended activities induce the kinds of learning that teachers and students need to meet the exigencies of the future. Nummela Caine and Caine conclude, "We are moved inexorably beyond the information-processing model as the predominant paradigm for learning" (1991, p. 87). Brain-based learning theory is more congruent with goals and objectives long held by social studies leaders.

Democracy and the Teacher of Social Studies

Leaders have variously defined the field of social studies since its founding in 1916 by the Commission on the Reorganization of Secondary Education (Gross, 1991). The spectrum has ranged from "a curriculum area organized around history and social sciences simplified for pedagogical purposes," to "subjects and lessons centered around social problems," to "educational reform" that teaches students "to manage change and crisis in a democratic society" (Gross, 1991; Barth, 1991). Some believe the field's major purposes are to transmit knowledge and train good habits, whereas others claim that the disciplines should be in the service of critical thinking and interactive, social problem solving (Engle, 1986; Evans, 1991).

"Citizenship education," a bone of contention, divides leaders in the field: Is it the central purpose of social studies, or the central purpose of the total school program? (Shaver, cited in Hertzberg, 1981; Davis, 1991). In some schools, "citizenship" grades reflect conduct and behavior, a measure of how well a student has conformed to the rules. Historically, the term has floated through several interpretations (Cornbleth, 1982). Initially, it meant creating a national identity by fostering commitment to democratic values and national loyalty. During the nineteenth century, it emphasized knowledge of government and the training of character traits such as hard work and honesty. With the influx of immigrants into the nation at the turn of the century, the concept broadened to include civic projects to improve the local community, as well as orientation and loyalty to American government.

According to Catherine Cornbleth, by 1982 the term had become no more than a slogan to acculturate youngsters "to accept prevailing democratic principles...and to adopt certain economic and social norms" (p. 260; also see Davis, 1991). In contrast, her concept, "democratic political education," suggests commitment not only to certain principles (for example, freedom, justice, equality, human rights, and dignity), but also to active participation in the governing process. Referring to the ideas of Thomas Popkewitz, B. Robert Tabachnick, and Gary Wehlage (1981), Cornbleth (1982) differentiates between illusory, technical, and constructive citizenship education. Constructive citizenship advocates these practices:

> [Encourage students] to pursue their own interests, engage in a variety of activities, and examine a broad range of political content and possibilities. Comprehension rather than memorization is sought, with content being integrated and related to students' experiences....[It] assumes knowledge is tentative, that there are multiple ways of knowing, and that different perspectives ought to be considered....The student role is an active one; learning activities...foster students' rights and responsibilities, and students are expected to demonstrate independence and initiative....[It] reflects a questioning orientation, one that encourages critical examination of the political system as well as effective participation in public affairs" (p. 261).

Research tentatively supported nonauthoritarian approaches. Cornbleth (1982) reported,

> An open classroom climate, in which controversial issues are freely discussed and students believe they can influence classroom procedures and events, shows a consistently strong, positive relationship with political and participatory attitudes...[and] lower political cynicism and alienation (pp. 262–263).

Despite these findings, teachers promoted unquestioned loyalty and obedience, and discouraged change-oriented participation. Cornbleth (1982) gave several reasons for these tendencies: (1) Special interest groups sought to impose their political morality; (2) the back-to-the-basics movement neglected participatory citizenship concerns; and (3) economic pressures limited resources for research in citizenship education.

Significant for teachers of social studies, research indicated a decline in citizenship and political knowledge held by American youth during the 1970s (Ehman, 1980 and Tyler, 1981, cited in Spring, 1989). Mary Tubbs and James A. Beane (1981, cited in Spring, 1989) reported survey findings of a decrease in the "teaching of social issues, student involvement in community service, and student involvement in curriculum planning" in American high schools since 1974 (p. 34). Arguing that the social studies had diminished as a school subject, James Davis (1984) beseeched educators to assume an advocacy role in defense of the field. He asserted that the most potent features of social studies programs are the participatory experiences that cultivate democratic citizenship.

Continuing the same theme, Walter W. Parker and John Jarolimek (1984) questioned the congruence of existing practices with the values professed by the society and its schools. Dialogue and creative problem solving, as well as knowledge and academic skills, are indispensable to socialize youth for active political participation. Urging teachers to summon the courage to oppose the accepted canon, the authors quoted the 1979 National Council for Social Studies Curriculum Guidelines:

> Whatever students of social studies learn should impel them to apply their knowledge, abilities, and commitments toward the improvement of the human condition (p. 13).

Although students learn participatory attitudes and skills by indirect and direct instruction, the social studies curriculum deliberately addresses the concern. For children of low socioeconomic backgrounds, their social studies classes may offer the only opportunities to discuss public issues and acquire participatory skills. Parker and Jarolimek contended that self-governance should be "a way of life" extending into all social relationships—clubs, organizations, unions, religious institutions, schools and so forth. Clearly, the two authors advocated a vision of constructive citizenship education.

In the Foreword to *CIVITAS: A Framework for Civic Education*, Ernest Boyer (1991) declared, "We are becoming civically illiterate as a nation" (p. xv). According to that publication, U.S. citizens possess neither sufficient knowledge nor confidence in their abilities to resolve social, political, and economic problems. As faith in the leadership and institutions erodes, Americans exhibit apathy in the public sphere. Less than half the eligible citizens vote today, compared with the 80 percent-plus turnouts in the nineteenth century. The U.S. voting record is among the lowest of Western democracies.

In a 1992 PBS interview, John K. Galbraith contended that people do not participate because they believe their opinions do not matter. Common consensus eludes an increasingly fragmented and polarized society. Boyer contends the society urgently requires civic education that emphasizes sophisticated communication, critical thinking, active decision making, involvement in the school's life, and knowledge of public affairs. R. Freeman Butts (1991) passionately argued that if democracy is to survive and flourish, the schools, both public and private, need to produce informed citizens who can participate effectively and critically in political discourse. The challenge for curriculum designers is to locate materials that will help students understand issues from several perspectives, as well as provide basic information needed to close the civic literary gap. An example of such a teaching resource was created in 1991.

The National Council for the Social Studies collaborated with the Center for Civic Education and the Council for the Advancement of Citizenship to create *CIVITAS* (Quigley and Bahmueller, 1991). This thick, detailed account is not a national curriculum proposal, but rather a guideline for curriculum developers who would promote civic competence, responsibility, and widespread participation of youth in the nation's political life. Ideological rhetoric and patriotism are not sufficient, *CIVITAS* contends. Students must feel "empowered" to monitor and influence public policy. They must be willing to set aside private interest and personal concerns for the sake of the common good, yet respect minority rights in the pluralistic society. To avoid disillusionment, they need to recognize that the process is not one of "win or lose," but one of continual negotiation and compromise in the allocation of scarce resources and distribution of power among factions. Their vistas must extend in empathetic appreciation and respect for the diversity found in the "global village." *CIVITAS* explores conservative and liberal viewpoints on a vast number of public issues. It is an invaluable resource for any who seek to reform American education in the 1990s. These recommendations require a conception of teaching and learning different from the dominant effective-teaching, process-product ideology.

Toward a Democratic Classroom Culture

The crisis facing American democracy in the 1990s differs greatly from that identified 20 years earlier. The system rests upon a shaky, weakened foundation. The religious right and commercial interests seriously challenge Horace Mann's vision of public education as a means to transcend socioeconomic differences (McCarthy 1994). If special interest groups or businesses come to dominate the schools, the nation may distort its commitment to social justice and civic participation. The society may veer toward the type of polarization it sought to escape more than two hundred years before. Without an informed citizenry disposed to participate in its own governance, a society cannot claim the title "democracy."

If the schools are to fulfill their historic mission to prepare citizens for active civic life, educators must create school cultures that encourage autonomous, responsible thought and action. They require flexibility rather than regimentation in both academic programs and classroom cultures. Just as the affective domain invades the cognitive processes, the "instructional program" inextricably connects to the system of "classroom management." The values, norms, resources, and individual talents of the school and larger community shape the unique culture of each classroom and school. No one system of discipline universally fits all situations. Nor can a code of conduct remain static. As in the larger society, the school's definition of acceptable behavior will change over time.

After more than a decade of strict controls and lower-level cognitive tasks, teachers and students will not shift easily to a less restrictive mode. As a preliminary step, educators need to reconsider basic assumptions about teaching and learning, as well as the central purposes of education and the vision of school as a community of learners. Sheldon Berman (1990) describes a conceptualization of community that coincides with what we have in mind.

> [A community is] a group of people who acknowledge their interconnectedness, have a sense of their common purpose, respect their differences, share in group decision making as well as in responsibility for the actions of the group, and support each other's growth....
>
> Creating a caring community...calls for developing a shared set of values or goals and establishing structures that allow...[for participation] in community decision making and in collective efforts that contribute...to mak[ing] a difference in the world....
>
> A sense of community requires affirmation. [It] means finding ways in which the community can affirm its members and acknowledge its own accomplishments....People become rich resources to each other. Communities need stories, heroes and heroines, rituals, and celebrations. These are the oil that makes a community function smoothly. They demonstrate that its members are valued and that people care about each other and about the group as a whole....
>
> They begin to understand the meaning of the common good, to appreciate that their efforts do make a difference, and to develop a sense of relatedness to the larger human community (p. 77).

In Berman's community, teachers shift from an attitude of "us-and-them" power struggle without relinquishing their responsibility to guarantee a safe, orderly learning environment. They do it in concert with the youngsters and administrators. An open, flexible setting requires a sense of trust and humor to minimize fear and stress. Good and Brophy (1991) observe that "open education is consistently inferior in its effects on students' achievement, although it may be somewhat superior to traditional education in its effects on student attitudes and other affective variables" (p. 353). The results of a well-controlled study by P.S. Fry and Jean Addington over three years demonstrated that students in open classrooms developed greater self-esteem, ego strength, and social problem-solving skills than those in the traditional settings (cited in Good and Brophy, 1991).

A Proposal: The "Think Tank" Metaphor

The image of the school as a factory inadequately represents the kinds of institutions required for present and future life in the United States. Both the political and economic sectors call for more than standardized "products" discharged from homogeneous molds and mindless conveyor belts. The image of teacher-as-technician—routinely loosening and tightening the machinery, compulsively checking for quality control—is also inadequate.

If futurologists predict correctly, the majority of adults will not occupy treadmill jobs. If government of, for, and by the people survives, its citizens will not play passive, obedient roles. Both the political and economic realms will require people who value and exercise intellectual accomplishment. They will ask probing questions and imaginatively sort out problems. They will responsibly initiate action, communicate persuasively, resolve conflicts, and appreciate human diversity.

However, a more important consideration than future needs of society should direct the discussion. What kinds of school experiences will help students make sense of the world they currently perceive and inhabit? By addressing that question first, then gearing the "instructional program" and "classroom management" to those answers, educators will have taken the first steps to authentic teaching and learning. They will also have taken the first steps to deal with the political and economic dilemmas facing the nation.

The "think tank" metaphor perhaps captures both the private and public functions of education. *Webster's New World Dictionary* defines the term as follows:

> [Slang] a group or center organized, as by government or business, to do intensive research and problem solving, esp. with the aid of computers and other sophisticated equipment (Guralnik, 1980, p. 1478).

Our conceptualization of the social studies classroom as a "think tank" recasts students and teachers as generators of knowledge and meanings, as problem solvers, rather than as processors and replicators of information or algorithmic skills. In such an institution, a central mission or area of concern defines the activities undertaken. The central mission of the class might simply be to help youth and teachers to make sense of the world in which they live. The metaphor suggests inquiry and expression in many human endeavors.

To retain credibility, participants in think tanks must adhere to basic principles. Committed to intellectual honesty, they probe issues deeply, and question basic premises or assumptions. To discern new patterns, causes, and effects, think-tank experts look at all the pertinent evidence in their quest for understanding. Their discoveries are meant to illuminate and influence public and private decision making; therefore, their communication must be clear, persuasive, reasonable. To be sure, the findings reflect the group's biases, preferences, and underlying values, but the merits of their solutions are weighed in the public sphere of debate and discussion. People from think tanks get out of the ivory tower and into the fray. They propose alternative solutions to problems and predict probable, possible, and preferable consequences to courses of actions. By their very existence, these institutions acknowledge the tentative nature of knowledge and the need for continuous inquiry, reflection, and evaluation.

What might it mean to think of social studies classrooms as think tanks? For one thing, teachers might eliminate the obsessive pressure "to cover it all" in a superficial manner. Just as think tanks select issues for investigation, teachers could opt for depth over breadth in designing curriculum, or deal with pressing issues of the day rather than a "prescribed program." One of the authors recalls observing a student teacher of social studies the day after the assassination of President Kennedy. The young teacher felt obliged to "review for the test" rather than deal with that momentous turning point in the history of the United States and the world. In a think-tank atmosphere, the teacher would have explored the more significant matter.

Students demonstrate the capacity to act responsibly and, with teacher guidance, to set norms of behavior conducive to learning. They carry out highly participatory activities related to social studies programs. They conduct model United Nations, congresses, court trials, and simulated press conferences, and presidential election campaigns. Such activities sprout to life in the imaginations of students and teachers. More often than not, projects begin as small-scale activities, then expand depending on the interests and commitments of the students and teachers. In a school climate that fosters discussion, creativity, and collaboration, administrators and curriculum supervisors take risks and accept trade-offs for "academic learning time" and "time on task." Brainstorming among students, teachers, parents, and administrators flourishes in a culture of collegiality.

As people increasingly rely on expert elites, "the replacement of democratic government by technocracy" poses a real threat (Boyer, 1991, pp. xv–xvi). In essence we devalue our own experiences or meanings and defer to other people's standards for *what* and *how* to present knowledge or solutions. If all students and teachers count as "experts" in a think tank, we acknowledge that their ideas and meanings are worthwhile, that they can generate understandings others will attend and perhaps put to use. What happens when that message is repeated year after year, class after class? Teachers might begin to ask more frequently, "What sense do you make of this?" instead of the traditional "Who, What, Where, When, Why and How?"

The idea conveys the message, "As a sentient, thinking creature, you deserve respect and dignity." In setting codes of behavior, schools and classrooms might take a line from Martin Luther King, Jr. as a guiding principle. From a jailhouse in Alabama, he wrote, "Any law that uplifts the human personality is just. Any law that degrades human personality is unjust…." A culture of courtesy and respect may replace one of repression and threat.

Interactive dialogue and conversation replace recitation and ritual as the major mode of operation in think-tank social studies classrooms. A great deal of research and theory supports the idea of discourse to develop complex thinking, higher levels of attention, and student involvement (Good and Brophy, 1991; Wilen and White, 1991; Vygotsky, 1978 cited in Wilen and White, 1991; and Cornbleth, 1991). Douglas Kellner (1990) cites the "Declaration of the Rights of Man and of Citizens," 1789:

> The free communication of ideas and opinions is one of the most precious rights of man. Everyone can therefore speak, write, and print freely, with the proviso of responsibility for the misuse of this liberty in the cases determined by law (pp. 11–12).

Open, unfettered discussion in social studies classrooms would help to overcome "the crisis in the public sphere" that threatens democracy. Identified by Jurgen Habermas, the concept claims that the public has been "transformed from participants in political and cultural debates into consumers of media images and information" (Kellner, 1990, p. 12). The reflective teacher, as lead researcher in the classroom think tank, will challenge with questions that get behind and beneath the shifting meanings, the images that blur reality and confound logical decision-making.

Think Tank Cultures Evolve

The interpretive paradigm for research assumes that cultural rules are generated, in part, by the participants whose interpersonal interactions shape the behavior in schools and classrooms (Cornbleth, 1991). The teacher, as a participant-leader occupies a unique position in creating the cultural rules that govern the learning situation. Community standards, students' and other educators' expectations, the goals of the curriculum, and school traditions exert powerful influences. Nevertheless, the individual teacher's vision of schools, learning, teachers, and pupils, as well as the terminology that represents that vision, will shape each classroom culture. Cinematographic images of *Stand and Deliver* and *Dead Poet's Society* illustrate the point.

The National Institute of Education (1985) reports the case of the McKnight Middle School in Renton, Oregon. In that low-income community, a strong behaviorist approach produced a dramatic reduction in vandalism, truancy, and incidences of student suspension for misbehavior. A highly structured academic program increased student achievement as measured by standardized tests. Parents, students, and teachers increased their involvement in the life of the school appreciably. The "instructional program" and "discipline system" apparently fit that community's expectations.

Richard L. Curwin and Allen N. Mendler (1988) provide useful rules of thumb, not the least of which are teachers' awareness of their own feelings and thresholds of tolerance for stress. Their 80-15-5 principle postulates that 80 percent of the youngsters rarely break the rules. Fifteen percent disobey on a somewhat regular basis, and 5 percent are chronically out of control. "The trick of a good discipline plan is to control the 15 percent without alienating or overly regulating the 80 percent and without backing the 5 percent into a corner" (p. 28). Students rarely misbehave if they are truly motivated, the authors conclude.

Under a punishment/obedience system, students do not learn to behave responsibly; they learn not to get caught. With a responsibility model, students and teachers develop the rules, that is, they reenact the creation of the social contract. Students learn the reasons behind the rules and recognize that freedom requires responsibility. Instead of rewards and punishments, Curwin and Mendler refer to "consequences," which are flexible and relative to the circumstances. The teacher retains certain prerogatives to assure that the "social contract" fits the overall school code. The authors contend, "[M]ost of the power of the social contract resides in the process, not the content (rules and consequences)" (p. 61). Rather than talk about the democratic process, the teachers and learners authentically participate in it.

In the context of fulfilling the United Nations Convention of the Rights of the Child, which declares children's participation in governance a basic civil and political right (Edmonds, 1992; Cantwell, 1992), European schools have implemented the social-contract approach. Hugh Starkey (1992) describes elementary schools in which children as young as six years draft charters or principles to guide the life of their classrooms. "Respect for process and law will increase if students are involved for the formulation of the rules and codes of conduct in their schools and classes" (p. 230). In European towns and cities, children have direct input in the governance of the total community. More than 350 children's councils operate in France alone. On June 29, 1992, National Public Radio reported that Cologne's "Office of Children's Interests" regularly consults youth about the kinds of community services and facilities they need, especially in the poor neighborhoods. At least some children in Europe are learning to participate actively, realistically, and responsibly.

Jo Ann Sweeney's work with high-school students in social studies confirms Curwin and Mendler's conclusion and mirrors the "authoritative" style described by McCaslin and Good (1992). She structured firm but flexible limits at the beginning of the semester. Students understood the reasons for the rules and the "jobs to be done." The academic content focused on contemporary social issues. Student committees had the responsibility to do research and present interesting reports. Bulletin boards had to be constructed. The fish had to be fed. The "interesting-things-to-do" table had to be updated with new readings, puzzles, and tapes. Discussion and debate flourished. By mid-semester the students had created their own classroom culture that spilled over into sessions before and after school hours. They had come "to see and internalize the rationales that underlie classroom rules and to operate within the rules on their own initiative" (McCaslin and Good, 1992, p. 11).

Intuitively, cognitively, and experientially, teachers craft classroom cultures to promote learning and responsible social participation. Contrary to this approach, the process-product paradigm fosters prescriptive, factory-like schooling whose graduates are unprepared to face the complex political and economic challenges of the nation. A growing consensus among reflective educators recognizes the inadequacy of the prevailing model. To supplant that paradigm, brain-based theories suggest other pedagogical elements: holistic, thematic learning; meaningful topics for discussion; varied, socially interactive projects; and nonthreatening classroom cultures that challenge in a state of "relaxed alertness."

Teachers and leaders of the social studies are alarmed at the decline in participatory attitudes, skills, and knowledge of public affairs. A model of democratic classroom culture, constructed from brain-based theories and progressive social studies objectives, can serve as a point of departure for reflection. To replace the factory representation, we propose the metaphor of the "think tank," where "everyone is a teacher, everyone is a learner."

We invite readers to close their eyes again and to reconsider the mental picture drawn at the beginning of the chapter. Has the vision changed?

CONCLUSION

The objective of this chapter was to discuss the discrepancies between professed goals and actual classroom practices. Traditionally, social studies has claimed as overarching goals the development of critical thought and social participation in the learning community. Nevertheless, by accepting the information-processing theory and effective teaching research as guides, educators in the field have achieved goals at the opposite ends of the pedagogical spectrum. Acquisition of culturally accepted knowledge and orderly, passive tasks in isolation characterize many social studies classes today. If teachers reflect about life in the classroom and the assumptions underlying their practices, they may begin to determine where they stand on the spectrum and to develop more congruence between creed and deed. More important, their instruction can involve a more authentic quest for understanding, a think tank culture in the preparation of future civic actors.

Reflective Questions

1. How do pupils and teachers tend to envision the learning process, as a step-by-step accumulation of information or as an ongoing construction of meaning, both spontaneous and deliberate, inside and outside the school?

2. In the selection of learning and teaching resources, do teachers and students rely predominately on textbooks and accompanying worksheets, or do they seek a variety of materials and experiences that reflect multiple points of view?

3. Do pupils and teacher collaborate in planning the use of class time, or does instruction follow predetermined rules and regulations?

4. Which factor is given more consideration in the organization of instruction: orderly classroom management, or engaging student curiosity and interest?

5. Does classroom communication tend to follow a pattern of dialogue and discussion, or a format of lecture and recitation?

6. Do pupils have opportunities to initiate, carry out, and present their own inquiry and creative projects, or is attention dedicated to covering a broad number of teacher-defined topics?

7. What efforts are made to balance teachers' explanations and pupils' interpretations and questions? Individual learning tasks and cooperative learning sequences? Periods of intense work and periods of relaxation and self-reflection?

8. Are provisions established to enable student resolution of conflict through discussion and negotiation?

9. How are current public issues infused in the curriculum?

GLOSSARY

brain-based education   Model of teaching and learning that draws on research concerning the brain's physiological functions and its influence on human behavior.

effective teaching research   (Also process-product research) A type of investigation that attempts to show relationships between teacher behaviors (process) and student achievement (product) as measured by standardized tests.

information-processing theory   Based upon social-cognitive and behaviorist research, this model of learning claims that humans acquire, store, and access knowledge similarly to the way a computer acquires, stores, and accesses data.

limbic system   Located in the center of the brain, this system monitors emotions and organizes new information in the locale memory system. It mediates between the R-complex and neocortex. Under stress and threat, the mediating function is inhibited. In states of challenge and "relaxed alertness," the limbic system is strengthened to respond imaginatively.

locale memory system   (Spatial memory system) The mental process believed to be controlled by the hippocampus, which organizes and monitors "mental maps" or meanings of incoming information. Rehearsal is not required to retain and recall elements of this system.

neocortex   The most "recent" region of brain evolution, it accounts for higher levels of thought. It "shuts down" under stress.

process-product research   (See effective teaching research)

R-complex   The most archaic part of the brain, which is concerned with survival and body functions. Under threat, this region tends to dominate. Typical responses are "ritualistic," automatic, without thought. This region is resistant to change and less adaptive.

taxon memory system   (Derived from "taxonomies" or lists) The mental process that requires rehearsal for the retention and recall of specific information. It is represented by the information-processing mode of learning.

"think-tank" metaphor   A representation of schools that emphasizes the generation of knowledge and the solutions to problems by all participants in an atmosphere of collegiality.

triune brain theory   A conceptualization that divides the brain into three evolutionary layers: the R-complex, the limbic system, and the neocortex.

ANNOTATED BIBLIOGRAPHY

Nummela Caine, Renate and G. Caine (1991). *Making Connections: Teaching and the Human Brain*. Alexandria, VA: Association for Supervision and Curriculum Development.

In the "Foreword," D.J. Carter, ASCD President (1990–1991), states: "The implications of this seminal work for teaching, testing, and remediation are far reaching....[It] may be the most powerful work written this year in terms of its potential to produce a long-range impact on education" (pp. v–vi). Complex ideas are clearly, simply stated. Conceptualization of learning and teaching fits overarching social studies objectives and goals.

Curwin, Richard L. and Allen N. Mendler (1988). *Discipline with Dignity*. Alexandria, VA: Association for Supervision and Curriculum Development.

As the title implies, the individual worth and esteem of each student and teacher should undergird all disciplinary decisions. Rather than a "system of management," the authors suggest principles and practical techniques that are congruent with democratic processes.

Edmonds, Beverly C. and William R. Fernekes, editors (1992). "The Convention on the Rights of the Child: A Challenge for Social Studies Education." *Social Education* 56(4):203–235.

The publication focuses on the substance, implications, and implementation of the United Nations Convention on the Rights of the Child. Twenty articles underscore the worldwide efforts of educators to involve youngsters in responsible participation in self-governance.

McCaslin, Mary and Thomas L. Good (1992). "Compliant Cognition: The Misalliance of Management and Instructional Goals in Current School Reform." *Educational Researcher* 21(3):4–17.

An excellent analysis of the inadequacies of simplistic "school reforms" based upon unrealistic or false assumptions. The authors criticize behavior modification as incompatible with problem-solving goals and suggest "authoritative" methods that permit increasing student self-control.

Quigley, Charles N. and Charles F. Bahmueller, editors (1991). *CIVITAS: A Framework for Civic Education* (National Council for the Social Studies Bulletin 86). Calabasas, CA: Center for Civic Education.

A framework for curricular reform, it is based on the premise that classrooms are the testing grounds for civic participation and political socialization. The volume explores in detail the conceptual, historic, and contemporary perspectives of many issues relating to civic education.

Scribner, Megan, editor (1992). "National Issues Forums." *NIF News* 1(1):1–8.

This organization provides research on fundamental issues, options, and rationales for resolving those issues and the training of moderators for public discussions. Its objective is "to counter the pervasive sense of political impotence and frustration." Teachers and others in the public sphere praise the materials and formats for promoting critical thinking. For further inquiry, write Victoria Simpson, 100 Commons Road, Dayton, Ohio 45459-2777.

REFERENCES

Aiken, W. (1942). *Adventure in American Education*, Vol. 1: *The Story of the Eight-Year Study: With Conclusions and Recommendations*. New York: Harper Brothers.

————. (Chairman of Commission on Relation of School and College of The Progressive Education Association) (1943). *Adventure in American Education*, Vol. 5: *Thirty Schools Tell Their Story: Each School Writes of its Own Participation in the Eight-Year Study*. New York: Harper Brothers.

Alexander, P.A., D.L. Schallert, and V.C. Hare (1991). "Coming to terms: How Researchers in Learning and Literacy Talk about Knowledge." *Review of Educational Research* 26:315–343.

American Society for Training and Development (1989). *Workplace Basics: The Skills Employers Want*. Washington, DC: Employment and Training Administration of the U.S. Department of Labor.

Barth, James L. (1991). "Curriculum Reform and the Foundations of the Social Studies." Pp. 8–15 in *Thinking about Social Studies: Some Specific Ideas about the Discipline*, Bulletin 83, edited by James L. Barth. Washington, DC: National Council for the Social Studies.

Beers, T. (1987). "Schema-Theoretic Models: Humanizing the Machine." *Reading Research Quarterly* 22(3):369–377.

Berman, Sheldon (1990). "Educating for Social Responsibility." *Educational Leadership* 48:75–80.

Blevins, D. (1991). "Social Studies: The Basics." Pp. 49–52 in *Thinking about Social Studies: Some Specific Ideas about the Discipline*, Bulletin 83, edited by James L. Barth. Washington, DC: National Council for the Social Studies.

Boyer, Ernest L. (1991). "Foreword." In *CIVITAS: A Framework for Civic Education* (NCSS Bulletin 86, pp. xv–xvii), edited by C.N. Quigley and C.F. Bahmueller. Calabasas, CA: Center for Civic Education.

Bracey, G.W. (1989). "Dangerous Practices." Pp. 247–253 in *Taking Sides: Clashing Viewpoints on Controversial Educational Issues*, 5th ed., edited by J.W. Noll. Guilford, CT: Dushkin.

Brophy, J. and T.L. Good, (1986). "Teacher Behavior and Student Achievement." Pp. 328–375 in *Handbook of Research on Teaching*, 3rd ed., edited by M.C. Wittrock. New York: Macmillan.

Bruner, Jerome S. (1990). "The Proper Study of Man." *Acts of Meaning*. Cambridge, MA: Harvard University Press.

Butts, R. Freeman. (1991). "A Personal Preface." Pp. xix–xxvi in *CIVITAS: A Framework for Civic Education*, NCSS Bulletin 86, edited by C.N. Quigley and C.F. Bahmueller. Calabasas, CA: Center for Civic Education.

Cantwell, N. (1992). "Conventionally Theirs: An Overview of the Origins, Content and Significance of the Convention on the Rights of the Child." *Social Education*, 56(4):207–210.

Cherryholmes, C.H. (1991). "Critical Research and Social Studies Education." Pp. 41–55 in *Handbook of Research on Social Studies Teaching and Learning*, edited by James P. Shaver. New York: Macmillan.

Clark, C.M. and P.L. Peterson (1986). "Teachers' Thought Processes." Pp. 255–296 in *Handbook of Research on Teaching*, 3rd ed., edited by M.C. Wittrock. New York: Macmillan.

Cornbleth, C. (1982). "Citizenship Education." Pp. 259–265 in *Encyclopedia of Educational Research*, 5th ed., Vol. 2, H.E. Mitzel. Washington, DC: American Educational Research Association.

————. (1991). "Research on Context, Research in Context." Pp. 265–275 in *Handbook of Research on Social Studies Teaching and Learning*, edited by James P. Shaver. New York: Macmillan.

Cuban, L. (1984). *How Teachers Taught: Constancy and Changes in American Classrooms 1890–1980*. New York: Longman.

Cuisick, P.A. (1991). "Student Groups and School Structures." Pp. 276–289 in *Handbook of Research on Social Studies Teaching and Learning*, edited by James P. Shaver. New York: Macmillan.

Davis, James E. (1984). "Foreword." In *Citizenship and the Critical Role of the Social Studies*, NCSS Bulletin 72, edited by Walter Parker and J. Jarolimek. Boulder, CO: ERIC Clearinghouse for Social Studies/Social Science Education & Social Science Education Consortium; Washington, DC: National Council for the Social Studies.

Davis, O.L., Jr. (1991). "Citizenship Education as the Central Purpose of Social Studies: The Heavy Load of a Dead Metaphor." Pp. 139–143 in *Thinking about Social Studies: Some Specific Ideas about the Discipline*, Bulletin 83, edited by James L. Barth. Washington, DC: National Council for the Social Studies.

Doyle, W. (1986). "Classroom Organization and Management." Pp. 392–431 in *Handbook of Research on Teaching*, 3rd ed., edited by M.C. Wittrock. New York: Macmillan.

Edmonds, B.C. (1992). "The Convention on the Rights of the Child: a Point of Departure." *Social Education* 56(4):205–206.

Eisner, E.W. (1979). *The Educational Imagination: On the Design and Evaluation of School Programs*. New York: Macmillan.

Engle, S.H. (1986). *What Ever Happened to the Social Studies?* Paper presented at Metcalf Colloquium, Urbana, IL.

Evans, R.W. (1991). "The Idea of Social Studies." Pp. 16–24 in *Thinking about Social Studies: Some Specific Ideas about the Discipline*, Bulletin 83, edited by James. L. Barth. Washington, DC: National Council for the Social Studies.

Evertson, C.M. (1987). "Managing Classrooms: A Framework for Teachers." Pp. 54–92 in *Talks to Teachers: A Festschrift for N.L. Gage*, edited by D.C. Berliner and B.V. Rosenshine. New York: Random House.

Finn, C.E., Jr. (Assist. Secy.) (1987). *What Works: Research about Teaching and Learning*, 2nd ed. Washington, DC: U.S. Department of Education.

Foley, D. (1990). *Learning Capitalist Culture: Deep in the Heart of Texas*. Philadelphia: University of Pennsylvania Press.

Gage, N.L. (1985). *Hard Gains in the Soft Sciences: The Case of Pedagogy*. Bloomington, IN: Phi Delta Kappa.

Gagne, R.M. (1985). *The Conditions of Learning and Theory of Instruction*, 4th ed. New York: Holt, Rinehart & Winston.

Good, T.L. and J.E. Brophy (1991). *Looking in Classrooms*, 5th ed. New York: HarperCollins.

Goodlad, John I. (1984). *A Place Called School: Prospects for the Future*. New York: McGraw Hill.

Gross, R.E. (1991). "The Social Studies: A Distinct Disciplinary Field or a Patchwork Umbrella?" Pp. 5–7 in *Thinking about Social Studies: Some Specific Ideas about the Discipline*, Bulletin 83, edited by James L. Barth. Washington, DC: National Council for the Social Studies.

Guralnik, D.B. (ed) (1980). *Webster's New World Dictionary of the American Language*, 2nd college edition. New York: Simon & Schuster.

Hertzberg, H.W. (1981). *Social Studies Reform: 1880–1980.* Boulder, CO: Social Science Education Consortium.

Hunt, J.B., Chairperson (1994) *Social Studies–History: Draft Standards for National Board Certification.* Washington, DC: National Board for Professional Teaching Standards.

Johnson-Laird, P.N. (1991). "Mental Models." Pp. 469–499 in *Foundations of Cognitive Science*, edited by M.I. Posner. Cambridge, MA: The MIT Press.

Johnston, W.B. (1989). *Demographics as Destiny: The U.S. Work Force in the Year 2000.* Washington, DC: Employment and Training Administration of the U.S. Department of Labor.

Kellner. D. (1990). *Television and the Crisis of Democracy.* Boulder, CO: Westview Press.

Kintsch, W. (1988). "The Role of Knowledge in Discourse Comprehension: A Construction-Integration Model." *Psychological Review*, 95:163–182.

Leming, J.S. (1989) "The Two Cultures of Social Studies Education." *Social Education.* (October) 53(6):404–408.

Marker, P.M. and D.J. Metzger (1991). "Democracy, Diversity and the Social Studies Methods." Pp. 166–172 in *Thinking about Social Studies: Some Specific Ideas about the Discipline*, Bulletin 83, edited by James L. Barth. Washington, DC: National Council for the Social Studies.

Marshall, J.D. (1995). "Review of *Enhancing Teaching*, by Madeline Hunter." In *The Educational Forum* 59(Winter):208–210.

McCarthy, M.M. (1994). "External Challenges to Public Education: Values in Conflict." American Educational Research Association Annual Meeting, New Orleans, LA (April). With permission from author.

McQueen, Theona V. (1992). *Essentials of Classroom Management and Discipline.* New York: HarperCollins.

Motorola Inc. (1991). *The Crisis of American Education.* Schaumburg, IL: Motorola.

Mukerji, C. and M. Schudson, editors (1991). "Introduction: Rethinking Popular Culture." Pp. 1–61 in *Rethinking Popular Culture: Contemporary Perspectives in Cultural Studies.* Berkeley: University of California Press.

National Institute of Education, editor (1985). "Success for Students Key to Improvement Programs at McKnight Middle School." *Profiles: Programs & Products: Goal Based Education*, No. 45. Portland, OR: Northwest Regional Educational Laboratory.

Parker, Walter and J. Jarolimek (1984). *Citizenship and the Critical Role of the Social Studies*, NCSS Bulletin 72. Boulder, CO: ERIC Clearinghouse for Social Studies/Social Science Education & Social Science Education Consortium; Washington, DC: National Council for the Social Studies.

Rachels, J. (1986). *The Elements of Moral Philosophy.* New York: Random House.

Reich, Robert B. (1991). "The Real Economy." *The Atlantic Monthly* 267(2):35–52.

Sadoski, M., A. Paivio, and E.T.Goetz (1991). "Commentary: A Critique of Schema Theory in Reading and a Dual Coding Alternative." *Reading Research Quarterly* 26(4):463–484.

Schallert, D.L. (1987). "Thought and Language, Content and Structure in Language Communication." Pp. 65–79 in *The Dynamics of Language Learning*, edited by J.R. Squire. Urbana, IL: National Conference on Research in English.

Shepard, L.A. (1991). "Psychometricians' Beliefs about Learning." *Educational Researcher*, 20(6):2–16.

Shulman, L.S. (1986). "Paradigms and Research Programs in the Study of Teaching: A Contemporary Perspective." Pp. 3–36 in *Handbook of Research on Teaching*, 3rd ed., edited by M.C. Wittrock. New York: Macmillan.

Smith, M.L. (1991). "Put to the Test: The Effects of External Testing on Teachers." *Educational Researcher* 20(5):8–11.

Snyder, D.P. and G. Edwards (1992). *America in the 1990s: An Economy in Transition, a Society Under Stress.* Paper prepared for the Foundation of the American Society of Association Executives: n.p.

Spring, J. (1989). *American Education: An Introduction to Social and Political Aspects.* New York: Longman.

Stanley, W.B. (1991). "Teacher Competence for Social Studies." Pp. 249–262 in *Handbook of Research on Social Studies Teaching and Learning*, edited by James P. Shaver. New York: Macmillan.

Starkey, H. (1992). "Teaching Children's Rights in Europe." *Social Education* 56(4):228–230.

Wilen, W.W. and J.J. White (1991). "Interaction and Discourse in Social Studies Classrooms." Pp. 483–495 in *Handbook of Research on Social Studies Teaching and Learning*, edited by James P. Shaver. New York: Macmillan.

Wilhelm, R.W. (1991). "Reflections on Social Studies Education." Pp. 61–65 in *Thinking about Social Studies: Some Specific Ideas about the Discipline*, Bulletin 83, edited by James L. Barth. Washington, DC: National Council for the Social Studies.

Willis, S. (1992, June). "Teaching Thinking: Educators Shift Emphasis from Recall to Reasoning." *ASCD Curriculum Update*, pp. 1–8. Alexandria, VA: Association for Supervision and Curriculum Development.

Wittrock, Merlin C., editor (1986). *Handbook of Research on Teaching*, 3rd ed. New York: Macmillan.

Zessoules, Rieneke and Howard Gardner (1991). "Authentic Assessment Beyond the Buzzword and Into the Classroom." Pp. 47–71 in *Expanding Student Assessment*, edited by Vito Perrone. Alexandria, VA: Association for Supervision and Curriculum Development.

Chapter Three

THE HIDDEN CURRICULUM AND SOCIAL STUDIES

Byron G. Massialas
Florida State University

THE BEGINNING OF THE SCHOOL YEAR, 1993–94, was highlighted by newspaper articles pointing to the fact that students entering middle school as sixth graders were to graduate from high school the year 2000 (Athans, 1993). It was expected that the class of 2000 was to "be watched by the world and sent off into the world at the turn of the century" (Athans, 1993, 4B). How did this statement impress the students as it is not only the turn of the century, but also the turn of the millennium? Julie is reported to have said, "Well I heard on TV that's when the world is going to end...I was watching *Beverly Hills 90210* and a commercial came on and said it. I know it's not true but that's what they say and it's kind of scary" (Athans 1993, 4B). After having said that, Julie proceeded with her friend, Abigail, to sign up for cheerleading.

Clearly the expectations are high for the "class of 2000," the expectation that something drastic is going to happen upon graduation. Yet schooling, including cheerleading, is expected to continue in the mode of "business as usual." The key questions are what is the business of schooling and is this business going to continue undisturbed by outside events?

Schooling, in virtually all formal statements issued by departments or ministries of education, worldwide, is expected to prepare future citizens to meet changes, anticipated and unanticipated, in their environment. Does schooling really do that?

Formal schooling plays a rather insignificant role in students' ability to meet the challenges of their rapidly changing environment. Formal schooling, consisting of the authorities' declarations of educational goals and means for achieving these goals, normally provides certification of time spent in school; it does not provide, however, certification for knowledge, attitudes, and skills needed by the students, all students, to cope successfully with change and be ineluctably part of it.

What is referred to as the hidden curriculum or the informal curriculum is an extremely powerful force that impacts students, positively or negatively, depending on the circumstances in which they find themselves. Yet this force is largely ignored by school administrators, teachers, parents, students, and the educational establishment, including textbook publishers.

We will discuss the key issues concerning the hidden curriculum as it relates to social studies teaching and learning.

1. Is the hidden curriculum in conflict with the formal curriculum? Should it be?

Many curriculum analysts "have focused on a discrepancy between what a curriculum says *ought* to be taking place in schools and what first hand observation reveals actually does take place. This discrepancy underlies the concept of the hidden curriculum..." (Gregg, 1988 p. 323). The hidden curriculum, what was once referred to by John Dewey as "collateral learning," consists of all learnings that take place in school as a result of actions by school personnel and students. These learnings are normally excluded from statements of what is to be learned through the formal program of studies specified in each school or school district.

One of the earliest studies of the hidden curriculum was conducted by Philip Jackson (1968) who established that elementary-school students learn to live with "crowds," "praise," and "power." To make it in school, students learn how to survive in the presence of many others, that is, students and teachers who also seek for themselves valued objects. In this process students learn to accept praise or reproof and they find out how power is distributed in school and what the role of the gate keepers is. In this environment students learn the "unpublicized features of school life" such as delay, denial, interruption, social distraction, and patience (Jackson, 1983, pp. 41–42). Yet the most important skill the students learn in school is how to deal with authority—usually this to be done through passivity and conformity to the rules. In this type of setting the hidden curriculum plays a significant role in student progress. "...Many of the rewards and punishments that sound as if they are being dispensed on the basis of academic success and failure are really more closely related to the mastery of the hidden curriculum" (Jackson, 1983, p. 56). Clearly the formal curriculum postulates the values of scholarship, academic learning, fairness, and democratic participation in decision making. The hidden curriculum, on the other hand, teaches students that those values are not quite realistic. To survive in school one needs to please the authorities, "apple polishing the teacher," and to comply with the institution's requirements. From this it is obvious that the formal curriculum does not contain realistic goals, while the hidden curriculum in fact delivers what students actually need to function in school effectively. The students soon learn that ignoring the hidden curriculum is a sure way to failure in school, both socially and academically.

Other authors assert that the hidden curriculum of the school, through the process prevailing in the classroom "militate against students developing a sense of community" (Giroux and Penna, 1983, p. 113). This happens primarily because "competition" and "individual striving" are emphasized. Although often schools through sections of their formal curriculum refer to the value of collectivity or the social good, the structure of the classroom, in actual practice, negates this objective. For example, students are always prompted to compete for good grades, for being the "teachers' pets," for being able to join the most desirable school clubs, and so on. Individualism is also fostered through the classroom seating arrangements where there is an attempt to have students be distanced from each other. In this milieu, the seats are arranged in rows, thus preventing students from establishing eye contact with other students, usually in the context of maintaining classroom discipline.

The response to the original question, whether or not the hidden curriculum is inimical to the formal curriculum, is that, as a rule, the two "curricula" are antithetical to each other. The formal curriculum preaches democracy, but the hidden curriculum imposes autocracy. The formal curriculum stresses academic knowledge and understanding; the hidden curriculum stresses the political process as a means of school achievement. But school and classroom dynamics are not the only purveyor of the hidden curriculum. As we shall examine later, hidden messages are conveyed through the formal curriculum as well. Standard textbooks, for example, convey implicitly a stereotypical picture of America—a two-child, nuclear, middle-class, white family. This portrayal indirectly legitimizes an institution that may appropriately represent only a fraction of the citizenry. As a result of this hidden message, students of the minority groups—or what is now referred to as microcultures—students of single-parent families, or students of low income backgrounds can develop feelings of inferiority, rejection, and loss of identity. In this context, then, the textbooks, as part of the formal curriculum, indirectly negate or contradict the traditional goal of American education, which is to provide equal opportunity to all children and youth to receive quality education and through it attain the "American Dream."

A recent study of commonly used American history textbooks revealed that the history of minorities is conveniently left out or distorted (Sugnet, Yiannousi, and Sommers, 1993). Significant events, such as the Columbus landing omit important facts about the treatment of native Americans and Africans. "…Although Eurocentric notions of Columbus heroically discovering an empty New World are slowly changing, even the best available textbooks have serious limitations" (Sugnet et al., 1993 p. 224). When evaluated against a multicultural, gender-inclusive checklist, the texts indicated an "overall mediocrity." In all, the diversity of American society and culture was not adequately presented. Given these hidden messages in textbooks, it is no wonder that many minorities feel excluded from the history of their own community and as a result begin to develop a sense of inferiority and a low self-concept. They feel that they do not belong.

It is apparent from this discussion that the hidden curriculum is generally in conflict with the formal curriculum. Naturally this conflict should not exist or, at least, it should be minimized. How can this conflict, however, be eliminated or reduced when the schools and their key players are resistant to any significant change? Through the additional issues that follow we will introduce some ideas about the changes needed to bring the formal and the hidden curricula in line with each other.

2. Is student learning affected by the hidden curriculum? Should it be?

Ever since formal schooling was instituted, educators assumed that teaching entailed learning. The idea was that teaching based on well-thought-out objectives and instructional methodologies would inescapably result in student learning. The studies referred to in this chapter, however, make this assumption unwarranted. It appears that the formal curriculum accounts for a relatively small share of learnings that students acquire in school. It is estimated that the share of these leanings is as little as 10 percent of all learning; the rest being attributed to the hidden curriculum (Massialas, 1989).

Student learning—as Philip Jackson, John Goodlad, Robert Dreeben, and others have demonstrated—is affected by the classroom and the general school climates in which students find themselves. After studying schools nationwide, one investigator concluded that inspite of the stated goals to this effect schools "did not place a high premium on experiencing democratic processes, independent thinking, creativity, personal autonomy, and learning for the sake of learning" (Goodlad, 1988, pp. 340–341). What students experienced in virtually all subject areas was a condition where those behaviors were fostered that sought "'right answers,' conforming and reproducing the known. These behaviors are reinforced daily by the physical restraints of the group and classroom, by the kinds of questions teachers ask, by the nature of the seatwork exercises assigned, and by the format of tests and quizzes" (Goodlad, 1988, p. 353). The rewards and punishments observed in the classrooms studied were geared to reinforce these types of student conforming behaviors. Particularly acute was the condition of students who were doing poorly in their lessons. These students were forced by the school environment not to feel good about themselves. Minority students were most likely to be affected by the hidden curriculum. Among students in the schools studied by Goodlad, 15 to 25 percent were expected not to finish high school, minority students being "overrepresented in this group" (Goodlad, 1988, p. 354).

The hidden curriculum impacts groups of students differently. A study of schools catering to students of different social-class backgrounds found that the hidden curriculum affected the learning of these groups of students in a number of ways (Anyon, 1988). For example, students who attended "working-class schools" engaged in mechanistic learning based on rote work. Very little or no explanation was given by the teacher of the phenomena studied in the various subjects, whether the subjects were language arts, social studies, or math. In contrast were the "affluent professional schools" and the "executive elite schools." In the former, student work is marked by "creative activity carried out independently. The students are continually asked to express and apply ideas and concepts" (Anyon, 1988, p. 378). In the latter school, students are taught to develop their "analytical intellectual powers...school work helps one to achieve, to excel, to prepare for life" (Anyon, 1988, p. 381). The investigator concluded that the hidden curriculum of the schools prepared students to enter the labor market: the working-class schools prepared students to be the laborers whereas the professional or elite schools prepared students to be the intellectuals and the professionals. Thus the students reproduced and reinforced the larger system of "unequal social relations." The age-old idea that schools through their curriculum contributed to the erosion of fixed social classes, membership in which prevented students from upward mobility, appeared to be a myth. In fact, schools, through the hidden curriculum, made it very difficult for even the most motivated students to break away from their destiny as it is prescribed by society. One side effect of the hidden curriculum, however, was to develop the "abilities and skills of resistance." Students resisted the monotony of the school, the day-in and day-out drill. Although this prevented them from learning "socially legitimate knowledge," they were able to acquire the methods that later on, in adult life, can be used to carry out a "slowdown," "subtle sabotage," or other forms of resistance in a place of work (Anyon, 1988, p. 385).

Although all schools offer promises of equality of opportunity for all, in actuality, as in the larger society, the school provides a system that treats students differentially. Social class, race, ethnicity, linguistic background, and gender are factors that impact the decision makers of the schools in organizing and delivering instruction. The hidden curriculum, manifested through the textbooks, the teachers, and the students themselves, affects what categories of students learn. Minorities learn to be obedient and passive. WASPs learn to be aggressive and involved.

Should the schools continue in this mode? Most educators would certainly abhor the status quo as described here and would recommend that the schools be restructured so that the cycle of schooling as a continuation and reinforcing element of the unequal distribution of opportunity be broken down. Attempts at this have been made, including such practices as designating certain schools with heavy enrollment of minorities and working-class youths as "magnet schools"—such schools emphasizing new areas of instruction such as telecommunications or global studies. Busing, of course, has been practiced for years, and its results on student learning are still disputed. The most important component in changing this stifling situation for minority students is the teacher because she or he controls the social dynamics of the classroom. To this teacher we turn our attention as we discuss the next issue.

3. Should "undesirable" elements in the hidden curriculum be replaced? How?

Knowledge or "cultural capital," values, and attitudes that accrue to an individual as a result of being a member of a group based on social class, race, ethnicity, and gender are difficult to change in school. However, certain things within the power of the teacher can be implemented—things that can make a difference in controlling the negative effects of the hidden curriculum.

Henry Giroux and Anthony Penna (1983) suggested a number of implementation strategies to be employed by teachers to alleviate the ill-effects of the hidden curriculum. These strategies include (a) the elimination of the "pernicious practice of 'tracking' students;" (b) the substitution of intrinsic for extrinsic rewards, especially avoiding using grades as a disciplining tool; (c) introducing a larger scale of group work that "represents one of the most effective ways to demystify the traditional, manipulative role of the teacher...it provides students with social contexts that stress social responsibility and group solidarity" (Giroux and Penna, 1983, pp. 155–116); (d) altering the way time is managed in schools, which is presently reminiscent of factory work, so that students can adopt a "modified self-pacing" procedure in the classroom—students can opt to work alone or in groups and develop a more personal communication line with the teacher; and (e) the establishment of "peer-leaders," students who are capable of fostering social relationships among peers so that the goals of the group can be attained without much teacher intervention.

A clearly defined strategy for using the hidden curriculum in a positive way was developed in connection with the application of the idea of the school being a laboratory for real-life experiences (Massialas and Hurst, 1978). Under this scheme students are to learn decision-making skills by actively participating in the distribution of power in the school. Students learn such participatory skills as proposing action, rule making, and voting. These skills are not learned theoretically, but rather they emerge from actual participation in school-related decisions that affect the student body, at large, or each student personally. Decision topics that emerge from the natural school setting include classroom seating arrangements, the grading system, disciplining, the use of passes, classroom assignments, textbook and materials use, school clubs operation, traffic movement in the halls, the quality and quantity of cafeteria food, the authority of the front office, peer relations, and so on. (See box). Teachers of all subjects, not only social studies, commit themselves to an in-depth involvement as part of their official task in the study topics that actually form the hidden curriculum. These decision topics change naturally every day and affect the students' lives. Thus students learn the skills they need to cope with their environment and participate in the major decisions that concern them. They learn how to identify the "gate keepers," or those who control power in the school (not always the principal), and how to deal effectively with them. As a result of this learning experience with the hidden curriculum of the school, students develop a relatively high sense of political and social efficacy, that is, they begin to understand how the system around them operates and feel competent in participating directly in that system and its decision-making mechanisms. Thus students, by being taught to not allow themselves to be manipulated by the system through the hidden curriculum, begin to control their environment rather than being controlled by it.

Needless to say, teachers for various reasons would be reluctant to apply a participatory program for students as a way of using the hidden curriculum for explicit learning. Teachers usually claim that the crowded school curriculum does not give them any flexibility to engage in such activities. If they do, they will be penalized by the system—by the administrators, the parents, the students. They will be criticized for not concentrating on academic subjects. Yet the demand for acknowledging the role of the hidden curriculum in learning and instruction is growing.

Decision Topics on Valued Objects

Ways for students to earn points—decision allowing them to evaluate for themselves.

Decision on what to do that day, especially on a Friday.

Giving a certain amount of work every day.

Decision on the seating they choose.

Decision on what to do with students who don't show up—should they go to the assistant principal?

Decision to carry on evaluation for next year and also for students to evaluate teacher.

Decision to send to the principal the boy who allegedly stole $15.

Give assignments to draw up pictures that they may make into slides.

Decision not to give free lunches—"no handouts."

Decision to use "contract method" to individualize classroom activity—three levels of activities: (1) basic skills; (2) higher skills, 2–3 digits; (3) top group, fractions.

Decision on raising hand.

Decision on "good behavior contest"—every time a teacher sees a student demonstrating good behavior to give student an award, for example, a dinner at the Holiday Inn.

Decision on disciplining—send them to the office, that's all you can do.

Decision to lecture on Greek and Roman civilizations.

Students don't like reading.

Decision to give students a set of questions on worksheets.

Decision to have a departmental syllabus.

Decision to take three boys to the office.

Decision to bring in older kids to tutor the younger.

Decision to call parents on discipline problems.

Decision to push for electives for younger kids.

Decision to put on tape student rights and responsibilities so that nonreaders can understand.

Decision never to send "discipline problems" to the front office.

Decision to have kids police themselves, for example, peer ridicule if they don't watch out.

Decision to give more options for student clubs or special-interest groups.

Decision to give credit for everything students do.

Decision not to use "home base" for anything important.

Decision not to paddle students.

Decision not to have clubs that are too structured.

Decision to talk it out with kids on discipline problems and send them to the office only if I can't handle them.

Call parent only when child is not doing well.

Byron Massialas and Joseph Hurst (1978). Social Studies in a New Era: The Elementary School as a Laboratory. *pp. 150–151, New York: Longman.*

An experimental program in Florida focusing on dimensions of the hidden curriculum found no appreciable interest among educators. The so-called Nims Project developed a series of 24 units on such topics as evaluation and grading, administrative decisions, student government, classroom rules, and so forth, which were to be used by teachers in involving students in direct decision making (Massialas and Hurst, 1978, pp. 367–368). Although the project evaluation established that the decision topics of the hidden curriculum provided students excellent spring-boards for learning participation and decision-making skills, teachers, as a rule, did not go out of their way to use the published program, *Skills in Democratic Participation.* Without a demand for it, the program, published in the form of 24 booklets for middle schools was eventually removed from the Title IV Innovative Projects dissemination list.

This example indicated that elements of the hidden curriculum, including the "undesirable" elements, such as tracking and punitive grading can be used as natural springboards for negotiations between teachers and students, thus providing for learning decision making in the school. Once the decision-making process is learned by the students, it can be transferred to decision objects outside the natural school setting—to the family as well as community contexts. It follows that both desirable and undesirable elements of the hidden curriculum could and should be used to advantage, provided they are made explicit and students are asked to use them as topics for practicing decision making.

4. Are there linkages between the hidden curriculum and social studies? If so, should social studies focus on the hidden curriculum?

Earlier in this chapter we examined how components of the hidden curriculum enter the realm of popular history textbooks used in American schools. These textbooks have, as a rule, excluded the stories of cultural minority groups—Native Americans, African Americans, Hispanic Americans, Asian Americans. Although the stereotypes of these groups have largely been removed from the textbooks, the exclusion of these groups from systematic treatment has produced negative effects on the students, especially minority students. These students experience a relatively low self-esteem; they feel as if they don't belong and that they are not part of the American culture and civilization. Ultimately these feelings can lead to such acts among these students as extreme deviant behavior, dropping out of school, engaging in criminal activity, and so on. "Members of racial and ethnic minorities are much more likely to drop out of school than white, Anglo students... "(Rumberger, 1987, p. 110). In-school factors such as poor academic performance and disliking school account for 56 percent of dropouts among Black, male students. Thus the hidden curriculum adversely affects the cultural minorities in the United States.

Earlier we discussed the overall influence of the hidden curriculum as it affects students in school catering to different social classes (Anyon, 1988). The way social studies was taught, however, appeared to make a significant difference on what students learned from the hidden curriculum in the different types of schools. In the working-class schools, social studies was taught in a mechanistic way, stressing memorization and copying from the teachers' notes on the board. For example, students had to copy the names of all the states, the state capital, the products of each state, and a "Fabulous Fact," such as "Idaho grew twenty-seven billion potatoes in one year...." (Anyon, 1988, p. 151). At times students would point to the geographic location of a state capital they were copying from the board, but no discussion of geographic principles ever took place. "Occasionally the children colored in a ditto and cut it out to make a stand-up figure (representing, for example, a man roping a cow in the Southwest). These were referred to by the teacher as their social studies 'projects.'" (Anyon, 1988, p. 151). In this class the teacher was clearly the authority and the authoritarian figure, continually issuing orders as to what students should be doing, using such words as "Shut-up," "Shut your mouth," "Open your textbook," and so on. All the courtesies that people use in everyday life were dispensed with by the social studies teachers in the working-class schools.

In the "affluent professional schools," on the other hand, students were asked to be creative and to develop and apply ideas and concepts about society and culture. For example, a fifth-grade class was asked to recreate an ancient civilization. "The children made an 8mm film on Egypt, which one of the parents edited. A girl in the class wrote the script and the class acted it out" (Anyon, 1988, p. 156). Students had a choice from a list of topics to conduct a project, some of which involved "graphic presentations of ideas." In the executive elite schools, students were encouraged to develop their intellectual powers. Students were asked to express their own positions on various matters. "Social studies work is most often reading and discussion of concepts and independent research" (Anyon, 1998, p. 160). Students are asked to analyze current social issues. Reasoning as opposed to pure opining is stressed. Questions such as "Why do workers strike?," "Why do we have inflation, and what can be done to stop it?" prevail (Anyon, 1988, p. 160).

It is obvious that social studies, perhaps more so than other school subjects, contains a sizable portion of the school's hidden curriculum. In the working-class schools, students learn obedience and respect for authority. They learn through rote memorization, never or rarely given the chance to question the world around them. Thus social injustices that affect them as members of the lower class, more likely to be racial and ethnic minorities, pass them by unexamined. The status quo is, willy-nilly, accepted. The boredom often created by this type of curriculum will force many of these students to drop out. In the affluent and elite type of schools, social studies is presented in the context of critical thinking and problem solving. Students learn skills as they participate in discussions on current social problems. They are taught to look at the world as a series of complex phenomena, phenomena that can be described and explained. They learn that social phenomena such as taxation, social welfare, criminal justice, health provision and so on are phenomena in which they have a stake and which are of concern to them. These phenomena or societal occurrences affect them directly. Students in these schools are expected to take an active part in supporting aspects or components of these social events that benefit them and in opposing components that are to their disadvantage. Thus the hidden curriculum of the school, especially the social studies, teaches the affluent students how to act out democratic principles to obtain their valued objects in life. Students from the low socioeconomic status and cultural minorities, on the other hand, learn how to follow orders, they learn how to recite the principles of democracy, but they are denied the opportunity to act them out. Thus cultural reproduction through the hidden curriculum is complete and realized in American schools. Social studies, more so than any other subject taught in school, is full of hidden messages that are constantly conveyed to the students. These hidden messages are contained in the textbooks and materials teachers and students use, in the culture of the school and the social studies classroom, and in the overall system of rewards and punishments. In a formal sense, social studies deals with such topics as social class, equality, democracy, political power, intergroup relations, culture diffusion, and the like. These topics are studied more often historically; rarely are they connected with the present. The hidden curriculum provides a golden opportunity for social studies teachers to connect the study of the formal content with the study of the nonformal or the hidden. When the different types of citizenship are studied, whether in classical Athens or Medieval Europe, the social structure of the school can also be studied to establish how students, themselves, are affected by this structure in the give-and-take of their daily routine. Are students from low SES treated differently from those in high SES? Why? What are the consequences of such treatment? Does it produce social inequality? If so, what can be done about it? How do factors such as gender, race, ethnicity, and linguistic background affect how people are treated in society and in the school? What can we do to remedy social injustices? What action plans can we formulate? How can we mobilize support to implement our plans? When students are consciously engaged in investigating these matters they "do" social studies in the best sense of the word. Thus the study of social studies becomes tantamount to the study of the hidden curriculum of the school. Students not only reflect on the issues involved, within a historical-spacial dimension, but they are also engaged in action to change those aspects of their own social-cultural environment that affect them adversely. Students are empowered through social studies focusing on issues of the hidden curriculum to retain the rights of citizenship, that is, the right of individuals to participate in decisions affecting them. This right should be exercised whether one is a member of a cultural minority group or a member of the privileged class. In this manner students can be engaged in creatively undoing the hidden curriculum that forces the reproduction of the dominant society. They negate it through what one author calls, "emancipatory rationality" (Giroux, 1983, p. 339). "Emancipatory rationality...is based upon the principle of critique and action. It is aimed at criticizing that which is restrictive and oppressive while at the same time supporting actions in the service of individual freedom and well being" (Giroux, 1983, p. 340). Students of the underprivileged classes in particular can benefit from school work that is based on emancipatory rationality, that is, they begin to think critically about their social conditions and then engage in calculated social action to bring about social and political change.

Social studies textbooks can be used by reflective teachers as springboards for students to identify and analyze authors' biases in describing historical or present-day events. These textbooks can be screened so that the hidden messages contained in them surface and are critically evaluated. A recent study of secondary-school student attitudes toward popular U.S. history textbooks found that students, when prompted, can identify biases and hidden messages in textbooks (Epstein, 1994). Although some students expressed believability in the content of the textbook, several detected lack of objectivity. Characteristically, one student said: "'I have to believe the facts but sometimes they present them in a way that America is always right and never makes mistakes....'" (Epstein, 1994, p. 43).

It is interesting to note that in spite of several studies on the importance of the subject, social studies educators tend to ignore the hidden curriculum, as such, as a powerful component of social studies. For example the NCSS *Curriculum Standards for Social Studies* (NCSS Bulletin 89, 1994) issued by a task force of well-known educators does not mention directly the hidden curriculum and its influence on student learning. Only indirectly can the teacher glean from the handbook material on how to handle messages and practices delivered through the hidden curriculum. For example, one content standard proposed by the task force for in-depth study is "Individuals, Groups, and Institutions" (p. 25). In this section students are asked, among other things, to find out "how institutions are formed, what controls and influences them, how they control and influence individuals and culture, and how institutions can be maintained or changed" (p. 25). The examples or performance following the thematic strands seem to suggest procedures and skills that students can use in their in-depth study of the subject. Students in the early grades, for instance, are asked to "give examples of and explain group and institutional influences such as religious beliefs, laws, and peer pressure on people, events, and elements of culture" and "identify and describe examples of tensions between and among individuals, groups, or institutions..." (p. 60). When engaged in this enterprise students in the early grades are expected, among other things, to strengthen their decision-making skills, that is, "recognize the values implicit in the situation and the issues that flow from them" and "identify alternative courses of action and predict likely consequences of each" (p. 149). The end result of this process is taking social action based on informed decisions. It should be noted, however, that though all these are related ideas and skills recommended by the task force, it is up to the teacher to draw examples primarily from the school and community environments that clearly demonstrate both positive and negative influences of the hidden curriculum student learning.

Conclusion

In this chapter we discussed various issues connected with the hidden curriculum of the school, focusing on the hidden curriculum of the social studies. We established that the hidden curriculum permeates all aspects of school life. This curriculum, which may account for as much as 90 percent of all student learning, can have both positive and negative effects. The effects can be positive when teachers acknowledge its existence and focus their instruction on an in-depth reflection of the hidden curriculum and its impact on students. For example, students discussing critically the absence of minority histories in social studies textbooks. Why are such histories absent? What are the effects on students who are members of minority groups? What can they do to have their histories become part of the formal curriculum? What actions must be taken by each student and by the group? Historically, what actions were taken by disenfranchised groups? What lessons can we learn from studying the actions of these groups?

The hidden curriculum has negative effects when it is ignored by teachers and administrators. For example, don't teachers know that minority students are bored and are likely to drop out of school when there are no references in the school curriculum to the contributions of their group to the American culture? Don't teachers know that academic tracking creates insidious distinctions among students, favoring the dominant class? Don't teachers know that the system of rewards and punishments is differentially administered to students? (Students of minorities and low SES are more likely to be punished than WASP students who are of high SES). Teachers who tacitly allow the hidden curriculum to exercise its influence on students without any intervention are contributing to the malaise that currently exists in schools—the school operating as a microcosm of the larger society reproduces and reinforces the social and cultural inequalities. Recent events nationwide centering on violent acts of youth, inside and outside the school, attest to this societal phenomenon. Schools are not considered safe anymore. The sanctuary that once these schools provided to children and youth has now been violated. Drugs, guns, fights, suspensions, arrests, massive drop-outs, and so on are common daily occurrences. Armed guards are policing the school premises. The hidden curriculum of the larger society has permeated the academy walls with far-reaching and often devastating consequences. The revolt of the masses has been reproduced in the nation's schools. Youth is now explicitly or implicitly crying for recognition by the adult society, for having attention paid to their needs for communication in human terms. Yet most teachers and administrators remain aloof to this call and operate on the assumption of business as usual. As this attitude by teachers continues, the alienation between youth and school personnel will grow to the point where schools will no longer be governed by the rule of reason and compassion, but rather by the rule of force and retribution. Schools will be like armed camps or prisons where only power relations prevail.

It appears that we are quickly approaching the breaking point within the school walls. Unless we make a complete turn around and attend immediately to the issues embedded in the hidden curriculum, we will witness a complete system breakdown. More and more violent acts in schools will be leading features in the local press. For example, front-page headlines in the *Sun-Sentinel* of October 21, 1993, proclaim: "Violence Erupts at School, on Bus" and "Teachers Protest Mayhem, Lack of Contract" (Athans, et al., 1993 and Daniels, 1993). The first article details two incidents in local schools: The first involved the stabbing of one student by another over an argument. The second incident involved a student who poked a bus driver in the face and threw away the bus keys, thus stranding the bus with 43 students for some time. The second article refers to teachers' demonstrations over the abuse teachers are receiving, and the demand to take new measures for "disruptive students."

A potentially very powerful instrument that has recently entered systematically the school scene is the philosophy and the methods of "cooperative learning." Cooperative learning is based on the idea that "if students want to succeed as a team, they will encourage their teammates to excel and will help them to do so." (Slavin, 1995, p. 4). Belonging to a group that is faced with a task or a problem to be solved contributes to an enhanced sense of camaraderie among students, which, in and by itself, promotes learning. "Team rewards, individual accountability, and equal opportunities for success" are the basic concepts of cooperative learning (Slavin, 1995, p. 5). Several research studies, summarized by Slavin, clearly support "the use of cooperative learning to increase student achievement, as well as such other outcomes as improved intergroup relations, acceptance of academically handicapped classmates, and increased self-esteem" (Slavin, 1995, p. 2). Although in the past educators have used some types of group learning techniques—that is, discussion groups, laboratory learning groups, and the like—group processes, for the most part, were not focused and there was an absence of clear-cut directions for completing the task. Under cooperative learning, students rely on each other, instead of competing with each other, to complete a task. Students "buy into" the objectives and the procedures of the cooperative learning group as they engage in positive social interaction with each other (Stahl, 1994). Thus the hidden curriculum of cooperative learning teaches students, among other things, the values of cooperation, interdependence, personal and group responsibility, and equal opportunity for success. This approach is in direct contrast with classroom approaches that emphasize competition, individualism, conflict, and, in many ways, discrimination against students who are members of minority groups or physically handicapped. The teacher who is seriously considering using the hidden curriculum in a positive way should carefully examine further the potential of cooperative learning strategies and their effects on students' values and behaviors.

Another promising tool for minimizing the destructive effects of the hidden curriculum—in so far as judging student performance in the classroom is concerned—is the use of "portfolio assessment." Portfolio assessment is based on a collection of a pupil's work. The term derives from "an artist's portfolio, which is a collection of the artist's work designated to show his or her style and range" (Airasian, 1994, pp. 262–263). In the classroom, the purpose of portfolios is "to collect a series of pupil performances or products that show the pupil's accomplishments or improvement over time" (Airasian, 1994, p. 263). Portfolio assessment deviates significantly from traditional types of assessment, such as paper-and-pencil tests based on multiple choice, true and false, and identification and matching questions. The traditional way of testing focuses on evaluation as a group process, based on group norms and or achievement at a point in time. Portfolio assessment, on the other hand, is based more on individual efforts, focusing on performance over a period of time, emphasing self-assessment and self-improvement. Portfolio assessment is more likely "authentic assessment" in that it "looks more like a real-life task rather than an activity constructed as a test that does not resemble much what happens beyond the test—let alone, beyond the classroom" (Farr and Tone, 1994, p. 10). This type of assessment, if properly practiced, encourages the students to control their own performance rather than being controlled by others. Teachers who use this assessment approach are more likely to reduce the tendency to make invidious comparisons among students; instead they judge each student's performance individually.

To avoid total mayhem in schools, social studies teachers must take the leadership and attend directly to the issues revealed by studying the school's hidden curriculum. Teachers must abandon the traditional curriculum—and the culturally obsolete textbooks and evaluation instruments used in it—and replace it with a curriculum based on current social and political issues, issues in which the students are personally involved. Teachers need to engage all students into programs that aim at learning decision-making skills in the natural settings of the schools. In other words, teachers of social studies need to become teachers of the hidden curriculum so that they can offer their students a true version of emancipatory rationality.

Reflective Questions

1. What are the basic premises underlying the theory of the hidden curriculum? Explain.

2. Do you agree or disagree with the proposition that the formal curriculum is antithetical to the hidden curriculum? Take a position on the issue and refer to examples that clarify your position.

3. Is student learning affected by the hidden curriculum? If it is, present examples other than those given in the chapter to demonstrate the point.

4. Do textbooks used in schools convey hidden messages to students? If you agree, provide some of these messages after carefully examining a social studies text used in grades 1 through 12.

5. Do you agree or disagree with the claim that minority groups (such as religious, racial, ethnic, linguistic, social, or gender-based) are most likely to be adversely affected by the hidden curriculum? Explain.

6. How can "undesirable" elements in the hidden curriculum be removed or replaced? For example, what parts of the classroom physical and social environments should be changed so that students have more of a chance to learn?

7. Are there connections between social studies and the hidden curriculum? If so, what can the social studies teacher do to uncover these connections and encourage his or her students to reflect on the issues and problems involved?

8. Is the practice of "tracking" part of the hidden curriculum? What are some direct and indirect effects on student learning?

9. What are the advantages and disadvantages of employing cooperative learning strategies in your classroom? Who is likely to benefit or be adversely affected by these strategies?

10. Does portfolio assessment help students escape from the tyranny of the hidden curriculum? Explain.

11. *How do the curriculum standards developed by various social studies groups, for example, NCSS, as well as organizations of historians and geographers, view the role of the hidden curriculum in social studies learning and instruction?*

12. *If you were advising a school board on strategies to deflect the negative influences of the hidden curriculum, what would you say? What would be your priorities and why?*

GLOSSARY

collateral learning   An expression originally used by John Dewey to refer to learning that is not clearly part of the formal program, that is, what is now referred to as the "hidden curriculum."

cooperative learning   In both its theoretical and practical dimensions, an approach to learning that emphasizes cooperation among members of a group of students as they identify and pursue common goals and processes. Cooperative learning groupings have a democratic base because participation in them is not centered on such factors as ethnicity, linguistic background, gender, or religious beliefs.

cultural capital   Knowledge that each individual accumulates as a member of a group or groups when ethnicity, religion, gender, social class, linguistic background, and so on play a major role.

emancipatory rationality   Procedures based on thinking and acting that empower individuals to participate directly in decisions affecting them.

formal curriculum   A statement of purpose and an outline of content themes and sponsored activities that presumably serve as a guideline of what is desirable in school. The formal curriculum is in direct juxtaposition to the hidden curriculum in that the goals or objectives of the latter are rarely spelled out.

hidden curriculum   Consists of experiences and learnings that are not contained in the formal pronouncements of school districts. These pronouncements include goals, objectives, programs of studies, instructional methods, materials, assessment procedures, and so forth.

peer teaching   A process by which students help others and learn from each other in carrying out the task of the school.

school-as-lab   A process whereby the political and social structure of the school is used as a basis of learning how to make decisions on valued objects and how to implement these decisions through reasoned action.

tracking   The process by which students are placed in classes or courses of study on the basis of an external criterion, usually academic performance or IQ scores.

ANNOTATED BIBLIOGRAPHY

Anyon, Jean (1980). "Social class and the hidden curriculum of work." *Journal of Education* 162:67–92.

Reports a study of different types of schools that cater to students from different socio-economic backgrounds. "Working class" schools prepare future blue collar workers whereas "executive elite" schools prepare future professionals in leadership positions. The hidden curriculum imparts different values for students in these schools. The first type of school stresses drill and recitation in instruction whereas the second type stresses reasoning and analytical thinking.

Dreeben, Robert (1969). *On What Is Learned in School.* Reading, MA: Addison-Wesley.

This classic book presents the theory of the hidden curriculum as it is implemented in the classroom and shows how the set-up of the school and the traditional classroom impart such values as individualism and competition.

Farr, Roger and Bruce Tone (1994). *Portfolio Performance Assessment.* Fort Worth, TX: Harcourt, Brace.

A good handbook of how to use portfolio assessment as a means of authentic assessment, that is, a process that helps teachers recognize the true potential of students in their quest for learning. Provides numerous examples for teachers after discussing the concept of portfolio assessment.

Goodlad, John (1984). *A Place Called School: Prospects for the Future.* New York: McGraw-Hill.

A comprehensive study of schools based on visits to one-thousand classrooms across the country. For each subject area, the book shows how the hidden curriculum imparts certain values that are different, often antithetical, to the values stated in the formal curriculum.

Henze, Rosemary C. (1992). *Informal Teaching and Learning: A Study of Everyday Cognition in a Greek Community.* Hillsdale, NJ: Lawrence Erlbaum Associates.

An anthropological study of children in a community in Greece that discusses "learning without teaching." Provides excellent examples that demonstrate the process of how children learn how to express emotions, how to use language, and how to learn about the political process.

Jackson, Philip (1968). *Life in Classrooms.* New York: Holt, Rinehart & Winston.

A classic study of interactions between students and teachers in the elementary school classroom. Jackson found that there is strong evidence of the influence of the hidden curriculum on all activities taking place in the classroom and in the school. Students learn through experience how to manipulate their informal curriculum to their advantage.

Nieto, Sonia (1992). *Affirming Diversity: The Sociopolitical Context of Multicultural Education.* New York: Longman.

An excellent resource for teachers for learning about the influences of the hidden curriculum on ethnic and linguistic minorities. Provides practical examples for use in the classroom to combat discrimination that is ingrained in the traditional curriculum. Proposes a model of multicultural instruction that is based on tolerance, acceptance, and respect. The end result of such instruction is "equity and social justice for all people."

Slavin, Robert E. (1995). *Cooperative Learning: Theory, Research and Practice*, 2nd ed. Boston, MA: Allyn & Bacon.

Presents the philosophy of cooperative learning and clearly summarizes the research related to applications of cooperative methods in the classroom. Provides case studies of teachers who have used these methods in their classrooms. Suggests strategies for "team building," cooperative problem solving, misbehavior, and so on.

Stahl, Robert J. (1994). *Cooperative Learning in Social Studies: A Handbook for Teachers.* Menlo Park, CA: Addison-Wesley.

Shows how a teacher can use cooperative learning strategies with heterogeneous groups to enhance learning. The approach is based on the assumption that such an arrangement minimizes the traditional instructional mode based on competition and invidious comparisons of students. Values and attitudes learned through cooperative learning methods include "positive interdependence," "positive social interaction behaviors," and "individual accountability."

REFERENCES

Airasian, Peter W. (1994). *Classroom assessment*, 2nd ed. New York: McGraw-Hill.

Anyon, Jean (1988). "Social Class and the Hidden Curriculum of Work." Pp. 366–389 in *Curriculum: An Introduction to the Field*, 2nd ed., edited by James R. Gregg. Berkeley, CA: McCutchan.

Athans, Marego, Chele Caughron, and Rich Pollack (October 21, 1993). "Violence Erupts at School, on Bus." *Sun-Sentinel*, p. 1A.

Athans, Marego (August 24, 1993). "Sixth-Graders Learn to Play by Different Rules in Middle School." *Sun Sentinel*, pp. 1B, 4B.

Daniels, Earl (October 21, 1993). "Teachers Protest Mayhem, Lack of Contract." *Sun Sentinel*, p. 1A.

Epstein, Terrie L. (1994). "America Revised Revisited: Adolescents' Attitudes Toward a United States History Textbook." *Social Education* 58(1):41–44.

Farr, Roger and Bruce Tone (1994). *Portfolio Performance Assessment*. Fort Worth, TX: Harcourt, Brace.

Giroux, Henry (1983). "Critical Theory and Rationality in Citizenship Education." Pp. 321–360 in *The Hidden Curriculum and Moral Education: Deception or Discovery?*, edited by Henry Giroux and David Purpel. Berkeley, CA: McCutchan.

Giroux, Henry and Anthony Penna (1983). "Social Education in the Classroom: The Dynamics of the Hidden Curriculum." Pp. 100–121 in *The Hidden Curriculum and Moral Education: Deception or Discovery?*, edited by Henry Giroux and David Purpel. Berkeley, CA: McCutchan.

Goodlad, John I. (1988). "What Some Schools and Classrooms Teach." Pp. 337–356 in *Curriculum: An Introduction to the Field*, 2nd ed., edited by James R. Gregg. Berkeley, CA: McCutchan.

Gregg, James R., editor (1988). *Curriculum: An Introduction to the Field*, 2nd ed. Berkeley, CA: McCutchan.

Jackson, Philip (1968). *Life in Classrooms*. New York: Holt, Rinehart & Winston.

Jackson, Philip (1983). "The Daily Grind…" Pp. 28–60 in *The Hidden Curriculum and Moral Education: Deception or Discovery?*, edited by Henry Giroux and David Purpel. Berkeley, CA: McCutchan.

Massialas, Byron G. and Joseph B. Hurst (1978). *Social Studies in a New Era: The Elementary School as a Laboratory*. New York: Longman.

Massialas, Byron G. (1989). "The Inevitability of Issue-Centered Discourse in the Classroom." *The Social Studies* 80(5):173–175.

National Council for the Social Studies (1994). *Curriculum Standards for Social Studies: Expectations of Excellence*. Washington, DC: NCSS, Bulletin 89.

Rumberger, Russell W. (1987). "High School Dropouts: A Review of Issues and Evidence." *Review of Educational Research* 57(2):101–121.

Slavin, Robert E. (1995). *Cooperative Learning: Theory, Research and Practice*, 2nd ed. Boston, MA: Allyn and Bacon.

Stahl, Robert J. (1994). *Cooperative Learning in Social Studies: A Handbook for Teachers*. Menlo Park, CA: Addison-Wesley.

Sugnet, Charlie, Evdoxia Yiannousi, and Meredith Sommers (1993). "Fourteen Ninety-Two in the Textbooks: A Critique." *Social Education* 57(5):224–227.

Chapter Four

QUESTIONS OF MOTIVATION FOR ACHIEVEMENT IN SOCIAL STUDIES

Ronald L. VanSickle
The University of Georgia

MANY TEACHERS OF SOCIAL STUDIES experience deep frustration because of their students' low levels of motivation to achieve. Insufficient student motivation is a problem for teachers in all subject areas; however, social studies is a particularly difficult case. Joan M. Shaughnessy and Thomas M. Haladyna (1985) reviewed several empirical studies of students' attitudes toward social studies and reached a dismal conclusion. "Most students in the United States, at all grade levels, find social studies to be one of the least interesting, most irrelevant subjects in the school curriculum" (p. 694). What are the sources of negative student attitudes toward social studies that students too frequently exhibit? What questions must teachers answer if students are to be motivated effectively to achieve in social studies? How might those questions be answered productively?

Social studies teachers are committed to teaching their students historical and social scientific knowledge that students can use in making effective decisions in their civic and personal lives. It is perplexing to many social studies teachers that their students are not more motivated to learn. After all, historical forces shape students' lives for better or/worse. They live in complex national and global societies full of opportunity and peril. Students are generally interested in people, particularly when those people believe their lives and values are in jeopardy, confront obstacles and dangers, and engage in interpersonal and intergroup conflicts. These conditions characterize much of the subject matter of social studies courses. Why, then, are many students motivated so little to study and to achieve in social studies?

Given classroom observations and student responses to interviews and questionnaires, social studies educators offer several hypotheses to explain students' lack of interest in the social studies. James Shaver, O.L. Davis, Jr., and Suzanne Wiggins Helburn (1979) claimed that poor, repetitive instruction in many social studies courses produces negative student attitudes. Fred M. Newmann (1988) observed that much social studies instruction is superficial, which prevents students from seeing the vitality of the subjects they study. Haladyna, Shaughnessy, and Al Redsun (1982) asserted that students' attitudes toward social studies are a function of their perceptions of the learning environment (for example, student relationships, classroom activities), teacher quality (enthusiasm, personal engagement), and student characteristics (self-confidence, perceptions of subject matter importance). They claim that these conditions in social studies classes tend to be even more problematic than in most other subject areas. Still other social studies educators focused on students' perceptions that the subject matter of social studies is unrelated to students' lives (Fernandez, Massey, and Dornbusch, 1976; Schug, Todd, and Beery, 1984). Students' attitudes and levels of motivation are a function of a complex set of variables.

The irrelevance explanation warrants further consideration because it might shed additional light on students' perceptions that contribute to low motivation. Celestino Fernandez, Grace Carroll Massey, and Sanford M. Dornbusch (1976) and Greg Farman, Gary Natriello, and Dornbusch (1978) investigated the irrelevance hypothesis with an ethnically and economically diverse sample of several hundred students in San Francisco high schools. They used a narrow definition of relevance, which they called "articulation." Articulation means "the extent to which students perceive that course work will be helpful to some future aspect of their (lives)" (Farman, et al., 1978, p. 27). The researchers wanted to know the extent to which the students in their sample believed mathematics, English, and social studies courses would help them achieve "happiness" in their future careers, marriages and families, and community work.

Overall, students tended to assess social studies as much less important for career happiness than mathematics and English. Students generally considered all three school subjects as unrelated to marriage and family happiness. However, they did regard social studies as more important for happiness through community work. Unfortunately, this last encouraging finding is not as good as it sounds. The researchers collected data regarding the personal importance to the students of the three areas of life. Future career was rated as very or extremely important by 94 percent of the students. Marriage and family was rated similarly by 69 percent of the sample. Only 33 percent of the students rated community work as very or extremely important. A large majority of the students appear to believe that the larger society, including the local community, has little to do with the quality of their lives. The implication of this perception for motivation to achieve in social studies is obvious and negative.

MOTIVATION TO LEARN

Because students ultimately must decide to be motivated, consider the nature of motivation to learn. Given a clear conception of student motivation, teachers can decide how best to influence students' motivational decisions. Motivation to learn is defined as a student's willingness to engage in efforts to achieve an academic goal and to persist in those efforts. Carol S. Dweck (1989) conceptualized motivation to learn as a function of three key judgments students make, which she called goal value, means value, and goal expectancy judgments. Students will be more highly motivated the more of these judgments they make positively and the stronger they feel about those judgments. Conversely, the fewer the positive judgments they make and the more weakly they hold the positive judgments, the lower their motivation. Later in this chapter, these three judgments will be used to organize ideas about how to influence students' motivational decisions (see Figure 4–1, p. 85).

Consider the goal value judgment. When a teacher presents students with an instructional goal to achieve, the students will explicitly or implicitly ask and answer the question: *How important is this for me to learn?* If students perceive no personal value in achieving the goal, then they will answer this question negatively. Consider the example of high-school world-history students who are asked to learn factual information about the national unifications of Italy and Germany in the nineteenth century. Unless some compelling reasons are presented for studying this topic, students are likely to think it has little to do with their lives. They might still be motivated for some reason to learn about Italian and German unification, but not because they think the knowledge is important.

Consider the means value judgment. When a teacher presents students with a task to perform to enable them to achieve an instructional goal, they will ask and answer the question: *How do I feel about participating in this learning process?* If students expect that the learning experience will be threatening, unreasonably burdensome, or boring, they probably will answer the question negatively and their motivation to learn will suffer. Many students do not value the following instructional activities: reading narrative textbooks for homework, listening to long lectures and taking notes, standing up and presenting oral reports to the class, and writing essays. Students might have to make multiple judgments about the instructional means a teacher selects. For example, students might enjoy a judicial role-playing activity and the follow-up discussion, but not the essay assignment that requires them to explain what they learned.

Consider the goal expectancy judgment. When a teacher presents students with a goal to achieve and a task to help them achieve it, they will ask and answer the question: *If I try, how likely am I to be successful and achieve the goal?* If students believe that failure is a likely outcome of their efforts, then they are likely to try to get the teacher to change the task, try to avoid having to do it, or try to come up with a plausible explanation for why they will not be successful that avoids personal responsibility. Suppose students are given a set of eyewitness and newspaper accounts of what happened at the Battle of Lexington Green in 1775. They are asked to evaluate the reliability and validity of each account, rank the accounts from most trustworthy to least trustworthy, and write an account of what actually happened. Further, suppose that the teacher announces that he or she will assign grades stringently based on how closely their judgments match those of historians. Unless students have unusual skills and self-confidence, they are likely to be pessimistic about their likely success. In that case, they might ask the teacher many questions to clarify and hopefully simplify the task. They also might begin pointing out aloud or internally to themselves how unreasonable it is for the teacher to expect them to achieve this goal. Student motivation to achieve the instructional goal is likely to be low to nonexistent.

According to this conception of motivation (Dweck, 1989), if students believe that an academic goal is personally important to achieve, that the activities involved in achieving the goal are desirable, and that they are likely to achieve the goal, then they will be highly motivated. On the contrary, if students believe that the goal is personally unimportant, that they are unlikely to achieve the goal, and that the activities are very burdensome or threatening, then they will have little motivation to learn. Of course, there can be combinations of the three conditions. For example, high goal value and goal expectancy judgments might produce a reasonably high degree of motivation to learn in spite of a low means value judgment (for example, boring reading materials). For a particular judgment (goal value), multiple influences can result in a net positive or negative judgment (see Figure 4-1). Articulating those influences

Figure 4–1. Motivation

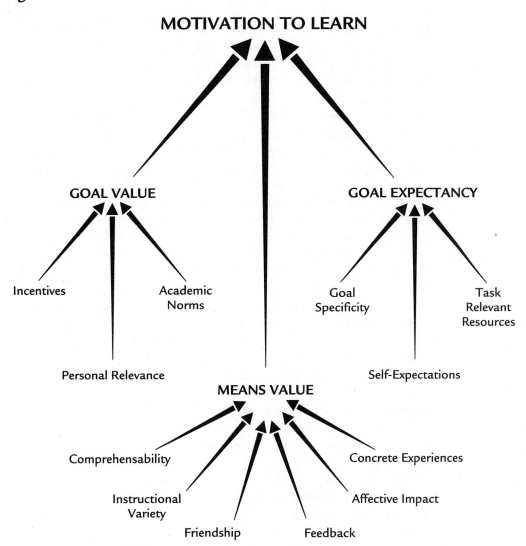

and clarifying the decisions teachers must make about them is a major task of this chapter. The following examples illustrate how students make the three motivational judgments.

A high-school student, Ben, had a very weak academic record that he was continuing in his last-period sociology class. Ben did very little work, participated hardly at all in class activities, and was very silent and unobtrusive. For several weeks his teacher tried without success to engage him in the work of the class. In early April, a directive came from the superintendent's office that all twelfth-grade social studies teachers would spend one week of class teaching the seniors to complete Internal Revenue Service Form 1040. The teacher was distressed but resigned himself to fulfilling the directive. As soon as he started the first class session, Ben became alert. Throughout the week, Ben worked diligently to complete the forms for several case studies. He stayed after class to continue working, he asked numerous questions, and he successfully achieved the goal of learning how to fill out income tax forms.

Viewed in terms of the three motivation questions, early in the course Ben appeared to have made a negative judgment about his likelihood of doing good work. That judgment was consistent with his poor academic record. He appeared to have made a negative means value judgment given his inattentiveness and his tendency to sleep. His teacher did not know what his goal value judgement might have been, but it was hard to imagine that Ben considered the class very important. What happened when Form 1040 entered the scene? In after school conversations, the teacher learned that Ben was working the night shift at a local foundry. For the first time, he was paying income taxes, and he was eligible to get a refund. To get that refund, he had to complete Form 1040. For this goal and task, he answered the goal value question positively and with great intensity. Given his struggles with the forms and directions, the learning process was very unpleasant for him. His questions and manner indicated that he was not confident about his ability to fill out the forms. However, the goal was so important that it outweighed the other negative judgments. The net result of Ben's answers to the motivation questions was positive and that translated into a level of motivated learning behavior that greatly surprised his teacher.

Robin, a third-grade student, was asked by her teacher to make a map of a real or imaginary community and to explain how it fit the definition of "community." The teacher had introduced her students to the concept of "community" and the class had briefly discussed examples of communities. The class then went to work on their maps. Robin was drawing a map of a town, but the work was going slowly because she was not very engaged in the task. She knew she could do it and she intended to fulfill her teacher's expectations, but the community map was just one more, not very interesting school task. Robin had made a positive goal expectancy judgment, a neutral or slightly negative means value judgment, and a negative goal value judgment.

Robin's teacher noted Robin's lack of enthusiasm and went over to talk with her. She remembered Robin's exciting report of her summer vacation at Sturgeon Lake in northern Michigan. She asked Robin if she had ever thought about Sturgeon Lake as a community. When Robin realized that Sturgeon Lake was a community, she was energized. She threw away the town map and quickly sketched Sturgeon Lake and located and labeled cottages, stores, the marina, the township hall, the constable's home, roads, and other features of a community. After the teacher's suggestion of focusing on Sturgeon Lake, one of Robin's favorite places, Robin changed her goal value and means value judgments strongly and positively. It is important to keep in mind that the sources of motivation will vary from student to student and often from topic to topic.

GOAL VALUE

Teachers can influence students' goal value judgments of an academic goal or task in several ways. They can provide incentives to increase the value students assign to an academic goal or task. They can make explicit the personal relevance of a goal or task to students' lives. They can attempt to modify anti-academic classroom norms and replace them with positive norms. All three approaches can work, but reservations held by some teachers must be considered.

Incentives

An incentive is a consequence students value that they receive for achieving a goal. Incentives can influence students to rate an academic goal more highly than they would otherwise because achieving the goal is a means to ends they desire. One type of incentive is an earned privilege that serves as an extrinsic reward for well-done work. For many students, grades are extrinsic rewards for academic achievement; they have a value apart from their function as feedback regarding performance. Some examples of other things that might serve as earned privileges are a library pass, an extra 10 minutes at lunch or recess, a special opportunity to play a computer game, and the option to skip an examination. Using earned privileges as a way of increasing students' judgments of the value of a goal requires that the teacher arbitrarily relate a desirable thing or opportunity with an academic goal so that students will work to acquire the incentive and incidently achieve the academic goal.

Social incentives are public positive judgments about students' competence that are intended to encourage or reinforce others' favorable judgments about the student. Public recognition of high-quality performance is a major type of social incentive. Examples include the teacher's public compliments about specific students' work and favorable comments in a class newsletter or on a bulletin board devoted to class news. Reports by students who have the job of identifying and announcing praiseworthy accomplishments of their peers can be especially rewarding and influential. Social incentives can be distributed in the form of opportunities for successful students to make decisions about classroom goals and activities. For example, students who have achieved well could be given choices about some topics to be studied or choices about some instructional procedures to be used. On a small scale, social incentives cause student achievement to lead to status and influence.

Issue: *Even if incentive systems work well, incentives raise a disturbing issue for many teachers.*

Critics of extrinsic incentives are concerned about what earned privileges and social incentives communicate to students about the importance of studying social studies. Do they communicate that the value of an academic goal is the short-term payoff in goods, opportunities, or status you get paid for achieving it? Students should be encouraged to see that the value of learning is becoming a more insightful and competent human being who will be better able to appreciate life and to deal with life's challenges. If students work to achieve academic goals because of short-run incentives teachers give them, they are likely to stop learning and thinking about social studies as soon as the incentives stop.

On the other hand, advocates of incentive systems observe that children and teenagers typically have notoriously short-term perspectives. It is better to motivate them with short-term incentives so they develop a record of academic success and a degree of expertise in the subject matter. Advocates argue that subjects become interesting and their values in life become apparent to people only when they have considerable experience with them. If social studies achievement is associated with pleasurable outcomes and recognition, some students will develop positive associations with the social studies and the internal motivation that all teachers hope for will develop. Incentives can motivate students in the early stages of their experience with social studies when they are unable to take a long-range view of the work. Students who never develop internal motivation to learn about the world through social studies will at least have acquired an intellectual base for thinking about the world even if they do not continue to develop it. From this perspective, incentives give students reasons to achieve goals when they cannot perceive the adult society's reasons for asking them to achieve. The way teachers resolve this issue has major implications for how they will structure courses.

Personal Relevance

Students who perceive that an academic goal is relevant to their personal lives in some way are likely to rate the goal as more important than they would otherwise. There are two ways that social studies academic goals might be personally useful (VanSickle, 1990). First, achieving the academic goal might enable one to assess the implications of conditions *within* one's immediate social environments (that is, face-to-face relationships) for making and implementing decisions to achieve one's personal goals. Second, achieving the academic goal might enable one to assess the implications of conditions *beyond* one's immediate social environments for making and implementing decisions to achieve one's personal goals. Students can perceive the personal relevance of a social studies goal if they understand how achieving it has implications for how they choose to act now or in the foreseeable future in pursuit of their own goals.

In 1990, I proposed a personal relevance framework for helping teachers and students to identify the personal relevance of social studies knowledge and skills. Four general motivations that influence much human behavior were identified; they are desires for a sense of security, sense of affiliation, sense of competence, and sense of influence. Also identified were five general goal areas in life in which these general motivations operate to shape human behavior: human relationships, occupation, health and safety, personal development, and finances. For example, within the occupational dimension of life, people seek an acceptable degree of security, productive and friendly relationships with others, confirmation of personal competence, and a reasonable degree of control over working conditions. If teachers help their students to see how a social studies goal can help them to achieve one or more of their personal goals as conceptualized in the personal relevance framework, they are likely to make positive goal value judgments. (See Figure 4-2.)

For example, suppose a teacher wants students to learn about the unification of Italy and Germany in the nineteenth century. Why should they care about Italian and German national unification? By studying Italian and German unification, students can begin to understand how nationalism and romanticism can produce tremendously intense, frequently violent social movements. Nationalistic movements endure over long periods of time in spite of great obstacles and generate high degrees of commitment by people who perceive their personal destinies as part of their "nation."

To take a recent example, the level of violence in the area that used to be Yugoslavia perplexed many people. Because of the atrocities committed, some people advocated that the United States and other nations take military action to stop the fighting. Understanding how nationalism and romanticism can bind people together in a struggle for nationhood should underlie citizens' assessments of whether the United States should intervene militarily in situations like this. A study of the political and military phases of German and Italian unification can contribute to that understanding. What do we want the United States government to do? Should the United States send troops with other United Nations members to try to end the violence? What will happen if some of the conflicting parties perceive U.N. relief efforts as disadvantageous and take military action against U.S. troops and others? Aside from military logistical considerations, there could be tremendous resistance to efforts to pacify the areas with outside military force. The various groups with their respective

Figure 4-2. **The Personal Relevance Framework**

	General Motivations			
Areas	**1. Sense of Security**	**2. Sense of Affiliation**	**3. Sense of Competence**	**4. Sense of Influence**
A. Human Relationships	A.1 • Support when needed • Predictable behavior • Freedom from disapproval	A.2 • Emotionally satisfying interaction • Inclusion in group activities	A.3 • To fulfill role responsibilities well • To receive recognition for role fulfillment	A.4 • To shape goals, procedures, resource allocations, people • To make significant contributions
B. Occupation	B.1 • Predictable employment • Physical safety • Freedom from intimidation	B.2 • Approval of occupational choice • Identification and status • Collegiality/peer inclusion	B.3 • To perform well • To be evaluated positively	B.4 • To influence working conditions, compensation, production process
C. Health and Safety	C.1 • Freedom from disease, unhealthy conditions, physical threat • Help when sick or injured	C.2 • Protection from health/safety threats • Cooperation to produce healthy/safe conditions	C.3 • To recognize physical threats • To act on knowledge of good health and safety	C.4 • To choose personal health/safety practices and risks • To influence health/safety conditions
D. Personal Development	D.1 • Clarity about identity, meaning of life, values, personal capacities	D.2 • Encouragement to develop • Interaction with others of similar values, interests	D.3 • To develop capacities, understanding • To act on values • To promote interests, values	D.4 • To generate support for interests, values • To obtain resources for development
E. Finances	E.1 • Short-run security • Long-run security	E.2 • Consensus on financial goals, roles, values, behavior	E.3 • To earn adequate income • To obtain good value • To increase financial resource base	E.4 • To obtain financial cooperation, recognition

traditions, histories, languages, and deep emotional commitments to restoring their lands to their "true" natures are likely to be very aggressive foes.

In the personal relevance framework, this is a health and safety issue. Students' safety or the safety of people important to them might be jeopardized if the United States commits troops to pacification efforts. If people support United States military intervention, they will understand that pacifying the Balkan area and many other areas of the world is likely to be very difficult and expensive because of the possibility of protracted guerilla warfare. Students might want to express their views to elected representatives or in the media to influence public opinion. Again, learning about nationalism and romanticism in nineteenth century Europe can enable students to understand that these phenomena characterize human behavior in many times and places. Achieving an academic goal in a world history course will be more important for some students because they understand how recurring historical phenomena can directly affect their lives.

Issue: *The personal relevance approach takes a very individualistic and utilitarian approach to persuading students that an academic goal is important.*

If the personal relevance approach is implemented wholeheartedly, then subject matter and academic goals that cannot be related easily to students' lives are likely to be deleted from courses. Some teachers believe that this is a problem because a society that aspires to be democratic needs citizens who think about the general welfare, not just their individual welfares. Many topics and issues are important to the welfare of our society and humanity generally—whether or not they affect particular individuals. On the other hand, advocates of the personal relevance approach claim that students are more likely to develop empathy and concern for the general welfare if they first learn that their lives are affected by social and historical forces beyond their immediate environments. The personal relevance approach is valuable in its own right and also because it can lead eventually to greater civic awareness.

Academic Norms

Academic norms are expectations shared by a group of people regarding what is worth learning and appropriate ways to go about achieving instructional goals. Consequently, norms operating in a classroom will influence students' willingness to work to achieve those goals. Examples of classroom norms are beliefs that homework over weekends is inappropriate, it is okay to ask other students for help when one does not understand something, there should be a lot of discussion in social studies classes, questions that require higher-order thought are not fair, seniors in college-preparation courses should do term papers, and students' grammar and spelling should not be graded in social studies classes. The effects of academic norms can be either positive or negative.

Sometimes the academic norms students bring with them to a class depress student achievement. For example, when a teacher presses for higher-order thought and intends to evaluate student performances, it is not unusual for students to resist. If so, a norm is operating that questions and projects that require higher-order thought are not appropriate. Students might express resistance by avoiding overt participation or trying to get the teacher off the subject. They might ask many questions to try to get the teacher to clarify the challenging task until it becomes a set of low-level, routine tasks (for example, how many pages, how many reasons, where can the answers be found, can the answers just be listed, can students work together, will partial credit be given, is there one right answer, what are the parts of the answer, how will it be graded). In some cases, students might overtly tell the teacher he or she has transgressed a norm: "Why do you keep asking us why?" "Nobody asks us questions like that!" "That's too hard."

Walter Doyle (1983) attributed the aversion to higher-order goals and tasks to students' desires to avoid risk and ambiguity. Higher-order goals tend to be at least somewhat open-ended and sometimes very unstructured. There are alternative ways of achieving the goal, and multiple ways of being unsuccessful or only partially successful. Considerable latitude is generally acceptable to students unless they are going to be evaluated. A bull-session discussion is no threat, but if the teacher is going to apply criteria to evaluate students' performances, then the risk of failure and appearing incompetent increases drastically. When achievement of a goal is ambiguous and the risk of clearly and publicly not succeeding is high, a norm of aversion often will begin to operate.

If a teacher highly values student higher-order thought and encounters this anti-achievement academic norm, then he or she will want to change it. The teacher must try to replace the unconstructive norm with a new one that supports higher-order thought. There are several approaches. The teacher can communicate frequently, clearly, and emphatically that higher-order thought is important through goal statements and rationales. Even when students resist, the teacher can persistently provide opportunities for students to engage in higher-order thought. Evaluative criteria for assessing student performance can be introduced, but their application for grading purposes can be phased in gradually. The teacher can emphasize to students that it is acceptable and even admirable to express ideas even if they turn out to be wrong as long as they are offered seriously. The teacher should reward serious but unsuccessful efforts, perhaps by means of participation points. Rewards and recognition for higher-order thought can be distributed frequently and for specific contributions. Through conversations outside of class, the teacher might enlist the help of more cooperative students who have strong peer influence. If high-influence students participate actively in discussions that require higher-order thought, they will model desirable student behavior and communicate to other students that engaging in higher-order thought is a good thing to do in spite of the risk and ambiguity. Over time, there is a good chance that the norm will begin to shift constructively.

Issue: *The school faculty should consider the state of academic norms among the students and among themselves as well.*

Efforts to change academic norms in positive ways will be much more effective if the school clearly communicates and promotes desirable expectations consistently from teacher to teacher, from one subject to another, and from one year to the next. This is likely to be trickier than it sounds. Expectations for students vary considerably from one teacher to another. For example, some teachers want to place much more emphasis on higher-order thought than do others. Once the discussion moves beyond coming to class promptly, bringing necessary supplies, and doing assignments on time, the faculty dialogue about desirable academic norms, how to promote them effectively, and specifically how to implement a schoolwide plan with accountability is likely to be very challenging.

MEANS VALUE

Teachers can influence students' means value judgments of an academic goal and task. Teachers can design a variety of instructional activities that require active participation and frequent performance feedback. They can increase the affective impact of the curriculum and instructional activities. They can take measures to increase the comprehensability of their teaching. They can use student relationships to increase students' willingness to participate actively in instruction. As with most good ideas, both costs and benefits should be considered.

Key Characteristics of Instructional Activities

Instructional activities can be designed in ways likely to influence students to rate instructional activities favorably, thus increasing the frequency and strength of positive means value judgments. Among these are the use of a variety of instructional techniques, concrete experiences, and frequent, systematic performance feedback (Brophy and Alleman, 1991). These are common recommendations that need to be reemphasized. Even if students think a goal is important, a repetitive, unavoidable learning process that varies little over weeks and months will dull anyone's enthusiasm for learning. Concrete experiences that allow students to view and participate in demonstrations (such as role playing, simulation gaming), examine artifacts (for example, maps, tools, artwork, letters), and interview real-life actors (for example, public officials, businesspeople, travelers) will increase the desirability of learning experiences for some students. Also, a learning experience will be more desirable for many students if they can assess how they are doing. In-progress feedback will give students the information they need to have a sense of security and a chance for some control over their final evaluation. The students whose attitudes toward social studies were investigated by Haladyna, Shaughnessy, and Redsun (1982) and Schug, Todd, and Beery (1984) supported instructional activities with these three characteristics.

Curricular Affective Impact

Why are soap operas, action/adventure, and police/emergency programs so popular among television viewers? One reason is that they focus on people in trouble. People are in situations in which they have a lot to lose. There is a high degree of risk that they will lose it. Often, they confront a lot of uncertainty about the best course of action. These conditions have a strong affective impact on viewers. As it happens, social studies teachers deal with subject matter and issues that frequently contain these elements. Curricular affective impact refers to the emotionally engaging effects of focusing students' attention on problems and dilemmas people have confronted and do confront that are represented in social studies subjects. Teachers who draw out the affective dimensions of what they teach can have a strong, positive impact on students' means value judgments.

Suppose fifth-grade students are studying the European exploration of the New World. One approach is to identify who the major explorers were, their motivations, what and who they discovered, their interaction with the native American inhabitants, the destruction of the Aztec and Incan civilizations, and so forth. This subject matter is fine, but what do we think about the explorers as people and their impact on the native Americans? How do we think Cortez and Pizarro should have made contact and interacted with the Aztecs and Incas? How should the Aztecs, Incas, and other native Americans have responded to the appearance of the Europeans so that catastrophe would not have followed? Should Cortez and Pizarro be considered guilty of human rights violations from our modern frame of reference or were they really heroes in a meaningful sense? Value questions like these are engaging and provoke thought and discourse about subject matter. They also can lead to consideration of issues that have great relevance in the world today.

Drama is another way to increase the affective impact of academic goals. If academic goals and their related tasks are sometimes presented dramatically, students are likely to rate instructional experiences more positively. Storytelling is one way. Much more than anecdotes, stories can place subject matter in a human context so that students can imagine real people facing real dilemmas struggling to find solutions to personal and social problems. Consider Prince Henry the Navigator of Portugal. Tell a story that describes Henry's situation as a junior prince in the kingdom and how a bloody crusade to North Africa fired his imagination of Eastern wealth. Describe his self-imposed near exile to Land's End, on the edge of the great world ocean. Describe how he broke traditions and prejudices as he organized the world's first research and development program to reach the East by ship. Explain the setbacks, crises, fears, and eventual successes as his captains groped farther and farther south along the west African coast. Describe how after Henry died, his ships finally reached the East, the new ocean trade shifted immense wealth from the Italian merchant cities to Portugal, and Europeans rapidly became planetary explorers (Boorstin, 1983). To do this well takes considerable thought and practice, but the focus on characters and plot can greatly increase the impact of the subject matter.

Another way to increase the dramatic dimension of instruction is to use case studies and role playing. A well-written case study of someone trying to keep his single frozen yogurt shop from going out of business because of increased competition from a frozen-yogurt chain is surprisingly engaging if it is about someone real in trouble. Again, some attention to character and plot is needed. If the case leads to a crisis of decision and students are asked to decide the protagonist's best course of action, a discussion of supply, demand, substitutability, complementary goods, and market structure can become animated and meaningful. Similarly, role playing can reveal real-life drama in mundane sounding events. When students take on the roles of people attending a zoning commission hearing on the location of a proposed parking lot, the level of feeling and involvement can be amazing. The teacher's task is to reveal the people and the dilemmas they face that form the heart of what historians and social scientists study and what we ask our students to study.

Issue: Although the ideas for increasing curricular affective impact look desirable, there is an important cost.

These ideas take time. They might take additional preparation time, and they certainly will take additional class time. Teachers must assess the opportunity cost of engaging students more intensely in efforts to achieve academic goals. If a teacher exerts much effort along the lines suggested, fewer academic goals can be addressed in a course. The familiar depth versus coverage issue arises. Skeptics express concern over the reduction of important goals and subject matter. They also question whether emphasis on the dramatic will tend to distort the subject matter to achieve an effect. How much dramatic license is justifiable? Advocates of increasing affective impact believe that students will achieve goals more effectively and have deeper, long-term commitments to learning if affective impact is increased. There is no simple resolution to this dilemma. Teachers must weigh the benefits against the costs in their situations.

Comprehensability

Comprehensability refers to the degree to which printed and verbal discourse is understandable in terms of knowledge students possess. If students cannot understand the reading material and discussion of a subject in class, they are likely to be very frustrated. Isabel L. Beck and Margaret G. McKeown (1988) analyzed four fifth-grade United States history textbooks for their comprehensability. They identified three problems. First, the narratives generally were not written with focused goals for student understanding at any level, ranging from paragraphs to chapters. Second, the narratives assumed previously learned knowledge that fifth-grade students do not typically possess. Third, explanations were inadequate. They stated cause and effect relationships, but generally they did not provide information that explained why major actors and events caused particular consequences. If the teacher is not sensitive to these problems, the most likely and reasonable response of students is to avoid participating in instruction as much as possible. That means their willingness to work toward achieving academic goals will be less than it would be if they could understand the subject adequately.

Beck and McKeown were specifically interested in how well the textbook presentations of the causes of the American Revolution took into account fifth-grade students' prior knowledge of the subject and their abilities to interpret the text. The following examples illustrate how the three problems pervaded the narratives. First, the French and Indian War was identified in the texts as a major cause of the Revolution, and the war itself was described. However, its linkage to the eventual outbreak of armed revolution more than a decade later was left vague. The specific information about the French and Indian War selected for presentation was not focused on the Revolution. Second, there were numerous statements about "No taxation without representation." However, none of the texts explained the nature of representative government, and very few of the fifth graders interviewed by Beck and McKeown could explain it. Third, Parliament repealed various taxes that angered the colonists except for the tea tax, and Parliament drastically lowered the cost of tea in the colonies. Most of the texts do not explain why a major reduction in taxes and a decrease in the cost of tea to colonial consumers led to the Boston Tea Party. How could fifth-grade students know that colonial tea wholesalers were cut out of the business and many colonists objected to Britain's continued claim that it could tax the colonies and rearrange the colonial economy whenever it chose? A teacher would be challenged to provide the additional information and missing linkages students would need to understand the Revolution's causes.

Textbook authors were the focus of Beck and McKeown's study. However, teachers also can make these same mistakes. The huge difference in quantity of knowledge between teachers and most students can make it difficult for teachers to perceive the difficulty levels of the goals and tasks they set for students. Also, and perhaps even more important, teachers see connections between events, people, places, and ideas that students cannot possibly perceive. In the day-to-day press of classroom teaching, a teacher must be very sensitive and conscientious about intellectually bridging the tremendous gap between his or her knowledge and the knowledge students bring to the class. The less effective a teacher is in bridging the gap, the more difficult and frustrating the class will be and the more negative students' means value judgments will be. Students' motivation to learn will suffer accordingly.

Friendship and Liking

The nature and quality of relationships between students can affect their desire to participate in a particular class. If students feel uncomfortable or rejected in a class, their willingness to work toward achieving academic goals is likely to be low (Schmuck and Schmuck, 1992). Some empirical evidence shows that students who are not liked in a class and know it tend to underachieve seriously (VanEgmond, 1960).

Several actions can be taken to be improve the emotional climate among students in a class. Cooperative learning techniques, such as Student Teams–Achievement Divisions and Teams-Games-Tournament, have been observed to increase friendship and helping behavior in classes (Slavin, 1986). It is difficult for teachers to see how liking choices operate in a classroom unless the teacher can watch students interact a great deal. A sociometric survey can reveal liking patterns and choices in a classroom that might not even be operational, just potential. If the teacher feels that some students are not engaged in the class group, the survey data can suggest possible groupings for classwork that could help (Schmuck and Schmuck, 1992). For example, if a relatively isolated student indicates that she likes another student and the second student does not indicate any dislike, it could be intrinsically satisfying for the first student to work with the second on a project or in a discussion. Students have a tendency to view each other only in terms of major school-related characteristics, such as academic status or athletic ability. Student interviews conducted occasionally can reveal nonschool interests and other dimensions of students' lives that could become the bases of new friendships among students. Each of these ideas could make the classroom a friendlier, less threatening place for students and have a positive effect on their means value judgments.

GOAL EXPECTANCY

Teachers can influence students' goal expectancy judgments regarding achievement of an academic goal. They can assure students that the resources they need to achieve a goal are available. They can state and communicate academic goals clearly. They can bolster students' self-expectations for strong achievement. The costs and benefits of implementing these recommendations are examined.

Task Relevant Resources

A variable affecting students' goal expectancy judgments is the availablity of task relevant resources. When students assess their probabilities of achieving an academic goal, they also assess the availability of resources necessary to achieve the goal. These resources include knowledge and skills necessary for the task, sources of information not already possessed (such as books), people who will assist the student (for example, teacher, peers, parents). This is especially important when a higher-order academic goal is posed for students because such goals tend to generate the previously discussed aversion to ambiguity and risk. Frances F. Voss, Terry R. Greene, Timothy A. Post, and Barbara C. Penner (1983) referred to this survey of relevant resources as the creation of a problem space. Students poorly prepared to address an academic goal might immediately determine that they have little or no personal knowledge or few skills appropriate to the task and almost instantly make a low goal expectancy judgment. Teachers need to help students identify knowledge and skills they already possess that is relevant to an academic goal and the human and material resources that are available to help them. If this is done, it is likely to influence students to make more positive goal expectancy judgments than they otherwise would make.

Goal Specificity

Students tend to want to avoid risk and ambiguity because of the danger that their class performances will be judged inadequate by the teacher or other students (Doyle, 1983). If students regard goals as unclear, their expectations for their own success are likely to be lower than if they clearly understand the goals. When students make goal expectancy judgments, they essentially are making risk assessments. Teachers can reduce the ambiguity students face and their perceptions of risk by stating goals very clearly. Behaviorally stated instructional objectives are one major way to state expectations very clearly. If a teacher is posing a challenging higher-order task, it will help to describe clearly the problem students are to solve and to announce explicitly the criteria for evaluating the adequacy of students' performances. Of course, sometimes teachers want their students to deal with situations that are less structured. As students gain knowledge and skill in an area, they should need less guidance. If they are to transfer their knowledge and skills to contexts outside of school, then they must learn eventually to deal with somewhat ambiguous problems and issues. The point is to minimize ambiguity when ambiguity is not an important part of the goal statement.

Issue: ***Some teachers object to high degrees of specificity and explicitness in stating learning expectations for students.***

These teachers fear that students will focus only on the specific objectives teachers state and will ignore everything else. They believe that behaviorally stated instructional objectives will lead to minimum expectations. On the other hand, advocates of clearly stated instructional goals argue that students who know little about a subject have difficulty identifying the important ideas and figuring out how to go about answering and solving challenging questions and problems. They claim that if students are achieving all the teacher's objectives, then the teacher should identify more goals or more challenging goals as the ends of instruction.

Self-Expectations

Students enter most instructional situations with general expectations about the likelihood that they can be successful in achieving the goals of the course. These self-expectations strongly influence whether students will exert enough effort to achieve instructional goals. Teachers can phrase the expectations they communicate to students as individuals or groups in ways that tend to increase achievement. Teachers should explain to students that an academic goal is challenging (assuming it is) and will require effort to achieve, but if students will work with the teacher and and work on the tasks, then students can expect to achieve the goal (Gage and Berliner, 1974). In contrast, telling students that a goal is easy to achieve will influence some students to underestimate the effort required to achieve a goal. Also in contrast, telling students that a goal is difficult without assuring them that the teacher actively will support their efforts will influence some students to make low goal expectancy judgments. As a result, some students will give up before they try to achieve the goal. The impact of the teacher's expectation statements will vary with the importance students assign to the teacher's opinion.

Social expectations, others' predictions of how likely a student is to achieve an academic goal successfully, also can influence students' self-expectations. If students are uncertain about their probabilities of success, others' opinions can provide cues for the students' predictions about themselves. Social expectations are likely to be most influential when students are most uncertain. Social expectations come from a variety of sources. If peers express expectations to each other that they can achieve a difficult goal, then they are more likely to believe that they can be successful. Even if peers do not express their expectations explicitly, their behavior can communicate their expectations. Along with the teacher's expectations, family and community expectations can affect students' self-expectations, again depending on the value the students assign to those sources.

Cooperative learning is one of the most straight-forward approaches to using social expectations to increase students' self-expectations and their positive goal expectancy judgments. If the tasks and rewards of cooperative learning groups are structured so that rewards are distributed based on the sum or combination of individual group members' performances, then students' expectations for each others' performances will tend to be high (VanSickle, 1992). If they receive rewards based on their individual performances or for a group product for which individuals cannot be held accountable, then the positive effect on interpersonal expectations is largely lost.

Issue: ***The emphasis in cooperative learning on student interdependence and individual accountability to peers worries some teachers.***

It seems unfair that students must depend on others to obtain classroom rewards, even if not grades, when they might be able to perform well alone. Also, being held accountable by student peers sounds questionable; teachers are responsible for holding students accountable for their work and behavior. Why should untrained students, some of whom lack maturity, be allowed to pressure their peers to perform? Advocates respond that school is one of the few places in life where people do not routinely work together to achieve goals; there is nothing radical about cooperative learning. They observe that students working together can help each other achieve academic goals even when the teacher is unavailable. If the teacher sees unacceptable behavior, he or she is responsible for intervening. The research on cooperative learning indicates that student relationships improve in quality and that mutual accountability has positive emotional outcomes. Teachers' views on independence, accountability, and motivation will determine whether they choose to use cooperative learning techniques.

ACHIEVEMENT ORIENTATIONS

The previous section discussed ways to increase students' motivation to learn social studies and some issues teachers must resolve as they consider the alternatives. Now, two more concepts are needed to interpret the implications for motivating students to achieve academic goals in social studies. Dweck (1989) identified two general orientations to achievement in school situations: a learning orientation and a performance orientation. Students with learning orientations generally focus on increasing their competence. They want to understand a subject, master the objectives of the curriculum, and learn something new. Acquiring new knowledge, developing a new skill, or refining a previously learned skill are achievements they want from instruction.

On the other hand, students with performance orientations generally focus on validating their competence. They want to obtain favorable judgments of their ability (such as grades, praise, peer recognition) or, at least, avoid unfavorable judgments. Success from a performance perspective is often normative, that is, based on comparison with others' performances. Consequently, performance-oriented students tend to assess achievement situations with social cues from others. Learning new knowledge or skills are of secondary concern to performance-oriented students; in some cases, learning is incidental to the main goal of obtaining positive judgments. The learning orientation and the performance orientation can be considered the opposite ends of a continuum. Most people are characterized by varying degrees of each achievement orientation; in addition, personal orientations can shift over time and from one achievement situation to another.

Consider the implications of the learning and performance orientations for students' judgments leading to motivation to achieve a higher-cognitive academic goal. With respect to goal value, strongly learning-oriented students probably will attend to the personal relevance of a higher-cognitive goal. In contrast, performance-oriented students will be likely to key in on personal competence judgments that will come with attempting to achieve the goal and accomplish its associated task. Also, performance-oriented students possibly will attend more than learning-oriented students to academic norms that provide cues to judging the importance of the higher-cognitive academic goal. Very different features of the goal and task are likely to influence the goal value judgments of the two kinds of students.

With respect to goal expectancy, learning-oriented students base their judgments on the availability of task relevant resources, their understanding of the task, and past experience with similar goals. Performance-oriented students will be very sensitive to ambiguity in the task because it increases the risk of being unsuccessful. They will also be more sensitive to social expectations as cues to what they can expect to achieve. If social expectations are negative or peer norms evaluate a goal and task as inappropriate or too hard, performance-oriented students are likely to make lower goal expectancy judgments than would otherwise similar learning-oriented students. Again, very different features of the situation are likely to influence the two kinds of students.

In terms of means value, learning-oriented students probably will be engaged by dramatic, value-based cognitive conflict because it is a challenge to clarify and resolve. Performance-oriented students' interest might well be captured by the conflict, but it will probably increase tension within them because the cognitive conflict poses a problem to which the solution is uncertain. This uncertainty could lead to their failure to perform satisfactorily. The more socially cohesive the class, the more performance-oriented students will use normative judgments to evaluate the higher-cognitive goal. The dramatic quality of the question or problem is likely to affect the two kinds of students similarly, unless it increases or decreases the ambiguity of the goal and task.

Persistence

Higher-order thought requires persistence, and the two achievement orientations have significant implications in this area as well. (See Figure 4-3.) According to research reviewed by Dweck (1989), learning-oriented students confronted by a question or problem decide how to begin and initiate work to accomplish the task. They continue to work when the teacher presents criteria for judging their work or provides critiques of their work in progress; the criteria or critiques will be incorporated into their thinking to help them decide how to proceed. When learning-oriented students encounter difficulty or fail to answer the question or solve the problem, they reassess what they have done, identify another approach, or seek assistance from the teacher or others. In the end, learning-oriented students are likely to achieve the goal satisfactorily.

In contrast, performance-oriented students, regardless of personal ability, have some danger points in the process. After beginning to work on a task, some students falter when the teacher provides evaluative information. The threat of failure becomes more salient and causes evaluation anxiety. The performance of students who suffer from evaluation anxiety often deteriorates. They express confusion, seek cues from peers and the teacher about how well they are doing, begin to think about their personal inadequacies, and think less about how to proceed with the task. As a result, they are more likely than learning-oriented students to underachieve.

Other performance-oriented students work well until they encounter difficulty with the task. They become frustrated and begin thinking about the fact that they are having difficulty rather than how to proceed or what kind of information or assistance they need. Consequently, their performance deteriorates, and they are likely to underachieve the goal. If they do not encounter significant difficulty, such students can achieve very well. The conceptualization of learning-oriented and performance-oriented achievement orientations can explain varying degrees of motivation to learn. Teachers can use these concepts to help interpret why particular students might be having difficulty

Figure 4–3. **Persistence**

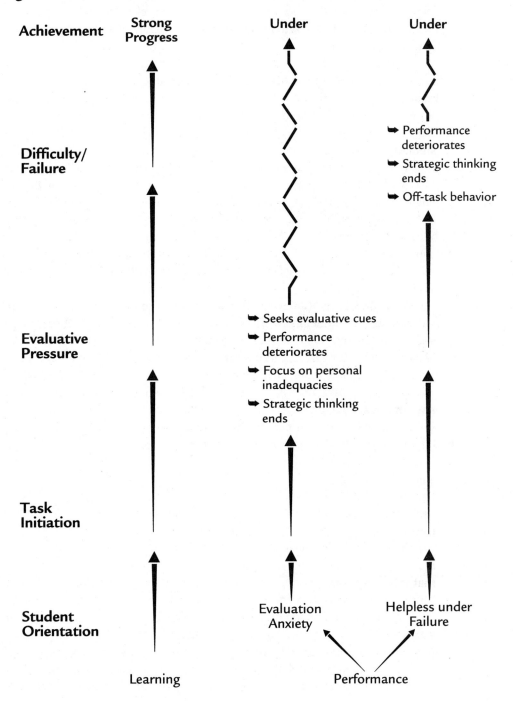

achieving an academic goal and why their motivation is flagging. Given an accurate diagnosis, teachers can attempt to counsel students experiencing frustration caused by evaluation anxiety or a sense of helplessness when confronted with difficulty.

Research indicates that students tend to shift from a learning perspective in the early grades to a more performance-oriented perspective in the later grades. It might be that the shift in orientation is a natural result of to students' cognitive development. One must be capable of perceiving social expectations, making interpersonal comparisons, and incorporating them into one's assessments of social situations before one can be strongly performance-oriented. Evidence exists that students in the earliest grades make interpersonal comparisons, but seldom use them for making judgments about themselves and social situations (Stipek, 1981; Stipek and Hoffman, 1980). Schools might reinforce social comparison and performance orientations, but they probably do not cause the shift from learning to performance orientations. A naturally occurring shift in achievement orientation could explain much of the decrease in student motivation to learn in the middle and secondary grades.

Systematic interventions to alter achievement orientations are not available, although experimental work is underway. An implication of the research is that challenging social studies academic goals and tasks should be introduced to students beginning in the early grades when they are most receptive to them. Even though a strong learning orientation looks ideal, information from the social environment can be valuable in assessing a situation, particularly an ambiguous one. A learning-oriented student with social awareness will probably be more successful than either an extremely learning-oriented student or an extremely performance-oriented student.

CONCLUSION

Students' motivation to learn is determined by students' answers to three questions: "How important is this for me to learn?" (*goal value*); "How do I feel about participating in this learning process?" (*means value*); and "If I try, how likely am I to be successful and achieve the goal?" (*goal expectancy*). Teachers can explore ways to influence students to make positive goal value judgments by providing a range of incentives (for example, earned privileges, social incentives), clarifying the personal relevance of academic goals, and reinforcing or altering academic norms to support goal achievement. Positive means value judgments can be promoted by incorporating variety, concrete learning experiences, and systematic feedback into instructional plans. Other approaches to increasing the means value of an academic goal are emphasizing the affective impact of the curriculum, attending to the comprehensibility of instruction, and promoting more friendship and liking relationships among students. Positive goal expectancy judgments can be encouraged by making sure students are aware of the availability of resources they need to achieve a goal, making goals specific, and communicating expectations in ways that influence students to expect to achieve a goal. Student motivation to learn is deeply affected by whether a student tends to approach an academic goal with a learning orientation or a performance orientation. Teachers who are sensitive to students' learning orientations possibly can help floundering students to regain their motivation and ability to achieve academic goals in social studies.

Reflective Questions

1. *Should students receive extrinsic incentives to encourage them to achieve academic goals?*

2. *Choose a social studies goal and develop a personal relevance rationale that might persuade students to value the goal.*

3. *To what extent are the individualistic and utilitarian aspects of personal relevance rationales problematic?*

4. *Identify a set of desirable academic norms you believe should operate in social studies classrooms.*

5. *Given that increasing the affective impact of instruction takes additional class time, decide and explain how much emphasis on affective curricular impact is justifiable.*

6. *To what extent do you believe the claim is valid that explicitly stated goals and objectives lead to a focus on minimum performance?*

7. *Why do you believe that student interdependence and peer accountability are constructive or destructive in social studies teaching and learning?*

GLOSSARY

academic norm   Expectations shared by a group of people regarding what is worth learning and appropriate ways to go about achieving instructional goals.

ambiguity   Lack of clarity regarding the nature of an academic goal, how to achieve it, or how to evaluate it.

comprehensability   Degree to which printed and verbal discourse is understandable in terms of knowledge students possess.

concrete experiences   Instructional activities in which students examine or participate in historical or social scientific phenomena.

curricular affective impact   The emotionally engaging effects of focusing students' attention on problems, and dilemmas people have confronted and do confront that are represented in social studies subjects.

goal expectancy   A student's judgment of the likelihood that he or she will achieve an academic end based on the question: "If I try, how likely am I to be successful and achieve the goal?"

goal specificity   Clearly stated learning outcomes.

goal value   A judgment of importance about an academic end based on the question: "How important is this for me to learn?"

incentives   A consequence students value that they receive for achieving an academic goal.

instructional variety   The use of several different teaching techniques rather than routine reliance on one or two techniques.

learning orientation   A student perspective on achievement characterized by a focus on increasing personal competence.

means value   A judgment about a learning experience based on the question: "How do I feel about participating in this learning process?"

motivation to learn   A student's willingness to engage in efforts to achieve an academic goal and to persist in those efforts.

performance orientation   A student perspective on achievement characterized by a focus on validating personal competence.

personal relevance   A student's perception that achieving an academic goal will help him or her achieve his or her goals in life.

risk   The probability that efforts to achieve an academic goal will be unsuccessful.

self-expectation   Prediction regarding the likelihood that one will achieve an academic goal.

task relevant resources   The knowledge, skills, materials, and people that students need to achieve an academic goal.

ANNOTATED BIBLIOGRAPHY

Beck, Isabel L. and Margaret G. McKeown (1988). "Toward Meaningful Accounts in History Texts for Young Learners." *Educational Researcher* 17:31–40.

Beck and McKeown analyzed four fifth-grade United States history textbooks and teacher materials. They found that the textbooks lacked clarity between content presented and instructional goals, were based on unrealistic assumptions about student background knowledge, and explained events and their relationships inadequately. The authors' analytical approach can be used to improve history instruction.

Brophy, Jere E. and Janet Alleman (1991). "Activities as Instructional Tools: A Framework for Analysis and Evaluation." *Educational Researcher* 20:9–23.

Brophy and Alleman identified issues relating to the design, selection, and evaluation of learning activities and reviewed research findings. They listed principles that can be used for designing, selecting, and assessing instructional activities.

Dweck, Carol S. (1989). "Motivation." In *Foundations for a Psychology of Education,* edited by A. Lesgold and R. Glaser. Hillsdale, NJ: Lawrence Erlbaum Associates.

Dweck reviewed much research on motivation to learn and developed a conceptualization of goal value, goal expectancy, and means value. She analyzed achievement motivation in learning and performance orientations and explored their implications for understanding age-related motivation issues.

Schmuck, Richard A. and Patricia A. Schmuck (1992). *Group Processes in the Classroom,* 6th ed. Dubuque, IA: Wm. C. Brown Publishers.

Schmuck and Schmuck explored the social psychology of classroom instruction in terms of expectations, leadership, friendship and class cohesiveness, norms, communication, and conflict. They described many activities and strategies for improving classroom climate and promoting students' academic productivity.

Slavin, Robert E. (1986). *Using Student Team Learning,* 3rd ed. Baltimore: The Johns Hopkins Team Learning Project, The Johns Hopkins University.

Slavin reviewed the extensive research literature on the cognitive and affective effects of cooperative learning. He explains in detail how to implement several cooperative learning techniques in elementary, middle, and secondary grades. The techniques explained include Student Teams–Achievment Divisions, Teams-Games-Tournament, Team Accelerated Instruction, Cooperative Integrated Reading and Composition, and Jigsaw II.

VanSickle, Ronald L. (1990). "The Personal Relevance of the Social Studies." *Social Education* 54:23–27, 59.

VanSickle explains the personal relevance framework and how to use it to develop persuasive rationales for the personal importance of historical and social scientific knowledge. The rationales can be used to increase students' goal value judgments. Several examples from history, government, and economics are presented as models for using the framework.

References

Beck, I.L. and M.G. McKeown (1988). "Toward Meaningful Accounts in History Texts for Young Learners." *Educational Researcher* 17:31–40.

Boorstin, D. (1983). *The Discoverers: A History of Man's Search to Know his World and Himself.* New York: Vintage Books.

Brophy, J. and J. Alleman (1991). "Activities as Instructional Tools: A Framework for Analysis and Evaluation." *Educational Researcher* 20:9–23.

Doyle, W. (1983). "Academic Work." *Review of Educational Research* 53:159–199.

Dweck, C.S. (1989). "Motivation." In *Foundations for a Psychology of Education,* edited by A. Lesgold and R. Glaser. Hillsdale, NJ: Lawrence Erlbaum Associates.

Farman, G., G. Natriello, and S.M. Dornbusch (1978). "Social Studies and Motivation: Articulation of Social Studies to Work, Family, and Community." *Theory and Research in Social Education* 6:27–39.

Fernandez, C., G.C. Massey, and S.M. Dornbusch (1976). "High School Students' Perceptions of Social Studies." *Social Studies* 67:51–57.

Gage, N. and D. Berliner (1974). *Educational Psychology.* Chicago: Rand McNally.

Haladyna, T., J. Shaughnessy, and A. Redsun (1982). "Relations of Student, Teacher, and Learning Environment Variables to Attitudes Toward Social Studies." *Journal of Social Studies Research* 6:36–44.

Newmann, F.M. (1988). "Can Depth Replace Coverage in the High School Curriculum?" *Phi Delta Kappan* 69:345–348.

Rholes, W.S., J. Blackwell, C. Jordan, and C. Walters (1980). "A Developmental Study of Learned Helplessness." *Developmental Psychology* 16:616–624.

Schmuck, R.A. and P.A. Schmuck (1992). *Group Processes in the Classroom,* 6th ed. Dubuque, IA: Wm. C. Brown Publishers.

Schug, M.C., R.J. Todd, and R. Beery (1984). "Why Kids Don't Like Social Studies." *Social Education* 48:382–387.

Shaughnessy, J.M. and T.M. Haladyna (1985). "Research on Student Attitude Toward Social Studies." *Social Education* 49:692–695.

Shaver, James P., O.L. Davis, and S.W. Helburn (1979). "The Status of Social Studies Education: Impressions from Three NSF Studies." *Social Education* 43:150–153.

Slavin, Robert E. (1986). *Using Student Team Learning,* 3rd ed. Baltimore: The Johns Hopkins Team Learning Project, The Johns Hopkins University.

Stipek, D.J. (1981). "Children's Perceptions of Their Own and Their Classmates' Ability." *Journal of Educational Psychology* 73:404–410.

Stipek, D.J. (1984). "Developmental Aspects of Achievement Motivation in Children." In *Research on Motivation in Education.* Vol. 1, *Student Motivation,* edited by R. Ames and C. Ames. New York: Academic Press.

Stipek, D.J. and J.M. Hoffman (1980). "Children's Achievement Related Expectancies as a Function of Academic Performance Histories and Sex." *Journal of Educational Psychology* 72:861–865.

VanEgmond, E. (1960). *Social Interrelationship Skills and Effective Utilization of Intelligence in the Classroom.* Unpublished dissertation. Ann Arbor: University of Michigan.

VanSickle, Ronald L. (1992). "Cooperative Learning, Properly Implemented, Works: Evidence from Research in Classrooms." In *Classroom Learning in the Social Studies Classroom: An Introduction to Social Study,* edited by R.J. Stahl and Ronald L. VanSickle. Washington, DC: National Council for the Social Studies.

VanSickle, Ronald L. (1990). "The Personal Relevance of the Social Studies." *Social Education* 54:23–27, 59.

Voss, J.F., T.R. Greene, T.A. Post, and B.C. Penner (1983). "Problem Solving Skill in the Social Sciences." In *The Psychology of Learning and Motivation: Advances in Research and Theory,* edited by G.H. Bower. New York: Academic Press.

Chapter Five

THINKING SKILLS INSTRUCTION IN SOCIAL STUDIES CLASSROOMS

William W. Wilen
Kent State University

SEVERAL YEARS AGO, this letter to the editor, entitled "Higher Priority Needed for Thinking Skills," appeared in an urban newspaper:

> In our present system of education, a great deal of emphasis is placed on memorization and much too little is placed on analysis of subject material. Our minds continue to be trained to memorize as opposed to being challenged by way of critical thinking. As a result, the dangerous reality is that the vast majority of students are graduating from their high schools with poorly developed interpretive skills.
>
> English teachers often complain about the lack of clarity and organization in students' writing. The fact is students do not write clearly because they do not think clearly.
>
> We pride ourselves on the existence of a writing lab where students may receive help on their papers, but we don't offer any type of 'thinking lab' where students could learn to think in a sensible and organized manner. Like anything else, thinking takes practice. The mere recounting of facts is so prevalent

in the majority of classes that our thinking skills are suffering. Learning should include much more than simply the relaying of facts. Knowledge is useless if the concept behind the facts is not understood.

Many of us will have the opportunity to sharpen our thinking abilities in college. However, the majority of high school graduates do not pursue advanced education.

The product that crosses the stage every June is certainly not capable of solving the pressing problems of our society. In fact the average high school graduate is one of the biggest problems our society faces. Demand is great for a better quality citizen.

The real conflict is rooted in the fact that analytical minds are needed to address and solve the problems of our system of public education. However, our system isn't producing enough minds capable of solving or even identifying significant problems (Yeargin, 1989, p. A4).

This articulate and insightful letter, as you may have realized, was written by a high school student.* Though it is a concerned student's plea to right a wrong, it also reflects a major unfulfilled need in social studies—the education of citizens who can think critically to make reasoned decisions and work to solve societal problems. This is not an isolated situation. Although thinking is a very natural act, researchers have consistently found that good thinking is a scarcity in the classroom. One of the most persistent problems in social studies is the absence of critical thinking in classrooms in spite of the numerous sources strongly advocating the use of higher-level thinking in a variety of forms (Banks and Clegg, 1990; Chapin and Messick, 1992; Mahood, Biemer, and Lowe, 1991; Martorella, 1991; Michaelis, 1988; Zevin, 1992)). If there ever has been a gap between theory and practice, this is a classic example!

Many issues related to teaching students to think in our social studies classrooms are directly and indirectly raised in the letter. The major one that serves as the primary focus for this chapter is how the skills of critical thinking can best be taught. Several key issue-related questions concerned with producing thoughtful students will serve as the outline for the chapter.

HOW CAN WE DISTINGUISH BETWEEN ORDINARY AND PRODUCTIVE THINKING?

Thinking is as natural as walking and most everyone thinks and most everyone walks. "If thinking is as natural as walking, why all the fuss about

---

*Rocco Yeargin, "Higher Priority Needed for Thinking Skills" (Letter to the Editor), *The* (Akron, Ohio) *Beacon Journal*, May 4, 1989, page A4. Reprinted by permission of the publisher. When he wrote this letter, Yeargin was a student, and student council president, at Central Hower High School in Akron.

teaching thinking?" (Perkins, 1987, p. xi). David Perkins raised this question in his "Forward" to Barry Beyer's (1987) book on thinking strategies. Perkins's answer to his own question is that the goal of teaching is to produce productive thinkers and productive thinking is a special achievement.

Robert J. Sternberg (1987a, p. 253) offers several characteristics of productive thinkers that have important implications for attaining the citizenship education goal of the social studies. Productive thinkers possess knowledge upon which to base thought because thinking cannot occur without information. Further, they can represent information from several points of view and understand multiple perspectives. Productive thinkers also have the motivation to use the thinking skills they have acquired. Finally, they can combine thought processes into strategies to solve problems. These characteristics seem essential if citizens are to confront issues and work to resolve problems.

Robert J. Swartz and David N. Perkins (1990) also conceptualize productive thinking and distinguish it from everyday thinking in specific outcomes and processes. Productive thinking yields such outcomes as more reliable conclusions, deeper insights, sounder decisions, and keener critical assessments. In process terms, productive thinking considers more possibilities, explores farther and wider, marshals more data, challenges assumptions, checks for errors, and maintains objectivity and balance, among others. Swartz and Perkins caution, though, that productive thinking will not result if students do not have an opportunity to engage in classroom activities that involve these processes and outcomes.

The most distinguishing characteristic of the productive thinker according to Francis P. Hunkins (1989) is the quantity and quality of questions asked. The productive thinker is a good questioner, and the driving force is an inquiring mind. He or she is an independent thinker, raising questions to create and use meaning, perhaps to identify problems that need investigation. "[I]n many schools, students are not challenged to make meaning; rather, they are asked to remember the meaning of others. The good thinker realizes that while some information originated with qualified others, much information and meaning is self-generated" (p. 16).

How Is Critical Thinking Productive Thinking?

Thinking, in the broadest sense, is the search for understanding. A problem of semantics is apparent when one tries to define the variety of forms of productive thinking, including critical thinking. Walter Parker (1991), upon reviewing the literature on thinking in social studies classrooms, found no consensus on the definitions of thinking and listed among the "contemporary clatter of terms": critical thinking, creative thinking, problem solving, decision making, and divergent and convergent thinking. Fred M. Newmann (1991b) rejected many familiar and specific forms of cognitive processes in favor of the term "higher-order thinking" for his research study because he considered it the broadest conception. All the other forms, he believed, could be subsumed under his conceptualization. Higher-order thinking was defined as "challenge and expanded use of the mind…[occurring] when a person must interpret, analyze, or manipulate information, because a question to be answered or a problem to be solved cannot be resolved through the routine application of previously learned information" (p. 325). Examples of higher-order thinking questions that are problem-related range from descriptive issue questions such as "How did the economy of the South depend on slavery?" to ethical ones, "Under what conditions, if any, can violence against a government be morally justified?" (Newmann, 1991a, p. 385). Lower-order thinking, in contrast, involves repetitive routines, mechanistic application, and similar memory level activity.

When teachers see or hear the term "higher-order thinking" many naturally think of the top three levels of Benjamin S. Bloom's *Taxonomy* (1956): Analysis, Synthesis, and Evaluation. Although Bloom and his associates devised the hierarchy to classify education objectives in the cognitive domain, the system has been used by theorists and researchers to describe teachers' questioning and students' thinking operations as they are displayed in the classroom setting.

Examples of questions at the three higher-order thinking levels are found in Table 5-1.

Table 5-1   Illustrative Questions

The following questions at the Analysis, Synthesis and Evaluation levels (Bloom's Taxonomy) are those a world-cultures teacher might ask after students had read *Distant Neighbors* by Alan Riding.

Analysis 1. How would you support the view that, in the interest of national security, the United States needs to understand Mexico, its "distant neighbor"?

Analysis 2. Examine the following newspaper editorial and try to figure out how Mexicans use formal and obscure language to hide emotions and avoid committing themselves.

Synthesis 3. You have been reading about the severe pollution problem in Mexico City. What would you include in a limited expenditure proposal to the government to reduce the high ozone levels?

Synthesis 4. If Mexicans revolt against their government in the near future, what might be some implications for the United States?

Evaluation 5. Do you agree with one assessment that Mexicans have been extraordinarily tolerant of bad and abusive government during the past 50 years? Why or why not?

Evaluation 6. If you had been a member of Congress in 1994, would you have voted in favor of the free-trade agreement with Mexico? Why or why not?

Although higher-order thinking can serve as the broad category for cognitive processes, it is useful to distinguish between other subcategories of thinking, including critical thinking. Critical thinking seems to be the most popular of the terms—so much so that many include other kinds of thinking under its rubric including decision making and problem solving. Beyer (1987) said that it "is one of the most abused terms...it means whatever its users stipulate it to mean" (p. 32).

Many social studies sources trace the definition of critical thinking back to John Dewey's (1910) conceptualization of reflective thinking: "active, persistent and careful consideration of any belief or supposed form of knowledge in the light of the grounds that support it and the further conclusions to which it tends" (p. 9). Current sources also cite Robert H. Ennis's interpretation of critical thinking that has implications for citizenship education: "...reasonable reflective thinking that is focused on deciding what to believe or do" (Ennis, 1987, p. 10.). Robert J. Marzano and colleagues (1988) interpreted "reasonable" in Ennis's definition as "...when the thinker strives to analyze arguments carefully, looks for valid evidence, and reaches sound conclusions" (p. 18). They went on to suggest the aim of teaching critical thinking is "...the cultivation of rational thinking for the purpose of guiding behavior" (p. 18).

John P. Patrick found critical thinking to be "...an essential element of general cognitive processes, such as problem solving or decision making, but is not synonymous with them" (Patrick, 1986, p. 1). Beyer (1988) is more specific. He considers critical thinking a cluster of specific intellectual operations that can be defined singly or in combination with each other. Critical thinking is not a strategy like decision making or problem solving because it does not consist of a generalized sequence of operations. Swartz and Perkins (1990) suggested some functions of critical thinking that coincide with the generally accepted definitions. Students engaged in critical thinking do the following:

- Aim at critical judgment about what to accept as reasonable and/or to do.
- Use standards that themselves are the result of critical reflection in making these judgments.
- Employ various organized strategies of reasoning and arguments in determining and applying these standards.
- Seek and gather reliable information to use as evidence or reasons in supporting these judgments (p. 38).

Barry K. Beyer (1988) lists a variety of specific critical thinking skills that are important in making decisions and solving problems and are the general focus of critical-thinking efforts in those social studies programs that have critical thinking as their commitment:

1. Distinguishing between verifiable facts and value claims
2. Distinguishing relevant from irrelevant information, claim, or reasons
3. Determining the factual accuracy of a statement
4. Determining the credibility of a source
5. Identifying ambiguous claims or arguments
6. Identifying unstated assumptions
7. Detecting bias
8. Identifying logical fallacies
9. Recognizing logical inconsistencies in a line of reasoning
10. Determining the strength of an argument or claim (p. 27)

The most recent interpretation of critical thinking in social studies was through the National Council for the Social Studies with issuance of its "Vision of Powerful Teaching and Learning in the Social Studies" document (NCSS 1993). The development of critical thinking skills is considered essential to achieve the goal of helping young people make informed and reasoned decisions for the public good. These thinking skills include the following:

1. Acquiring, organizing, interpreting, and communicating information
2. Processing data to investigate questions, develop knowledge, and draw conclusions
3. Generating and assessing alternative approaches to problems and making decisions that are both informed and justified according to democratic principles
4. Interacting with others in empathetic and responsible ways (p. 160)

COULD THE TEACHING OF THINKING BE JUST ANOTHER SOCIAL STUDIES FAD?

The development of students' ability to think has always been regarded as an important and ambitious goal in education. Even during times when it was not at the top of the educational agenda, a certain persistency has helped maintain its underlying importance. We only need to go back a little more than 30 years to begin to demonstrate the recurring interest in the teaching of thinking. The National Education Association, in a 1961 report, stated that "the purpose which runs through and strengthens all other educational purposes—the common thread of education—is the development of the ability to think" (pp. 11–12). During the 1960s most reform curriculum projects in mathematics and the behavioral and social sciences had as their goal the development of students' thinking abilities. In social studies this was particularly the case with the emphasis on teaching the findings and thought processes of historians and social scientists. During the 1970s we entered a period of economic instability while students' standardized test scores began to decline and the public began demanding more accountability. The result was a back-to-basics movement with an emphasis on academic skills. Although the "three R's" were emphasized, many wondered if the pendulum hadn't swung back too far and if reasoning shouldn't be the fourth R.

Since the early 1980s the pendulum has swung again, and there has been a renewed interest and innovation in the teaching of thinking. Several reasons contributed to this trend, of which the primary seem to be the several major national reports supporting the need for the development of students' thinking skills. The decade began with a major report being issued by the National Commission on Excellence in Education (1983). It prompted the call for higher standards after documenting students' poor performance on higher-order thinking skills. Other studies of high schools documented the lack of attention toward activities requiring reflective thinking (Boyer, 1983; Goodlad, 1984; Sizer, 1984). Another important contributor to the renewed interest in student reasoning is the substantial increase in national conferences, programs, and workshops focusing on thinking skills and the increase of research and theoretical literature on thinking.

This growing interest has coincided with the movement toward constructivist teaching and learning principles in the 1990s. Reflective thought plays an important part because the focus is on encouraging students to *understand* subject matter rather than just to *know* it as has been the traditional emphasis. Constructivist and "best practice" principles call for teachers to use methods that encourage students to study subject matter in depth and learn by connecting new to prior information and applying learnings in authentic situations. The result is more meaningful learning. Students reflect on what is being taught and use critical thinking to make applications particularly in decision-making and problem-solving situations (Brooks and Brooks, 1993; Zemelman, Daniels and Hyde, 1993).

WHY TEACH THINKING SKILLS?

The primary reason is to better prepare students for today's highly complex and rapidly changing world of work, education, and communication. The inference is that the probability of success in these areas is increased if citizens possess reasoning proficiency (Voss, Perkins, and Segal, 1991). Raymond S. Nickerson (1987) offered other reasons that he readily admitted could not be substantiated: reasoning proficiency contributes toward "one's psychological well-being," and we need to learn to think because it is our nature. It is our nature because, "we want students to become good thinkers because thinking is at the heart of what it means to be human; to fail to develop one's potential in this regard is to preclude the full expression of one's humanity" (p. 32).

The primary reason to teach thinking in social studies is the preparation of democratic citizens. The National Council for the Social Studies Curriculum Standards (1994) states that the purpose of social studies is citizenship education: "to help young people to develop the ability to make informed and reasoned decisions for the public good..." (p. 3). The outcome is civic competence, which is "...the knowledge, skills and attitudes required of students to be able to assume 'the office of citizen'..." (p. 3). Our democratic society is based on the freedom to think and express ideas and further, to act on decisions related to those ideas. Rational citizens are informed, reflect on public issues, and work to democratically resolve problems for the purpose of improving society. Citizens' participation in public life is essential to the well being of our democratic system. Student possession of a wide range of thinking skills is essential if they are to interlock knowledge and beliefs with decision-making and problem-solving action. In many respects, "good thinking is a prerequisite for good citizenship" (Nickerson, 1987, p. 31).

WHY DO TEACHERS FAIL TO TEACH FOR CRITICAL THINKING?

In his review of the research on thinking in social studies, Parker (1991) had this to say about the acceptance of critical thinking as a goal by theorists, researchers, and educators while being rejected as practice by teachers at all levels:

> Specifying thinking and decision-making objectives, planning for their achievement, lamenting their absence in practice, and exhorting teachers to devote themselves to the task are together a time-honored tradition in social studies. No other objectives have been espoused so persistently or with such enthusiasm for their anticipated effects on students and society alike. And perhaps no others have been so consistently underachieved (p. 345).

What barriers do teachers experience that inhibit the promotion of higher-order thinking in their classrooms? One researcher who is participating in Newmann's ongoing Higher Order Thinking Study involving a questionnaire, interviews, and nearly 500 classroom observations of 56 teachers in 16 social studies departments nationwide, found six dominant barriers (Onosko, 1991). They are summarized as follows:

1. *Teaching as Knowledge Transmission.* The primary goal of social studies teachers is student acquisition and reproduction of knowledge. With the instructional emphasis on students as passive receivers of information, little opportunity is left for them to be thoughtful participants.

2. *Broad, Superficial Content Coverage.* Teachers experience internal and external pressure to cover vast amounts of information at the expense of going into depth on select topics. The coverage barrier is noticed in conjunction with the knowledge transmission barrier. Little time is left for students to reflect on what has been covered.

3. *Teachers' Low Expectations of Students.* Teachers possessing this negative perception engage in instruction that emphasizes factual information because students are perceived as unable or unwilling to think at the higher cognitive levels. This barrier can also be a consequence of the coverage barrier.

4. *Large Numbers of Students.* Large numbers of students within classes and as part of a full load generates real and imagined concerns about classroom management. One important consequence is the lack of confidence in conducting large or small group discussions that can help facilitate thinking. Large class size reinforces knowledge transmission because lecture and recitation, by their very nature as instructional methods, control students' behavior.

5. *Lack of Teacher Planning Time.* Teachers typically have only one planning period per day and very little other than routine planning and preparation can be accomplished in this short time. With little time to prepare for indepth lessons and instructional approaches that encourage higher-order thinking, teachers resort to simplistic textbook-based knowledge transmission. The result is little challenge of students' thought capabilities.

6. *A Culture of Teacher Isolation.* As a result of teachers spending their day with students, they have little extended contact with fellow professionals. Lost are opportunities to share curricular and instructional ideas potentially related to developing students' critical thinking. Isolation also screens teachers from constructive criticism and commendation about their instructional practices.

These barriers are closely interrelated and therefore feed on one another to create a kind of meta-barrier, or even more insurmountable barriers to developing students' reflective thought. Joseph J. Onosko (1991) elaborated on this interconnectedness:

> Large total student load and large class size limit opportunities for thoughtful interaction between teachers and students, which, in turn, contributes to low student expectation on the part of teachers. Instruction by transmission tends to foster a curriculum of coverage, and, in reciprocal fashion, the demands of content coverage necessitate instruction by lecture (transmission) to ensure that everything gets covered. Little planning time for teachers to exchange ideas with colleagues helps to ensure the continuation of a culture of isolation and traditional methods of instruction. Many additional linkages between the barriers could be identified (p. 360).

TO WHAT EXTENT CAN ALL STUDENTS BE TAUGHT CRITICAL THINKING SKILLS?

The full range of students from 5 to 6 years old to adult and low ability to very high ability can learn the skills associated with critical thinking, assuming appropriate instructional approaches are applied. Research has shown that low-to medium-ability students' thinking can be improved in all subject areas whereas the thinking of high-ability students can be improved in particular subject areas (Swartz and Perkins, 1990). Research has also shown that students are not limited in developing thinking skills by their intelligence or developmental level of intellectual competence. Although IQ predicts academic achievement well, it measures only a part of intelligence. Research shows that IQ scores can be raised and thinking can be improved (Swartz and Perkins, 1990).

Closely related is the relationship between culture and reasoning processes. Regarding IQ test scores, Sternberg (1987b) reported on research that shows that cultures perceive intelligence differently and this results in varied performances on similar tests. People do not agree about what is intelligent. In his review of research, Dalton Miller-Jones (1991) concluded that reasoning for some members of a culture may be independent of the context or situation whereas other members' reasoning is situational. His study of inner-city children found that high and low achieving African-American kindergarten children used different reasoning processes that emerged from specifics related to the situation presented in the tests. Among the implications for educational practice Miller-Jones projected was that teachers should encourage students to develop awareness of their own reasoning processes and to share them with each other as they solve problems, for example.

Another concern is the supposed limiting effect of students' developmental levels. According to Jean Piaget, levels of intellectual competence are based on developmental stages. For example, theoretically students would not be able to engage in higher level, more abstract, thinking operations until the formal operations stage starting at age 11. Current research, though, shows that Piaget's developmental theory cannot be completely substantiated. Although the idea of broad stages can generally be demonstrated, students develop at different times. Research has also disconfirmed the proposition that students are unable to reason formally until the final state. Swartz and Perkins (1990) advise that teachers should try teaching any kind of thinking at any age. The only problem is younger students may have trouble with the complexity of information because of limited short-term memory. To summarize, "neither IQ nor Piaget's developmental perspective imposes strong limits on the opportunity to develop students' thinking" (Swartz and Perkins, 1990, p. 15).

SHOULD THINKING SKILLS OR CONTENT BE TAUGHT FIRST?

The argument for teaching content first is that, for students to think, they need to think about something. But this does not mean they need to have a vast store of basic knowledge and fundamental techniques. Students can engage in problem solving in social studies classes based on the experiences and knowledge they currently possess. For example, primary grade children can plan for the collection of metal, glass, plastic, and paper products to start a recycling program in their classroom, just as senior-high government students can hypothesize ideas, gather data, and devise a plan for a recycling program to be presented before city council.

The reasoning behind the idea that learning different kinds of thinking will enhance content mastery is that the use of thinking processes facilitates knowledge acquisition and application. This may be true to some extent, but new content is not easily and quickly assimilated. Thinking skills help master new content, but the learning cannot be routine. Thinking needs to be adapted to new content just as new content forces thought to be reorganized (Swartz and Perkins, 1990). Swartz and Perkins (1990) logically suggest that thinking and content be learned together because each reinforces the other. For example, to develop skill in formulating an opinion and supporting it, students have to practice forming an opinion about something such as an election issue. An opinion about an issue must be knowledge-based as is the support for the opinion. We cannot think critically about something without knowing about it. Catherine Cornbleth's (1985) review of research also supports the idea that the development of critical thinking skills is highly knowledge dependent.

WHAT IS THE BEST APPROACH TO TEACH FOR CRITICAL THINKING?

A variety of approaches have been identified to teach critical thinking skills, and many have been implemented in social studies classrooms at all levels. Four approaches will be presented here based on the research review by Scott Willis (1992) and the ideas of Carl Bereiter (1984). Willis (1992) identified three of the most common approaches (p. 1):

1. Creation of a classroom environment that fosters thinking, without direct teaching of thinking skills
2. Infusion of thinking skills into regular classroom instruction
3. A separate course for teaching thinking

A fourth alternative proposed by Bereiter (1984) is the following:

4. Permeation of the total instructional program with thinking activities.

Environmental Impact Approach

The environmental impact approach emphasizes creating a classroom intellectual atmosphere that encourages students to engage in higher-order thinking without direct instruction in critical thinking skills. This is primarily accomplished through the use of teacher and student questions, particularly within the framework of discussion. Teachers create a thoughtful environment by asking questions at the higher cognitive levels to encourage students to use and apply the knowledge they have learned. A variety of questioning techniques is employed to stimulate thinking and interaction including wait time. Encouraging students to ask questions, which is an important component of the inquiry method, is also essential for a thoughtful environment. Higher-order thinking is accomplished as the teacher and students interact over issues and problems during which students are expected to formulate and support their positions and explain their reasoning (Willis, 1992).

Newmann and his associates at the University of Wisconsin are currently conducting what promises to be the most influential study of classroom thoughtfulness and higher-order thinking since the Hilda Taba and Harvard Social Studies Projects of the 1960s (Parker, 1991). To investigate the successes and failures of promoting higher-order thinking in social studies classrooms, Newmann and his associates conducted almost 500 classroom observations and interviews with social studies teachers, departmental chairs, and administrators from 16 high schools during the past five years. The emphasis of this ongoing study is to understand what social studies departments do to promote higher-order thinking and contrast successful departments with those that do not specifically promote higher-order thinking. In essence, he is trying to find out what teachers do to create classroom environments that foster thinking (Newmann, 1991b).

Newmann has used the data he has collected to create a broad conceptual framework for the teaching of thinking so that it might serve as a base for knowledge on the teaching of thinking. The basis of the conceptualization is that, for students to think productively, they need a combination of in-depth knowledge of subject matter, intellectual skills in processing information, and dispositions of thoughtfulness. Although knowledge is essential to understanding, skills are important for students to be able to apply the knowledge to solving of new problems. Dispositions of thoughtfulness also need to be developed. They are attitudinally based and refer to students' tendency to be reflective, curious, and flexible as they deal with knowledge in an inquiring fashion (Newmann, 1991a).

How can higher-order thinking be described during social studies lessons? Rather than focusing on specific thinking skills, knowledge, and attitudes, as other researchers had done, Newmann (1991b) identified generic "indicators of thoughtfulness" that are observable qualities of classroom activity and talk that facilitate students' development of subject matter understanding, thinking skills, and dispositions of thoughtfulness. Fifteen indicators were initially identified and used to rate the lessons observed during the research project. Eventually six dimensions were selected as the most fundamental criteria for classroom thoughtfulness (pp. 330–333):

1. There was sustained examination of a few topics rather than superficial coverage of many.
2. The lesson displayed substantive coherence and continuity.
3. Students were given an appropriate amount of time to think, that is, to prepare responses to questions.
4. The teacher asked challenging questions or structured challenging tasks (given the ability level and preparation of the students).
5. The teacher was a model of thoughtfulness.
6. Students offered explanations and reasons for their conclusions.

Newmann's broad conceptualization of higher-order thinking and identification of "generic" indicators of classroom thoughtfulness are characteristic of the environmental impact approach to teaching thinking. He feels that the direct teaching of thinking skills, decontextualized from subject matter, will make the process too mechanistic. To think productively, students also need, along with thinking skills, in-depth subject knowledge, and dispositions of thoughtfulness. Too much emphasis on thinking skills can diminish the importance of the other two components. All three areas need equal attention (Willis, 1992).

Parker (1991) suggests that Newmann has made a major contribution with his broad focus on higher-order thinking because a foundation of thoughtfulness in the classroom may be a necessary requisite before serious attention toward developing thinking strategies can be initiated. These strategies include decision making and problem solving. "[T]he creation of thoughtful classrooms is an enormously helpful step, albeit an intermediate one between mindless social studies lessons on the one hand and the vision of social studies classrooms as laboratories of democracy on the other" (p. 352).

Infusing Skills Approach

The second approach to teaching thinking is the infusing-skills approach. It is the most popular. Advocates of this approach say that creating a thoughtful classroom environment is not enough and that thinking skills must be directly taught. One related issue in connection with this approach is whether to teach the skills in the context of subject-matter content or to teach general thinking skills outside the content (Willis, 1992).

Critical thinking improves when direct instruction on critical thinking is involved rather than instruction on the standard course content. This was the conclusion Parker (1991) drew after his review of eleven studies based on four major programs of research over the past 50 years. The programs included the Harvard jurisprudential studies, Taba's cognitive task studies from the 1960s, and Newmann's classroom thoughtfulness study, which is ongoing. Both the Harvard and Taba projects emphasized content-specific thinking and decision making (Parker, 1991).

Another important component of the Harvard and Taba projects was their focus on developing students' depth of understanding as opposed to superficial coverage on content. Few believe that students will develop thinking skills as a result of studying standard course content as it is currently taught using the standard textbook. Most social studies curricula emphasizes breadth of content coverage rather than in-depth understanding. One position is that immersing students in an in-depth examination of subject matter content will allow them to develop a thoughtful understanding of social studies issues and problems, for example. Although specific thinking skills are not taught, in-depth study builds analytical power that could not be possible if a great variety of topics is taught or if the emphasis is on thinking skills training (Parker, 1991).

Infusing thinking skills into existing curriculum entails integrating content and skills equally to maintain a balance of the two. Although skills are taught in the context of the subject matter, the intent is to retain their individual identity (IRT Communication, 1991). Among the advantages to this approach that Sternberg (1987a) sees are that (1) the thinking skills learned are applied to the content and, therefore, run less of risk of not being applied than if skills were taught as part of a separate program; and (2) thinking skills are reinforced throughout the subject rather than thinking skills being thought of as separate from the subject. Beyer (1988) adds that research shows that better motivation is provided when thinking skills are taught at the time they are needed to achieve subject objectives. Also, if the skills are taught and reinforced throughout the semester or year, retention of the skills and processes occurs. Furthermore, research shows that students learn the skills and subject matter better as measured on final examinations if they are taught concurrently.

Beyer (1988) advocates infusing the teaching of thinking skills and strategies along with the subject matter. He strongly recommends the following (p. 81):

1.   The content used should be that of regular, subject matter courses.
2.   Learning thinking skills should be as explicit and publicly affirmed a goal of teaching and learning in these courses as is subject matter learning.

3. Whenever it is time to use a new or important thinking skill to achieve a subject matter goal (to learn some information, a concept, an understanding, or a generalization), the teacher should take the time to introduce or provide guided practice in the skill or help students transfer the skill.

Beyer believes that unless the infusion effort takes into account these recommendations, little will change, and students will not learn the thinking skills (1988).

Patrick (1986) is another supporter of the position that the teaching of critical thinking in social studies is most effectively accomplished when subject matter and thinking skills are interrelated. His reasoning is that critical thinking cannot be facilitated without students' knowledge of appropriate facts and concepts related to the issue or problem being taught. Successful critical thinkers must be able to draw on several subjects from history and the social sciences for evidence to support propositions. Effective critical thinking involves, among other things, knowing about how to combine a variety of skills into strategies for application in solving problems and making decisions. For this reason Patrick suggests that teaching discrete skills would be ineffective in developing student's critical thinking abilities.

Separate Course Approach

The separate course approach emphasizes teaching thinking skills outside the context of regular classroom content. It is the least common approach—probably because many programs require students to take a separate course, which will naturally have its own class period. For example, two such programs are Higher-Order Thinking Skills (HOTS) and Philosophy for Children (Willis, 1992). HOTS is aimed at at-risk students in grades 3 to 6 and helps them develop general thinking skills. Students participate in HOTS four days per week for 35-minute lessons. Philosophy for Children is designed to improve students' higher-order thinking skills through discussion of philosophical questions. Intended levels are kindergarten through high school, and students meet two and a quarter hours weekly for the full year (Beyer, 1988; Willis, 1992).

Selection of a particular program should depend on what is best for the school, targeted academic programs, and the needs of students because all the programs are different. Sternberg (1987a) suggests that some general advantages of using separate programs are (1) they will likely have more impact because they are not lost in content-based curriculums; (2) they permit students to focus heavily on thinking skills as the priority while other learnings being relegated to secondary status; and (3) they can be evaluated more easily than if they were infused into specific content courses. Beyer (1988) adds that if a separate course on thinking skills is to be taught by a few teachers, staff development problems of logistics, time, and expense are minimized.

Employing a separate thinking course approach also has some major disadvantages. It can be very difficult for many districts to insert another course into the scope and sequence of the existing curriculum. Teachers selected to teach the special course will also need training to implement the thinking skills program. Content area teachers will need inservice training to follow-up by transferring, applying, and extending the generic thinking skills from the separate course to the subjects they teach (Beyer, 1988).

Although many programs to teach thinking skills are available to schools through publishers, they are very different. No one program is best for all students, programs, or schools. Sternberg (1987a) summarized the variability in programs he has found:

> Some programs are more suited to older children, some to younger; some are more suited to urban children, others to rural children; some programs are more suited to brighter students, others to less-bright students; some programs emphasize analytic thinking skills, others emphasize synthetic thinking skills; some programs require extensive teacher training, others require very little teacher training; some programs require multiple-year interventions, others require as little as a semester (p. 257).

Because of the numerous programs available, Barbara Z. Presseisen (1986) advises that teachers learn about a variety of programs and try some of the procedures and materials before making decisions about their advantages and disadvantages. Also, it is important to review the evidence available to determine the impact the particular programs had on specific student populations.

Beyer (1988) identified 20 of the more popular thinking skills programs in his review of the literature. Although only one is specifically oriented to social studies, all have as their goal the learning of a variety of thinking strategies and skills appropriate for social studies. Each is described in his book in terms of its major goal, intended audience, assumptions, targeted thinking skills, training process and materials, time involved, developers, and where information can be obtained. Those most appropriate for social studies are listed here:

- Basics
- Building Thinking Skills
- CoRT (Cognitive Research Trust)
- Creative Problem Solving (CPS)
- Critical Analysis and Thinking Skills (CATS)
- Critical Thinking, Books I and II
- Critical Thinking in American History
- Future Problem Solving
- Higher-Order Thinking Skills (HOTS)
- Instrumental Enrichment

- Junior Great Books
- Making Changes
- Making Judgments
- Odyssey
- Olympics of the Mind
- Philosophy for Children
- Strategic Reasoning
- Talents Unlimited

A more extensive description of many of these programs, and others, by their authors, can be found in Arthur L. Costa (1985).

Some published programs can be infused into existing school curricula. The advantages of these programs are (1) they do not require a separate course that may not fit into existing school programs; (2) they increase the chances that the thinking skills will be applied to knowledge; and (3) they promote the idea that thinking skills are to be reinforced throughout the curriculum rather than being separate. Sternberg (1987a) suggests that schools consider adopting a thinking skills program that combines the advantages of both models: "The points raised by both sides are persuasive enough to argue for a mixed model in which thinking skills are taught as a separate course at the same time that they are infused and reinforced throughout the entire curriculum" (p. 255).

Beyer (1988) supports the idea of a mixed model and suggests a combination of both separate courses and infusion of thinking skills teaching in subject-matter courses spanning the K to 12 curriculum. As an illustration, a model thinking skills program particularly appropriate for social studies based on the information gathered by Beyer (1988) could begin with Philosophy for Children for kindergarten through third grade. The purpose of this program is to develop students' reasoning by having them read special novels with inquisitive children as characters. They then discuss underlying ideas and concepts. During the intermediate fourth through sixth grade phase, CoRT could be implemented because it is "relatively light handed, focusing more on heuristics or rules of thumb useful in triggering thinking than on detailed, step-by-step instruction in specific thinking skills...CoRT is easily integrated into existing classroom teaching and into any subjects" (p. 89). During the junior high years, Creative Problem Solving might be implemented because its goal is to develop students' abilities and attitudes necessary for problem solving. Another possibility is that teachers could develop a special course of their own with a particular focus on incorporating problem-solving or decision-making skills. At the high school level, social studies teachers could reinforce and extend the critical thinking skills students have learned in their specific subject areas. Another alternative is to include another commercial program such as Critical Analysis and Thinking

Skills (CATS) because it aims to teach how to apply a critical thinking process in analyzing issues and problems in American and world history, government, and other subjects. Another option in American history is Critical Thinking in American History, which consists of supplementary materials for a one- or two-year course in American history. Among its goals is "to make students better, more skeptical citizens" (p. 300). Considering the number of programs available, a curriculum with a major emphasis on thinking skills could be easily be constructed given the resources of the school.

Are the commercial programs effective in achieving the goals they purport to achieve? Sternberg and Kastoor Bhana (1986) conducted an extensive review of research related to five of the most well-known and, generally, most widely-used thinking skills programs: Instrumental Enrichment, Philosophy for Children, Structure of the Intellect (SOI), Problem Solving and Comprehension: A Short Course in Analytical Reasoning, and Odyssey. The findings were disappointing because few valid and reliable studies have been conducted, including no evaluations that could be used in determining the extent that the programs worked. Of the studies and materials that were reviewed related to the five programs, Sternberg and Bhana concluded, "Some thinking skills training programs are probably not a whole lot better than snake oil, but the good ones, although not miracle cures, may improve thinking skills" (p. 67). They advised that school districts interested in evaluating the effects of a program will need to conduct their own assessments because success of programs is based on many factors related to implementation. A trained program evaluator can be obtained to assess outcomes in an unbiased manner.

Permeation Approach

A particularly pessimistic view about the future of thinking skills instruction was expressed by Bereiter (1984):

> Perhaps no one will be so indiscriminate as to call thinking skills instruction a frill, but it is often treated as one, just one more burden on an already heavily loaded curriculum, one more competitor with the things teachers are held accountable for. Consequently, no matter how readily teachers agree that more should be done to promote thinking skills, it is reasonable to predict that thinking skills instruction will tend to be passed over by more standard activities directed toward the three R's and subject-matter instruction (Bereiter, 1984. p. 75).

What has not worked, in his experience, is treating thinking skills as enrichment, or treating them as special and added on, rather than integrated with academic substance. Treating thinking skills as subject matter where they are superficially memorized and applied in exercises is also a failed approach. Bereiter urges that two strategies be implemented to increase the probability that the teaching of thinking skills will be successful: (1) integrate thinking skills objectives with other, already accepted instructional objectives, and (2) permeate the instructional program thoroughly with thinking skills activities. The first results when content objectives are made contingent on activities that also promote thinking. The second results when thinking skills are promoted throughout the school curriculum in all aspects of the instructional program. "Success in teaching thinking skills results when content objects are contingent on activities that also promote thinking and when thinking skills permeate the entire curriculum" (p. 75).

The underlying idea of the permeation approach is that "…the promotion of thinking skills should be deeply embedded in the whole fabric of an instructional program" (p. 77). It cannot be done if the teaching of thinking skills occupies a week in the instructional program or a few pages in a textbook. A big problem is that social studies teachers rely heavily on the text, particularly at the secondary level. Textbook publishers try to simplify something that is complex and, of course, few educational outcomes are more complex than encouraging and challenging thinking. Publishers need to be pressured by school administrators and teachers to permeate their texts with thinking-skills instruction. Each page of every text needs to represent the teaching of thinking in some way (Bereiter, 1984). Though Bereiter stated this position in 1984, and others have stated it as well, there is no evidence these statements have influenced publishers, and little evidence they have influenced teaching practices.

WHAT ARE THE BEST METHODS AND TECHNIQUES TO APPLY WHEN TEACHING FOR CRITICAL THINKING?

Although many techniques and strategies can be applied when teaching for higher level thinking, the approach not to take is that which has dominated social studies instruction for so many years. Lecture and recitation, with its emphasis on low cognitive level questions, is more appropriate to encourage students to learn the basic facts and understandings related to a topic. Kevin O'Reilly (1991) referred to this approach as the three T's: "teachers and texts impart information to students, who passively memorize it to be regurgitated on tests" (p. 364). Critical thinking generally requires students to be actively involved in discovery and constructing information related to topics, issues or problems by responding to and asking questions at the higher cognitive levels. Discussion is one of the primary instruction methods most associated with the encouragement of higher-level thought.

Traditional social studies instruction has emphasized teaching *about* something. Effectively encouraging students to engage in and develop critical-thinking skills and strategies involves teaching for thinking and the teaching of thinking. Swartz and Perkins (1990) pursue their idea further by describing how teaching for thinking involves purposely creating a classroom climate that stimulates and supports student thinking. Important considerations they identified for teachers are the following (p. 168):

- Allowing students to discuss things openly in the classroom, rather than to speak only when they think they have the right answer
- Asking thought provoking questions rather than just asking questions that prompt the recall of facts
- Providing more hands-on and exploratory activities rather than relying solely on paper-and-paper tasks and worksheets
- Bringing students problems to be solved rather than simply giving out information

Two well-known curricular projects from the 1960s had teaching for thinking as an important objective and seemed to address the classroom climate considerations discussed. The Harvard Social Studies Project (Oliver and Shaver, 1974; Newmann and Oliver, 1970) and the Taba projects (Taba, 1966; Taba, Levine and Elzey, 1964) were both concerned with the development of reasoning through the direct instruction of thinking skills. Further, both projects emphasized curriculum depth over coverage and teaching thinking skills as content-dependent. The Harvard Projects had as their goal encouraging secondary students to think systematically about controversial issues. Teachers used the "recitation-analytic" strategy to review students' understanding of the issue and to clarify and examine value dimensions of the issue, while the "socratic-analytic" strategy encouraged students to take a stand on the issue and to support and defend it (Parker, 1991).

Taba's experimental curriculum was designed to develop elementary students' reasoning using a variety of teaching strategies. Basic cognitive tasks were identified to encourage students to think and construct social studies knowledge. Teaching functions that facilitated student performance on the cognitive tasks and influenced student thinking were applied (Parker, 1991). Essential to the success of both the Harvard and Taba project was the role of interaction between teachers and students and the use of different kinds of questions and questioning techniques to stimulate thinking.

Bruce Joyce (1985) proposed teaching thinking by employing a variety of models of teaching rather than the standard recitation approach that dominates the instructional scene in most schools. A strong advocate of the permeation approach as presented previously, Joyce urged that the teaching of thinking should be an important component of every instructional activity for several reasons: a substantial storehouse of teaching models exists that are appropriate for directly teaching both content and reasoning in all subject areas, including social studies, and at all levels; the models are more effective than traditional approaches to teach the content and thinking related to basic school subjects; and the models teach the subjects and thinking together, eliminating the traditional dichotomy between content and intellectual activity. Joyce applied the last reason to teaching social studies: "There is no inherent conflict between teaching the fundamentals of citizenship in a democratic society... and learning to think" (Joyce, 1985, p.6). The content of subjects such as social studies needs to be taught simultaneously with thinking. Joyce lists thinking processes and skills and illustrations of several of the models of teaching he has proposed in his instructional program (Joyce and Weil, 1992). Those particularly appropriate for the social studies are the following:

- Attack problem inductively: concept formation models
- Attain concepts and analyze their thinking strategies: concept attainment models
- Analyze social issues and problems: jurisprudential and role playing models
- Think divergently: group investigation
- Work together to generate and test hypotheses: group investigation model
- Reason causally: inquiry training, group investigation, simulation
- Master complex bodies of information: memory model, group investigation
- Analyze personal behavior, set personal goals, and conduct independent inquiry: nondirective teaching, awareness training
- Analyze social situations and develop flexible social skills: role playing, simulation, group investigation, nondirective teaching

Joyce suggests that extensive training is necessary to learn, practice, and feel comfortable with the models. He advises that teachers need to master four or five of the models to effectively teach thinking in a course. This is a critical step to permeating a curriculum with instruction on thinking.

It seems particularly appropriate to focus on teachers' use of different types of questions and questioning techniques because of their potential to engage students in higher-order thinking. All of the instructional approaches presented previously as essential components of the Harvard, Taba, and models of teaching programs as ways to encourage student thinking rely on teacher questioning to engage students' thought processes. The importance of questioning was specifically stressed by Taba and associates (1964): "The role of questions becomes crucial, and the way of asking questions by far the most influential single teaching act" (p. 53) because of the way they encourage students to think critically. But questions are not asked within a vacuum; they are asked within the context of instructional methods, most notably in social studies classrooms in the form of recitation and discussion. Recitation, because of the teacher's emphasis low cognitive level questions within the highly structured teacher question-student response-teacher reaction interaction pattern, is most appropriate for determining the extent to which students have learned key facts, concepts, and other information related to an issue, problem, or topic. Discussion is the instructional approach that has very high potential to stimulate students' reflective thinking (Wilen and White, 1991).

What does the research say to teachers about how their approaches to questioning can stimulate student thinking? Researchers recommend using higher-cognitive questions if developing critical thinking skills is an important curricular goal (Gall and Rhody, 1987). Questions having the potential to stimulate critical thinking are generally defined as above memory, using the familiar Norris M. Sanders (1966) variation of the Bloom (1956) system of classification. The most intellectually demanding questions are at the analysis, synthesis, and evaluation levels. Barry K. Beyer (1987) referred to these cognitive operations as "micro-thinking skills" because they are the building blocks of the problem-solving, decision-making, and conceptualizing-thinking strategies. Although it is recommended that higher-cognitive questions be asked if critical thinking is desired, research also shows that there is only about a 50 percent congruency between the cognitive level of question asked and level of student response. In other words, high-level questions do not necessarily lead to correspondingly higher levels of student thinking as indicated by their responses (Mills, Rice, Berliner and Rousseau, 1980; Dillon, 1982).

Teachers have at their disposal several influential questioning and alternative non-questioning techniques to encourage students to think at the cognitive levels intended. The most powerful in its potential to stimulate thinking is wait time. Wait time can occur immediately after a teacher asks a question and before a student responds and immediately after the student responds and the teacher reacts. Research has shown that the quality of students' responses improves dramatically as teachers increase their wait time to 3 to 5 seconds. Specifically, the length of students' responses increases and their responses reflect higher level, more complex, and more reflective thought (Atwood and Wilen, 1991; Rowe, 1986; Tobin, 1987). After a student has responded to a question the teacher can also probe the student's response to encourage him or her to clarify or expand a response, support a point of view or extend thinking to a higher level. Teachers can also redirect their questions to other students to encourage greater participation and thinking (Wilen, 1991).

Using a variety of alternative, non-questioning, techniques to encourage higher level thinking is also recommended, although based on a limited body of research. In his studies of secondary social studies classrooms, James T. Dillon (1988, 1990) found that using a variety of statement forms, wait time, and student questions resulted in more student participation and talk, more student-student interaction, and more student questions. Considerable interest has been generated in trying to find approaches that encourage students to formulate questions because student questioning is such an important part of decision making and problem solving (Strother, 1989). Several educators have recommended that teachers train their students to formulate and ask questions (Dantonio, 1990; Dillon, 1988; Hunkins, 1989). Although the impact of such non-questioning alternatives as the use of statements and student questions on student thinking is not certain, these techniques are essential for encouraging discussion and other methods designed to promote higher-order thinking.

Using discussion method has significant potential for creating the conditions and intellectual environment appropriate for stimulating higher-order thinking in social studies classrooms. One problem is that teachers tend to label any teacher-student interaction, including recitations, as discussions. Gage (1969) defined discussion as a teacher's involvement of "two or more learners in a cooperative examination and comparison of views in order to illuminate an issue and contribute to learners' understanding" (p. 1454). Dillon's (1994) more recent definition extends Gage's to include as a purpose facilitating a group's "…appreciation or judgement, their decision, resolution or action over the matter at issue" (p. 8). The term "conversation" is important in the definition of discussion because the interaction pattern needs to be informal, involving the exchange and sharing of thoughts and feelings (Wilen, 1990). This contrasts with the highly structured interaction pattern of recitation. Conducting discussions in social studies classrooms almost seems essential because it is so compatible with such democratic values and processes as rationality, decision making, commitment to fairness, and respect for others' opinions and feelings (Bridges, 1979; Wilen, 1994). Meredith D. Gall (1985) found that use of the discussion method was generally effective in achieving several citizenship education goals including promoting higher-order thinking, changing students' attitudes, and involving students in group problem solving.

The most distinguishing characteristic of discussion, in addition to the teacher's use of higher cognitive questions, is the variable interaction pattern. Instead of the highly structured pattern characteristic of recitation, there is more interaction between students. The teacher talks less and students talk more, including asking more questions. The pace of interaction slows and both teacher and student utterances become longer. The interaction becomes more open, less structured, and more conversational as teacher and students explore different points of view, stimulate and expand ideas, refine and support opinions, and generally learn from each other (Wilen and White, 1991). Newmann (1988, 1991a) found in his study of higher-order thinking in social studies classrooms that the teachers of the most thoughtful classrooms engaged their students in discussion that was characterized by a high degree of student interaction, extensive questioning, students' explanations of their reasoning, and use of sources other than the textbook. This was in contrast with teachers of less thoughtful classrooms who relied more on lecture, recitation, and the textbook.

An excerpt of an actual discussion of a social issue from an eleventh grade classroom has been included in Table 5-2 to illustrate the distinguishing characteristics of discussion. In this excerpt, the teacher and students are discussing the curfew law recently enacted in an northeast Ohio urban area. Before this phase of the lesson the teacher had reviewed the provisions of the curfew as described in a newspaper article distributed for homework the night before and the perceived reasons for the law.

The driving force behind this discussion was the higher cognitive level question encouraging inferential thinking related to possible problems caused by the curfew law. The students were applying the facts they had learned to think about the issue in a different way. The other major characteristic was the interaction pattern, which is teacher-student-student-student-student-teacher. Much more student-talk than teacher-talk was apparent; students were not just talking to the teacher, they were talking to one another. This was evident when

---

Table 5–2 Excerpt of a Classroom Discussion

The following is an excerpt of an eleventh-grade class discussion of a local community social issue:

(15 minutes into the period)

T: Can anybody think of some problems that the curfew might cause? Problems of enforcement or problems with the implications?

Leslie: Once you're 18 you're legally an adult and you can do whatever you want. Most people's curfew for our age is between 11:30 and 12:00. If you're out for your prom, and your eating out in Canton, if you get back at 11:35 then you're breaking the law. You're not allowed out after that. Well, it's not about vandalism. Kids are going to do it anyways.

Rhonda: I don't think the police are going to do that. After so long they're going to get tired of just pulling kids over.

Amy: How can they tell who to pull over? Are they just going to pull anyone over who looks over 18? How can they tell who's over 18?

Salvador: The police are not enforcing it. They usually get pulled over for a violation and then they'd get caught if they were not 18.

T: If the police are worried about pulling people over whom they suspect of being under 18 they might not be able to take care of other more serious problems. And that might be a problem. Any suggestions if we're the police and concerned about young people out until 2:00 in the morning? Might there be a better way to handle this?

(discussion continues)

a student asked a question that another student answered. At this point students began to assume some discussion leadership. The teacher's role was to initiate and facilitate this conversation. This segment ended with another higher cognitive level question.

The instructional approach and materials used in the Critical Thinking in American History project (CTAH) (O'Reilly, 1991) serve as a good illustration of generally how critical thinking can be taught and specifically the role questioning and discussion plays in achieving this goal. Although CTAH was developed for high-school students, the materials have been successfully adapted to junior-high school and college classes (Beyer, 1988). O'Reilly's rationale for CTAH is that "Good reasoning is at the heart of serious history" (p. 364), and the purpose of the project is to directly teach the skills of reasoning using historical problems and interpretations. The materials, in the form of booklets, were designed to serve as supplementary materials for a one- or two-year course in American history and vary in difficulty for low ability, average, and advanced students (Beyer, 1988). The skills emphasized in the critical thinking program are these:

- Identifying and evaluating evidence
- Distinguishing conclusions from premises
- Identifying unstated assumptions
- Identifying imprecise words
- Identifying connections among parts of an argument
- Evaluating ethical claims

The instructional approach is varied, but heavily uses higher-order questions and discussion. Typically a skill is first demonstrated in the context of familiar everyday problems. For example, a teacher's introduction of the skill of identifying and evaluating evidence begins with five students role playing a robbery in the hallway outside the classroom. The event is analyzed through questioning and eventually the students are led to a discussion of the nature of evidence. Training continues with a gradual progression of exercises involving increasingly more difficult historical problems and interpretations. After focusing on the interpretations written by others, students eventually construct their own interpretations from original course materials. The discussion method is essential in the training process as students develop their reasoning skills through interaction with the teacher, materials, and with each other (O'Reilly, 1991).

CONCLUSION

Rocco Yeargin, the student who wrote the letter to the editor introducing this chapter, directly described what theorists and researchers have been advocating about the teaching of critical thinking and what teachers have been practicing in our social studies classrooms. Although critical thinking has always been recognized as an important component in achieving the goal of citizenship education, it never has been a curricular or instructional priority in the schools. Karen Rosenblum-Cale (1987) expressed this contradiction: "Thinking is a very natural act. What is unnatural is its scarcity" (p. 45). The emphasis in our social studies classrooms has been on coverage of subject matter and recall of basic knowledge and understandings. If students are to be prepared to reflect on and work toward dealing with the pressing issues of our society, they need to be trained to critically think and have opportunities to practice these skills. Good thinking and good citizenship go hand in hand.

The literature supports teachers providing for students at all levels, regardless of their ability, opportunities to think because they are capable. Students can think at the higher cognitive levels given their current knowledge and experiences. Thinking and content should be learned together because students cannot think critically about an issue or problem under consideration without adequate knowledge. Critical thinking and content are dependent on one another, and they reinforce each other.

Although there are several major approaches, and many variations of these approaches, for teachers to teach critical thinking skills, the literature favors the infusion approach of directly teaching critical thinking skills as part of subject-matter content in the classroom context. Also, considerable attention must be given to creating a positive classroom environment. Critical thinking skills must be developed in an environment that also strongly emphasizes in-depth study of subject matter and creation of student dispositions of thoughtfulness.

Critical thinking can best be taught when students are encouraged to speak openly; ask thoughtful questions; engage in hands-on, and minds-on, learning activities; and focus on issues and problems. Among the instructional behaviors teachers can employ to facilitate critical mindedness are asking higher level and challenging questions related to a limited number of topics, issues, and problems; using wait time to encourage students to think, and offering support for their opinions and conclusions. It also seems very important that teachers genuinely attempt to model thoughtfulness knowing that their influence can be a powerful stimulator for learning at all levels.

The questioning behaviors of teachers and students are particularly influential in helping create an environment conducive to stimulating critical thinking. Teachers who emphasize asking higher cognitive level questions and using a variety of questioning and alternative nonquestioning techniques will increase the probability that their students' responses, comments, and questions will be thoughtful. This is particularly the case in discussions that can have as a primary purpose the development and practice of such thinking strategies as decision making and problem solving. Discussion, by its very nature, also has the potential to provide opportunities for students to learn, experience, and practice democratic processes. What better way to begin to prepare students for reflective and active citizenship?

It is too optimistic to predict that the conditions in the schools will change in the near future. Though schools' philosophies and goals, as listed in courses of study and curriculum guides, will continue to stress the need to develop students' critical thinking skills, teachers generally will continue emphasizing reproductive thinking. Enlightened social studies teachers and departments such as those discovered during Newmann's (1991a, 1991b) valuable and ongoing study on higher-order thinking hopefully will model what is essential and possible in teaching for productive, or critical, thinking. What is needed is a concerted effort by schools to reduce the barriers to the promotion of critical thinking that teachers so often experience. It probably won't happen, though, until the public values, advocates, and supports thoughtfulness. James F. Voss, David N. Perkins and Judith W. Segal (1991) expressed our current state of affairs: "…although we have succeeded in making secondary education available to all young people, we have never seriously accepted the challenge of teaching all members of this diverse population how to become competent thinkers and reasoners" (p. viii). When we do address that challenge, Rocco Yeargin and his peers of the American school system may be satisfied with, and even enthusiastic about, the education they received.

Reflective Questions

1. *How can we tell the extent to which students are critically thinking?*

2. *How many critical thinking skills should be taught?*

3. *Should students of all cultures know universal critical thinking skills? If so, which skills are most important?*

4. *How important is language development in learning to think critically?*

5. *To what extent are there differences in the capability of students representing different cultures to think critically?*

6. *How can the barriers to promoting thinking in the classroom be reduced?*

7. *To what extent do critical thinking skills transfer to other subjects and situations?*

8. *What is the best way to assess critical thinking?*

9. *What role can the computer play in teaching students to think critically?*

10. *How can teacher education programs best provide a critical-thinking skills program?*

GLOSSARY

critical thinking   Reflective application of skills involved in examining information, observation, behavior, or event; analyzing an issue; forming and supporting an opinion; making a decision; or solving a problem.

higher-order thinking   General reasoning involving the interpretation, analysis, or manipulation of information.

lower-order thinking   Recall of knowledge, information, observations, and experiences.

thinking   Search for understanding.

ANNOTATED BIBLIOGRAPHY

Baron, Joan B. and Robert J. Sternberg, editors (1987). *Teaching Thinking Skills.*
New York: W.H. Freeman.

This book presents a comprehensive look at the nature and instruction of thinking. Twelve essays represent diverse perspectives from leaders in the field including Ennis, Nickerson, Perkins, Quellmalz, Swartz, Paul, and Sternberg. The essays emphasize translating theory and research into classroom practice.

Beyer, Barry K. (1987). *Practical Strategies for the Teaching of Thinking.* Boston: Allyn & Bacon.

A comprehensive presentation of methods, techniques, and strategies related to directly teaching for thinking. Beyer's philosophy is to make thinking skills the focus of learning with subject matter a secondary consideration. The companion volume to this book is *Developing a Thinking Skills Program* (Beyer, 1988).

Newmann, Fred M. (1991). "Promoting Higher Order Thinking in Social Studies: Overview of a Study of 16 High School Departments." *Theory and Research in Social Education* 19(4):324–340.

Five articles report the results of the federally funded Project on Higher Order Thinking in the High School Curriculum conducted by Fred Newmann and his colleagues at the University of Wisconsin from 1985–1990. The study examined the extent social studies departments in 16 high schools around the United States encouraged higher-order thinking in classrooms and also examined the barriers to promoting thinking.

Parker, Walter C. (1991). "Achieving Thinking and Decision-Making Objectives in Social Studies." Pp. 345–356 in *Handbook of Research on Social Studies Teaching and Learning,* edited by James Shaver. New York: Macmillan.

Review of research related to the teaching for thinking in social studies, including a historical focus on two major programs: Harvard Social Studies and Taba Projects. Also reports on the Newmann Project on higher-order thinking in U.S. high schools.

Rosenblum-Cale, Karen (1987). *Teaching Thinking Skills: Social Studies.* Washington, DC: National Education Association.

A review of the literature on teaching for thinking with a particular focus on the theory and practice of teaching for thinking by level: primary, elementary, middle/junior high school, and high school.

Strother, Deborah B. (1989). "Developing Thinking Skills Through Questioning." *Phi Delta Kappan* 71(4):324–327.

Generalized research findings are presented from a resource panel of experts on using classroom questioning as a means to stimulate the development of student thinking.

Swartz, Robert J. and David N. Perkins (1990). *Teaching Thinking: Issues and Approaches.* Pacific Grove, CA: Midwest Publications.

A comprehensive introduction to the field of teaching for thinking covering types of, and issues related to, thinking; planning and instructional approaches for thinking; and assessment of thinking. Particular emphasis is placed on how to teach thinking using the separate program and infusion of thinking skills approaches. This volume is very useful for educational practitioners because it is written in basic terms.

Voss, James F., David N. Perkins, and Judith W. Segal, editors. *Informal Reasoning and Education*. Hillsdale, NJ: Lawrence Erlbaum Associates.

Informal reasoning is defined as "contextualized reasoning" or thinking that is not restricted to abstract mathematical or logical reasoning. This volume presents the contexts and characteristics of reasoning and the problems of teaching reasoning in the classroom. The chapters by O'Reilly and Newmann directly focus on thinking in social studies classrooms.

Wilen, William W., editor (1990). *Teaching and Learning Through Discussion*. Springfield, IL: Charles Thomas.

A variety of perspectives on the theory, research, and practice related to the discussion method are presented by well-known experts in the area of discussion including Bridges, Gall, and Dillon. Part of the focus of each chapter is on thinking.

Wilen, William W. (1991). *Questioning Skills for Teachers*. 3rd ed. Washington DC: National Education Association.

A brief, but comprehensive, review of past and current research findings related to the oral questioning behaviors and practices of teachers as they impact student thinking and achievement. The bibliography lists 138 sources.

Willis, Scott (1992). "Teaching Thinking." *Curriculum Update*. Alexandria, VA: Association for Supervision and Curriculum Development.

Review of the three major approaches to teaching for thinking: environmental impact, infusing skills, and separate course approaches. Also examines related issues, including teaching for transfer and developing metacognition.

REFERENCES

Atwood, V.A. and William W. Wilen (1991). "Wait Time and Effective Social Studies Instruction: What Can Research in Science Education Tell Us?" *Social Education* 55(3):179–181.

Banks, J.A. and A.A. Clegg, Jr. (1990). *Teaching Strategies for the Social Studies: Inquiry, Valuing, and Decision Making*, 4th ed. White Plains, NY: Longman.

Bereiter, C. (1984). "How to Keep Thinking Skills from Going the Way of All Frills." *Educational Leadership* 42(1):75–77.

Beyer, Barry K. (1987). *Practical Strategies for the Teaching of Thinking*. Boston: Allyn & Bacon.

Beyer, Barry K. (1988). *Developing a Thinking Skills Program*. Boston: Allyn & Bacon.

Bloom, B.S., M.D. Englehart, E.J. Furst, W.A. Will, and D.R. Krathwohl, editors (1956). *Taxonomy of Educational Objectives, Handbook I: Cognitive Domain*. New York: David McKay.

Boyer, Ernest L. (1983). *High School: A Report on Secondary Education in America*. New York: Harper & Row.

Bridges, D. (1979). *Education, Democracy and Discussion*. Windsor, England: National Foundation of Educational Research.

Brooks, J. and M. Brooks (1993). *The Case for Constructivist Classrooms*. Alexandria, VA: Association for Supervision and Curriculum Development.

Chapin, J.R. and R.G. Messick (1992). *Elementary Social Studies*, 2nd ed. White Plains, NY: Longman.

Cornbleth, C. (1985). "Critical Thinking and Cognitive Process." Pp. 11–63 in *Review of Research in Social Studies Education: 1976–1983*, edited by W. Stanley. Washington, DC: National Council for the Social Studies.

Costa, A.L., editor (1985). *Developing Minds*. Alexandria, VA: Association for Supervision and Curriculum Development.

Dantonio, M. (1990). *How Can We Create Thinkers?* Bloomington, IN: National Educational Service.

Dewey, John (1910). *How We Think*. Boston: D.C. Heath.

Dillon, J.T. (1982). "Cognitive Correspondence Between Question/State and Response." *American Education Research Journal* 19:540–551.

Dillon, J.T. (1990). "Conducting Discussion by Alternative to Questioning." Pp. 79–96 in *Teaching and Learning through Discussion*, edited by W.W. Wilen. Springfield, IL: Charles Thomas.

Dillon, J.T. (1988). *Questioning and Teaching: A Manual of Practice*. New York: Columbia University, Teachers College Press.

Dillon, J.T. (1994). *Using Discussion in Classrooms*. Buckingham, England: Open University Press.

Ennis, R.H. (1987). "A Taxonomy of Critical Thinking Dispositions and Abilities." Pp. 9–26 in *Teaching Thinking Skills*, edited by J.B. Baron and R.J. Sternberg. New York: W.H. Freeman.

Gage, N.L. (1969). "Teaching Method." Pp. 1446–1258 in *Encyclopedia of Educational Research*, edited by R.L. Abel, 4th ed. London: Macmillan.

Gall, M.D. (1985). "Discussion Methods of Teaching." Pp. 1423–1427 in *International Encyclopedia of Education*, Vol. 3, edited by T. Husen and T.N. Postlethwaite. Oxford: Pergamon Press.

Gall, M.D. and T. Rhody (1987). "Review of Research on Questioning Techniques." Pp. 23–48 in *Questions, Questioning Techniques, and Effective Teaching*, edited by W.W. Wilen. Washington, DC: National Education Association.

Goodlad, John I. (1984). *A Place Called School: Prospects for the Future*. New York: McGraw-Hill.

Hunkins, F.P. (1989) *Teaching Thinking Through Effective Questioning*. Boston: Christopher-Gordon.

IRT Communication Quarterly (1988, Fall). "Teaching Higher Order Thinking in Social Studies." p. 1.

IRT Communication Quarterly (1991, Winter). "The Immersion Approach to Developing Thinking." p. 2.

Joyce, B. (1985). "Models for Teaching Thinking." *Educational Leadership* 42:4–7.

Joyce, B. and M. Weil (1992). *Models of Teaching*, 4th ed. Boston: Allyn & Bacon.

Mahood, W., L. Biemer, and W.T. Lowe (1991). *Teaching Social Studies in Middle and Senior High Schools*. New York: Macmillan.

Martorella, P.H. (1991). *Teaching Social Studies in Middle and Secondary Schools*. New York: Macmillan.

Marzano, R.J., R.S. Brandt, C.S. Hughes, B.F. Jones, B.Z. Presseisen, S.C. Rankin, and C. Suhor (1988). *Dimensions of Thinking: A Framework for Curriculum and Instruction*. Alexandria, VA: Association for Supervision and Curriculum Development.

Michaelis, J.U. (1988). *Social Studies for Children*, 9th ed. Englewood Cliffs, NJ: Prentice-Hall.

Miller-Jones, D. (1991). "Informal Reasoning in Inner-City Children." Pp. 107–130 in *Informal Reasoning and Education*, edited by J. Voss, D.N. Perkins, and J.W. Segal. Hillsdale, NJ: Lawrence Erlbaum.

Mills, S., C.T. Rice, D.C. Berliner, and E.W. Rousseau (1980). "The Correspondence Between Teacher Questions and Student Answers in Classroom Discourse." *Journal of Experimental Education* 48:194–204.

National Commission for Excellence in Education (1983). *A Nation at Risk*. Washington, DC: Government Printing.

National Council for the Social Studies (1993). "A Vision of Powerful Teaching and Learning in the Social Studies; Building Understanding and Civic Efficacy." *Social Education* 57:213–223.

National Education Association (1961). *The Central Purpose of Education*. Washington, DC: NEA.

Newmann, F.M. (1988). *Higher Order Thinking in High School Social Studies: An Analysis of Classrooms, Teachers, Students and Leadership* (Report by the National Center on Effective Secondary Schools). Madison: University of Wisconsin, Madison.

Newmann, F.M. (1991a). "Higher Order Thinking in the Teaching of Social Studies: Connections Between Theory and Practice." Pp. 381–400 in *Informal Reasoning and Education*, edited by J.F. Voss, D.N. Perkins, and J.W. Segal. Hillsdale, NJ: Lawrence Erlbaum Associates.

Newmann, F.M. (1991b). "Promoting Higher Order Thinking in Social Studies: Overview of a Study of 16 High School Departments." *Theory and Research in Social Education* 19(4):324–340.

Newmann, F.M. and D.W Oliver (1970). *Clarifying Public Controversy*. Boston: Little, Brown.

Nickerson, R.S. (1987). "Why Teach Thinking." Pp. 27–37 in *Teaching Thinking Skills*, edited by J.B. Baron and R.J. Sternberg. New York: W.H. Freeman.

Oliver, D.W. and J.P. Shaver (1974). *Teaching Public Issues in the High School*. Logan: Utah State University Press. (Original work published 1966).

Onosko, J.J. (1991). "Barriers to the Promoting of Higher-Order Thinking in Social Studies." *Theory and Research in Social Education* 19(4):341–366

O'Reilly, K. (1991). "Informal Reasoning in High School History." Pp. 363–379 in *Informal Reasoning and Education*, edited by J.F. Voss, D.N. Perkins, and J.W. Segal. Hillsdale, NJ: Lawrence Erlbaum Associates.

Parker, Walter C. (1991). "Achieving Thinking and Decision-Making Objectives in Social Studies." Pp. 345–356 in *Handbook of Research on Social Studies Teaching and Learning*, edited by James Shaver. New York: Macmillan.

Patrick, J.P. (1986). *Critical Thinking in the Social Studies*. Bloomington, IN: Eric Clearinghouse for Social Studies/Social Science Education.

Perkins, David N. (1987). "Foreword." P. xi in *Practical Strategies for the Teaching of Thinking*, edited by B. Beyer. Boston: Allyn & Bacon.

Presseisen, B.Z. (1986). *Thinking Skills: Research and Practice*. Washington. DC: National Education Association.

Rosenblum-Cale, K. (1987). *Teaching Thinking Skills: Social Studies*. Washington, DC: National Education Association.

Rowe, M.B. (1986). "Wait Time: Slowing Down May Be a Way of Speeding Up!" *Journal of Teacher Education* 37(1):43–50.

Sanders, N.M. (1966). *Classroom Questions, What Kinds?* New York: Harper & Row.

Sizer, T. (1984). *Horace's Compromise: The Dilemma of the American High School*. Boston: Houghton Mifflin.

Sternberg, R.J. (1987a). "Questions and Answers about the Nature and Teaching of Thinking Skills." Pp. 251–259 in *Teaching Thinking Skills*, edited by J.B. Baron and R.J. Sternberg. New York: W.H. Freeman.

Sternberg, R.J. (1987b). "Teaching Intelligence: The Application of Cogntive Psychology to the Improvement of Intellectual Skills." Pp. 182–218 in *Teaching Thinking Skills*, edited by J.B. Baron and R.J. Sternberg. New York: W.H. Freeman.

Sternberg, R.J. and K. Bhana (1986). "Synthesis of Research on the Effectiveness of Intellectual Skills Programs: Snake-Oil Remedies or Miracle Cures?" *Educational Leadership* 44(2):60–67.

Strother, D.B. (1989). "Developing Thinking Skills Through Questioning." *Phi Delta Kappan* 71(4):324–327.

Swartz, R.J. and David N. Perkins (1990). *Teaching Thinking: Issues and Approaches*. Pacific Grove, CA: Midwest Publications.

Taba, H. (1966). *Teaching Strategies and Cognitive Functioning in Elementary School Children* (Cooperative Research Project No. 2404). San Francisco: San Francisco State College.

Taba, H., S. Levine, and F.F. Elzey (1964). *Thinking in Elementary School Children* (Cooperative Research Project No. 1574). San Francisco: San Francisco State College.

Tobin, K.G. (1987) "The Role of Wait Time in High Cognitive Level Learning." *Review of Educational Research* 57(1):69–95.

Voss, J.F., D.N. Perkins, and J.W. Segal (1991). "Preface." P. vii in *Informal Reasoning and Education*, edited by J.F. Voss, D.N. Perkins, and J.W. Segal. Hillsdale, NJ: Lawrence Erlbaum Associates.

Wilen, W.W. (1990). "Forms and Phases of Discussions." Pp. 3–24 in *Teaching and Learning Through Discussion*, edited by W.W. Wilen. Springfield, IL: Charles Thomas.

Wilen, W.W. (1991). *Questioning Skills for Teachers*, 3rd ed. Washington DC: National Education Association.

Wilen, W.W. (1994). *Democracy and Reflective Discussion in Social Studies Classrooms*. Paper presented at the Third International Social Studies Conference, Nairobi, Kenya.

Wilen, W.W. and J.J. White (1991). "Interaction and Discourse in Social Studies Classrooms." Pp. 483–495 in *Handbook of Research on Social Studies Teaching and Learning*, edited by J. Shaver. New York: Macmillan.

Willis, S. (1992). "Teaching Thinking." *Curriculum Update*. Alexandria, VA: Association for Supervision and Curriculum Development.

Yeargin, R. (1989, May 4). "Higher Priority Needed for Thinking Skills" [Letter to the editor]. Akron, OH: *Beacon Journal*, p. A4.

Zemelman, S., H. Daniels, and A. Hyde (1993). *Best Practices: New Standards for Teaching and Learning in America's Schools*. Portsmouth, NH: Heineman.

Zevin, J. (1992). *Social Studies for the Twenty-First Century*. White Plains, NY: Longman.

Chapter Six

TEACHING VALUES IN SOCIAL STUDIES EDUCATION—PAST PRACTICES AND CURRENT TRENDS

James S. Leming
Southern Illinois University

IT HAS NEVER REALLY BEEN MUCH OF AN ISSUE with the American people whether the schools should teach values. The schools, after all, have always taught values. The most basic activity of schools, imparting knowledge, is teaching children that knowledge is to be valued over ignorance. Also, the patterns of organization of school life teach children that social order is to be valued over social disorder. One persisting expectation of the American people has been that the schools will bring a diverse set of people into a common understanding and respect for basic American values. The most prominent instructional approach of the eighteenth and nineteenth centuries used to achieve this goal was basic readers such as *The New England Primer* and *McGuffey's Eclectic Readers*. These textbooks featured moral exhortation within the content of the reading materials.

Although there is little disagreement among the American people regarding whether the schools should teach values, the field of values education still contains considerable controversy. This chapter explores some issues that are

145

associated with the field of values education. The most significant of these are: What values should be taught?; How are values learned?; How should values be taught?; What works?; What is the best approach?; and, What should the role of the teacher and the school be in the process? To assist you in reaching your own position on theses issues, information will be presented on the history of values education and the research related to the teaching and learning of values in schools.

During the past thirty years, American education has rediscovered values education. Three approaches to values education have received considerable attention among educators and the general public alike. These approaches have been referred to as values education, moral development, and character education. Later in this chapter I will discuss the three major recent approaches to moral education and the research that supports each of the approaches. But first, some background information is presented on the history of moral education in this century.

VALUES EDUCATION IN THE TWENTIETH CENTURY

The first three decades of this century saw character education become a major preoccupation of schooling. Such factors as increasing industrialization and urbanization, a continuing tide of immigration, World War I, the Bolshevik Revolution, and the spirit of the Roaring 20s, all contributed to a mood among the population and educators that something needed to be done about the apparent threat to social stability and vitality posed by the decline of moral standards. As is traditional in this country, when social needs are identified, the schools are expected to respond, and respond they did. Surveys conducted in the 1920s (cited by Yulish, 1980, and Chapman, 1977) indicated that virtually every school in America was responding in some way to the educational goal of developing character.

In 1922, the Religious Education Association initiated a study of the effects of religious education. Between 1924 and 1929, the Institute of Social and Religious Research, funded by John D. Rockefeller and housed at Teachers College, Columbia University, undertook the most detailed and comprehensive effort to date to assess the impact of schools on character. The Character Education Inquiry direction was initially set by Edward Thorndike, with Hugh Hartshorne and Mark May heading the final project. The report of the Character Education Inquiry was published in a three-volume series entitled: *Studies in the Nature of Character* (Hartshorne and May, 1928–1930). Among the many disturbing findings within the 1,782 pages was the following:

> [T]he mere urging of honest behavior by teacher or the discussion of standards and ideals of honesty, no matter how much such general ideals may be

"emotionalized," has no necessary relation to conduct...there seems to be evidence that such effects as may result are not generally good and are sometimes unwholesome...the prevailing ways of inculcating ideals probably do little good and do some harm (Vol. 1, p. 413)

The 1930s saw a rapid decline in interest in character as a prominent objective in education. Although the publication of findings of the Character Education Inquiry alone did not account for the demise of the Character Education movement, it undoubtedly played an important role.

Following a 30-year period of dormancy, the mid-1960s through the early 1990s saw a resurgence of interest in the values held by youth among both the public and educators. Among the current reasons offered for character education are disturbing trends in youth conduct (suicide, homicide, increased sexual activity, drug and alcohol abuse, and delinquency), the disintegration of the two-parent family and the resultant weakening of the family unit as a transmitter of core values, the growing epidemic of psychosocial adjustment problems of youth, the declining academic performance and work habits of youth resulting in an "at-risk" competitive position for the nation, and a host of highly visible national figures whose public behavior presents poor character images to youth.

Thus, like the early part of the century, the social stability and vitality of our nation appear in danger, and once again the schools are called upon to respond to this very real social need. From 1965 to 1980, this movement was commonly referred to as "moral" or "values education" (MVE). Around 1980, a shift in emphasis occurred and character education, after a hiatus of 45 years, again became the term of choice to describe the school's role in shaping the values of youth. Character education was the term chosen to describe the new educational movement because it denoted a focus more on virtues or character traits such as honesty, integrity, and self-discipline, whereas MVE focused primarily on decision making or thinking about moral questions. For MVE, inculcation and indoctrination were pejorative terms. For character education, no such negative connotations were associated with those terms.

THE MORAL/VALUES EDUCATION MOVEMENT AND RELATED RESEARCH

Two approaches dominated the values education movement from 1960 through the mid-1980s.

In 1958, both Sidney Simon and Lawrence Kohlberg completed their doctoral dissertations, Simon at New York University and Kohlberg at the University of Chicago. Eight years later each published his first work dealing with moral or values education. Simon, collaborating with Louis Raths and Merrill Harmin, coauthored *Values and Teaching*, the highly influential first statement of the theory and technique of values clarification (Raths, Harmin, and Simon, 1966). Kohlberg, in an article in the *School Review*, for the first time linked his cognitive-developmental theory of moral reasoning with the practice of moral education in schools (Kohlberg, 1966). These two approaches to moral education dominated the field of moral or values education for the next 25 years, with values clarification (VC) enjoying more popular success in schools, and the cognitive-developmental approach receiving more attention and acclaim from scholars and researchers. As is typically the case with educational movements, it is difficult to judge exactly how much impact these two approaches had on educational practice; however, given the sheer volume of journal articles, curricular materials, and books centering on these two approaches, it is safe to assume that in the eyes of most school personnel, the cognitive-developmental approach and values clarification have been synonymous with moral or values education throughout the past two decades.

Although the two approaches were different in many ways, they both emphasized that moralizing was not to be included in the teacher's role as moral educator.

Values Clarification

In VC, the goal was for each student to achieve greater clarity regarding his or her values by following the prescribed seven-step valuing process. The teacher was expected to be only a facilitator of the valuing process and, for fear of influencing students, was to withhold his or her own opinions. Whatever values the student arrived at, they were to be respected by the teacher.

The theory of values clarification recognizes that people today have difficulty "pulling themselves together." It is a difficult world in which to grow up. As a consequence, some people flounder in confusion, apathy, or inconsistency. They can not understand their values; they have no clear values that serve as guides for action in a complex and often confusing world. The purpose of values clarification is to help people understand their values. If people are clear about their values, then their behavior should also change; they should show less confusion, apathy, or inconsistency. The VC methodology has four key elements:

1. *A focus on life.*   The approach focuses people's attention on aspects of their own lives that may indicate things they value.
2. *An acceptance of what is.*   To clarify values one must accept others' positions nonjudgementally.
3. *An invitation to reflect further.*   Not only must others' position be accepted, but individuals must also be encouraged to reflect in some depth on those positions.

4. *A nourishment of personal powers.* Values clarification not only encourages the exercise of clarifying skills, but also nourishes a sense of possibility for self-direction. That is, people, if they know what they value, can take charge of their lives.

From an instructional point of view, to clarify values means to apply in the classroom the process of valuing. Valuing involves three processes that comprise seven criteria. Unless something satisfies all seven criteria, it is not called a value, but rather a belief or attitude or something other than a value. The three processes that comprise values clarification are choosing, prizing, and acting. The seven-step valuing process is presented here:

- Choosing
  1. freely
  2. from alternatives
  3. after thoughtful consideration of the consequences of each alternative
- Prizing
  4. cherishing, being happy with the choice
  5. enough to be willing to affirm the choice to others
- Acting
  6. or doing something with the choice
  7. repeatedly, in some pattern of life

During the 1970s and 1980s values clarification was the most popular approach to values education. One book of values clarification strategies sold more than 600,000 copies (Simon, Howe, and Kirshenbaum, 1972). The classroom described in Box 6-A is an example of the values clarification strategy in action.

Although popular with teachers, the VC approach was also the subject of scathing criticism. The criticisms focused on two major issues: privacy and moral relativism. Critics questioned whether teachers had the right to inquire into personal areas of one's values and have students discuss these in an open forum. Critics also questioned whether any value position, such as the value of cheating on tests, was a legitimate outcome of the educational process.

The Kohlberg Approach

In Kohlberg's moral dilemma discussion approach (MD), the teacher's role also was to serve as a facilitator of student reasoning, to assist students in resolving issues of moral conflict, and to ensure that the environment in which the discussion took place contained the conditions essential for the development of moral reasoning. The moral development approach to moral education has been referred to by a variety of names: the Kohlbergian approach, the dilemma-discussion approach, and the cognitive developmental approach to moral education. This approach is the product of the talents and creative abilities of Harvard psychologist Lawrence Kohlberg.

Box 6–A   Values Clarification

At Cleveland Middle School, Mr. Jones, a U.S. history teacher, is disturbed by the rising incidence of cheating that he has detected on unit tests. He decides to confront this issue head on and use a values education strategy that he had heard about this summer at a teachers' workshop.

Mr. Jones: So some of you think it is best to be honest on tests, is that right? (Some heads nod affirmatively). And some of you think dishonesty is all right? (A few hesitant and slight nods). And I guess some of you are not certain. (Heads nod). Well, are there any other choices, or is it just a matter of dishonesty versus honesty?

Sam: You could be honest some of the time and dishonest some of the time.

Mr. Jones: Does that sound like a possible choice class? (Heads nod). Any other alternatives to choose from?

Tracy: It seems to me that you have to be all one way or all the other.

Mr. Jones: Remember now, we're looking for alternatives on the issue first, next we will look at consequences. Any more alternatives? (silence). OK, now I'm going to list the alternatives on the board and you examine them for consequences to see which one you prefer. Later in small groups you will have a chance to discuss your view with others.

Ginger: Does that mean that we can decide for ourselves whether we should be honest on tests here?

Mr Jones: No, that means that you can decide on the value. Although you may choose to be dishonest I shall insist that we be honest on our tests here. In other areas of your life, you may have more freedom to be dishonest, but one can't do anything any time, and in this class I shall expect honesty on tests.

Ginger: Well, I think I've decided that I'll cheat everywhere I can.

Mr. Jones: How does that decision make you feel about yourself?

Ginger: I'm not sure.

(Adapted from Raths, Harmin, and Simon, 1978)

In 1956 Lawrence Kohlberg undertook a longitudinal study of the moral development of 58 early adolescents in the Chicago area. At intervals of three years he returned to the same individuals to assess any changes regarding how they reasoned about moral dilemmas.

Kohlberg identified five stages of reasoning that some members of his sample progressed through sequentially. Some sample members progressed more slowly than others, but no one stood still and no one regressed. The reasons for doing right associated with each of the stages are briefly presented:

Stage 1:   *Heteronomous morality.*   Avoid punishment and deference to the superior power of authorities.

Stage 2:   *Instrumental purpose and exchange.*   Serve one's own needs and recognize that others have needs also. Return good for good and evil for evil.

Stage 3: *Mutual interpersonal expectations.* It is important to be a good person in your own eyes and the eyes of others.

Stage 4: *Social system and conscience.* Obey laws to keep the social system going. The alternative is social chaos.

Stage 5: *Social contract and individual rights.* A feeling of contractual commitment freely entered into is the basis of moral obligation. One source of one's obligations is the morality of the U.S. Constitution, it's conception of the social welfare, and its emphasis on individual rights.

Kohlberg's educational approach arose from the finding that when individuals are exposed to cognitive conflict and, simultaneously, examples of the next highest stage of moral reasoning, moral development occurs. As a result, the key aspects of his approach to moral education are moral dilemmas and classroom discussion. The teacher's role is to ensure that each student confronts the moral issue in the dilemma and has the opportunity to hear other perspectives on the issue. The classroom described in Box 6-B is an example of this approach in practice.

Criticisms of the dilemma-discussion approach have centered around issues of moral relativism and the connection between gains in moral development and changes in behavior (Fraenkel, 1976).

Although the values clarification and cognitive developmental approaches to MVE were not the only approaches advocated during the past 25 years, they were the only two approaches researched extensively. Other approaches to MVE typically focused on the rational analysis of the values claims behind positions on social issues. Typical of such approaches were value analysis developed by Jerrold Coombs, James Chadwick, and Milton Meux (Metcalf, 1971), the jurisprudential approach (Oliver and Shaver, 1966) and the reasoning with democratic values approach (Lockwood and Harris, 1985). Research on these approaches was sparse and inconclusive. Values clarification and the moral discussion approach, on the other hand, were the focus of hundreds of empirical investigations, and now, in the early 1990s, one can talk with confidence regarding the impact of these approaches on students.

The Research Base for Values Clarification and Moral Dilemma Approaches

The research on the moral discussion approach to moral education represents a real success story in educational research. All the reviews of the moral discussion research program have reached similar conclusions (Enright, Lapsley, and Levy, 1983; Lawrence, 1980; Leming, 1981, 1985; Lockwood, 1978; Schlaefli, Rest and Thoma, 1985); namely, that when students are engaged in

---

Box 6–B   Moral Development

Ms. Spicer, senior American Government teacher, is teaching a small unit on government regulation and medical ethics. She has just presented the case of Ben and Betty Peters to the class. The Peters have just found out that their newborn child has Downs Syndrome. In addition to being retarded the child also has a badly damaged heart. The doctor has informed them that even if the operation is successful to repair the damaged heart, the infant will likely die at an early age. The doctor has told Mr. & Mrs. Peters that it might be best to let nature take its course. The doctor needs to know their decision in the next two hours. What should they decide?

Ms. Spicer: Well class, what do you think? First let's look at the morality of the case.

Robert: They might really want the baby, and they should try to save it.

Ms. Spicer: Suppose they really didn't want a baby right then, are you saying then it would be OK to let it die?

Robert: I guess so. I'm not really sure.

Ms. Spicer: OK. Hector, have you formed an opinion?

Hector: I think they should let the baby die. You see, if they let it live, it would have a really horrible life. It would be the nicest thing to do.

Liz: I disagree. I'm with Robert 100 percent. It's the parents' child and they should do what they want and they'll probably want to keep it.

Ms. Spicer: Liz, you seem to agree pretty much with Robert.

Liz: Yeah, hard to believe isn't it?

Ms. Spicer: Gary, do you have a position?

Gary: They have no choice but to save it. Physicians have a moral obligation to save life.

Ms Spicer: Could you expand on that for me, Gary?

Gary: The fact is that it's written into law in the Hippocratic oath that they have sworn to uphold. It's the doctor's moral obligation to keep the child alive at all costs. If he breaks the oath then anything goes as far as what doctors can do.

Anne: But Gary, you're missing the point. It would be a cruel thing to do to prolong the suffering of the child. The doctor's moral obligation would be to let the child die.

Ms. Spicer: Let's quickly summarize the perspectives that we have at this point before we go on. Robert and Liz, it seems to me that you are saying that the Peters should do what they want—it's basically their child and their decision. Hector and Anne, you seem to think that the Peters should do what a good and decent person would do, and Gary, you seem to think that the most important thing is for the doctor to stay true to the oath that he has made to save life.

(Adapted from Arbuthnot and Faust, 1981)

---

the process of discussing moral dilemmas accompanied by cognitive disequilibrium and exposure to examples of the next highest state of moral reasoning, and when the treatment condition lasts at least a semester in length, a shift in student reasoning of one-quarter to one-half stage will result in approximately 80 percent of the studies. Also detected was an increase of 4 to 5 percentage points in principled moral reasoning as measured by the Defining Issues Test

(Rest, 1979)—principled moral reasoning is reasoning at stage five. The research on the moral discussion approach, while including many studies based in social studies classrooms, also includes studies in a variety of other subject areas and research with college-aged and adult samples. The pattern of findings in social studies classrooms was consistent with those found in other areas.

The extent of research on the values clarification approach to MVE, well over 100 studies, is equal to that of the MD approach. The pattern of the research findings of the VC approach is also highly consistent. The difference, however, is that with the MD approach, the hypothesized changes in moral reasoning were found; with the VC approach there was a consistent pattern of failure to find significant changes in the dependent variables (Lockwood, 1978; Leming, 1981, 1985, 1987). Similarly to the MD research, many VC studies were conducted in social studies classrooms. Again, there were no differences in the patterns of findings across areas.

The contrast between the research on the values clarification approach and the moral discussion approach is stark. Whereas the MD approach typically involves only a single dependent variable (stage of moral reasoning), the VC research program contains a bewildering array of dependent variables such as values thinking, self-concept, school attitudes, dogmatism, value related behavior, and so forth. Although the percentage of the studies finding the predicted results varies from dependent variable to dependent variable, the success rate is in the 0 percent to 20 percent range.

In answer to the query "What works?," when using the available research from the MVE movement, it is safe to say the moral discussion approach works, and the values clarification approach does not. This generalization, however, needs some qualification, as do most attempts to draw conclusions from research. First, the stage growth found as a result of the moral discussion approach is in the stage two, three, and four range and is generally quite small—usually less than one-third of a stage for interventions of at least one semester. Second, none of the MD studies reviewed have used any form of social or moral behavior as a dependent variable; therefore, the success reported relates to development in reasoning, not character. The claim by Kohlberg and his associates that moral reasoning and moral behavior are related at the principled level (Kohlberg and Candee, 1984) is based on statistically weak associations (Blasi, 1980). Thus, even though the MD approach "works," it appears to be of little help planning for K to 12 curricula if that curriculum has as an objective influencing students' personal and social behavior.

Within the values clarification research literature are a handful of studies that have as a dependent variable what the researchers call value-related behavior. The findings of these studies are inconclusive. So, although one of the two approaches to MVE that dominated the past 25 years was somewhat successful in attaining its desired educational goal, the movement of this period offers little assistance in planning for character education when changes in student behavior is a central objective.

What is true for the moral education movement in general has also been true for moral education efforts within the social studies curriculum. The emphasis to this point has been almost exclusively on reasoning about questions of values and morality, and the research results have indicated that these efforts have had negligible impact on student values or behavior. One perspective on this state of affairs is that morals, values, and character are not purely cognitive constructs; how they become internalized, and how they might subsequently be altered, involves more than reasoning. This point will be presented in more detail later.

ADDITIONAL RESEARCH PERSPECTIVES ON SCHOOLS AND VALUES

In this section I will examine a sample of other perspectives that involve research on schools and values. These perspectives analyze the standard or traditional school curriculum, nontraditional programs, school climate, and social issues approaches.

The Research Base for the Traditional School Curriculum

Couldn't one argue, however, that traditional school curricula, especially in social studies and English, that inescapably involves a focus on human behavior and values, have some influence on student values and character? By the traditional school curriculum I am referring to teaching school subjects in a manner that is teacher-centered and involves extensive use of textbooks, lectures, and testing. This is, after all, the dominant pattern of instruction in American schools.

The evidence for the potential influence of traditional school curricula on student values is drawn primarily from two sources. First, in nearly every study that has attempted to evaluate the influence of MVE curricula, the comparison or control group has consisted of traditional instruction. For example, in one typical VC study, VC activities are introduced into the history curriculum. Both the treatment (VC) group and the comparison group are pre- and post-tested on a battery of values-related variables. If the traditional history curriculum has any impact it should show up as a gain in moral reasoning for the control group on the dependent variable(s). In educational research literature, one finds hundreds of studies that have assessed the influence of new innovative curricula on students' attitudes and values. One almost never encounters a statistically significant change in attitudes or values in the control groups used in these studies.

A second source of data regarding the potential for the traditional curriculum to influence attitudes or values is drawn from research on the influence of textbook biases on youth. A traditional approach to character education has been to use books that reflect traditional values or present a dominant social/moral ideology, for example, presenting traditional sex roles within family units, pointing out the positive character traits of great Americans, and the like. The assumption among pro-character advocates has been that literature or history containing pro-character themes will result in pro-character attitudes and values among students. However, this conclusion does not appear warranted when the available research is examined.

Sylvia-Lee Tibbets (1978), in a review of studies on the effects of sexist reading material on youth, concluded that the effects are "extremely individual, personal, varied, and unpredictable" (p. 167). Candace Schau and Kathryn P. Scott (1984), in one of the most complete reviews of the influence of sex role stereotyping in educational materials on sex role attitudes, found evidence for some short-term changes in gender equity attitudes, but little evidence that these changed attitudes persisted or generalized beyond the content of the materials. James Banks (1991), reviewing the effects of racially biased materials on youth, found the research to be of generally poor quality and the results equivocal.

John Guthrie (1983), in a general review of the literature on learning values from textbooks, found the tone surrounding the theme and the mindset of the reader to be the primary determinants of value formation. The theme of the text and the educators' teaching strategies determine student evaluations of material and therefore whether the material will reinforce or change an individual's values. Royal Grueneich (1982) also eschewed simple claims for the effects of biased materials on children's attitudes or values. Her review of the literature indicates that "Children virtually never form an internal representation of the story which is identical to the explicit content of the story, and furthermore, children of different ages may form different interpretations" (p. 41).

The research conducted by Hartshorne and May in the 1920s left the field of character education in apparent disarray in that it appeared that traditional directive methods of teaching for virtue did not work. The research on the recent MVE movement that examined programs that emphasized student reflection and choice, although in some cases successful at influencing reasoning related to values, failed to find any related influence on character or virtue. Is all lost? Is it possible that the values of youth lie beyond the realm of the influence of school curricula? Four additional areas of research about schools that may prove helpful in answering this question should be considered. These areas of recent research are cooperative learning strategies, community service/social action programs, just community settings, and school climate research.

The Research Base for Nontraditional Programs and Approaches

Cooperative learning

The research on cooperative learning strategies represents one of the major educational research success stories over the past decade. In cooperative learning students are placed in small groups where group learning (achievement) assumes importance and students assume responsibility not only for their own learning, but also for the learning of others. The results of this type of learning environment organization on students' achievement and positive social values and behavior are impressive. Reviews of the extensive literature on this topic, involving more than 100 studies (Johnson, Maruyama, Johnson, Nelson, and Skon, 1985, and Slavin, 1990) have found that in addition to increased academic achievement, students engaged in cooperative learning activities also developed more positive social attitudes and behavior. In general, it was found that students learned to better get along with students of other races and ethnic groups, students were found to be more accepting of mainstreamed students in the classroom, students demonstrated greater mutual concern for each other, and students were more likely to engage in prosocial behavior.

Community Service

Social action or community service programs place students outside the school and in the community where they assume participatory roles with social consequences. These roles can range from performing public service activities to direct participation in social action designed to exert a positive influence on the community. The major sources of data regarding the influence of such programs on student values and behavior come from Dan Conrad and Diane Hedin (1981, 1982), Allyce Holland and Thomas Andre (1987), Ruth Jones (1974), and Robert Rutter and Fred M. Newmann (1989). The results from these studies regarding program effects on students' sense of civic responsibility, when detected, are small. This pattern of results may be partly caused by the inability to control the nature of the students' experiences in the field setting, resulting in uneven and less than desirable experiences for many students. In addition, these programs are usually electives, and student motivation for participating in them and commitment to the programs are varied.

Just Community

Kohlberg, as a result of the growing realization that moral educators can not wait until youth reach the highest stages to be concerned about behavior and as a result of the need for schools to sanction certain behaviors, and not others, revised his perspective on moral education in the late 1970s (Kohlberg, 1978). Part of this revision incorporated an emphasis on collectively derived social norms as a goal of moral education (Power, Higgins, and Kohlberg, 1989). This emphasis on collective norms rather than the individual values grew out of Kohlberg's experiences in alternative schools where he chronicled the development of democratically derived norms required to organize the social environment necessary for group functioning.

The just community approach of Kohlberg and his associates evolved primarily within small alternative school settings, usually involving 50 or fewer students and a faculty-to-student ratio of 10 to 1 or less. In the just-community approach, within the framework of schoolwide community meetings, real problems related to social organization are confronted and discussed and decisions are reached. The result is that the group itself develops the norms by which group life is organized. For example, in a four-year study of the Cluster School in Brookline, Massachusetts, F. Clarke Power and Joseph Reimer (1978) identified four problematic areas that emerged in the life of the school: social interaction (race relations), respect for property (stealing), drug usage, and attendance (absenteeism). Through a process of collective deliberation, which included the teachers, norms were proposed, agreement reached, expectations for behavior advanced, and finally compliance with the norms enforced by the group. According to Power and Reimer, because this approach harnessed the strong motivational factor of peer pressure within a democratic context, it was found that students eventually modified anti-social behavior to comply with mutually agreed upon social norms. For the Cluster School, Power and Reimer reported group compliance in three of the four normative areas. No collective norm emerged for drug usage, in large part because the students did not share the perception of the teachers that such a norm was needed. The teachers had, in fact, adopted advocacy positions on an issue that had little salience to the students.

School Climate

Although the just-community research is based on an atypical educational setting, there are encouraging data from research on school climate in more typical school settings. One of the most extensive is the pioneering study by Patricia Minuchin, Barbara Biber, Edna Shapiro, and Hebert Zimiles (1969). They found that in progressive schools—schools that emphasize experience in peer groups such as extensive discussion group problem solving, democratic ways of social functioning, and activities designed to formulate codes of social behavior—higher levels of social conduct and moral behavior were achieved as contrasted with students from schools organized in the more traditional manner. David Boesel (1978), in the "Safe Schools Study," reported a clear relationship between school climate and organization and the rate of school violence and crime. Schools with low rates of school violence, in contrast with schools with high rates of violence, were schools where students rated classrooms as well disciplined, where school discipline was seen as fairly administered, where classroom instruction is seen as relevant and meaningful, and where students believed that they can influence what happens in their lives by their efforts rather than feeling that things happen to them that they can not control.

James Coleman, Thomas Hoffer, and Sally Kilgore (1981) in the "Private and Public Schools Study" found that the more academically effective schools, both public and private, had two characteristics in common: their structure enabled them to impose discipline, and they held high academic standards. In more effective schools, discipline was not merely imposed, but was on the whole accepted by the students as legitimate—worthy of commitment. Another large-scale study relevant to school atmosphere was conducted in England. Michael Rutter, Barbara Maughan, Peter Mortimore, Janet Ovston, and Alan Smith (1979) in *Fifteen Thousand Hours* studied 12 inner-city schools over a five-year period. The authors found, holding social background constant, substantial differences among schools in students' learning and behavior. The most important factor in explaining these differences was the school's character as a social institution. In schools that emphasized defined responsibilities of students, had a strong emphasis on academics, and provided clear incentives and rewards, students did better in school, attended more regularly, and behaved more responsibly outside of school. In the previous four studies, schools that seemed to have an impact on student character were based on an ideal of respect for the student, real student participation in the school life, the expectation that students behave responsibly, and the opportunity to do so. The discipline is not always imposed from without, but students are provided the opportunity to develop an internalized orientation.

Summing up, what we currently know from school-based research with school-aged youth about what works and what doesn't work regarding MVE and character education is as follows:

What Works:
- Moral dilemma and discussion strategies will result in small increments of growth in the stage of moral reasoning, but no change in character-related behaviors.
- Cooperative learning environments in which students assume responsibility for their own learning and behavior and the learning and behavior of others will result in positive changes in selected prosocial character traits.

- Classroom and school climates that embody such factors as clear standards, mutual respect between students and teachers, and shared governance has been found to be associated with positive student character.

What Doesn't Work:

- Values clarification appears to not influence attitudes, values, or behavior of students. The evidence regarding other decision-oriented and value-free approaches to MVE indicates they likewise are not effective in this regard.
- Traditional approaches that involve the standard curricula and moralizing by teachers do not appear to have any major influence on the development of character.

CHARACTER EDUCATION: THE APPROACH TO VALUES EDUCATION OF THE 1990s

Many Americans concerned about the values of youth have rediscovered character education. There are many historical parallels between the time periods that gave rise to character education in the 1920s and the 1980s. In both periods there was a shift in the people's thinking to a more politically conservative stance, with more conservative views regarding social stability and an emphasis on traditional values. In the 1980s the Reagan administration—through William Bennett, Secretary of Education—refocused the educational debate away from the value neutral approaches of the values education movement of the 1970s and 1980s. The major difference between the approaches of the 1970s and 1980s and the character education movement was the emphasis on the inculcation of specific character traits or virtues in children.

What is character? One influential proponent of character education, Edward Wynne (1985), defined character as follows:

> Character is simple, immediately observable, good conduct; either the performance of words or physical acts, or the refraining from certain words or acts. The good conduct involved consists of demonstrating certain virtues; tact, honesty, obeying legitimate authority, perseverance, displaying a good sense of humor, loyalty, and so on (pg.4).

Character education differs from the two approaches discussed previously in that it begins with a list of specific character traits or virtues that constitute its goals. VC and MD do not have specific virtues or character traits to instill in youth. The methods used by character educators also differ from the previous approaches. Exhortation, modeling, lectures, print and media illustrating positive values, opportunities to perform virtuous acts such as helping others, rewards for appropriate behavior, writing essays to illustrate why one should

---

Box 6–C   *Character Education*

Music teacher Carolyn Barrett is determined that her fourth graders don't grow up to imperil humankind. So, in a classroom at Lincoln Elementary School (Clovis, CA), she raises her baton and puts the tots through the usual paces. They sing about equality, racial tolerance, and reliability. "Most of all, you can count on me! me! me!" the less-than-harmonious belt out, as 40 children point at their chests. For the grand finale, the children interlock hands, sway in unison and sing, "We are the future: We stand for love."

"This class will stand for the right things," Ms. Barrett tells the children between songs. She coaxes the children to share what they think

are the right values. A boy's hand shoots up. "Not doing drugs," he say proudly. "Caring for other people," says a girl. Ms. Barrett beams.

In the classroom, Lincoln Elementary School promotes seven values—honesty, responsibility, respect, dedication, perseverance, self-respect, and concern for others. One second-grade teacher selects a value-of-the-month and a famous person who exemplifies it. Typically, one boy and one girl are picked who exhibit the traits of that value, and they are honored at monthly school assemblies.

(Adapted from Nazario, 1992).

---

adopt certain virtues, and the like are all part of the repertoire of a teacher whose goal is the development of his or her students' character. Character education gives far less attention to students' abilities to reason about their value choices. An example of what a character education classroom might look like is presented in Box 6-C.

Two major issues within the contemporary character education movement have yet to be resolved: What virtues should be taught, and what methods should be used to teach them? All the advocates of character education believe that general agreement can be reached regarding a core of basic values that compose a central part of the shared social lives of Americans. These advocates recommend that educators involve the local communities in the refining and more precise definition of these virtues into their educational goals. In Box 6-D you will find three lists of virtues proposed by contemporary proponents of character education.

LESSONS FROM THE PAST: THREE VIEWS ON HOW TO TEACH VALUES

In the mid 1920s, the National Education Association, as a result of the perception of a decaying moral situation in society, initiated a Committee on Character Education. This committee sent an inquiry to 300 cities to solicit ideals as to how character education could be improved. It was concluded from this survey:

Box 6–D   List of Virtues

William Bennett (1993)	Ed Wynne & Kevin Ryan (1993)	Thomas Lickona (1991)
compassion	justice	responsibility
self-discipline	prudence	respect
responsibility	temperance	tolerance
friendship	fortitude	prudence
work	faith	self-discipline
courage	hope	helpfulness
perseverance	charity	compassion
honesty	duty	cooperation
loyalty		courage
faith		honesty
		fairness
		democratic values

That efforts at Character Education across the country were "seemingly feverish, anxious, and even frantic in character." It was impossible to discover anybody of settled convictions as to experiences needed or subject matter preferred. There was little evidence of carefully thought-out, well-tested techniques of procedure which could be employed in securing character results. Thus while the schools of the country were giving universal and definite attention to the development of good character, there was some confusion and lack of clear knowledge as to how best to go about the problem of character education (Yulish, 1980, p. 117).

Undoubtedly, as the current character education movement gains steam, the same kind of pluralism regarding methodology will be present. If a research base to inform practice is not developed, a similar lack of clear knowledge as to how best to proceed may well again become the norm. One finds three possible approaches to the practice of character education woven through the new movement. These approaches and their limitations are discussed in the next pages.

The Traditional/Indoctrinative Approach

This approach to character education was the dominant model practiced in the movement of the 1920s and is the primary method used by pro-character social organizations today (for example, scouts, religious organizations, the military). If implemented in schools, this approach would result in students being expected to recite pledges; study the lives of great people; read morally relevant and hopefully inspiring stories, such as those found in *McGuffey's Readers* and

Horatio Alger stories; master appropriate historical perspectives; listen to vigorous moralization by teachers; participate in ceremonial occasions and public service activities; and the like. The content of character education would be a secular catechism.

That such a "character education redux" view is very much a possibility is apparent in the writings of some individuals currently advocating the new character education. Wynne (1986), for example, has stated that "...the interesting question is not 'should we preach?' Rather, it is, 'How has preaching fallen into such disrepute and how can it be revitalized?'" (p. 1). In another place Wynne (1984) argued for pledging allegiance to one's school and what it stands for, as "a good idea, and a wonderful example of the capability of the human imagination (in harnessing) the community and team building virtues of the pledge" (p. 1). Certainly such a catechistic approach can not be dismissed out of hand, for history shows that some religious groups have been able to successfully inculcate religious character in their adherents, and most historians agree that the *McGuffey's Readers* were an important factor in melding a diverse collection of immigrants into a cohesive nation.

Today one of the most popular approaches to character teaching is through the use of stories, historical or fictional, that contain morally uplifting and exemplary examples of good character. William Bennett's best selling *The Book of Virtues* is testimony to the widespread acceptance of this approach (Bennett, 1993). But the question of how character is learned from literature is not clear. Today, there are two general positions about how character education should use literature.

First, Mark Tappan and Lyn Brown (1989) have argued that children's moral storytelling creates authorship of moral choices, actions, and feelings. According to Tappan and Brown, narrative is how individuals give meaning to their life experiences. The stories of our lives are imbued with moral value, and the telling of these stories to others leads to an increased sense of moral responsibility for our actions. Effective character education from this perspective urges that teachers encourage students to tell the moral stories of their lives. Examples of the many different moral voices of children can be found in Robert Coles (1986) and Carol Gilligan (1982).

Second, Paul Vitz (1990) argues that an appreciation for the power of stories in character education has been lost. For Vitz, the focus is not the personal stories of the students, but rather the morally inspiring stories of others. He argues that there is little direct practice in morality that schools can offer for students. What is possible, from his perspective, is that students can experience moral conflict and witness morally exemplary behavior through narrative. This narrative will usually be through the study of history or of literature. Examples of how stories might be used to foster character can be found in Robert Coles (1989a) and Susan Parr (1982). To date no research supports the claims that narrative can be an effective method for character development; however, it is clearly an approach deserving careful consideration and further study. Several considerations, however, caution against an overreliance on traditional and indoctrinative methods.

The evidence that such methods have a socially beneficial effect within school contexts is minimal. The findings of Hartshorne and May have not been challenged in this regard. The most recent evidence—for example the influence of Catholic schools on student character (Benson, Donahue and Guerra, 1989), or the impact of the traditional lecture-recitation approach to the teaching of social studies on students' political attitudes (Leming, 1985)—suggests that directive approaches to character education simply do not change values and shape character-related behavior. This position should not be taken as an expression of the perspective that schooling has no effect on the values or character of growth. Clearly, the experience of schooling has an impact on the values of youth. The question I am raising is regarding the importance of the role of explicit curricular efforts in the process.

One important reason that explicit curricula may have little effect on student's values may be that the attitudes, values, and behavior that children are instructed to learn by adults frequently have little meaning or salience for the students. David P. Ausubel (1968) discussed this phenomena from the perspective of "phony concepts"—concepts used in writing or speaking without an understanding of the basic meaning. Phony concepts are learned largely through imitation or rote, and children use them solely because they pass for learning and bring rewards. Additional explanations for the failure of directive approaches to character education are the salience to youth of the issues deemed important by teachers and the potential of teachers to serve as moral examples. When high-school juniors and seniors were recently asked to list to whom they turn when making important decisions (Schultz, 1989), they listed, in order, friends (55%), parents (47%), relatives (10%), and teachers/advisors at school (5%). Another current national survey of American youth (Girl Scouts Survey of Beliefs and Moral Values of America's Children) concluded that "One finding emerges clear and strong: The issues most cited in newspaper headlines and most aggressively voiced by experts and activists as the source of youth crises are simply not an immediate concern to most children" (Coles, 1989b, p. 34). If both the message and the messenger in schools lack moral salience to students, then it appears unlikely, on the face of it, that values can be easily transmitted in this manner.

Although difficult to imagine a school where one would not teach children that cheating is wrong and helping others is good, too frequently the results of such efforts are teachers' smug righteousness, and the acquisition of phony concepts by students—knowledge without understanding or a motivational component. Another reason that these directive lessons and experiences may not "take" is that the messages may be unacceptable to the student and therefore resisted (Willis, 1977). Anyone who has ever taught in the public schools and dealt with character-related issues knows well the strong influence on youth of alternative norms based in the home or the peer group.

There is also little evidence that simply presenting information about the dangers of certain behaviors or the benefits of alternative behaviors has much of an influence on students. For example, traditional approaches to sex education and drug education have been spectacularly consistent in their inability to change in youth behavior in the desired directions (Schapps, Dibartalo, Moskowitz, Palley, and Churgin, 1981; Stout and Rivera, 1989). In addition, the mounting fear persists among many parents and educators that such efforts can have an iatrogenic impact; that is, sex education may in fact lead to greater sexual activity, and drug education to increased drug use. The values we as teachers wish to instill sometimes are not what students learn. As Richard Merelman (1980), a perceptive observer of the political socialization process, has noted, schools attempt to instill a respect for authority; however, the opposite lesson is sometimes learned. That is, repeated exposure to teacher mediocrity results in students learning a very different lesson about authority.

The Reasoning One's Way to Character Approach

One of Benjamin Franklin's many perceptive observations about Man was "So convenient a thing it is to be a reasonable creature, since it enables one to find or make a reason for everything one has a mind to do" (Franklin, 1981, p. 42). Franklin's observation is one of many possible explanations for the failure of curriculum researchers to find any significant impact on values or behavior of decision oriented approaches to MVE. Another explanation is that the content of the reasoning is typically far removed from the real-life experiences in which moral behavior occurs. A further explanation is that character is the result of habit or other nonrational motivational dynamics, not reason. For example, maintaining positive relations with others clearly motivates much of children's behavior. Approaches to MVE that emphasize rational decision making have not been shown to effectively influence character among school-aged youth. This is not to say that pedagogical approaches to character education should not accord an important place for the development of thoughtfulness, but rather that the assumptions that prior approaches have made regarding the causal relationship of reasoning to behavior need careful reanalysis.

The Classroom and School Atmosphere Approach

If there is one small finding of the Character Education Inquiry that holds promise for the informed practice of character education, it is that in incidences of deceit, differences between classrooms were the rule rather than the exception (Hartshorne and May, 1928, pp. 324–329). These differences in student behavior were also found in follow-up data collected the next year. These differences in deceit were not accounted for by differences in age, intelligence, or home background and were found regardless of the type of school (progressive or traditional). Hartshorne and May speculated that the teachers' respect for the students' personalities may have been the factor that accounted for these effective "character educators." Teacher attitude and the resultant classroom climate apparently had a significant and lasting impact on one form of moral behavior.

To sum up, the most significant factors in the school regarding character development appear to lie not within the formal school curricula and traditional approaches, but rather with the school atmosphere (what has sometimes been called the latent or hidden curriculum). Essential to the development of character, therefore, are the personal characteristics of the teacher and the role he or she assumes, the kinds of relationships he or she forms with the students, and the resultant classroom climate. In the final section of this paper I will discuss some directions that offer promise for successful character education, some potential pitfalls to be avoided, and some suggestions for future research. First, I will present a useful theoretical perspective for viewing the practice of character education that will provide a framework for the subsequent discussion.

A THEORETICAL PERSPECTIVE ON THE SCHOOLS' ROLE IN CHARACTER FORMATION

One of the many problems facing the development of effective character education is the atheoretical nature of thinking and research on the topic. Currently the writing and research in the field consists of disparate bits and pieces of sociology, philosophy, child-development research, and socio-political analyses. Although such diversity is inevitable and in some sense beneficial, a more coherent view, one that can integrate the available research, has the potential to provide the necessary focus to the movement and to guide the curriculum planning and research in a way that yields cumulative knowledge regarding the schools' role in fostering character. The best theoretical perspective to date on moral or character education is that of Émile Durkheim (1925/1973). Durkheim's perspective incorporates the social and political framework, recognizes the importance of developmental stages in children's development, and describes a learning process that is consistent with current basic and applied research on the learning of character. Durkheim argued that there were three essential elements to morality and that each of these elements requires developmentally appropriate responses by teachers and adults.

The first element is discipline. Discipline is the disposition that regularizes conduct within the totality of moral rules that operate within society. It is the willful assent to conform to the social order. Essential to the concept of discipline is the individual's propensity for regularity and, therefore, the need to yield to the moral order, and the need to restrict impulse or inclination. That is, conduct must become orderly, follow social mores, and transcend impulse and suggestion. Society requires that impulse be controlled. For civic life to succeed, the individual must be free from the incessant search for appropriate conduct. Discipline is the controlling of that impulse, the recognition of the authority of the moral law, and the willful subjugation of the individual to that law.

The second morality element is attachment to the group. According to Durkheim, discipline and the collective ideal are two reflections of the same reality. Moral authority is social in origin, so attachment to the group is society conceived as that which is desirable and good, that which attracts us. Discipline, on the other hand, is society conceived as that which commands us.

The third morality element is autonomy or self-determination. One fundamental axiom of morality is that the human being is the "sacred thing par excellence." It follows that any restriction on individual conscience is immoral because it violates individual autonomy. Durkheim avoids the apparent contradiction between individual autonomy and the necessary subjugation of the individual to the collective interest by holding that the conformity embodied in morality in its mature form is not the result of physical restraint or external imposition. Instead it is the result of individual reflection that deems conformity as good because it is judged that there exists no other alternative for social life. This recognition is not one of resignation, but rather is based upon enlightened allegiance. Liberation occurs through the individual's willful assent to society and morality, recognizing that there is no other basis for either personal or social life. This does not mean that any social arrangement is acceptable. The individual, through his or her reason, is able to judge the extent to which the moral order is based upon respect for the individual and, to the extent that it is found as such, freely conform.

The goal of moral education is, therefore, to develop in the child the elements of morality: discipline, attachment to group, and autonomy. Durkheim cautioned against viewing morality as a personal artifact whose configurations, from childhood, are totally created by the individual. He recognized that both the rational as well as the nonrational play significant roles in the moralization of the child. Durkheim suggested that among the very young, the teacher's role necessarily involves the use of some nonrational activities, for example, the use of the teacher's authority to convey rules in a powerful manner and the use of punishment to signal vigorous disapproval of the violation of moral rules. Later in the child's development, when conceptual and reasoning powers are more fully developed, the role of reasoning becomes more the teacher's province.

Durkheim does not make the mistake of assuming that what constitutes full-blown adult morality should define the goals and practice of moral education with the very young. The process of moral and character education should strive to gradually shift the child's initial deference to moral authority instilled in the early years toward an internal self-chosen moral orientation. Two attributes of young children—their suggestibility and preference for regularity—should be used by the teacher to achieve the early goals of education. Early on, according to Durkheim, the teacher must state orders regarding moral rules and social order with firmness and resolution. Through the teacher the morality of the classroom (in effect, a social group with an existing moral code) is revealed to the child. Because moral violation, the breaking of the moral code, undermines and diminishes the social morality, the teacher must clearly and forcefully censure that act to preserve the worth of the rules. Vigorous disapproval is therefore the essence of punishment.

From the Durkheimian perspective, the teacher's role is to structure the class in such a way as to ensure that moral sentiments develop and that they are reinforced through a sense of unity that grows out of common enterprise. All children have altruistic sentiments. Giving the child an idea of the group that he or she belongs to, and attaching him or her to these groups through collective life and efforts, helps to ensure that the altruistic will triumph over the egoistic and the impulsive. The love of the collective life is to be developed in the young children through (a) gradually broadening the consciousness of the child to infuse it with the ideals of the social groups to which he or she belongs, (b) linking these ideas with the greatest number of similar ideas and feelings, (c) communicating these group ideals and feelings with warmth and feeling, and (d) developing the power of moral action through exercise—group effort in the collective interest.

The classroom plays an important role in the moral education process because it represents an intermediate step between the affective morality of the family and the more impartial morality of the society; in the classroom the child begins to lose some of his or her uniqueness by being treated more impartially than in the family (Dreeben, 1968). This initial subjugation of the child to an impartial moral code is critical if the child is to develop and finally, upon reaching adulthood, function as a morally responsible manner. The school can contribute to children's moral development in a manner that the family cannot. Within the family, the bonds of solidarity are developed from blood relationship and are reinforced by constant contact and interaction. Political society, ideally constituted, is not predicated upon personal relationships. The school's proper function is to bridge the gap between the moral system of the home, based on love and intimacy, and the moral system of the society that is largely impersonal and based on collective self-interest. School is more than the transmission of knowledge and modes of thinking. If society remains only an appearance, a far off ideal to the child, then he or she is likely to call into question the devotion and sacrifice that is at the root of moral life—because the referent is unclear. Society must be fleshed out to the child. The knowledge of the social sciences and the humanities provides insights that allow the child to move to a mature morality. Morality that is originally based upon a degree of fear and deference to powerful authority gradually broadens to include attachment to groups and finally, through reason and study, develops into autonomous allegiance to the social order.

In general, contemporary research on the development of character in schools supports the developmental framework presented by Durkheim. The finding that character is fostered by clear rules, fairly enforced, and by orderly classroom and school environments, suggests that discipline is in fact an essential element of moral education. The influence on student character of cooperative learning methods and just community environments suggest mechanisms by which the school can use the dynamics of attachment to groups in a positive pro-character manner. Additionally, the newest wave of sex and drug education interventions—programs that incorporate peers, parents, and community in defining and supporting appropriate behavior—have been found to be the most effective to date in changing student behavior (Leming, 1992).

Finally, the moral dilemma discussion methodology provides a means by which schools can assist youth in developing their moral reasoning so that as adulthood approaches they develop the capacity for principled moral reasoning consistent with a respect for human rights within a democratic social framework. Clearly moral life consists of neither an endless series of moral quandaries nor rigid dispositions that remain inflexible regardless of the situation. Contemporary society contains many choices for young people where the right thing to do is not transparently clear. Deciding on the right course of action when values are in conflict, or the application of values is ambiguous, is a significant goal of character education. A recent exemplary social studies curriculum in this regard is *Reasoning with Democratic Values* (Lockwood and Harris, 1985).

PRINCIPLES FOR FUTURE PRACTICE AND RESEARCH

In the remainder of this paper I wish to present some principles that should guide practice and research in values and character education. The first of these centers on the place of reason in the development of values.

One weakness of any approach to character education that relies on student decision making such as the VC and MD approaches of recent history, is clearly evident from Durkheim's perspective as well as from the findings of recent research. Approaches that only ask youth to think about moral questions fail to teach children how they ought to behave. Young children must, as Aristotle (1981) suggested "....be brought up from childhood to feel pleasure and pain at the proper things... (p. 37)." Although reason should necessarily be a part of all character education, it must be recognized that a full understanding of our moral system and one's duties within it must await adulthood. R.S. Peters (1966) has referred to this phenomena as the paradox of moral education: "The palace of reason has to be entered through the courtyard of habit (p. 214)." A perspective on the teachers' role in the development of students' rational powers is presented later.

A second principle central to effective character education deals with the teacher's role. All teachers have a moral responsibility to control student behavior under their supervision. Through these actions, the teacher reveals the differences between what is considered good character and what is considered poor character. The methods by which teachers accomplish this responsibility are example (modeling), signaling to students approval and disapproval of their behavior, and explanation (giving reasons).

The use of example, either through one's own behavior, or by reference to that of another, is a universally agreed upon method. Bettleheim (1985) has recently captured one dynamic by which this process takes place:

> Probably the only way for an undisciplined person to acquire discipline is through admiring and emulating someone who is disciplined. This process is greatly helped if the disciple believes that even if he is not the favorite of the master, at least he is one of the favorites. Such a belief further motivates the disciple to form himself in the image of the master—to identify with him (p. 54).

The teacher must be a model for the behaviors expected of the students. Children's attention must be drawn to the appropriate behaviors as manifested in their social world, and teachers must explain, in language that children understand, the reasons for appropriate behavior(s). The teacher is not the only source of models. Literature, film, peers, and the actions of others also serve as models. For a teacher, or for anyone, to be an effective model requires that

1. He or she be perceived as possessing a high degree of competence, status, and control over resource (model saliency).
2. He or she be perceived as nurturant and caring (mutual positive affect).
3. The model and behaviors be perceived as familiar—one of us, not alien.
4. The beneficial consequences of the modeled behavior should be apparent.
5. The behaviors modeled should be shared by other salient individuals: there should be repeated exposure.

This list is adapted from Bronfenbrenner (1970) and Bandura (1977).

It is a tall order for teachers to be expected to continually exhibit morally exemplary behavior to children. Some teachers undoubtedly do not make good models for children for they lack the perceived salience, affect, or understanding of youth required. For more teachers to become effective in this regard will require a greater sensitivity on their parts to how they are perceived by students, awareness of opportunities to model or draw children's attention to proper behavior, and skill at communicating meaning regarding these events to children. Meaningful communication must inevitably mean that teachers understand the differences in language at different stages of cognitive development and be able to present arguments to students at levels that are both attractive and comprehensible. Tom Lickona's book *Raising Good Children* (Lickona, 1983) is a rich source of strategies and examples about how to effectively communicate with children, taking into account their cognitive development levels. Children should be taught and should come to accept that having good reasons for our actions is an important part of behaving in a socially acceptable manner. Children should be taught to recognize the good and also to know why it is good.

A third general principle central to the practice of effective character education relates to the concepts of school atmosphere, climate, or ethos. One of John Dewey's more cited observations is that "The school cannot be a preparation for social life, excepting as it reproduces, within itself, typical condition of social life (Dewey, 1909/1975, p. 14)." Dewey was a major critic of the directive approaches to character education in the 1920s. These approaches emphasized direct moral instruction/catechical instruction and the use of rules, slogans, creeds, codes, and pledges. Dewey argued that social order and the school atmosphere were the salient dimensions of school life for the purposes of character education. The research just discussed suggests that the ethos of schools offers a significant opportunity to influence character.

CONCLUSION

A number of factors need attention if the character education movement of the 1980s and 1990s is not to befall the same fate as the character education movement of the 20s. These factors are the quality of new curriculum, the characteristics of teachers, agreement about values to be taught, and characteristics and size of schools.

Although I recognize the need for appropriate pro-character instructional materials for use in classrooms, I am skeptical that classroom lessons alone will be of much assistance in achieving the goals of character education. One such curricula developed by the American Institute for Character Education (Goble and Brooks, 1983) is conceptually muddled and has only a weak research base. For example, the AICE curricula, though professing to be directive in spirit, frequently uses open-ended discussion methods that appeared to be borrowed from both values clarification and the moral discussion approaches. The approach now claims to be in 33,000 elementary classrooms in 45 states. Does it work? The only evidence presented by AICE is a series of glowing testimonials from school administrators from districts that have adopted the curricula. Testimonials, however, are among the weakest forms of social-science evidence, especially when used to verify causal claims.

There are, however, some encouraging efforts being made in curriculum development. One such program is the Child Development Project (Watson et al., 1989). This K to 6 program has a clear, research-based rationale and has adopted a comprehensive and multidimensional approach toward education for character development. Instruction designed to foster character takes place in the classroom, within the school at large, and in cooperation with the home and community. From an instructional perspective, the program features highlighting core values, developmental discipline involving children and adults in mutually shared expectations, opportunities for helping others, cooperative activities, and regular reflection on other points of view.

Can teachers become a significant contributing factor in developing character in youth? First, we need to recognize that little is known regarding the attributes and practices of teachers who are effective character educators. We can draw upon information from such sources as studies on modeling and autobiographic accounts of great teachers, but there are few, if any studies conducted in real schools that attempt to explain classroom differences in student character in terms of differences between teachers. Clearly such knowledge is needed if effective character education programs are to be developed. Based on our limited knowledge of modeling behavior, teacher pre-service and in-service programs will need to be developed to sensitize teachers to the appropriate behaviors and skills. Undoubtedly some teacher characteristics relevant to effective character education, for example, sensitivity and attractiveness, are less susceptible to modification than others; however, such skills as being able to develop positive classroom atmosphere and teacher communication skills are probably more malleable. One can not underestimate the importance of the type of relations that the individual teacher develops with students in his or her classroom. Attempting to add to the repertoire of skills expected of teachers must be undertaken carefully. Many teachers in the past have stayed away from values education because of the inherent political dangers, the press of the existing curriculum and accountability for cognitive outcomes, and the complex new skills necessary to master some of the classroom dynamics, such as class discussion.

There is a need at the community, state, and national levels for the practice of character education to contain some basic agreement regarding appropriate goals and practice. Character education must become an activity with clear community support, with resources provided for its implementation, and with clear rewards for teachers who take its goals seriously and develop the necessary competencies. The willy-nilly character of the 1920s movement failed to result in increased knowledge regarding the practice of character education. Some agreement must be reached regarding the central virtues that underlie character education and how those virtues can best be achieved. However, as Alan Lockwood (1991) has pointed out there are problems associated with lists of virtues; namely, contemporary life is complex and such lists do not always provide clear guidelines for action, nor do they always provide guidance about how to handle situations when values conflict. A continuing dialogue within schools, and between schools and communities, is essential to avoid fractious and debilitating debate.

Finally, the development of effective character education programs must go beyond the explicit curricula and include classroom and school atmosphere as a major focus. Schools will need to encourage greater student participation and responsibility for the organization of school life. Clear standards of student behavior must be set and students must come to appreciate the need for those standards and accept them as "fair." Participation in the creation and enforcement of these rules through democratic means will probably be the most effective way to achieve this goal. To accomplish this in schools of thousands of students may be very difficult. Smaller schools, or smaller units within schools, may be necessary for effective character education.

Reflective Questions

1. *Proponents of multicultural education suggest that we teach youth to respect the values of those from backgrounds different from ours. Can we teach that certain virtues are preferable and at the same time respect the values of others that don't share that view? How can this conflict be resolved?*

2. *Under what conditions might the teachers and administration not wish to incorporate values into the curriculum that community members want taught? What would be the best way for the school to handle this matter?*

3. *What is the best way for schools to decide which values they should teach, and which values they should not teach?*

4. *Should a teacher ever attempt to indoctrinate? When might it be appropriate and when might it not?*

5. *Are there any dangers associated with attempting to use peer-group norms to support the values education of youth? If so, what might they be, and how might they be overcome?*

6. *In what ways is character education different from values education and moral development education? What are the strengths and weaknesses of each of the approaches.*

7. *Because an approach might be proven effective, is that sufficient warrant for its adoption by a school district? If an approach has no research to support it, should a school not consider it?*

8. *What is the relationship between classroom discipline and values education? Is it possible for them to work at cross purposes? If so, in what way? How can this be avoided?*

9. *Should principles such as telling the truth be taught as absolute principles (that is, always the case) or as qualified principles (that is, sometimes the case). Explain.*

10. *Are there character issues such as sexual behavior that should not be discussed in class because of the potential privacy issues involved? If yes, explain. If no, how can the issue of privacy be handled?*

GLOSSARY

autonomy   When individuals are free to understand and accept the legitimacy of the moral rules and norms that serve as the basis of social life.

character education   An approach to education in which the primary focus is the development of virtues and patterns of conduct that are widely held in society to be worthwhile.

cognitive disequilibrium   A mental state of puzzlement or curiosity brought on by exposure to information that challenges currently held assumptions.

cognitive moral development   A psychological perspective on human development, commonly associated with Lawrence Kohlberg, that holds that under the proper conditions all individuals, over the life span, have the potential to progress through an invariant series of five stages of reasoning about moral issues.

community service   Programs in schools that involve students in the local community engaged in activities that make a positive contribution to that community.

inculcation   To teach or impress through frequent repetitions or exhortations; to fix in the mind.

indoctrination   The intentional effort to teach, as truth, concepts, or ideals about which differences of opinion exist; to attempt to get students to accept specific content regardless of the evidence.

moral values   That subset of values that are concerned with the consideration of other people's well-being and interests.

social action   Educational programs that attempt to engage the students in direct citizen action.

values   Standards and principles for judging worth; ideals that all individuals hold regarding the good, and the bad, that serve as guides for behavior.

ANNOTATED BIBLIOGRAPHY

Arbuthnot, Jack B. and David Faust (1981). *Teaching Moral Reasoning: Theory and Practice.* New York: Harper and Row.

Contains a thorough description of the theory and practice of the moral discussion approach. The book is comprehensive in its treatment of all aspects of the methodology. Contains sections on assessment of outcomes and special problems associated with implementing the approach.

Brandt, Ron, editor (1993). "Character Education" (Special Issue). *Educational Leadership* 43(4).

A collection of eighteen articles on a wide range of issues related to character education. Such topics as service learning, affective education, program descriptions, and critiques of character education are featured.

Kirshenbaum, Howard (1992). "A Comprehensive Model for Values Education and Moral Education." *Phi Delta Kappan* 73:771–776.

A current appraisal of what went wrong with the values clarification movement by a leading figure in the field during its peak period of popularity. The proposed comprehensive approach to values education is a synthesis of traditional and newer approaches. Recommendations are that values education focus on a variety of issues using a variety of approaches and take place not just within the classroom, but also involve the entire school and community.

Lickona, Thomas (1991). *Educating for Character: How our Schools can Teach Respect and Responsibility.* New York: Bantam.

This book will in all likelihood become the classic text on the character education movement of the 1990s. It opens with a discussion of the need for character education and the role that schools and the home must play in the endeavor. Next, specific strategies are presented for classroom use. The final section discusses how to create a schoolwide climate that fosters character.

Lockwood, Alan L. and David Harris (1985). *Reasoning with Democratic Values: Ethical Problems in United States History* (3 volumes). New York: Teachers College Press.

This is one of the best efforts to integrate the study of values into the U.S. history curriculum. Forty-nine cases based on true historical events show how individuals faced conflicts between basic democratic values. The cases are arranged chronologically and, are engagingly and intelligently written. The initial volume provides background and suggested activities for use in the classroom.

Power, F. Clarke, A. Higgins, and Lawrence Kohlberg (1989). *Lawrence Kohlberg's Approach to Moral Education.* New York: Columbia University Press.

The title of this book is misleading, but that should not detract from its value. This book deals only with the just community stage of Kohlberg's work in moral education. (For a guide to the moral discussion approach, see Arbuthnot and Faust cited previously.) This book contains the definitive statement of the theory, practice, and research on the just community approach. Practical examples are cited from democratic classrooms and schools.

Raths, Louis E., Merrill Harmin, and Sidney B. Simon (1978). *Values and Teaching*, 2nd. ed. Columbus, OH: Charles E. Merrill.

This is a well-written, well-organized, and thorough presentation of the theory and practice of values clarification. The emphasis is practical throughout, with many examples of lessons and descriptions of the approach in practice.

Simon, Sidney B., Leland W. Howe, and Howard Kirshenbaum (1972). *Values Clarification: A Handbook of Practical Strategies for Teachers and Students*. New York: Hart.

This volume sold more than 600,000 copies; a tribute to the interesting and engaging activities to be found within. This was the Bible for those teachers committed to values clarification in their classrooms, and contains 79 teaching strategies that have been found to be engaging to students.

Vitz, Paul C. (1990). "The Use of Stories in Moral Development: New Psychological Reasons for an Old Education Method." *American Psychologist* 45:709–720.

This article argues that narratives (stories) and narrative thinking should be the central focus for moral education. According to Vitz, the mistake of many contemporary moral education programs has been too much focus on propositional thinking and verbal discussion of abstract cases. The article is very technical at points because of the incorporation of detailed psychological literature.

Watson, Marilyn, Daniel Solomon, Victor Battistich, E. Schaps, and Judith Solomon (1989). "The Child Development Project: Combining Traditional and Developmental Approaches to Values Education." Pp. 51–92 in *Moral Development and Character Education*, edited by L. Nucci. Berkeley, CA: McCutchan.

Contains a description of one pioneering districtwide effort at character education within the K to 6 grades of the San Ramon Valley Unified School District in California. The five components of the approach (highlighting core values, developmental discipline, helping, cooperation, and understanding others) are described in detail. Examples of how the principles are put into action are presented.

REFERENCES

Arbuthnot, Jack B. and David Faust (1981). *Teaching Moral Reasoning: Theory and Practice*. New York: Harper & Row.

Aristotle (1981). *Nicomachean Ethics*. Indianapolis: Bobbs-Merrill.

Ausubel, David P. (1968). *Educational Psychology: A Cognitive View*. New York: Holt, Reinhart & Winston.

Bandura, Albert (1977). *Social Learning Theory*. Englewood Cliffs, NJ: Prentice-Hall.

Banks, James A. (1991). "Multicultural Education: Its Effects on Students' Racial and Gender Role Attitudes." Pp. 459–469 in *Handbook of Research on Social Studies Teaching and Learning*, edited by James P. Shaver. New York: Macmillan.

Bennett, William (1993). *The Book of Virtues*. New York: Simon & Schuster.

Benson, Peter L., Michael J. Donahue, and Michael G.J. Guerra (1989). "The Good News Gets Better." *Momentum* 20:40–44.

Bettleheim, Bruno (1985, November). "Punishment Versus Discipline." *Atlantic Monthly* 256(5):51–59.

Blasi, Augusto (1980). "Bridging Moral Cognition and Moral Action: A Critical Review of the Literature." *Psychological Bulletin* 88:1–45.

Boesel, David (1978). *Violent Schools–Safe Schools: The Safe-School Study Report to Congress* (ED Publication No. ED 149 464, 466). Washington, DC: U.S. Government Printing Office.

Bronfenbrenner, Uri (1970). *The Two Worlds of Childhood*. New York: Russell Sage.

Chapman, William E. (1977). *Roots of Character Education: An Exploration of the American Heritage from the Decade of the 1920s*. Schenectady, NY: Character Research Press.

Coleman, James S., Thomas Hoffer, and Sally Kilgore (1981). *Public and Private Schools*. Chicago: National Opinion Research Center.

Coles, Robert (1986). *The Moral Life of Children*. New York: Free Press.

Coles, Robert (1989a). *The Call of Stories: Teaching and the Moral Imagination*. New York: Houghton Mifflin.

Coles, Robert (1989b). *Girl Scouts Survey of the Beliefs and Moral Values of America's Children*. New York: Girls Scouts of the United States of America.

Conrad, Dan and Diane Hedin (1981). *Executive Summary of the Final Report of the Experiential Education Project*. St. Paul: University of Minnesota, Center for Youth Development and Research.

Conrad, Dan and Diane Hedin (1982). "The Impact of Experiential Education on Adolescent Development." *Child and Youth Services* 4(3–4):57–76.

Dewey, John (1909/1975). *Moral Principles in Education*. Carbondale and Edwardsville: Southern Illinois University Press.

Dreeben, Robert (1968). *On What is Learned in School*. Reading, MA: Addison-Wesley.

Durkheim, Emil (1925/1973). *Moral Education*. Glencoe, IL: Free Press.

Enright, Robert, Daniel Lapsley, and Victor Levy (1983). "Moral Education Strategies." Pp. 43–83 in *Cognitive Strategy Research: Educational Applications*, edited by Michael Pressley and Joel Levin. New York: Springer-Verlag.

Fraenkel, Jack R. (1976). "The Kohlberg Bandwagon: Some Reservations." *Social Education* 40:216–222.

Franklin, Benjamin (1981). *The Autobiography of Benjamin Franklin.* New York: Random House.

Gilligan, Carol (1982). *In a Different Voice: Psychological Theory and Women's Development.* Cambridge, MA; Harvard University Press.

Goble, F.G. and B.D. Brooks (1983). *The Case for Character Education.* Ottawa, IL: Green Hill Publishers.

Grueneich, Royal (1982). "Issues in the Developmental Study of How Children Use Intention and Consequence Information to Make Moral Evaluations." *Child Development* 53:29–43.

Guthrie, John T. (1983). "Learning Values from Textbooks." *Journal of Reading* 26:574–576.

Hartshorne, Hugh and Mark May (1928–1930). *Studies in the Nature of Character.* Vol. 1, *Studies in Deceit.* Vol. 2, *Studies in Self Control.* Vol. 3, *Studies in the Organization of Character.* New York: Macmillan.

Holland, Allyce and Thomas Andre (1987). "Participation in Extracurricular Activities in Secondary School: What is Known, What Needs to be Known?" *Review of Educational Research* 57:437–466.

Johnson, David W., Geoffrey Maruyama, Roger T. Johnson, Deborah Nelson, and Leron Skon (1981). "Effects of Cooperative, Competitive and Individualistic Goal Structures on Achievement: A Meta-Analysis." *Psychological Bulletin* 89:47–62.

Jones, Ruth S. (1974). "Changing Student Attitudes: The Impact of Community Participation." *Social Science Quarterly* 55:439–450.

Kohlberg, Lawrence (1966). "Moral Education in the School." *School Review* 74:1–30.

Kohlberg, Lawrence (1978). "Revisions in the Theory and Practice of Moral Development." Pp. 52–73 in *New Directions for Child Development: Moral Development*, edited by W. Damon. New York: Wiley.

Kohlberg, Lawrence and Daniel Candee (1984). "The Relationship of Moral Judgment to Moral Action." Pp. 498–581 in *Essays on Moral Development*, Volume II, *The Psychology of Moral Development*, edited by Lawrence Kohlberg. New York: Harper and Row.

Lawrence, J.A. (1980). "Moral Judgment Intervention Studies Using the Defining Issues Test." *Journal of Moral Education* 9:178–191.

Leming, James S. (1981). "Curricular Effectiveness in Moral/Values Education: A Review of Research." *Journal of Moral Education* 10:147–164.

Leming, James S. (1985). "Research on Social Studies Curriculum and Instruction. Interventions and Outcomes in the Socio-Moral Domain." Pp. 123–213 in *Review of Research in Social Studies Education: 1976–1983*, edited by W.B Stanley. Washington, DC: National Council for the Social Studies and Social Science Education Consortium.

Leming, James S. (1987, April). *Values Clarification Research: A Study of the Etiology of a Weak Educational Research Program.* Paper presented at the meeting of the American Educational Research Association, Washington, DC.

Leming, James S. (1992). "The Influence of Contemporary Issues Curricula on School-Aged Youth." Pp. 100–151 in *Review of Research in Education*, edited by G. Grant. Washington, DC: American Educational Research Association.

Lickona, Thomas (1991). *Educating for Character: How Our Schools Can Teach Respect and Responsibility.* New York: Bantam.

Lickona, Thomas (1983). *Raising Good Children: From Birth Through the Teenage Years.* New York: Bantam.

Lockwood, Alan L. (1991). "Character Education: The Ten Percent Solution." *Social Education* 55:246–248.

Lockwood, A.L. (1978). "The Effects of Values Clarification and Moral Development Curricula on School Age Subjects: A Critical Review of Recent Research. *Review of Educational Research* 48:325–364.

Lockwood, A.L. and David Harris (1985). *Reasoning with Democratic Values: Ethical Problems in United States History* (3 volumes). New York: Teachers College Press.

Merelman, Richard M. (1980). "Democratic Politics and the Culture of American Education." *The American Political Science Review* 74:319–332.

Metcalf, Lawrence E., editor (1971). *Values Education: Rationale, Strategies and Procedures.* Washington, DC: National Council for the Social Studies.

Minuchin, P., E. Biber, E. Shapiro, and H. Zimiles (1969). *The Psychological Impact of School Experiences.* New York: Basic Books.

Nazario, S.L. (September 11, 1992), "Right and Wrong." *The Wall Street Journal.*

Oliver, Donald W. and James P. Shaver (1966). *Teaching Public Issues in the High School.* Boston: Houghton Mifflin.

Parr, Susan R. (1982). *The Moral of the Story: Literature, Values and American Education.* New York: Teachers College Press.

Peters, Robert S. (1966). *Ethics and Education.* Glenview, IL: Scott Foresman.

Power, F. Clarke, A. Higgins, and Lawrence Kohlberg (1989). *Lawrence Kohlberg's Approach to Moral Education.* New York: Columbia University Press.

Power C. and J. Reimer (1978). "Moral Atmosphere: An Educational Bridge Between Moral Judgment and Action." In *New Directions for Child Development* (No. 2), edited by William Damon. San Francisco: Jossey Bass.

Raths, Louis E., Merrill Harmin, and Sidney B. Simon (1966). *Values and Teaching.* Columbus, OH: Charles E. Merrill.

Raths, Louis E., Merrill Harmin, and Sidney B. Simon (1978). *Values and Teaching,* 2nd ed. Columbus, OH: Charles E. Merrill.

Rest, James R. (1979). *Development in Judging Moral Issues.* Minneapolis: University of Minnesota Press.

Rutter, M., B. Maughan, P. Mortimore, J. Oriston, and A. Smith (1979). *Fifteen Thousand Hours.* Cambridge, MA: Harvard University Press.

Rutter, R.A. and F.M. Newmann (1989). "The Potential of Community Service to Enhance Civic Responsibility." *Social Education* 53:371–374.

Schapps, E., R. Dibartalo, J. Moskowitz, C. Palley, and S. Churgin (1981). "A Review of 127 Drug Abuse Prevention Program Evaluations." *Journal of Drug Issues* 11:17–43.

Schau, C.G. and K.P. Scott (1984). "Impact of Gender Characteristics of Instructional Materials: An Integration of the Research Literature." *Journal of Educational Psychology* 76:183–193.

Schlaefli, Andre, James R. Rest, and Stephen J. Thoma (1985). "Does Moral Education Improve Moral Judgment? A Meta-Analysis of Intervention Studies Using the Defining Issues Test." *Review of Educational Research* 55:319–352.

"Schools' Role in Developing Character." (1986). (Special issue). *Educational Leadership* 43(4) (Entire issue).

Schultz, John B. (1989). "AHEA's Survey of American Teens." *Journal of Home Economics* 81:27–38.

Simon, Sidney B., Lelane Howe, and Howard Kirschenbaum (1972). *Values Clarification: A Handbook of Practical Strategies.* New York: Hart.

Slavin, Robert (1990). *Cooperative Learning: Theory, Research and Practice*. Englewood Cliffs, NJ: Prentice Hall.

Stout, James W. and Frederick P. Rivera (1989). "Schools and Sex Education: Does it Work?" *Pediatrics* 83:375–379.

Tappan, Mark B. and Lyn M. Brown (1989). "Stories Told and Lessons Learned: Toward a Narrative Approach to Moral Development and Moral Education." *Harvard Education Review* 59:192–205.

Tibbetts, Sylvia Lee (1978). "Wanted: Data to Prove that Sexist Reading Material has an Impact on the Reader." *Reading Teaching* 30:158–165.

Vitz, Paul C. (1990). "The Use of Stories in Moral Development: New Psychological Reasons for an Old Education Method." *American Psychologist* 45:709–720.

Watson, M., D. Solomon, V. Battistich, E. Schaps, and J. Solomon (1989). "The Child Development Project: Combining Traditional and Developmental Approaches to Values Education." Pp. 51–92 in *Moral Development and Character Education*, edited by L. Nucci. Berkeley, CA: McCutchan.

Willis, Peter (1977). *Learning to Labor*. New York: Columbia University Press.

Wynne, Edward (1984). "Another Pledge of Allegiance." *Character II* 3(5):1.

Wynne, Edward (1985). "A Definition of Character." *Character II* 4(6):4.

Wynne, E. (1986). "The Relevance of Preaching." *Character II* 5(3):5.

Wynne, E. and K. Ryan (1993). *Reclaiming our Schools: A Handbook on Teaching Character, Academics, and Discipline*. New York: Merrill.

Yulish, Stephen M. (1980). *The Search for a Civic Religion: A History of the Character Education Movement in America, 1890–1935*. Washington, DC: University Press of America.

Chapter Seven

THE CHALLENGE OF A GLOBAL AGE

Jan L. Tucker and Anna M. Evans
Florida International University

> In the final analysis, our most common link is the fact that we all inhabit this planet. We all breathe the same air. We all cherish our children's future. And we are all mortal.
>
> John F. Kennedy

FOUR TYPES OF ISSUES WILL BE ADDRESSED in this chapter: philosophical, historical, political, and practical. These issues are framed by four questions. First, what is education for a global perspective? Second, why has education for a global perspective emerged as a strong force in education in the United States? Third, should the social studies help to develop a global perspective for students? Fourth, how can the social studies contribute to the development of a global perspective? The terms *education for a global perspective* and *global education*, although differing in exact meaning, shall be used interchangeably.

WHAT IS EDUCATION FOR A GLOBAL PERSPECTIVE?

The conclusive answer to the question of what is education for a global perspective has not been settled, but that is not surprising because it is a comparatively new field. Definitional questions in education are numerous and generally difficult to resolve, but the process of education manages to develop nonetheless. Indeed, the field of social studies itself, although dating back to the early years of the century, is still struggling with questions of definition. The basic philosophical question about global education is whether it is a curriculum or whether it is a social movement.

Global Education as a Curriculum

In 1977, Ernest L. Boyer, United States Commissioner of Education, established the Task Force on Global Education to examine the national need for global perspectives in education. Following two years of extensive data collection and discussion, the report concluded that there was a need (U.S. Commissioner of Education's Task Force on Global Education, 1979). The Report defined global education as occurring through

> [L]earning experiences, formal or informal, that increase the individual's ability to understand his or her condition, in the community and in the world. It includes the study of nations, cultures, and peoples, with a focus on understanding how these are interconnected, how they change, and what the individual's responsibility is in this process. It draws on the various disciplines and expands them to meet changing circumstances. It provides the opportunity to develop realistic perspectives on world issues, problems, and prospects, and awareness of the relationships between enlightened self-interest and the concerns of people throughout the world, and the basic knowledge and skills essential for life in a global age (p. 4).

The federal recommendations included a special program of incentive grants and contracts to improve and expand education for a global perspective. The report, however, got lost in the shuffle of presidential administrations. In November 1980, Ronald Reagan defeated Jimmy Carter in the presidential election, and the national government's support for global education ended—at least for the time being. Nevertheless, programs in global education at the local and state levels sprang up around the country, and these programs developed definitions of global education not unlike the one contained in the U.S. Commissioner's Report.

The State Plan for Global Education in Florida (Florida Department of Education, 1982), accepted by the Florida State Board of Education as a framework for developing global education programs at the local level, defined global education as a curriculum and a process that

Provide students and individuals with the knowledge, skills, and attitudes which are necessary for them to meet their responsibility as citizens of their community, state, and nation in an increasingly interdependent and complex global society. In addition, education for a global perspective includes at least the following components:

- The ability to conceptualize and understand the complexities of the international system;
- A knowledge of world cultures and international events; and
- An appreciation of the diversities and commonalties of human values and interests.

The goal of global education is to expand an individual's perception of the world. Persons with a global awareness are sensitive to the multicultural and transnational nature of the human condition. They exhibit an intellectual curiosity about the world that transcends local and national boundaries.

The Michigan *Guidelines for Global Education* (Michigan Department of Education, n.d.) described global education as student outcomes and suggested specific means by which schools can help students reach these goals:

Global education in a school system will equip the student with an understanding and an awareness of global interdependence by providing encouragement and opportunity to

- Acquire a basic knowledge of various aspects of the world: geographic, cultural, racial, linguistic, economic, political, historical, artistic, scientific, and religious.
- Develop a personal value and behavior system based on a global perspective....
- Understand problems and potential problems that have global implications.
- Explore solutions for global problems.
- Develop a practical way of life based on global perspectives.
- Plan for alternative futures.
- Participate responsibly in an interdependent world.

The Florida and the Michigan plans both emphasized the *infusion* of a global perspective into the existing curriculum across all subject areas, including social studies. New York, by contrast, developed a curriculum plan more specific to the social studies (New York State Education Department, 1987).

In New York students are offered a two-year course of study called *Global Studies:*

The [New York] syllabus for grades 9–10 provides students with the opportunity to study other nations and their cultures within a framework that is designed to develop a global perspective. This approach aims to cultivate in students knowledge, skills, and attitudes needed to function effectively in a world characterized by ethnic diversity, cultural pluralism, international and domestic violence, and increasing interdependence....

An even more explicit emphasis upon global and multicultural education in the social studies was recommended recently in New York amidst a storm of public controversy (New York State Social Studies Review and Development Committee, 1991).

One Nation, Many Peoples: A Declaration of Cultural Interdependence affirmed that:

> Beginning in the earliest grades social studies should be taught from a global perspective. The earth is humankind's common home. Migration is our common history. The earth's peoples, cultures, and material resources are our common wealth. Both humankind's pain and humankind's triumphs must be shared globally. The uniqueness of humankind is our *many ways of being human*, our remarkable range of cultural and physical diversity within a common biological unity (p. 1).

Willard Kniep (1989) developed a global curriculum framework that was adopted by the National Council for the Social Studies as one of three alternative approaches for organizing the social studies curriculum from kindergarten through the twelfth grade. The Kniep model is the most extensive and detailed statement regarding the relationship of a global perspective as it could be incorporated into the social studies curriculum. He recommended a curriculum organized around four essential elements of study: systems, including economic, political, ecological, and technological systems; human values, both universal and diverse values; persistent issues and problems, including local, national, regional, and global problems; and global history. Five conceptual themes are included in the Kniep curriculum: interdependence, change, culture, scarcity, and conflict. These concepts serve as curriculum organizers because they "are essential to the development of a global perspective" (p. 401).

Global Education as a Social Movement

Some global educators characterize global education as a social movement rather than a curriculum. Lee Anderson (1990) argues that global education is unlike subject specializations such as mathematics education, science education, foreign-language education, or social studies education. Rather, according to Anderson, global education is

> [A] reform movement within contemporary American education that seeks to alter schools, universities, and non-formal educative institutions in ways that provide children and adults with the basic intellectual competencies needed to deal effectively and responsibly with a twin reality of American life. That reality...is the fact that the United States is becoming an increasingly globalized society embedded in a world that as a whole is becoming increasingly interconnected and interdependent as a consequence of the growth of worldwide ecological, economic, political, cultural, and technological systems (p. xvii).

Those who view global education as a social movement are apt to link their work in the schools with a set of values related to perceived changes taking place in the world. Barbara Benham Tye and Kenneth Tye (1992), in describing their work in the Orange County, California, schools observed

> It is clear that global education is a value-oriented movement in that it is part of a larger societal change which involves a new view of how our nation (or any nation) relates to the rest of the world....
>
> This move away from a competitive, individualistic view of the world toward a more interdependent, cooperative one is a major change for our society. However, viewed from the perspective of other values we hold—cooperation, democracy, fair play, the golden rule, and the like—it is not. The idea that global education is somehow a left-wing movement is simply wrong. It draws on rich cultural themes deeply imbedded in the fabric of our society....Marxist theory calls for a radical rupture with the past while American society has a tradition of social movement which builds on that which goes before. Global education is one current manifestation of such a social movement (p. 67).

Global education conceived as a social movement rather than a specific curriculum spawns certain corollaries. Possibly the most important is that global education can become a mechanism for implementing change at a school level, encompassing the activities and the actors in one school or collection of schools such as a high school and its feeder-pattern middle and elementary schools. Such an approach requires great emphasis on the leadership of the school principal and lead teachers in combination with extensive staff development, student and parent involvement, networking, clinical support and public information. Global education as a social movement is labor-intensive, localized, and likely to be an interdisciplinary effort involving the participation of many individuals both inside and outside the school.

Global education defined as a social movement tends to annoy educators whose interest is mainly in curriculum—for example, social studies educators who see the separate disciplines of history and the various social sciences as the basis of the social studies curriculum. Their objections range from anxiety about zealousness and indoctrination to worries that the integrity of disciplines such as United States history may be at risk within a global education environment.

Concerns about global education as a social movement are analogous to disagreements about the origins of social studies itself. Conventional wisdom holds that the social studies owes its existence to a culminating consensus on differing approaches to teaching history—as described in the landmark 1916 NEA report on social studies in secondary school. David Warren Saxe (1992, p. 272) argues, however, that "the real foundations of social studies must push...back into the formation of the social welfare *movement* [emphasis added] in the 19th century." If global education as a social movement is a contemporary extension of social studies as a social movement—as a dynamic field of study for cultivating civic competence in a global age—then, "the history of social studies," as Saxe suggests, "is just beginning" (p. 273).

The question of whether global education is a curriculum or a social movement is important and should be carefully considered by every teacher. But the classroom application of global education does not require that there be mutually exclusive positions on the issue. One can believe that global education is primarily a curriculum and be a very fine teacher. Or, one may believe that global education is a social movement and also be a fine teacher. A mature teacher must take into consideration the strengths and weaknesses of each point of view. A good global teacher must be able to create and practice the curriculum manifestations of global philosophy. And a good global teacher must be able to determine the philosophical implications of concrete curriculum applications. Although starting at different points, two teachers could easily end up doing similar things in the classroom. The concepts and practices of global education are dynamic, and the global teacher changes with new experiences and new insights—just like the world itself.

WHY HAS EDUCATION FOR A GLOBAL PERSPECTIVE EMERGED AS A FORCE IN EDUCATION IN THE UNITED STATES?

Social Foundations of Global Education

By formulating the scientific concept of culture and destroying the myth of race as a determinant of behavior, cultural anthropologists beginning in the 1920s laid the intellectual foundations for global education. Franz Boas, Ruth Benedict, Margaret Mead, and their colleagues provided a "scientific basis for dealing with the crucial dilemma of the world today: how can peoples of different appearance, mutually unintelligible languages, and dissimilar ways of life get along peaceably together" (Kluckhohn, 1949, p.1)? This understanding of ourselves as a species capable of creating and carrying culture opened the way for thinking and believing more inclusively about the world. But it was not until the 1960s and 1970s that the image of a global perspective burst upon our consciousness. Visionary thinkers, best-selling books, and unexpected events sharpened and expanded our *weltanschauung*.

Rachel Carson (1962) astonished the public with the harmful consequences of the use of pesticides. Marshall McLuhan (1964) described a global village with its people linked through communications technology. Pierre Teilhard de Chardin (1964) wrote of the convergence of human aspirations and history into the *noosphere*—a progressive unification of humankind and intensification of our collective consciousness. Barbara Ward (1965) and R. Buckminster Fuller (1969) conceived the metaphor of Spaceship Earth as a closed life-support system with its inhabitants accelerating through time and space dependent upon each other for survival. Paul Ehrlich (1968) called our attention to the stunning exponential growth rate of world population and impending ecological catastrophe. Alvin Toffler (1970) warned of impending future shock. Barbara Ward and René Dubos (1972) coined the now-familiar notion of "thinking globally, acting locally." The Club of Rome (1972) ignited a global controversy regarding the rapid depletion of our nonrenewable resources. And biologist Lewis Thomas (1974) portrayed Earth as a single living cell.

Critical events on a global scale played an important role in raising our consciousness. In 1963, people around the world witnessed on broadcast television the assassination of President John F. Kennedy and the subsequent murder of his accused killer, Lee Harvey Oswald—events that still deeply trouble the nation. In 1968, offshore drilling failures washed vast quantities of crude oil onto Santa Barbara's unspoiled beaches and initiated a public outcry. Throughout the 1960s, American astronauts and Soviet cosmonauts reported on the radiant beauty of Earth as seen from space. In the winter of 1972–1973, angry motorists spent hours waiting for a gasoline fill-up as a consequence of the global oil embargo by the member nations of the Organization of Petroleum Exporting Countries (OPEC). This new public awareness of global interdependence was bound to find its way into education. The concept of global education for the schools began to take shape.

Global Education Emerges in the Schools

The idea of global education in the schools was introduced in a landmark report by the Foreign Policy Association, funded by the U.S. Office of Education, entitled *An Examination of Objectives and Priorities in International Education in U.S. Secondary and Elementary Schools* (Becker, 1968).* The

---

* Jan Tucker attended the Northern California Curriculum Conference, Sausalito, September 28–30, 1968, where James Becker and Lee Anderson introduced the report of the Foreign Policy Association. Tucker's most vivid memory of the conference is the skeptical response to the report by the participants who were preoccupied with the stunning life events around them in 1968: the assassinations of Martin Luther King, Jr. in Memphis and Robert Kennedy in Los Angeles; the race riots in American cities, including Washington, D.C.; the violence surrounding the Democratic National Convention in Chicago; the student anti-war protests on the campuses of the San Francisco Bay Area and the brutal police reactions. The year 1968 was a precarious environment for the introduction of global education and serves today as a powerful reminder of the influence of contemporary societal events on educational change. The Sausalito participants were in no mood to hear about global interdependence when across the Bay college students were soon to face the bayonets of the National Guard—even though those very local events were the direct consequence of our involvement in Vietnam.

report argued that revolutionary changes on a global scale had outpaced a static curriculum and that the concept of "international" was losing its accuracy and utility. "The change from a collection of many lands and people to a system of many lands and peoples," according to Anderson (1968), "was a profound change in the human condition." It became clear that a new term was needed to describe the changes. The idea of global education was born.

Other important voices added their convictions to the transformation. Harold Taylor (1969) urged teachers to use the world as the main context for their profession and as the principal content for their classroom instruction. Edwin O. Reischauer (1973), prominent historian of East Asian civilization, argued for a fundamental restructuring of education.

> A...basic reform in education will be necessary. This I believe should be a conscious effort to get away from the assumed, even if unspecified, unit of our own nation and its culture as the almost exclusive focus of education. To put it in more positive terms, we should broaden the focus to include all humanity and the whole of the human experience....(p. 182).

Another important step toward the idea of global education was the publication of *Schooling for a Global Age* (Becker, 1979). Leading educators, including Lee and Charlotte Anderson, John Goodlad, Bruce Joyce, David King, Robert Leestma, Judith Torney, and Ken Tye, marshaled a powerful prescription for introducing a global perspective into the school curriculum. Despite a national legacy of isolationism, Horatio Alger righteousness, ethnocentrism and a domestic marketing outlook, Goodlad was optimistic:

> Many national educational organizations representing teachers, administrators, and policy makers have explicitly committed themselves to furthering the aims of global education. The local, state, and national context for global education grows more promising (Becker, 1979, xvi).

Another influential volume was *International Human Rights and International Education* (Buergenthal and Torney, 1976). Based on the 1974 UNESCO *Recommendation Concerning Education for International Understanding, Co-operation and Peace and Education Relating to Human Rights and Fundamental Freedoms*, the authors placed emphasis upon the importance of the study of international human rights in the schools (p. 152–162).

Professional education organizations, including the National Council for the Social Studies (1981), adopted policy statements that urged schools to become effective agents of citizen education for a global age. The social studies program was assumed to have a special leadership responsibility for this important task (Remy, Nathan, Becker, and Torney, 1975):

> It is important that social studies educators become increasingly self-conscious about the images of the world which underlie their teaching—that is, their own

world view. In addition, it is important that they have an understanding of the process of children's learning about the world outside the United States (p. 3).

Global Education After the Cold War

Fundamental global changes occurred in the late 1980s and early 1990s that accelerated the introduction of global education into the schools. "Future historians almost certainly will hail the last years of this century as a watershed in world affairs," stated Zbigniew Brzezinski (1989, p. 6), head of the National Security Council during the Carter administration. In response Thomas H. Kean (National Governors' Association, 1989), former governor of New Jersey, observed "We must make international education a priority in this country. I have no illusions about the difficulty involved in this. But neither do I doubt the consequences if we do not. America can't afford to wait a generation."

William Jefferson (Bill) Clinton (Tye and Tye, 1992), then Governor of Arkansas and Democratic candidate for President, representing the first of the 50 states to mandate global education, wrote,

> As the world continues to grow smaller and more interdependent, there is a greater need for global education. Our economic, political, social, and environmental systems have become interconnected to such a degree that we must develop a world awareness. This means understanding the interconnectedness of world systems as well as different values and points of view (p. xi).

Albert Gore (1992), then Senator from Tennessee and Democratic Vice-Presidential candidate, identified the rapid deterioration of the global ecology as our primary security threat. He held that the future and education should play a major role in restoring the balance.

> For civilization as a whole, the faith that is so essential to restore the balance now missing in our relationship to the Earth is the faith that we do have a future. We can believe in that future and work to achieve it and preserve it, or we can whirl blindly on, behaving as if one day there will be no children to inherit our legacy. The choice is ours; the earth is in the balance (p. 368).

Global Realities Within the United States

With a window on the world, students gain an informed and informal global perspective, geographic literacy, language skills, and cultural sensitivity (Morton, 1991). The wide distribution of education has given more people an introduction to many forms of data, thus greatly enhancing the possibility of innovation for the well-being of many societies. In the United States, integrating global realities within an existing social studies curriculum meets the needs of an ever-changing, ethnically diverse, increasingly interdependent, international community. As mentioned earlier in this chapter, global education responds to a number of events on the world stage: the environmental crisis, shortages, the population explosion, the influx of refugees, terrorism, human rights, worldwide inflation, just to name a few. All of these events manifest that activities outside of our national borders increasingly affect the daily lives of our people, and events in our society affect people in other countries (Alger and Harf, 1986).

Responding to the global realities as they occur is a necessity for the survival of any group of people. In 1958, after the launch of the Russian satellite, Sputnik, the United States recognized the global reality that its citizenry might not be competitive, in as much as they may have lacked some skills. The federal government provided federal funds to improve instruction in mathematics, science, and modern language as an answer to a global reality (Armstrong, Henson, and Savage, 1989).

Robert W. Ritchey (1973) contended that:

> The National Defense Education Act represents an expression of the federal government's concern over the fact that the long struggle of the free world against communism could be won or lost in the classroom. Particular interest was shown first in improving mathematics, science, and foreign language instruction and then extending the work to civics, history, geography, and reading. Thus the federal government encouraged improvement in these and other educational areas by offering financial incentives to the states (pp. 410–411).

The demographical "browning of America" and the United States' hope of recapturing its global economic and technological dominance are global realities and are often given as reasons why innovative curriculum infusions or social movements such as global education are now receiving serious attention (Henry, 1990). The discussion of race, class, migration, gender issues, and other topics of this nature are increasingly more popular to the general population.

The world is becoming smaller every day, and a greater knowledge of our global community is fundamental. Studying population dynamics should broaden perspectives and assist people with understanding the interconnectedness of each society (Hodgkinson, 1985). Listed here are census data from the 1990 United States Census.

The population of the United States in 1990 was 248.7 million people (*World Almanac Book of Facts* 1992, 1991):

- Asian/Pacific Islanders are the fastest growing minority group. In 1990, this group accounted for 2.9 percent of the population, up from 1.5 percent of the population in 1980. During the 1990 United States Census, 7.3 million people identified themselves as Asian/Pacific Islander.
- The nation's Hispanic population growth exceeded that of the Asian/Pacific Islander in total numbers, but not in percentages. Hispanics

grew from 6.4 percent in 1980 to 9 percent of the population in 1990. The total Hispanic population is 22.4 million people.

- The percentage of Black Americans increased from 11.7 in 1980 to 12.1 in 1990, or 30 million people.
- The American Indian, Eskimo, Aleut population grew from .6 percent in 1980 to .8 percent in 1990, or two million people.
- Approximately 25 percent of the United States growth comes from immigration; the remainder of the United States population growth comes from births.

Global education advocates and multiculturalists must be reminded that the two entities are not mutually exclusive. Both educational formats should stand for freedom and universal values, essential concepts in today's ethnically polarized and troubled world. There would not be any multiculturalism without global education. Rose Duhohn-Sells (1991) wrote that the culturally diverse populations of this country should be used to strengthen the fiber of America in preparation for the twenty-first century. The richness of each ethnic group can contribute to creating a nucleus of knowledge that will be beneficial to all. With the growing minority populations, America is the "Land of Many Nations."

In 1990, the population of the world was: 56 percent Asian; 21 percent European descent; 9 percent African; and 8 percent Latino (South American). The United States has a constituency that represents every racial and cultural group from around the world. From the 1990 world census, 6 percent of the global population is North American (*World Almanac Book of Facts* 1992, 1991).

Claire Gaudiani (1991) contends that the

[L]ast decade has seen the development of a borderless global economy, the shift from a bipolar economy to a multi-polar power structure, and the expansion of a global environmental science and telecommunications systems. As this new globally interdependent period emerges, the case for global multicultural education seems clear. Nevertheless, resistance to diversifying the curriculum remains strong (p. 124).

Teachers educating for the twenty-first century should encourage students to become active participants in a pluralistic democracy by instilling the civic virtues necessary for personal liberty in a global community (Guadiani, 1991). Social studies should be aimed primarily at teaching young people to be responsible future global citizens in a multicultural society. The social studies program is responsible to the young people for their potential influence on educational policy as adults, their function as parents and informed citizens of their states, nations, and the emerging global community. When the social studies is taught, the teacher can stimulate one's awareness to situations in the global arena.

In the post-Cold War era, the question "Should global education be included in social studies?" has run its course. Being curious about the world and being an American are no longer incompatible; in today's world of interdependence and cultural pluralism, the two are congruent and mutually reinforcing.

SHOULD THE SOCIAL STUDIES HELP STUDENTS DEVELOP A GLOBAL PERSPECTIVE?

Many social studies teachers are skeptical about using social studies content as a vehicle for developing a global perspective, despite strong leadership by professional organizations such as the National Council for the Social Studies (NCSS, 1994) and the Association for Supervision and Curriculum Development (Anderson, Nicklas, and Crawford, 1994).

NCSS maintained that to achieve excellence in social studies:

> Students should be helped to construct a *global perspective* that includes knowledge, skills, and commitments needed to live wisely in a world that possesses limited resources and that is characterized by cultural diversity. A global perspective involves viewing the world and its people with understanding and concern. This perspective develops a sense of responsibility for the needs of all people and a commitment to finding just and peaceful solutions to global problems (p. 7).

Goodlad (1984) reported, however, that the typical social studies program offered very little global content. More than half the students believed "that foreign countries and their ideas are dangerous to American government."

> [Many social studies teachers] appeared not to have sorted out the curricular and instructional ingredients of a social studies program designed to ensure understanding and appreciation of the United States as a nation among nations and its relationship to the social, political, and economic systems of other countries (pp. 212–213).

The gap between the exponential rate of change in global realities and the capacity of social studies programs to deal with these changes has widened in recent years—despite efforts by scattered schools and educators to deal with the problem. Probably, as Goodlad suggested, the reticence of social studies teachers to be more assertive "merely reflects ambiguity in the surrounding society regarding our nation's role in a world of growing interdependence—the world in which our people live and will live as adults" (p. 213).

Tye and Tye (1992, p. 103) reported a broad spectrum of attitudes by teachers generally toward global education. Those attitudes indicative of acceptance for global education ranged from a cautious "needs to see that global education is politically safe" to an enthusiastic "open to the idea of global education, open to exploring new things, will do extra work." Attitudes reflecting resistance to global education began with a comparatively mild "being too busy with other innovative ideas" to an intense ideological belief "that global education is un-American and/or a secular humanist plot."

Vestiges of the "we versus they" mentality of Cold War still exist in the nation, and global education in certain areas may still be perceived as a subversive, "one-world" approach to social studies education. According to Steven L. Lamy (1988), world views may be classified as system-maintenance, system reformation, and system transformation. System transformers can represent political opposites: the alternative left and the alternative right.

During the mid-1980s, some global education programs came under very heavy attack from the alternative right, including the Center for Teaching International Relations (CTIR), University of Denver, one of the oldest and most respected centers for global education research and development. Thomas G. Tancredo, representative of the United States Department of Education in the Denver regional office, commissioned a study of CTIR that was published as "Blowing the Whistle on Global Education." (Cunningham, 1986). The study characterized CTIR global education materials as biased toward "naive world order values such as peace, social justice, and economic unity" (Tye and Tye, 1992, p. 63).

During the Cold War, global education was characterized sometimes by the alternative right as a left-wing variety of system transformation—as un-American. These charges were untrue at the time, and as Anderson (1990, p. 33) has pointed out, the world has shifted and education for a global perspective is now mainstream, conventional stuff. Indeed, in some parts of the world, global education may be viewed by educators as system maintenance—an attempt to preserve American economic and cultural dominance in the world. Within the United States, however, the ideological argument is between the radical right and system reformers—between those who wish to create an authoritarian political and economic system and those who seek cooperative multilateral efforts aimed at responding to inequities in the global system. With the end of the Cold War, these right-wing attacks on global education have diminished, and the radical right has shifted most of its attention to criticisms of multicultural education.

Even during the Cold War, most surveys of social studies teachers indicated at least a verbal support of global education. In a local study of social studies teachers in the Dade County Public Schools, Tucker (1983) found, for example, that 90 percent of the respondents believed that global education was "an important part of social studies," "a necessity," "increasing in importance in the future," and "needing greater emphasis than is currently the case in the social studies." The overwhelming majority saw no ideological barriers to the introduction of a global perspective in the social studies curriculum.

Global Education in Schools

Global education faces more serious problems in the schools. The crowded daily school schedule and the need to meet the standards of the existing curriculum cause many teachers, understandably, to resist the introduction of anything new, especially if it is also viewed as taking extra time. Moreover, very few social studies textbooks are written with a global view. Therefore, global education is unlikely to be incorporated on a large scale into any school as a separate or a new curriculum.

If, however, teachers and schools become convinced that global education can help them accomplish other goals in an already taxing schedule, it is likely to be infused into the existing curriculum through a wide variety of means ranging from individual teachers to an entire faculty, from the formal curriculum to the informal curriculum, from the social studies and foreign-language departments to all the disciplines, and across all grade levels. Global education tends to be more easily accepted in schools and in teacher training programs when it is linked theoretically and practically to other school reform movements such as school-based management and shared decision making; multicultural education; theme schools; whole language teaching; writing across the curriculum; media centers as the central focus of a school; and cooperative learning (Freeman, 1986; Tye, ed., 1990a; Tye, ed., 1990b; and Merryfield, 1992).

A Social Studies Teacher's Leadership Role in Global Education

The role of a teacher of social studies (K to 12) in implementing global education will vary according to the school's circumstances and environment. At one end of the scale are the few social studies teachers who have received formal training in global education; they are equipped to induce change in their own classrooms with little or no need for outside assistance. Whether they do so is largely a matter of individual preference and choice. With a little encouragement and experience, they can also be leaders for reform on a larger, more comprehensive scale within the social studies department and the entire school. The initiative for global program development at a school level, however, can spring from literally anywhere. Social studies teachers may find themselves following leaders from other disciplines such as science or language arts.

School administrators will typically turn to social studies teachers for leadership in global education. When it dawns on a critical mass of parents, students, and administrators, as it has already in some locations, that our schools must respond to the dynamics of American citizenship and productivity in the global village, a social studies teacher reluctant to embrace global education stands to be shunted away from the mainstream of professional development in schools. But if social studies teachers fail to accept the challenge, schools will likely seek leadership elsewhere. What the social studies can contribute to global understanding will cease to be a relevant question. Rather it will be: What can global understanding contribute to the social studies? This ironic twist would be unfortunate, for the backgrounds social studies teachers have in history and the social and behavioral sciences offer much to global education and to the process of school change. Hopefully, social studies teachers will seize the coming professional leadership opportunity.

How Can the Social Studies Contribute to the Development of a Global Perspective?

Incorporating a Global Perspective into the Social Studies

Recent national reports and state curriculum recommendations on social studies, as noted earlier, have documented a need for students in the United States to know more about the world around them, especially through more instruction in history and geography. Such content knowledge, although desirable, is an insufficient condition of global education. And this difference between desirable and sufficient may be *all* the difference in ensuring for ourselves a workable and promising future.

Global education begins with the premise that information and knowledge about the rest of the world must inform our own consciousness so that we can better understand ourselves and our relationships to each other and to other peoples, cultures, nations, and global issues. Knowing oneself better is an essential outcome of education for a global perspective. Recent scholarship in developmental psychology suggests that developing a balanced and healthy personality requires an understanding of the complexities of an increasingly complex and interdependent world (Csikszentmihalyi, 1993). From an earlier era, Rudyard Kipling put it well: "How can he know England, who only England knows?"

The Importance of a Conceptual Understanding of Global Education

A conceptual understanding of education for a global perspective is critically important to its successful classroom implementation. A conceptual understanding enables a teacher to reconstruct one's existing content knowledge into a more flexible and useful database for developing global lessons and provides a context for introducing fresh teaching strategies such as computer-based communications applications linking students and schools around the world.

In a 1974 working paper called "An Attainable Global Perspective," Robert Hanvey, anthropologist by inclination and educator by profession, developed an integrated notion of a global perspective that has been widely used as a framework for developing global education programs.* Paraphrased by Kenneth Tye and Barbara Benham Tye, the Hanvey Model consists of five dimensions that represent a closely linked aggregation of interdisciplinary content themes, beliefs, and intellectual skills.

- *Perspective Consciousness:* An awareness of and appreciation for other images of the world, and recognition that others have views of the world that are profoundly different from one's own.
- *State-of-the-Planet Awareness:* An in-depth understanding of prevailing global issues, events, and conditions.
- *Cross-cultural Awareness:* A general understanding of the defining characteristic of world cultures with an emphasis on understanding differences and similarities.
- *Knowledge of Global Dynamics:* A familiarity with the nature of systems and an introduction to the complex international system in which state and nonstate actors are linked in patterns of interdependence and dependence in a variety of issues areas; consciousness of global change.
- *Awareness of Human Choices:* A review of strategies for action on issues in local, national, and international settings (Tye and Tye, 1992, pp. 86–87).

The Hanvey Model has many applications for developing educational experiences. These range from teacher training programs in university settings to school settings where teachers can create global classroom lessons and units of study, infuse global concepts and content into existing courses such as United States History, and develop interdisciplinary programs across entire schools. (Refer to the organizations listed at the end of this chapter for additional information about global materials and publications.)

One example of the potential power of the Hanvey Model combined with computer-communications technology is the following project called "Find a House with a Mouse" developed by students and teachers in Aveiro, Portugal, and transmitted internationally in October 1992 via the Apple Global Education (AGE) computer network that links more than 100 schools located throughout the world. Aveiro is a city of 75,000 inhabitants on the Atlantic coast whose livelihood depends on tourism, growing and selling flowers, and fishing. Escola Secundária de José Estêvão is a junior and senior high school (grades 7 to 12) with 3,000 students, most of whom are preparing to go on to college and university training. The material can be easily adapted for use at the elementary level. To convey the full flavor of the project, the text is printed as it was downloaded from the AGE network. [Note: The AGE network has undergone changes since

---

* The Hanvey Model of Global Education has been translated into several languages, including Russian and Spanish, to facilitate training in global education on an international level. For example, global education has been formally adopted by the Russian Ministry of Education as an integral part of its post-Cold War program for the radical reform of its education system.

Project Find a House with a Mouse

FOREWORD:

José Estêvão High School has collaborated in AGE last year under the motto "getting to know diversity in order to make the unity stronger."

Our school has participated in several projects and suggested others. As a consequence of this previous work we have been present at the Askov Conference last August and have presented the "Find a House with a Mouse" and other participants also added their own ideas.

TARGET:

Identifying the common points the students have about their different houses in order to build the "Global Home" as a symbol of union.

WHO THE PROJECT IS AIMED AT:

14–16 year-old students (9th–10th grades)—one class in each school. [Note: Elementary students could use the information also.]
DURATION: from October till May

HUMAN RESOURCES:

1. In each school there should be teachers responsible for the coordination of the activities and a first systematization of data.
2. José Estêvão High School is responsible for:
   a. the global coordination;
   b. examining and compiling the results;
   c. publishing of the book with the work developed and the analysis of the results.
3. Multisubject work which involves Geography, History, Art, Drawing, English, the mother tongue.

This project is divided in 6 different stages.

STAGE 1: The student situation in his own house.

Target: acknowledging the objective conditions of the relation—student-to-home.

This task is to be done in each class, answering the following items:

1. Identify your country and city/town.
2. Identify your school.
3. Describe your house as a physical space:
3.1. Identify the surrounding area.

3.2. Identify type of house—single family house, flat/apartment.
3.3. Draw the exterior of your house.
3.4. Identify the building materials and colour of the exterior of the house.
3.5. Draw a plan of the houseplan, number of storeys and the total area.
3.6. Mention heating (in case there is) and specify type.
4. Describe a picture of the house as a living space.
4.1. Mention your family:
number of people
ages
4.2. Describe your room.
4.3. Mention the part of the house in which the family spends most of the time.
4.4. Mention the languages spoken at home.
4.5. Mention the cost of the housing (dollars).

This stage will take place during October till 15th of November.

The teacher or teachers responsible for the project in each school will have to select the most significant answers and send them to José Estêvão High School until 15th of November.

STAGE 2: The house and its symbolical aspects.

1. Target: comparing the subjective relations student/house in the different social/ cultural spaces.
2. Tasks to be performed by the students.
2.1. What meaning has the house you live in for you?
2.2. What does your room mean for you?
2.3. What meaning do you give to "leaving Home"?

Project   *Find a House with a Mouse, continued*

2.4. What is the relation about house/job?

This stage will take place between 15th of November and the 15th of December.

The results should be sent to José Estêvão High School by the 15th of December.

In each school a teacher or teachers will have to select the most meaningful answers.

STAGE 3: Relation of the traditional home with the nature environment and the community.

1.   Target: acknowledge the value of the memory of the traditional home as a symbol of the culture and identity.

2.   These tasks to be done by the students in case there is a traditional house where they live.

2.1. Draw the outside of the house.

2.2. Mention the building materials and the colour.

2.3. Draw the house plans.

2.4. Mention in case there is any relation between the type of the house and the weather.

2.5. Mention the way of living in connection with the house.

2.6. Establish the relation between the traditional house and the family.

This task will have to be carried out during January and the results will have to be sent to José Estêvão High School till January 30th.

STAGE 4: Building the dream house.

1.   Target: assemble the symbols the students associate to the house.

2.   Work to be carried out by students:

2.1. Draw the façade of your dream house and mention the materials to be used and its colour.

2.2. Draw your dream house plan.

2.3. Identify the central part of the house.

2.4. Identify the persons you would like to live with in the dream house.

2.5. What would please you most to have in the inside the house?

2.6. What is the meaning of the dream house to you?

This stage will take place between February and March 15th. The results should be sent to José Estêvão High School till March 15 by the coordinator.

STAGE 5: Building the "Global Home."

1.   Target: creation of the global home in each school based upon the knowledge of the "dream houses" and using different traditional houses.

2.   Different tasks to be done.

2.1. José Estêvão High School, the coordinator school, will inform the other schools about the perspectives of the "dream house" and of the traditional houses which will serve as inspiration to the building of the global home.

2.2. Building of the global home by the different schools. This will be the product of a teamwork with a total freedom of creativity.

The final results will be sent to José Estêvão High School till April 8th.

STAGE 6: José Estêvão High School will be in charge of the organization of a book which will be sent to all the schools involved in the project. This book will include:

1.   The different perspectives of the global home.

2.   The students attitudes according to the different geographical and cultural spaces. The environmental aspects, different positioning in the world.

The coordinators: Arsélio Martins, Carmo Leitão, Céu Cruz, Delfim Diaz from the AGE network. [Note: The AGE network has undergone changes since 1992. For current information contact Apple Computer directly.]

This project from Portugal contains many elements of the Hanvey Model and demonstrates the model's power to add value to social studies instruction. The project can be used in conjunction with the Hanvey Model by teachers at all grade levels in the United States and elsewhere to convey and reinforce the acquisition of a global perspective.

"Find a House with a Mouse" itself is an object lesson in *Global Dynamics*— the growing technological interdependence of the world. More than simply reading and discussing technological interdependence, students can actually participate in an international communications network—a powerful first-hand experience with Hanvey's *Global Dynamics*. In terms of *State-of-the Planet Awareness*, students can participate in developing their own database about housing on a global scale. They will be able to ascertain different levels and degrees of *Perspective Awareness* about housing according to the preferences indicated by the responses. The students in Portugal may learn about the serious global issue of homelessness—in the discovery that not everyone has access to a home in the traditional sense implied in the project. The intention to develop a "global home" as a result of the research is a vivid example of *Awareness of Human Choice*—the conscious use of systemic knowledge to ascertain long-range and wide-range effects in planning human action. *Cross-Cultural Awareness* is an integral part of the project design. In addition, students are encouraged to work in teams to use and further develop the skills needed to design, implement, and evaluate a complex cross-cultural project—extending the idea of cooperative learning and decision making to a global level.

As an educational project, "Finding a House with a Mouse" stands firmly on its own merits. Its global learning potential, however, is greatly enhanced by using the Hanvey Model to use, analyze, and extend the project beyond its initial design. The Portuguese project may seem beyond the capacity of most social studies classrooms in the United States today. If so, the problem lies not with the project. Education for a global perspective will be greatly enchanced when our educational capacity in the social studies begins to catch up with the technological potential. Awaiting that time, most global education will occur within the framework of more traditional settings. Much can be accomplished.

Fresh Global Scholarship for a Changing World

The fierce controversy over the United States and World History national standards developed by the National Center for History in the Schools, University of California at Los Angeles (1994 a,b,c), has overshadowed the growth of important new scholarship in the discipline of history itself. As a discipline, historical scholarship is yielding to the questions of the present—more and more of which are global in nature. In the long run, this globalizing trend will greatly influence instruction in social studies classrooms. A creative social studies teacher can start now by using history to think globally.

We can begin to think globally in the social studies by challenging the conventional wisdom that social studies content, including citizen participation, ought to be separately organized into knowledge enclaves of "domestic" and "foreign." In the typical social studies program the curriculum and supporting materials are classified into United States or European or world history and into United States or world geography. Forty-five percent of secondary social studies teachers are teaching United States history; another 20 percent teach European/world history (Rutter, 1986).

The social sciences are much the same. Government as a subject is almost exclusively devoted to our national government, with state and local government sometimes sprinkled about. Economics is usually based upon an out-dated domestic model with very little recognition of the linkage between our national and global economies. Sociology is laced with case studies drawn from our own national experience; on the other hand, anthropology normally focuses exclusively on other cultures and other peoples, inhibiting the application of its central and powerful concept of culture to our own society. Even ethnic, multicultural studies tend to be organized within the national context, often at the expense of the global experience that continues to nourish our diverse and pluralistic culture.

Historians of a global persuasion are demanding a larger voice in the profession. For example, Theodore von Laue (1987), emeritus professor of history at Clark University, noted that the discipline of history is struggling through a "profound transition":

> On the one side, powerfully entrenched, lies the professional tradition of local history, national history, specialized history....That history probes into the past in even greater detail, producing more evidence about smaller subjects....On the other side...loom the larger contexts of meaning created by the global framework into which life is now set. It is in that world where our students, our young faculty, our public have to find their way....Our history...must be global history, history viewed in all its aspects from a global perspective.

History is, and always has been, the flagship of the social studies curriculum. This intellectual ferment among historians comes at a critical time. Embedded in this discourse may be the potential for a reformulating and restructuring of social studies itself. The importance of a fresh global perspective on historical scholarship for American citizenship education, and consequently for rethinking the social studies, can hardly be overemphasized.

Walter LaFeber (1989), professor of history at Cornell University, asserted

> [Global] changes require us to rethink not just the foreign policies we have pursued since the advent of the Cold War, but also our scholarship and the

curriculum we teach....fresh scholarship and curriculum changes are needed to understand properly the roots and meanings of these [global] transformations.

For example:

Scholars will have to ask new questions of those pre-1914 years when the United States had to survive as one of a half-dozen great powers; when Americans confronted a world being rapidly remade by new technology, and when Washington and other capitals had to deal with revolutionary nationalism in Latin America, the Middle East, Africa, and Southeast Asia.

Through the prism of global turning points of the 1990s, additional examples of a refocusing of historical scholarship become apparent. The concept of the trading state (Rosecrance, 1986), for example, can be useful to seek aspects of our own history that resemble current realities in the interdependent global economy. During the years of the famous clipper ships in the late eighteenth century, New England, especially Massachusetts, was an important part of a global trading network. Using concepts from anthropology such as culture exchange, we can see clearly the significant influence of the clipper ship trade upon New England, using as examples the influences of Chinese culture on Boston and other seaport communities—that are still felt today.

Using this historical database, students can hypothesize about the potential cultural effects of contemporary international trade on cities like Norfolk, Houston, Miami, New Orleans, Jacksonville, Charleston, Savannah, Seattle, and Chicago. Students can then analyze the pros and cons of the effects of the trading state on local communities in the United States. A recent example of the culture exchange concept at work is the influence of the Japanese culture upon local communities around the nation that serve as sites for Japan's automotive industry. One result is that local community leaders, including teachers, have been invited to Japan to learn more about Japanese culture so they can integrate more study about Japan into the curriculum of the local schools. Regrettably, there has been a dark side, also. Following the opening in Tennessee of the very first high school in the United States built for Japanese students, a cross was burned in the school's front lawn, bringing into sharp focus the sometimes violent intersection of international culture exchange with our own domestic history.

Old and new, these two examples of the relationship between the rise of the trading state and culture exchange have roots that run deep in our history. If global concepts are established in the classroom, then students can begin to understand current history and to place analogous historical events such as the voyages of Columbus in a broad intellectual perspective. The examination and testing of analogies is a sturdy intellectual tool and an exciting teaching technique made possible by the rich context of global history. Similar rich teaching and learning scenarios can be constructed, using as a point of departure contemporary global turning points such as the end of the Cold War, the ascent of the Pacific Rim nations, and the United States as a world nation.

Pre-collegiate textbooks in United States history seldom treat our international relations between the Civil War and World War I as being terribly important. Domestic concerns such as the closing of the frontier, Reconstruction, industrialization, big business, and the growth of labor unions almost completely overshadow our international connections even though they were very important to the building of America. For example, the construction of our railroads would have been severely retarded without the investment of English capital or the labor of the Irish, Chinese and German Russians.

The American Revolution itself was a global event, as described by the late Barbara Tuchman (1988). The critical moment in the eventual success of the colonists came when Admiral Count de Grasse sailed from Brest with the great French fleet to join forces eventually with General Washington for the showdown in the Chesapeake Bay and the final battle at Yorktown. The infusion of French support shifted the strategic balance of power and enabled the Colonists to emerge victorious. Less well known is the vital role of the Spanish Caribbean toward ensuring the safe and successful passage of de Grasse on his way to the Colonies.

> In the West Indies during July [1781], de Grasse completed his preparations for the campaign, except for the last necessity of money. The loan he had hoped to raise from the inhabitants of Santo Domingo having been thwarted, he turned to another local Spanish source, the population of Cuba....the population of Havana, remembering the assault on their city by the British less than twenty years before, were glad of the opportunity to retaliate. By popular subscription, the money for de Grasse is said to have been raised in less than 48 hours, with the help of Cuban ladies who contributed their diamonds, and was promptly delivered to his flagship....On August 15, 1781...de Grasse sailed from Cap-Français for America and Chesapeake Bay with the money...three Saint-Simon regiments and all 28 ships of his fleet (pp. 238–239).

In United States history textbooks, our global connections during the early and middle periods are practically a non-event, with important exceptions like Manifest Destiny, the Mexican War, the Spanish-American War, and "walk softly, but carry a big stick." When our global linkages manage to come to the surface, they generally reflect only the American perspective and are footnotes in our relentless march to national unity and world power. For most Americans, our involvement with the world began in earnest with World War I, and even then we are portrayed as reluctant players on the world stage. This global myopia typically found in United States history textbooks may have served an American citizenship education function during a period when the nation was seeking its distinctive identity among the world's nations, but it becomes increasingly counterproductive during the global era when cooperation and consensus better serve our national interests (American Foreign Policy: Coping with the Diffusion of Power, 1989).

Historical questions raised through the lens of the new global realities can provide a more complete picture of our early and continuing engagement with the rest of the world. A global picture of our own history will help dispel the prevailing attitude of "splendid isolation" that today impedes the desired *rapprochement* between global education and American citizenship education efforts. If our own history turns out to be much more global than we have been taught, our new understanding should provide a firm foundation for enabling American citizens to deal more eagerly and confidently with the interdependent world we have entered. Being interested in the world and being an American will no longer be incompatible; instead, they will be congruent and mutually reinforcing.

Contradictory Reform Efforts in the Social Studies

In parallel, but running slightly ahead of the new global historical scholarship, a mostly additive, quantitative, and static model of history has been recommended for the social studies curriculum by prestigious national commissions such as the Bradley Commission on History and the Schools (1988), and by widely publicized statements like *Education for Democracy: A Statement of Principles* (1987), released as a joint project of the American Federation of Teachers, Freedom House, and the Educational Excellence Network. At the state level, the model is being implemented in California through its *History–Social Science Framework.* (California State Department of Education, 1988).

Paradoxically, some of these reports strongly advocate the teaching of "myths, legends, and tall tales" in the social studies curriculum at the primary grade level to "fire student imagination" and to develop student interest in history and the humanities (California State Department of Education, 1988, pp. 4–5). On the face of it, this recommendation appears innocent enough. A deeper understanding of the global history of the twentieth century reveals, however, that "myths, legends, and tall tales" in the hands of anti-democratic forces, be they ideologies of the extreme left or right, can be twisted easily to serve the purposes of the state (Blackburn, 1985).

By whom and according to what criteria will these "myths, legends, and tall tales" be chosen? Will impressionable students, their imaginations stirred by fantasy, subsequently be able to distinguish between fiction and fact in grade four when they study state history, in grade five when they learn about United States history, or in grade six when students turn their attention to the cradles of civilization—and so on into the upper grades. Where will students be taught the important distinction between value judgments and statements of fact, the intellectual building blocks of critical thinking? Are "myths, legends, and tall tales," when offered as history, a proper social studies foundation for democratic citizens who live in a complex world and who starve for reliable knowledge? Will the introduction of history through myths provide a respect for grounded knowledge, the role of evidence, and the rules of objective inquiry—paramount goals of American citizenship education? In what way are "myths, legends, and tall tales" different from "the things that go bump in the night" and the superstitions that ruled human behavior before the Enlightenment? "Myths, legends, and tall tales" taught as literature *within the context* of history are one thing; but taught *as* history—are quite another and a most dubious matter.

A more encouraging effort can be found in the report *Charting a Course: Social Studies for the 21st Century* (National Commission on Social Studies in the Schools, 1989). *Charting a Course* integrates a global perspective into social studies content, especially in grades 9 to 11 where United States and world history are combined into one three-year sequence. This global reconstruction of history as a subject in the schools is deeply embedded in its goal statement and in its recommended curriculum scope and sequence.

> It is important that social studies help students understand that our entire history has taken shape in response to significant foreign contributions, threats, and resources. Our future is likely to see an elaboration of this link (p. 13).

Importantly, the qualitative ferment in historical scholarship based upon a global perspective, underway in the academy for the last decade, is for the first time introduced by the Commission into the K to 12 social studies curriculum as a serious alternative to the quantitative, additive approach.

Global Classroom Materials and Curricular Approaches

The curricular approach recommended by the National Commission on Social Studies in the Schools is encouraging. The time lag, however, between this fresh historical scholarship and the traditional approach that pervades the educational reform movement, is far too great. One may wonder if "the horse is already out of the barn."

New classroom materials will be required; teachers must be trained. Textbooks must be written to reflect accurately the correlation of the historical experience of the United States with the rest of the world. It is a matter of national urgency to close the gap. The federal government ought to advance global historical scholarship by making it a priority for funding. This lag in bringing globally oriented historical scholarship to bear on the social studies curriculum is a deplorable state of affairs. Unless something is done to speed up the process to rejuvenate historical scholarship with a global framework, we may well lock another generation of students into a social studies curriculum out of touch with the times, a fate we can ill afford in these rapidly changing times.

The quantitative argument for just more history—made by the Bradley Commission and others—in the social studies curriculum is not the answer. The rationale for history in the curriculum must be based upon something other than "history is good and we need more of it." The fundamental questions about the study and the teaching of history are analytic and qualitative, asked with an eye toward how history can be made into a vital part of the school curriculum—rather than the deadly review, recite, and regurgitate syndrome that currently places history at the bottom of student interest. How can the study of history, with a global perspective, contribute to democratic citizenship? Can history be made more meaningful to the everyday lives of students? How can we deal with conflicting historical interpretations? How can history assist us in examining unexamined assumptions and making "puzzles of facts," as Henry Steele Commager has urged? How can history make us more critically aware of the human condition and of our own society?

Paul Kennedy (1988), historian at Yale University and author of the controversial best seller, *The Rise and Fall of the Great Powers*, provides a contemporary United States analogy to what Kipling may have been suggesting for England at the turn of the century. Kennedy noted, "You only properly understand your own country when you remove the ethnocentric spectacles, examine the history of other countries, and put your own nation within the larger context of global developments" (p.1).

Professor Kennedy is highly critical of the current crop of educational reformers, meaning national politicians and administrators, who decry the lack of historical knowledge among our young people and who would cure the situation by emphasizing "traditional, inward-looking, American history alone."

An even more profound issue, according to Kennedy, is the lack of knowledge of world history and our nation's place in it by our political leaders themselves. He forecast that our presidential candidates would go through the 1988 campaign "believing that they have nothing to learn from history but a few platitudes about Manifest Destiny, the American Way, 'appeasement' and the...like." Who among us today will deny the accuracy of his prediction?* And he asks, "Is it too much to ask today's politicians to put history into their own curriculum, as well as recommending it for all 15-year-olds?" And for politicians and students alike, Kennedy's core curriculum must contain more than a

> [B]asic corpus of historical facts about the nation's Constitution, its presidents, its chief political developments. [It is also necessary to understand] the larger economic and strategical changes that have occurred on this planet over the past few centuries (p. 1).

---

* For example, see Sidney Blumenthal, *Pledging Allegiance: The Last Campaign of the Cold War.*

The further development of a fresh, globally-oriented knowledge base in history and its rapid infusion into the social studies curriculum will greatly assist us in understanding the complex era that has opened up before us.

Leften Stavrianos (1989) has developed a global framework for understanding world history. His motivation as a historian is to find "a usable past." He identified four conceptual themes of contemporary life that represent a method to extract from history certain "lifelines from our past." They are ecology, gender relations, social relations, and war. He develops these concepts within the context of three historic time periods: kinship societies, characterized by a hunting and gathering economy; tributary societies, found in the origins of agriculture in the river valley societies; and capitalism (commercial capitalism, 1500–1770; industrial capitalism, 1770–1940; and high-tech capitalism, 1940–present). For example, the relations between men and women in kinship societies were much more egalitarian than now. During the agricultural period when labor became specialized, gender hierarchies were established with men typically holding the dominant status. This global framework of understanding can readily be used by a social studies teacher as an introduction to the study of world history—thus providing an organizing idea for sorting out the complexities of world history.

A gifted curriculum writer or teacher can add other variables to the framework to fit the local circumstances and the interests and abilities of the students. For example, one might add racism based on skin color as a fifth factor to be examined in kinship, tributary, and capitalist societies. This idea lends itself to an examination of the anthropological meaning of race and culture. Such an approach will bring the tools of social science to bear on an understanding of world history and will help students better sort out the acrimonious debates about multiculturalism that have split the scholarly community, the schools, and the nation. Annette Weiner (1992), president of the American Anthropological Association, argues that we must "find intellectual models that support cultural diversity without erecting battle lines that discourage understanding and tolerance and that breed racism" (p. B1). In a more futuristic example, students can be challenged to create a hypothetical post-capitalist society (for example, one based on information and technology) and speculate about the nature of ecology, gender relations, social relations and war (plus racism) in that future situation. This type of project would qualify for what Theodore Sizer (1992) calls an "exhibition"—a major work that demonstrates a comprehensive grasp of content and serves as a means of assessment.

The Stavrianos approach inherently invites students to consider the study of history in pragmatic terms and helps answer the question: What's in it for me? By seeking meaningful patterns or schema—always in a competent and responsible manner—history becomes a more useful discipline. Stavrianos cautions that patterns of history are not predictive; instead, their usefulness derives from the capacity to understand human flexibility and potentiality— offering the student the perspective of history in a profoundly humanistic sense. In the final analysis, Stavrianos maintains, "each generation must write its own history, not because past histories are untrue but because in a rapidly changing world new questions arise and new answers are needed" (p. 13).

Ross Dunn (1989), professor of history at San Diego State University, urges that world history be taught as the human community as a whole. This approach "stresses in each era of the past the larger-scale patterns of change that have brought the world to its present state of complexity and interdependence" (p. 220).

> Such a global history would be chronologically organized—that is, it would have a narrative structure, though a looser one than U. S. and European surveys often have. Students would follow a world time line that stirs awareness of the interrelations of societies from one century to the next and that invites continuous comparison of events occurring in different parts of the world. Each primary unit of the course would be organized around an important chain of events...whose impact was wide enough to involve peoples of differing cultures in a shared experience. These "big" events would provide the common reference point for investigating and comparing other events and trends that relate more narrowly to particular civilizations and cultural groups (p. 220).

Thinking Globally and Acting Locally

Education for a global perspective can occur on the local level and is more than merely learning about other people in other places at other times. According to Lee Anderson (1990):

> A student need not be studying things foreign or international, as we have conventionally thought of these terms, in order to be involved in a global education. There are ways in which a student can be studying his or her own community and be as much involved in global education as when he or she is studying a community in another part of the world (p. xvi).

Civic and community participation and service activities offered through social studies programs, as recommended by Ernest Boyer (1983), ought to be conceived with a global dimension in mind. It is increasingly difficult to imagine a local participation activity without a global connection. Wall Street has its 24-hour stock market, so that brokers and investors can keep up with the London, Tokyo, and Hong Kong exchanges; these global changes are reflected in economic and investment activity at the local level. The local public hospital will reflect a network of global links, both in its human dimensions of staff and patients and in its research programs. How about a community research project on the homeless or local unemployment?

The student investigation may reveal, as Robert Reich (1989), Harvard political economist and Secretary of Labor in the Clinton administration, pointed out, a global connection to the problems of the homeless and unemployment in the United States. The richest 20 percent of the population in the United States saw their share of national wealth increase significantly during the 1980s while the share of the poorest 20 percent decreased. Reich argues that our low-wage earners are now in competition with low-wage earners around the world—and this is a losing struggle. He urges that we refocus our efforts on developing new, high-quality products that will add value to the global economy—products that will be purchased by others because they represent a better idea, a higher quality. Trying to produce more of the same, he predicts, will doom the United States to permanent underclass status. His conclusion is that poverty in the United States is now a global problem, and only massive investments in the nation's infrastructure, education, health, housing, transportation, and communications will enable us to compete with nations that are doing better in developing and nourishing their human resources.

Conclusion

Will the rest of the world, developing economically and politically at break-neck speed, permit the United States the luxury of an entire generation to readjust to the new international scheme of things? Probably not. They will proceed with or without us. Our self-interest is served by being vitally involved in world affairs.

The rapid infusion of a global perspective into the social studies curriculum will greatly assist in understanding the complex era that has opened up before us.

For further information about programs that link social studies and global education, you can contact these organizations:

- The American Forum for Global Education
  120 Wall Street, Suite 2600
  New York, New York 10005
  (212) 742-8232
- The Association for Supervision and Curriculum Development (ASCD)
  225 North Washington Street
  Alexandria, Virginia 22314
  (703) 549-9100
- Center for Human Interdependence
  303 W. Katella, Suite 302
  Orange, California 92667
  (714) 633-8173
- Center for Teaching International Relations (CTIR)
  University of Denver
  Graduate School of International Studies
  Denver, Colorado 80208
  (303) 871-3106
- Children's Museum
  300 Congress Street
  Boston, MA 02210-1034
  (617) 426-6500, extension 223
- Consortium for Teaching Asia and the Pacific in the Schools (CTAPS)
  East-West Center
  1777 East-West Road
  Honolulu, Hawaii 96848

- Global Awareness Program
  College of Education
  Florida International University
  Miami, Florida 33199
  (305) 348-2664
- Hitachi Foundation
  1509 22nd Street, N.W.
  Washington, DC 20037
  (202) 457-0588
- International Education Consortium
  6800 Wydown Boulevard
  St. Louis, Missouri 63105
  (314) 721-3255
- LINKS (Linking International Knowledge with Schools)
  106 Stuart Hall
  George Washington University
  Washington, D.C. 20052
  (202) 676-7543

- National Council for the Social Studies (NCSS)
  3501 Newark Street, N.W.
  Washington, D.C. 20016
  (202) 966-7840
- REACH Center
  180 Nickerson Street, Suite 212
  Seattle, Washington 98109
  (206) 284-8584
- Social Studies Development Center
  Smith Research Center
  Indiana University
  2805 East 10th Street
  Bloomington, Indiana 47405
  (812) 335-3584
- Stanford Program on International and Cross-Cultural Education (SPICE)
  300 Lausen
  Littlefield Center, Room 14
  Stanford University
  Stanford, California 94305-5013
  (415) 725-1489

Reflective Questions

1. *To help students become more marketable in a global society, what courses do you believe should be emphasized in the student curriculum?*

2. *Why must we educate students to live in a global community?*

3. *Read the origins of global education and identify the most plausible and compelling scenarios you find for the need of global education. Explain the basis of your selection.*

4. *Evaluate the relative merits of characterizing global education as a social movement rather than a curriculum.*

5. *Of the different definitions of global education discussed in this chapter, which are likely to influence the curriculum during the 2000s? Explain your decision.*

6. *What steps would one need to take in developing global education in the present day curriculum?*

7. *What are the possible consequences of embracing global education as a part of the social studies?*

8. *Although Tye and Tye found in their study that teachers had an attitude of acceptance for global education, they also found resistance to global education. Why?*

9. *Cite several reasons why global education might face problems in some schools. Evaluate the reasons.*

10. *In view of the findings in this chapter, indicate several ways a teacher of the social studies could implement global education in the classroom.*

11. *How do Stavrianos' conceptual themes promote global education thinking?*

12. *How can the following statement by Lee Anderson be interpreted: "a student need not be studying things foreign or international, in order to be involved in a global education?"*

13. *What types of curriculum changes are needed to prepare students to live in an ever-changing, more international, multicultural, and multiethnic society?*

GLOSSARY

culture Anthropologists define culture as the totality of *learned* attitudes, values, beliefs, traditions, and tools shared by a group of people to give order, continuity, and meaning to their lives.

ecological catastrophe A condition among interdependent organisms that threatens the existence or fruitful balance of all organisms in that environment.

global education The process by which people acquire the ability to conceptualize and understand the complexities of the international system: a knowledge of world cultures and international events; and an appreciation of the diversity and commonalties of human values and interests.

global interaction As large scale phenomenon, a characteristic of the modern world with its global interchanges of raw materials, technology, people, energy, capital, manufactured goods, information, and culture.

global interdependence The concept of a shared reality regarding world resources, technology, and cultures.

global perspective Consists of the information, attitudes, awareness, and skills, that, taken together, can help individuals to understand the world, how they affect others, and how others affect them.

global village A world linked together by the electronic media.

globalizing The process by which one develops an awareness of world affairs.

multicultural education Education that focuses on providing real opportunities for students whose cultural or language patterns make it difficult for them to succeed in traditional school programs; many multicultural programs also emphasize positive intergroup and interracial attitudes and contacts.

OPEC Organization of Petroleum Exporting Countries. This cartel among nations that export petroleum controls the sale price and availability of oil on international markets.

Post-Cold War Era The era in which we've witnessed the disintegration of the Soviet Union and the fragmentation of ideological warfare between the "Capitalistic West" and the "Communist East."

race Anthropological division of the human species into subgroups on the basis of biological traits and characteristics. The concept of race is used to differentiate between various human subgroups. Anthropologists have pointed to the fundamental differences between the concepts of race and culture.

racism Mistaken belief that humans, individually and in groups, inherit certain mental, personality, and cultural characteristics that make them either superior or inferior and determine their behavior. Historically used by dominant societal groups as a justification for anti-social behavior, including slavery and institutional discrimination.

UNESCO United Nations Education, Scientific and Cultural Organization. It provides technical assistance, training programs, and field services to developing nations.

ANNOTATED BIBLIOGRAPHY

Backman, Earl L. editor (1984). *Approaches to International Education*. New York: Macmillan Publishing Company.

This book explores the subject of international education at various universities. The editor points out five obstacles to establishing an international education program. This book should be of interest to those who seek advanced degrees in the areas of international education.

Banks, James A. (1991). *Teaching Strategies for Ethnic Studies*. Boston: Allyn & Bacon.

This book explores the classroom tactics needed to instruct students from many ethnic groups. The author further discusses the concepts, strategies, and materials that relate to planning and developing a multicultural curriculum.

Becker, James M., editor (1979). *Schooling for a Global Age*. New York: McGraw-Hill.

With chapters by leaders in the field of global education, the primary strength of this book is its presentation of a broad spectrum of thinking on global education. This is the first major book on global education.

Center for Educational Research and Innovation (1989). *One School, Many Cultures*. Paris: Organisation for Economic Co-Operation and Development (OECD).

This report takes a critical look at the development of educational policy under the pressure of cultural and linguistic movements in OECD countries. The report recognizes the complexity and sensitivity of the issues that it considers.

Collins, H. Thomas. (1990, January). "Strengthening the International Curriculum: The Principal's Role." *NASSP Bulletin*. 74:80–88.

The author points out that instructional leaders and principals can ensure that international education becomes a strong component of the curriculum. He contends that Americans lack knowledge about specific events in the area of international education. The author offers several specifications to help students become "internationally literate."

Daniel, Neil and June Cox (1992). "International Education for High Ability Students: An Avenue to Excellence." *NASSP Bulletin*. 76:87–94.

The authors ask that we examine external evidence concerning international education for the specific needs of gifted students. Two questions were advanced:

1. What's happening around the world?
2. Are we doing as much as we can, or as much as other nations are doing to offer appropriate education to our most able learners?

The authors believe that the implicit competition our country and other nations are facing add to the perceived need for celebrating diversity for students of high ability.

Diekmann, Robert (1990, January). "Resources for International Education." *National Association of Secondary School Principals* 74:75–78.

The author lists samples of resources for international programs that are readily available to secondary-school educators. Suggestions are made for principals who are interested in strengthening their student exchange programs. The Council on Standards for International Standard for International Educational Travel (CSIET) publishes an annual directory of exchange programs, available for $6.50 from CSIET, 3 London Street, S.E., Suite 3, Leesburg, VA 22075.

Hanvey, Robert G. (1974). *An Attainable Global Perspective*. New York: Center for Global Perspectives, Inc. a.k.a. The American Forum for Global Education.

Hanvey's essay has become a classic in the field. He posits five dimensions of awareness, knowledge, skills, and attitudes that together constitute a global perspective. The Hanvey conceptual framework can be used in a variety of ways: lesson and program development; learning outcome evaluation.

Husen, Torsten (1990). *Education and the Global Concern*. Oxford, England: Pergamon Press.

This book delves into the growing realization that the schools are beset by problems. The background of several chapters is to designate curricula and programs which aim to achieve global learning.

Kniep, Willard M. (1989). "Social Studies Within a Global Education." *Social Education* 53(6)385, 399–403.

A description of a total K to 12 curriculum in social studies that has global education as the organizer. The author concentrates on the subject matter changes necessary to achieve a global perspective within the social studies.

Morris, Pamela (1991, April/May). "Distance Education for Caribbean Social Studies Teachers." *Social Education* 55(4):235–238.

This article demonstrates the important role social studies can play in Caribbean nation building. The idea of "correspondence or distance education" is not new. Courses have been offered for many years in Europe and the United States, primarily through written correspondence. Students have found the programs both interesting and useful. The programs are not, however, without pitfalls. Planning units for distance teaching demands that details in a lesson plan be written out completely, and clearly. Students and teachers interested in distance education in the Caribbean can contact the University of the West Indies, Mona Campus, Jamaica.

National Council for the Social Studies (1994). *Expectations of Excellence: Curriculum Standards for the Social Studies*, Bulletin 89. Washington, DC: NCSS.

These suggested national standards were developed by NCSS independent of any federal funding, unlike other national standards projects in history, geography, and social studies. The standards are designed to serve three purposes, by providing the following:

- A framework for social studies program design from kindergarten through grade 12 (K to 12)

- A guide for curriculum decisions by providing student performance expectations in the areas of knowledge, processes, and attitudes
- Examples of classroom activities that will help guide teachers as they design instruction to help their students meet performance expectations

Reardon, Betty A. (1988). *Educating for Global Responsibility: Teacher Designed Curricula for Peace Education: K–12*. New York: Teachers College, College Press.

This book is designed to help students develop a global identity and a planetary perspective as a framework for international education. The main purpose of this book is to present a collection of teacher-designed peace education curricula. Many of these curricula have been tested and refined over several years of use. All of these materials are on deposit in the curriculum resource center at Teachers College, Columbia University.

Tucker, Jan L. (1988). "Social Studies for the 21st Century." *Social Education* 52(3):209–214.

Tucker argues that social studies ought to become more cognizant of the impact of global interdependence on the purpose and content of the field. National Council for the Social Studies (NCSS) presidential address in November 1987.

Tye, Kenneth A., editor (1990). *Global Education: School-Based Strategies*. Orange, CA: Interdependence Press.

Case studies of the successful infusion of global education into the existing curriculum in schools throughout the United States, written by the individuals who were responsible for the development at the local level. Introduction by John Goodlad.

Tye, Kenneth A., editor (1990). *Global Education from Thought to Action*. Alexandria, VA: Association for Supervision and Curriculum Development.

This ASCD yearbook defines global education, explains its importance, describes its implementation, and demonstrates its uses for school improvement. The book is divided into two parts: the first part deals with the context necessary for understanding and teaching with a global perspective, and the second part deals with the practices in global education.

Tye, Barbara B. and Kenneth A. Tye, (1992). *Global Education: A Study of School Change*. Albany: State University of New York Press.

Tye and Tye present the research results of a four-year project designed to infuse global education into selected schools in Orange County, California. Chapters deal with issues relating to conducting research in school settings, global education viewed as a social movement, the conditions in schools that favor and oppose the introduction of global education and the pivotal role of the principal. Foreword by then Governor Bill Clinton and Introduction by Professor Lee Anderson.

References

Alger, C. and J. Harf (1986). "Global Education: Why? For Whom? About What?" In *Promising Practices in Global Education: A Handbook with Case Studies*, edited by R.E. Freeman. New York: National Council on Foreign Language and International Studies.

Ambrose, S.E. (1985). *The Rise to Globalism: American Foreign Policy Since 1938*, 4th ed. New York: Penguin Books.

"American Foreign Policy: Coping with the Diffusion of Power" (1989). *Carnegie Quarterly* 34(1):1+.

Anderson, Charlotte, with S. Nichols and A. Crawford (1994). *Global Understandings: A Framework for Teaching and Learning*. Alexandria: Association for Supervision and Curriculum Development (ASCD).

Anderson, Lee F. (1968). "An Examination of the Structure and Objectives of International Education." *Social Education* 32(7):639–647.

Anderson, Lee F. (1990). "A Rationale for Global Education." Pp. 13–34 in *Global Education from Thought to Action, 1991 Yearbook of the Association for Supervision and Curriculum Development*, edited by K.A. Tye. Alexandria: ASCD.

Armstrong, David, K. Henson, and Thomas Savage (1989). *Education: An Introduction*. New York: Macmillan.

Becker, James M. (1968). *An Examination of Objectives, Needs and Priorities in International Education in U.S. Secondary and Elementary School*, (Contract No. OEC-1-7-002908-2029). Washington, DC: Office of Education, Department of Health, Education and Welfare, Bureau of Research (ERIC Document Reproduction Service No. ED 026 933).

Becker, James M., editor (1979). *Schooling for a Global Age*. New York: McGraw-Hill.

Blackburn, G.W. (1985). *Education in the Third Reich: Race and History in Nazi Textbooks*. Albany: State University of New York Press.

Blumenthal, Sidney. (1990). *Pledging Allegiance: The Last Campaign of the Cold War*. New York: HarperCollins.

Botkin, J.W., M. Elmandjra, and M. Malitza (1979). *No Limits to Learning: Bridging the Human Gap: A Report to the Club of Rome*. New York: Pergamon Press.

Boyer, Ernest L. (1983). *High School: A Report on Secondary Education in America*. New York: Harper & Row.

Bradley Commission on History in Schools (1988). *Building a History Curriculum: Guidelines for Teaching History in Schools*. Washington, DC: The Educational Excellence Network.

Brzezinski, Zbigniew (1989). *The Grand Failure: The Birth and Death of Communism in the Twentieth Century*. New York: Charles Scribner's Sons.

Brzezinski, Zbigniew (June 16, 1989). "Toward a Grand Strategy for a World in Flux." *International Herald Tribune*. P. 6.

Buergenthal, T. and Judith V. Torney (1976). *International Human Rights and International Education*. Washington, DC: Department of State, U.S. National Commission for UNESCO.

California State Board of Education (1988). *History–Social Science Framework for California Public Schools*. Sacramento: California Department of Education.

Carson, Rachel (1962). *Silent Spring*. Boston: Houghton-Mifflin.

Club of Rome (1972). *The Limits to Growth: A Report for the Club of Rome Project on the Predicament of Mankind.* New York: Universe Books.

Csikzentmihalyi, M. (1993). *The Evolving Self: A Psychology for the Third Millennium.* New York: HarperCollins.

Cunningham, G. (1986). "Blowing the Whistle on Global Education." Unpublished report. Washington, DC: U.S. Department of Education, Region VII.

Duhohn-Sells, Rose (1991). "Visions of Multicultural Education for the 21st Century." In *Toward Education that is Multicultural*, edited by C. Grant. New Jersey: Silver, Burdett, Ginn.

Dunn, Ross E. (1989). "Central Themes for World History." Pp. 216–233 in *Historical Literacy in the Schools: The Case for History in American Education*, edited by P.G. Gagnon and the Bradley Commission in the Schools. New York: Macmillan.

"Education for Democracy: A Statement of Principles" (1987). *American Educator* 11(2):10–18.

Ehrlich, Paul R. (1968). *The Population Bomb.* New York: Ballantine Books.

Florida Department of Education (1982). *State Plan for Global Education in Florida.* Tallahassee: Florida Department of Education.

Freeman, R.E., editor (1986). *Promising Practices in Global Education: A Handbook with Case Studies.* New York: National Council on Foreign Language and International Studies.

Fuller, R. Buckminster (1969). *Operating Manual for Spaceship Earth.* New York: Simon & Schuster.

Goodlad, John I. (1984). *A Place Called School: Prospects for the Future.* New York: McGraw-Hill.

Gore, Albert (1992). *Earth in the Balance: Ecology and the Human Spirit.* Boston: Houghton Mifflin.

Guadiani, Claire (1991). "In Pursuit of Global Civic Virtues: Multiculturalism in the Curriculum." *Liberal Education* 77(3):12–15.

Hanvey, Robert G. (1974). *An Attainable Global Perspective.* New York: Center for Global Perspectives. a.k.a. The American Forum for Global Education.

Henry, W.A. (1990). "Beyond the Melting Pot." *Time* 135(15):28–31.

Hodgkinson, H.C. (1985). *All One System: Demographics of Education, Kindergarten through Graduate School.* Washington, DC: The Institute for Educational Leadership.

International Population Reports (1990). Washington, DC: The U.S. Department of Commerce and U.S. Census Bureau.

Kennedy, Paul (1988). *The Rise and Fall of the Great Powers: Economic Change and Military Conflict from 1500 to 2000.* New York: Random House.

Kennedy, Paul (January 24, 1988). "The U.S. and World History." *The Miami Herald* Section F. Pp. 1+.

Kluckhohn, C. (1949). *Mirror for Man: The Relation of Anthropology to Modern Life.* New York: Whittlesey House.

Kniep, Willard M. (October, 1989). "Social Studies Within a Global Education." *Social Education* 53(6):385, 399–403.

LaFeber, Walter (1989). "We Need Fresh Scholarship to Understand Changed World Realities." *The Chronicle of Higher Education* 35(37):A40.

Lamy, S.L. (1988). "Worldviews Analysis of International Issues." Pp. 1–25 in *Contemporary International Issues: Contending Perspectives*, edited by S.L. Lamy. Boulder: Lynne Rienner Publishers.

M'Bow, A.M. (1983). "Where the Future Begins." *The UNESCO Courier* 36(1):4–9.

McCarty, P. (1991). "Bring the World into the Classroom." *Principal* 71:8–10.

McLuhan, Marshall (1964). *Understanding Media: The Extensions of Man.* New York: McGraw-Hill.

Matrianos, E. (1988). "A Humanizing Force in Global Curriculum Building." In *Toward a Renaissance of Humanity*, edited by T. Carson. Alberta: University of Alberta Press.

Merryfield, M.M. (1992). "Preparing Social Studies Teachers for the Twenty-First Century: Perspectives on Program Effectiveness from a Study of Six Exemplary Teacher Education Programs in Global Education." *Theory and Research in Social Education* 20(1):17–46.

Michigan Department of Education (n.d.). *Guidelines for Global Education.* Lansing: Michigan Department of Education.

Morton, C. (1991). "A Global Training Session." *Media and Methods* 28(3):34.

Morris, Pamela (April/May 1991). "Distance Education for Caribbean Social Studies Teachers." *Social Education* 55(4):235–238.

National Center for History in the Schools (1994a). *National Standards for History: Expanding Children's World in Time and Space, Grades K–4.* Los Angeles.

National Center for History in the Schools (1994b). *National Standards for United States History: Exploring the American Experience, Grades 5–12.* Los Angeles.

National Center for History in the Schools (1994c). *National Standards for World History: Exploring Paths to the Present, Grades 5–12, Experimental Edition.* Los Angeles.

National Commission on Social Studies in the Schools (1989). *Charting a Course: Social Studies for the 21st Century.* Washington, D.C.

National Council for the Social Studies (1981). *Global Education.* Position statement prepared by International Activities Committee. Washington, D.C.

National Council for the Social Studies (1994). *Expectations of Excellence: Curriculum Standards for Social Studies.* Bulletin 89. Washington, DC.

National Governors' Association. (1989). *America in Transition: The International Frontier.* Washington, DC.

New York State Education Department. (1987). *9 & 10 Social Studies, Global Studies, Tentative Syllabus.* Albany: Bureau of Curriculum Development.

New York State Social Studies Review and Development Committee. (1991). *One Nation, Many Peoples: A Declaration of Cultural Interdependence.* Albany: New York Education Department.

Parekh, B. (1986). *Strategies for Improving Race Relations: The Anglo American Experience.* Manchester: Manchester University Press.

Reich, Robert B. (May 1,1989). "As the World Turns." *The New Republic*: 200(18):23.

Reich, Robert B. (1991). *The Work of Nations: Preparing Ourselves for 21st-Century Capitalism.* New York: Alfred A. Knopf.

Reischauer, Edwin O. (1973). *Toward the 21st Century: Education for a Changing World.* New York: Vintage Books.

Remy, R.C., J.A. Nathan, J.M. Becker, and J.V. Torney (1975). *International Learning and International Education in a Global Age.* Bulletin 47. Washington, DC: National Council for the Social Studies.

Richey, R.W. (1973). *Planning for Teaching: An Introduction to Education*. New York: McGraw-Hill.

Rosecrance, R. (1986). *The Rise of the Trading State: Commerce and Conquest in the Modern World*. New York: Basic Books.

Rutter, R.A. (1986). "A Profile of the Profession." *Social Education* 50(4):252–255.

Saxe, D.W. (1992). "Framing a Theory for Social Studies Foundations." *Review of Educational Research*. 62(3):259–277.

Sizer, T. (1992). *Horace's School: Redesigning the American High School*. Boston: Houghton Mifflin.

Stavrianos, Leften F. (1989). *Lifelines from Our Past: A New World History*. New York: Pantheon Books.

Taylor, Harold (1969). *The World as Teacher*. Garden City: Doubleday.

Teilhard de Chardin, Pierre (1964). *Future of Man*. Translated by N. Denny. New York: Harper & Row.

Thomas, Lewis (1974). *The Lives of a Cell: Notes of a Biology Watcher*. New York: Viking Press.

Toffler, Alvin (1970). *Future Shock*. New York: Random House.

Tuchman, Barbara (1988). *The First Salute: A View of the American Revolution*. New York: Alfred A. Knopf.

Tucker, Jan L. (1983). "Teacher Attitudes Toward Global Education: A Report from Dade County." *Education Research Quarterly* 8(1):65–77.

Tucker, Jan L. (1988). "Social Studies for the 21st Century." *Social Education* 52(3):209–214.

Tucker, Jan L. (1991). "Global Education is Essential to Secondary School Social Studies." *Bulletin, NASSP* 75:43–51.

Tye, Kenneth A., editor (1990a). "Global Education from Thought to Action." *Yearbook of the Association for Supervision and Curriculum Development*. Alexandria, VA: Association for Supervision and Curriculum Development.

Tye, Kenneth A., editor (1990b). *Global Education: School-Based Strategies*. Orange, CA: Interdependence Press.

Tye, B.B. and K. Tye (1992). *Global Education: A Study of School Change*. Albany: State University of New York Press.

UNESCO (1974). "Recommendations Concerning Education for International Understanding, Cooperation and Peace and Education Relating to Human Rights and Fundamental Freedoms." In *International Human Rights and International Education*, edited by T. Buergenthal and J. Torney. Washington, DC: U.S. National Commission for UNESCO.

U.S. Commissioner of Education's Task Force on Global Education (1979). *Report with Recommendations*. Washington, DC: U.S. Office of Education.

von Laue, Theodore H. (1987). "A Plea for True Global History." *World History Bulletin* 4(2):1 +.

Ward, Barbara (1965). *Spaceship Earth*. New York: Columbia University Press.

Ward, Barbara and René Dubos (1972). *Only One Earth: The Care and Maintenance of a Small Planet*. New York: W.W. Norton.

Weiner, Annette B. (1992). "Anthropology's Lessons for Cultural Diversity." *The Chronicle of Higher Education*. Pp. B1–2.

World Almanac Book of Facts, 1992 (1992, 1991). New York: Scripps Howard Co.

Chapter Eight

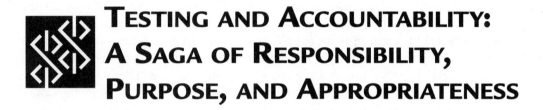

Testing and Accountability: A Saga of Responsibility, Purpose, and Appropriateness

Wilma S. Longstreet
University of New Orleans

The Issues and Their Background

School accountability, as measured by national and state tests, has dominated the educational reform movement of the 1980s and 90s (Salganik, 1985). In the past few decades, we have experienced a veritable explosion in the use of testing and in the demands that schools be held accountable for the inadequate performances of their students. All levels of schooling from kindergarten to the university have experienced the increasing use of tests not only as a means for assessing students' ability, but also as a way of determining how well schools are doing. According to the Congressional Office of Technology Assessment (1992), revenues from test sales increased by 150 percent between 1960 and 1989 while K to 12 enrollments grew by only 15 percent.

School Responsibility

In its efforts to achieve equal educational opportunity for all children, the American judicial system has accepted the view that testing, typically in a standardized format, is a fair way of determining the quality of school outputs. For example, on June 8, 1989, the Kentucky Supreme Court ruled that a school system whose students are educated inadequately is "inherently inequitable and unconstitutional" (Foster, 1991, p. 34). The Court then set forth certain goals for students and required the state legislature to establish a system for assessing student performance *in terms of these goals* so that the schools could be held accountable for the results of instruction. Under the Court's order, students' test scores—in this case based on performance events, portfolios, and projects as well as on more traditional measures—became central to determining how well the schools were delivering education to their rural, mostly white, and, presumably, poorly educated students.

Numerous objections could be made to the position taken by the Court, not least of which is the *non*recognition of such critical sociocultural factors as health care, nutrition, and the educational background of parents. Factors such as these have a demonstrable impact on student performance while remaining essentially beyond the control of the schools (Goodlad, 1992).

Possibly even more important in the context of judicial decision making are the persistent differences found among the group achievement scores of diverse minorities. Peter Airaisian (1987), for example, cites the 1983 scores for Florida's state graduation examination. African-Americans constituted 57 percent of those failing the examination while they represented only 20 percent of the high-school senior class. At the broader, federal level, *The National Education Goals Report* (1994) found that the proportions of white and minority students meeting the Goals Panel reading performance standard in the twelfth grade "differed by 16–27 percentage points" (p. 36) in favor of the whites. Bias in favor of the middle-class white majority of high-school seniors appears to be an explanation for such results, and this is often assumed to be the case. However, the case has not been proved. As Carlos Ovando and Virginia Collier (1985) noted, "Until more is known, we can make only subjective judgments of what is and what is not cultural" (p. 250), and, to continue the thought, of what is and what is not bias in testing.

Notwithstanding our many doubts about the real meaning of test scores, the Kentucky Supreme Court, among others, has chosen to use them as an instrument of accountability. To hold schools responsible, indeed, to blame them for students who do not reach an acceptable level of achievement, as typically determined by one or another standardized test, is certainly questionable in light of the many complex factors impacting student performance. When the cultural diversity of minority groups is brought into the equation, our understanding of what is meant by accountability diminishes exponentially. Can any single test score or even a set of test scores accurately represent the myriad of activities and expectations associated with schooling? It is, to say the least, highly unlikely.

The very idea of accountability of schooling is a marked break with our past. Educational opportunity for all has not historically meant equal academic achievement for all (Foster, 1991, pp. 34–35). In fact, when the bell curve is used to compare students' test scores, and this has long been our scholastic tradition, a certain percentage of students are expected to fail.

The Nature of Testing

For this entire century, public schools have been involved in a major controversy. On the one hand, there are those, represented by Edward L. Thorndike (1913) and B.F. Skinner (1953), who believe the curriculum can be subdivided into clearly delimitable components, then translated, as part of curriculum planning or "engineering," into specific performance objectives, and finally, evaluated by the "scientific" testing of what students have achieved in light of the pre-established, clearly defined objectives. On the other hand, there are those, represented by John Dewey (1910; 1963), Elliot W. Eisner (1985) and Howard Gardner (1983), who believe that learning must be understood in terms of holistic experiences that can only be fully described in context and *after* students have actually engaged in learning. Given this conception, objectives are typically broad and somewhat open-ended. Evaluating holistic outcomes usually involves qualitative and subjective forms of assessment.

The relatively recent reform movement in testing, *authentic assessment*, like Eisner's (1985) connoisseurship, assumes that holistic performance must be and can be evaluated in holistic, humanistic ways. However, though continuing to gain momentum, authentic assessment remains little more than a minor player in the twentieth century history of testing. Although certainly worthy of our attention in this chapter because of its potential to lead to significant testing reform, the standardized, objectively conceived version of evaluating learning has undoubtedly dominated American education and continues to do so in the latter years of the twentieth century.

Standardized Testing

Standardized tests that permit comparisons of one student's score with that of another according to a bell curve distribution are known as *norm-referenced tests*. This type of objective test has characteristically been used in determining accountability. Norm referencing, is accomplished by using percentile scores that represent the percentage of individuals in a standardization sample who fall below a given raw score. For instance, if 15 percent of subjects taking a test obtain fewer than 20 correct answers on a test, a raw score of 20 is equivalent to the fifteenth percentile. Students' responses to items used in a norm-referenced test are carefully monitored to determine whether the distribution of right and wrong responses continues to support the assumption of a bell curve distribution. In those instances where the items are judged as not sustaining the assumption of a bell curve, they are either adjusted or abandoned (Berlak, 1992, p. 10). Thus, norm-referenced tests have built into their very design that a certain percentage of students will fail. It is hardly reasonable to blame the schools for such failures, albeit that has, in recent times, often been the case.

In 1963, Robert Glaser proposed using *criterion-referenced tests*, which would assess mastery of a specified content domain rather than compare the performances of students. Criterion-referenced tests are based on established benchmarks for learning that everyone is assumed *able* to achieve and ought to achieve. That is, a given population is not used as the basis for interpreting test scores, but rather some pre-established conception of what students ought to know about a content area is used. Criterion-referenced tests have been widely used in recent decades by school systems as a means of determining whether their students have achieved minimum competency, say, in the basic subjects. Nevertheless, norm-referenced tests, such as the California Achievement Test, dominate the testing administered in our schools and remain the primary instrument for assessing school accountability.

Both norm- and criterion-referenced tests share two basic assumptions, as has been noted by Lauren B. Resnick (1990). One is that knowledge can be decomposed into discrete elements that lose little in their isolation from other related elements. For instance, the Bill of Rights can be usefully memorized without students understanding the reasons why a democracy could become oppressive to the individual unless there were some form of protection. The other is that knowledge can be decontextualized, that is, skills or insights acquired in one context can be easily transferred to other contexts. For example, knowing how to think logically in mathematics contributes to thinking logically in questions of citizenship. Both these assumptions (decomposability and decontextualization) enable standardized tests to ask clear, delimited questions having very specific responses.

Despite differences in how normed- and criterion-referenced tests are designed, the items used in each are practically indistinguishable (Berlak, 1992 p. 11), being primarily multiple choice questions requiring the selection of a single correct answer. Regardless of the often avowed intent to develop creative, evaluative, and problem-solving skills in our youngsters, our standardized tests tend to emphasize ground-covering memorization based on specific, clearly delimited objectives. An analysis conducted by the

Mid-Continent Regional Educational Laboratory of multiple-choice test items included on the Stanford Achievement Battery revealed that "inferring" was required in only 6 percent of all items; "summarizing" was included in approximately 2 percent; "ordering" was found in 6 percent; "transposing" appeared in only 4 percent; and "representing" was essential in 7 percent. On the other hand, such a low-level skill as "retrieving" (involving the recall or recognition of information) was required for 100 percent of all items (Marzano and Costa, 1988). A parallel examination of the California Test of Basic Skills revealed comparable findings (Marzano and Costa, 1988). In sum, objective, standardized tests consistently evaluate a fairly low level of thinking. Their growing use as instruments of accountability encourages schools to emphasize simple, isolated skills over more complex, holistic ones.

Performance-Based, Holistic Testing: Authentic Assessment

In discussing traditional standardized tests, Grant Wiggins (1993) takes the position that they inadequately prepare the young for the "real, 'messy' uses of knowledge in context..." (p. 202). He goes on to say, "It makes no intellectual sense to test for 'knowledge' as if mastery were an unvarying response to unambiguous stimuli" (p. 202). The authentic assessment movement would remedy this by bringing complex, somewhat unpredictable contexts together with the inherently personal, intellectual performances of students so that the quality of students' judgment and their behavior can be evaluated in situations resembling real-world experiences. Developing portfolios—that is, of collections of students' works organized around a purpose or theme—and projects—that is, the assignment of problematic situations requiring multiple, real-world activities for resolution—are among the innovative approaches to evaluating holistic performance that are currently being pursued under authentic assessment.

The Role of Testing in School Reform

In the "bell curve" tradition that has dominated most of the twentieth century, the schools filled the role of gatekeepers, determining individual success and failure well beyond the school years. Those who could go on to college because they were able to engage in advanced intellectual activity were far more likely to succeed. Less gifted students academically would drop out by the eighth grade or with a high-school diploma. The now widely accepted view that everyone has a right to be prepared well enough to go to college or at least well enough to function effectively in business and industry has led to the current emphasis on the mastery of a minimum set of skills and content, and, unhappily, to "minimum" expectations as well.

Historically, schools were held responsible for the inputs of education and for the processes they pursued, but not for the outputs. Because of the preeminence that is now given to outputs, accountability has come to mean the attainment of clearly articulated learning objectives. Achievement scores have become the single most important means for holding schools accountable for the instruction they deliver.

Minorities especially have felt that the public schools have failed them and have demanded improved output for their youngsters. It is rather ironic that the instruments of accountability—the Iowa Tests of Basic Skills, the California Achievement Tests, the Metropolitan Achievement Tests, to name a few of the most widely used—have often been viewed as biased and culturally insensitive toward minority groups.

The question of test bias has hardly been resolved, but efforts to deal with bias have been redirected. Instead of trying to develop "culture-free" tests, as R.B. Cattell did in 1940 and Allison Davis and Kenneth W. Eels did in 1953, an undertaking generally considered futile today (Ovando & Collier, 1985), recent efforts have been turned toward achieving "culturally fair" examinations. Items that are judged to be "culturally loaded" are being eliminated from standardized tests. For example, an item asking about the color of a fruit such as the persimmon would not be used in areas where the fruit is not native. Items receiving a disproportionate number of correct or incorrect responses in association with a minority group would be modified in future test versions to control the statistical bias. Instructions for tests have already been modified to avoid the passive voice and language that is abstract in favor of active, concrete expression. Steps such as those just described have the purpose of giving children of diverse backgrounds an equal chance to perform well on standardized tests by limiting the inevitable effects of culture through the use of traits likely to be shared and easily understood by the vast majority of students taking the test. As noted earlier, the complexity of sociocultural factors impacting student performance is so considerable that we have been unable to produce much evidence of bias beyond our own observations and opinions, and we are by no means sure that, if test bias does indeed exist for America's minorities, we can identify or control it.

America/Goals 2000

We are now in the midst of a movement that would establish national standards for student learning through a federally-supported, nationwide system of assessment. In 1989, testing and its linkages to accountability were made the centerpiece for national educational reform. The well-publicized education summit between former President Bush and the state governors led to a reform strategy based on nationally administered standardized achievement tests and the recognition that "what gets tested gets taught" (Willis, 1992). The strategy was included as a part of the *America 2000* plan put forth by President Bush in accord with the nation's governors, among whom, it should be noted, was then-Governor Clinton. President Clinton has, for the most part, continued the program under the heading, *Goals 2000*.

One premise underlying this strategy is that the administering of well-designed tests and the dissemination of the results nationally will help the states improve the level of academic standards held for students as well as actual student achievement. Our historical experience with the ever-increasing use of standardized tests appears to be contrary to this idea. In fact, the decline in test scores has persisted for most of the second half of the twentieth century despite more testing and more newspaper comparisons of the performances of local schools.

Goal 3 of *America 2000* proposes that all students, "...leave grades four, eight, and twelve having demonstrated competency in challenging subject matter including English, mathematics, science, history, and geography" (U.S. Department of Education, 1990, p. 1). Early on, it became clear to the resource committee assigned to Goal 3 by the Goals Panel that curricular frameworks establishing the academic bases for the proposed national tests would be necessary and would need to be sustained by a broad, national consensus. Frameworks for mathematics and science were developed first; these were to be followed by history, the framework for which was completed in 1994 with funding from the National Endowment for the Humanities and the Department of Education. It was subsequently censored by the U.S. Senate because of the impression that America's role in history was too negatively portrayed. A federal grant was given to the National Council of Teachers of English (NCTE) to develop the language arts standards, which, however, was suspended in 1994 because of negative reactions to the Council's first draft. The Council decided to continue its development of language arts standards in collaboration with the International Reading Association (IRA).

The National Assessment of Educational Progress (NAEP), a research office originally established in 1969 by Congress to produce a descriptive profile of national educational performance, had its charge re-directed toward determining and then testing "what students should be able to do" (National Assessment Governing Board, 1991, p. vii). The NAEP, long prohibited from ranking or comparing schools either by districts or states, was authorized by an Act of Congress (P.L. 100–297) to engage in a limited, experimental effort to produce state-by-state comparisons of student performance first in mathematics and reading, and subsequently in history (Rothman, 1990c). In fact, in December 1989, the NAEP governing board adopted a resolution asking Congress to remove entirely the prohibition against utilizing "NAEP items and test data at the district and building levels." Furthermore, according to Chester E. Finn, former head of NAEP, the efforts of the President and the state governors to establish national goals led NAEP to adopt a plan to set national standards for student performance on the tests they administer.

In 1992, the Senate passed a bill called the Neighborhood Schools Improvement Act that placed into law the six goals of *America 2000*. In addition, both houses of Congress authorized and codified the Goals Panel (Jennings, 1992). Under the Clinton Administration, the Goals 2000: Educate America Act was passed. Among its various measures was the establishment of the National Education Standards and Improvement Council (NESIC), a panel of bipartisan experts designed to endorse the standards, which would then serve as the bases for national tests. As of February 1995, the growing criticism of the work on standards has led to a delay in appointing members to NESIC and the Republican-led Congress is considering its elimination before any members are seated. The entire standards enterprise may become a private effort. However, despite acrimonious debates concerning the work on standards of several, federally funded groups, the piloting of nationally oriented tests has proceeded on schedule, and it does not appear likely that the strategy for school reform based on national testing will be abandoned any time soon.

Although plans for national testing were under development, negative reactions to standardized testing were becoming a significant concern for those dedicated to the national testing movement. Thirteen states declined to participate in the initial NAEP pilot studies in mathematics conducted in March 1990 (Putka, 1990). Pittsburgh, a major industrial city, refused to join its state in submitting to the NAEP pilot tests. According to Paul LeMahieu, director of testing in the Pittsburgh public schools and former president of the National Association of Test Directors, the NAEP governing board "ignored many educators' requests for assessments that include fewer multiple-choice items and more writing or other demonstrations of progress" (Putka, 1990, B-1). Clearly, these were the stirrings of a movement to reconceptualize the nation's approach to testing.

NAEP accommodated the demands by undertaking four pilot studies involving performance-based, authentic assessment techniques. In the writing portfolio study, a nationally representative sample of fourth and eighth graders participated in the standard approach to writing assessment and also submitted portfolios of their best writing. The results of the evaluation of students' portfolios, issued in February 1995, were "not very good," according to Gary W. Phillips, associate commissioner at the National Center for Education Statistics, which oversees NAEP (Olson, 1995, p. 5). This was hardly surprising. More important, the "study found little relationship between how students did on the portfolio writing and their scores on the regular writing assessment…" (Olson, 1995, p. 5). Although the study demonstrated that writing and evaluating portfolios could be conducted on a large scale, it appears that different aspects of writing are examined when portfolios are used than under NAEP's traditional format. To use portfolio assessment as a means of meeting the federal goal for national testing, the differences in the two results must be understood more thoroughly than appears to be the case currently.

Debates and Dissension

Inevitably, debates about the usefulness and appropriateness of testing have reached levels of intensity in the 1990s unknown in prior decades (Olson, 1991; Wolk, 1992). Certainly, empowering the NAEP to pursue testing in such a way as to set standards for student performance nationwide is a significant source of dissension especially among educational professionals, many of whom feel their input has been short circuited by the nation's political leadership. The basic issue underlying these many debates is whether the standardized test—be it norm-referenced to fit a bell curve distribution or criterion-referenced to establish universal benchmarks for learning—or even holistic performance with efforts to standardize its qualitative, often subjective judgments should be used as an accountability instrument and, if so, for what purposes. The related issue is whether we should have a national curriculum, and if so, ought it be established through testing.

These issues compose the fulcrum for a whole series of related questions and debates. For example: Who or what agency shall take the schools to task for student performances deemed unacceptable? Who shall decide the extent and nature of the content to be tested? Are there learnings and goals established for schooling that are not measured appropriately by current testing methods? Ought the federal government hold local schools responsible for performances established at the national level, or is that the proper role of states or even of parents? Are standardized tests, typically based on multiple choice items, requiring students to recognize correct answers, valid instruments for school accountability? Are they valid representations of the goals we hold for schooling?

The federal government has been in recent years particularly prone to using the results of tests as justification for financial support. Such federally sponsored programs as Chapter 1 have been expected to meet stricter standards of performance than in the past, as measured by nationally normed tests. Schools failing to achieve higher performance standards have been required to sign program improvement agreements or lose their Chapter 1 funding (Lewis, 1992). Given the truly terrible fiscal state that a majority of American schools find themselves in, the awarding or denial of funds is tantamount to an iron grip over the curricula of the public schools and their implementation. The federal government's role in the engrandisement of the testing movement has inevitably been a part of the debates and will no doubt be exacerbated as the reforms of *America/Goals 2000* continue to be pursued, as appears quite likely under the Clinton presidency.

It should be noted in the context of education's ongoing fiscal crisis that NAEP has contracted with a privately-owned corporation, Educational Testing Service (ETS), to conduct the initial phases of national testing. The development and distribution of tests have generally been under the purvue of private companies. Testing has become a profitable, multibillion dollar industry. This must inevitably lead us to question the role that profits have had in the veritable explosion of testing and demands for school accountability. Are we testing to benefit our students or are our concerns for accountability urged on by a profitable and hungry industry?

This chapter cannot possibly explore all the many significant issues related to the testing/accountability reform movement in general or even within the more narrow context of social studies. The remainder of this chapter will, however, develop a series of perspectives from which these numerous issues can be viewed. It will attempt to examine the fit between standardized testing and the goals and content of social studies. It will examine issues related to the movement toward a national curriculum, especially as it impacts social studies. It will also look into the authentic assessment movement and the alternative tests that are being proposed as a way of overcoming the standardized test limitations, especially with regard to social studies.

PERSPECTIVES ON TESTING AND ACCOUNTABILITY: AN OVERVIEW

Not many classroom teachers or school administrators support testing as it is now being pursued. For the most part, professional educators are well aware that schooling is a multilevel process that can be fundamentally altered by decisions made at any level of the organization (Barr and Dreeben, 1983). The number of students assigned to a class, the busing of students to a school, or the presence of an active Parent Teacher Association (PTA) are examples of decisions having profound effects on learning while often being beyond the control of either the teachers or administrators who are, nevertheless, held accountable. What is more, tests representing the simplest forms of learning are being used to evaluate their work.

Generally, the arguments opposing standardized tests for school accountability can be viewed from at least five distinct perspectives: (1) legal and other sources of legitimacy for accountability; (2) the nature of goals for the curriculum and how they are developed; (3) the validity and appropriateness of using measuring instruments for school accountability; (4) fiscal responsibility;

and (5) benefit(s) to students. A brief exploration of each is undertaken here for the purpose of establishing the context within which debates about accountability and standardized testing in social studies occur. The effort will then be to redirect and expand these debates for the unique content and purposes associated with social studies.

Legal and Other Sources of Legitimacy for Accountability

The first of these five perspectives revolves around the U.S. Constitution and the fact that the founding fathers gave authority over education to the states and not to the federal government. For most of our history, the federal government remained uninvolved in educational policy, especially at the elementary and secondary levels. Indeed, a cabinet office at the presidential level for education was not established until 1979. Essentially, education developed as a community-based undertaking guided by locally elected school boards. That was what was legally provided for in the Constitution. It is a grass-roots approach often considered to be crucial to American democracy and the cultural diversity that has been its embodiment for most of its history.

In the 1960s and early 1970s, the Federal government enacted a series of programs that were intended to influence how the states conducted education. Because there was no legal authority to affect change, the government used grants and other forms of funding to entice compliance by the states. Both Democrats and Republicans—liberals and conservatives—have since then supported a variety of federally funded educational initiatives from drug education to vocational training and early childhood education. Federal evaluation of the results of these programs have come to be seen as important input for developing future educational policy. The federal government's use of standardized testing to establish national standards and, by implication, a single national curriculum, is a logical continuation of earlier federal policy that would bring about change in public education through funding. It is, however, one more step away from the original intent of the Constitution and from that local involvement often considered crucial to the success of education. The opposition is well represented in this statement by John Taylor Gatto (1992, p. S14): "The first 200 years of U.S. history reveal the true public consensus on schooling—the more kinds the better for all of us."

In fairness to the nationally oriented testing and accountability reform movement, and certainly in a uniquely American way, everyone is getting in on the act (Anrig, 1992, p. S7). Numerous organizations have become involved in efforts to develop a national testing system, each with a somewhat different perspective on how standards and assessments should be achieved. All, however, envision the voluntary involvement of the nation's schools. Among them are, to mention but a few, the following: Education America Inc., a private organization founded to promote and possibly develop a mandatory high-school achievement test; the New Standards Project, a joint effort of the National Center on Education and the Economy and the Learning Research and Development Center to create a voluntary examination system; the Core Knowledge Foundation, established by E.D. Hirsch in 1990 to disseminate cultural literacy nationwide and pilot two examinations at the sixth and twelfth grade levels; and, of course, the National Assessment Governing Board established by Congress to set policy for NAEP in its endeavors to develop national standards through a testing program. Perhaps diversity in education is built deeply enough into our American traditions, as George R. Anrig (1992), president of Educational Testing Service, suggests, so that even a national movement led by two U.S. presidents cannot be implemented in a singular fashion.

There remains, nevertheless, a question of legitimacy that goes beyond legal and organizational considerations, and even supercedes whatever limits may be associated with standardized testing. What are parents' rights over the minds of their children (Sizer, 1992)? Should parents hold the schools responsible for the textbooks used and the library books stored on their shelves? Is it legitimate for one parent or even a large, albeit minority, group of parents to demand changes in the school's curriculum because of their dissatisfaction with what is happening in the schools? Who ought to be responsible for the moral, emotional, and intellectual development of children? School people? Parents? The federal government? When do children become accountable for themselves?

These questions of legitimate authority over children's development do conflict in important ways with the current testing and accountability reform movement. To the extent that a small group of parents or a special interest group of any kind believes they have the legitimate authority to re-direct, limit, or change school instruction, the schools themselves cannot be held accountable, especially for the performances of students on standardized tests designed for a single national curriculum. *Creationism*, a so-called scientific movement that was politically notable in Louisiana in the late 1980s, would have placed the teaching of biblical creation along side the theory of evolution. The fundamental conflict with national, standardized testing must surely be obvious. There is, on the one hand, the legitimate authority of parents and local groups over the development of their children and, on the other hand, the increasing responsibility being assigned schools for the development of children. Where national academic standards fit into this picture is not at all clear.

The Nature of Goals for the Curriculum and How They are Developed

Goals are the school-based translations of society's aims for education. They represent the philosophy and the vision of what people hope education will do for their children. Ideally, goals are not imposed on the schools through testing, but are rather supported by the locally elected school-board members, their appointed administrators, and the traditions that have grown up around schooling. Goals are ultimately turned into clearly articulated sets of learning activities that are expected to contribute to the achievement of the goals. Testing and measurement of what students have actually learned has become the standard approach to evaluating the successful implementation of the objectives, and, by implication, the goals. The use of testing to influence the nature of goals is quite a reversal of the usual process.

The focus on learning objectives as measurable outputs has its roots in the work of Ralph Tyler who, in the 1930s, headed a major national project examining student learning known as the Eight-Year Study (Stufflebeam and Shinkfield, 1985). According to Tyler (1949), evaluation was best accomplished by ascertaining how well specific instructional objectives had been mastered. This particular form of output evaluation based on linking specific objectives with student achievement put forth by Tyler has dominated modern educational evaluation and our interpretation of accountability until this most recent reform movement. For the first time in our history, it is being proposed that evaluation lead the development of goals rather than vice versa.

The clearly articulated, precise nature of the objectives used as the bases for standardized testing necessarily impact the depth, scope, and complexity of the curriculum, limiting what is studied to what is observable and measurable. Appreciating artistic creativity, grasping the central thrust of a work, reflecting on the underlying meaning for society of a set of historical events must all be transformed into behaviors that are measurable on the traditional standardized test. Students must "identify," not "reflect"; they must "select" or "list," not "realize" or "value." Being complex, reflective and holistic are unsuitable characteristics for the traditional standardized test. The very nature of the content, regardless of subject, is often changed and narrowed to make it fit the requirements of standardized testing and the dominant multiple-choice item.

Of course, some content areas are more suitable to such modification than are others. Mathematics and the sciences appear to benefit from the narrowing and increased rigor typically introduced by standardized tests; there are, however, many professionals in mathematics and the sciences who find current tests counterproductive in terms of the problem solving that they believe needs to characterize their respective fields. Subjects such as social studies, fundamentally rooted in the uncertainties and complexities of social and political interaction, may be required to alter their qualitative nature to fit the requirements of test item structure.

In addition to narrowing the traditional areas of study, standardized tests have unwittingly become impediments to change in the curriculum. For example, there is currently a movement to include statistics in the high-school curriculum. However, unless statistics becomes a subject for standardized testing, little real attention is likely to be given to the subject. Not being the object of a national test undermines the attention that would otherwise be given to a content area. Mathematics and science are included in the NAEP efforts whereas art and music are not; in social studies, history is included whereas economics and political science are not (Viadero, 1991). If teachers and the schools are to be evaluated on the basis of test scores, it must surely be obvious that art and music and economics and political science are likely to be omitted from the curriculum and, in any case, would be instructionally neglected.

In sum, on the one hand, the nature of the content (and of the goals as well) in the various subjects is limited, even trivialized, by the kinds of test items employed; on the other hand, the range of subject areas included in the curriculum is limited by the range of subjects targeted for standardized testing. The conceptualization and implementation of new areas of academic studies are greatly restricted under such circumstances. Nationally based, standardized testing contributes to the narrowing of the existing curriculum as well as to the continuation of a status quo curriculum.

The Validity and Appropriateness of Using Standardized Tests for School Accountability

Beyond the issues related to whether testing should be allowed to influence the nature of the curriculum and its goals, is the question concerning how accountability for the schools ought to be pursued. Although current measuring instruments focus on the academic performances of students, schools are burdened with responsibilities that range from developing traditional values and appropriate social behaviors to caring for under-nourished, poor rural and inner-city children. Increasing numbers of children come from broken homes, violent neighborhoods, and drug-infested streets. They frequently work or watch television into the early hours of the morning only to sleep through classes at their desks. These are circumstances the public schools cannot ignore; the schools are responsible whether they like it or not. How should responsibilities of this sort be brought into the accountability equation, or should these be ignored as they are now through the widespread use of standardized tests? The underlying meaning of our current approach to school accountability is that what counts in determining the quality of a school is the academic performance of the student body. All else appears to be irrelevant.

How valid are the tests we are using to measure the performance of schools in the real world? George R. Anrig (1992), president of Educational Testing Service, opposes using test scores to determine accountability. In his view, "If we want information about how schools are doing, then let's get information, not simply scores from a single test"(p. S7). The evaluation of one of society's most complex institutions, education, has been reduced to a set of scores representing mostly low-level skills as measured by multiple-choice items. Can anyone seriously believe this is an appropriate approach to accountability?

Fiscal Responsibilty

Standardized testing has become a multibillion dollar industry. Financially-strapped school districts have been required to spend an increasing portion of their budget to demonstrate that they are effective. Of course, the more money and time spent on demonstrating effectiveness, the fewer the resources available to help schools become effective. It is not uncommon to encounter school people who feel they are expending more energy on being accountable than on improving instruction or classroom conditions.

Is this money for testing well-spent? Would it be fiscally more responsible if the money were spent on resources or, possibly, on finding out what students *do* know so that the knowledge they bring to school can be built upon? At present, standardized tests tell us what students have not learned in subjects that have long been the mainstay of the curriculum. Holistic performance assessment would allow greater variety of student input, but this may not become a part of the assessment, which, to obtain national comparability, must be regularized according to some "standardized" format. Whether we like it or not, students and teachers put all their efforts into performing well on the tests, and these have been almost entirely directed toward the traditional academic subjects. Perhaps significant reform could be achieved if we were to direct the fiscal resources now dedicated to testing and accountability toward a fuller understanding of what our students know and need; toward the development of evaluative tools that encourage rather than impede change; and toward establishing new, more relevant curricular directions.

Benefit(s) to Students

Possibly the single most important perspective that needs to be explored in the testing and accountability reform movement is whether the benefits derived from testing compensate students sufficiently for the negatives that typically accrue. Achievement scores are indeed useful in diagnosing student academic performance and helping teachers to direct their instruction where the academic "need" is greatest. But significant resources are deflected from students to cover the costs for testing, resources that could be dedicated to improving the curriculum and its instructional delivery.

Furthermore, tests are now given to all students nearly every year, consuming precious instructional time. Indeed, in some states, tests are being administered to kindergarten children as a requirement for entering first grade. According to Jean Harris and Joseph Sammons of the New York Public

Interest Research Group (1989), 75 percent of New York schools surveyed test their kindergarten pupils. By the second grade, 93 percent of the students are tested. To paraphrase Anrig (1992), what can possibly be learned from a ninety-minute test administered to a five-year-old child that a teacher and parents working months with a child do not already know well enough to make judgments about placement and promotion (p. S7). On the other hand, children who are tested and do not move on may be emotionally scarred by the experience, indeed, "turned off" to schooling in general and the pressure brought on by the undue emphasis on test results and what they do not know.

We also need to remember that although schools may be held responsible for the inadequate performances of their students, it is the students who will be held back a grade or denied graduation or viewed as lacking in native ability. Whether the traditional bell curve, mastery, or holistic performance underlies the interpretation of test scoring, allowances for cultural and personal differences are rarely made. Socioeconomic background and cultural diversity are considerations put forth by those resisting educational reform based on standardized test scores. These, however, are often set aside by current reformers who claim they are no more than excuses for ineffective schools that have unacceptably lowered their expectations for poor and culturally diverse children. Those resisting counter that this pressure to have students perform well on tests has led to a narrowing of curriculum offerings and to more meager content (Corbett and Wilson, 1990).

Comparing the test scores of school districts can have other detrimental effects as well. Imagine attending a school whose average test score is below the city/state/national average. You understand that your school is a nearly impossible one to teach at, and the test scores prove it. The situation is bound to lower your self-esteem especially after average school scores are published by the local newspaper. It may even induce you to avoid your school all together. Is the meager information derived from test scores worth the potential devastation of self-esteem? What are the benefits to students that justify putting them at such substantial risk? This author is certainly hard-pressed to justify the explosion in test usage that has characterized schooling in the past several decades.

THE SOCIAL STUDIES, THE REFORMERS, AND NATIONAL TESTING

The debates generally associated with the accountability and testing reform movement are relevant as well to the field of social studies. Should nationally based tests be the primary instrument for accountability in social studies? Are the tests we typically use appropriate measures for what we intend to accomplish in social studies? Should we allow the curriculum to change to fit the test requirements? Are the benefits that may accrue from testing worth the negatives? Are our limited resources being wisely spent on testing? What legitimate authority underlies what we propose to do in social studies with tests?

These questions could be validly asked about any of our school subjects. However, every field has certain unique characteristics that ought to be explored in greater depth and assigned greater weight whatever the plan for reform may be. In social studies, concerns related to control of the curriculum by a nationally devised set of standardized tests are especially relevant. Professionals in mathematics, science, and English may debate a particular sequence or the curricular inclusion of a topic or two, but they already have a broad consensus concerning the content and structure of their respective curricula. It is quite another story for social studies.

Since the establishment of social studies as a school subject in 1916, there have been numerous controversies regarding the nature of the social studies and its appropriate content. By developing standardized tests in history and geography, important issues about the way the social studies curriculum ought to be organized are being short-circuited, and professionals in the field are being handed *de facto* decisions that render discussion and debate irrelevant. Although the development of curricular frameworks for geography and history have been undertaken by the NAEP as a necessary first step in structuring standardized tests, the omission of other social-science disciplines, of issue-centered studies, and of critical evaluation disregards years of work and research in the field and imposes the status quo curriculum that has long dominated public-school practice. If, for example, a school system wished to give prominence to social problems related to current events, it would find that the nationally distributed, standardized tests ignore this kind of content. In effect, the standardized tests have made the *de facto* curricular decision that the study of social problems is not important. At the very least, the study of social problems could not meet Goal 3 of *America 2000* because it would be difficult to demonstrate.

Authentic assessment with its emphasis on evaluating holistic performance does have the potential of dealing with "real, 'messy' uses of knowledge in context" (Wiggins, 1993, p. 202), and, most certainly, knowledge associated with the practice of citizenship in a democracy is "messy"!

The 1995 debates over appropriate history and language arts standards, which found Congress directly involved in opposition to the standards developed by content experts, may impede the use of authentic assessment in social studies. Realistic demonstrations of democratic citizenship in action hold considerable potential for offending the sensitivities of many groups—from arch conservatives who believe the development of patriotism is of foremost importance to liberal groups demanding "politically correct" public discourse. Grant Wiggins (1993) illustrated performance assessment following a history unit on the Revolutionary War. Only a section of his example is reproduced here, but it is sufficient for the reader to consider the kinds of controversies that might arise.

> You are a prosecutor or a defense attorney in a trial brought by a parent group seeking to forbid purchase by your high school of a U.S. history textbook, excerpted below....You will present a 10-minute oral case (supported by a written summary of your argument), in pairs, to a jury, taking either side of the question. (p. 202)

Content Validity

In the context of reforming education by using tests that yield nationally comparable scores, Wiggins' example poses a crucial problem. How can the multitude of disparate responses possible be assessed in a form that is comparable among literally millions of respondents? The obvious answer is that certain major criteria would be established and experts would review responses on the bases of standards set within the criteria. Unfortunately, realistic performance related to the use of knowledge as citizens of a democracy is messy. The liklihood is that messy knowledge will be avoided or made to conform to predicatable limits. If, as reformers hope, school subjects will be influenced by what is tested, the study of controversial issues related to the exercise of democratic citizenship are likely to be curtailed.

Ignoring the kinds of content that could be important to reforming the study of citizenship, and that are, as well, unique to the subject, would place the content validity of the tests being administered at risk. Content validity refers to what a test measures. In other words, how well does the test content represent the domain of content that is the object of measurement? If, for example, reading comprehension is being assessed, a score based on the ability to spell is only minimally related to the domain being measured. If students in social studies are asked to know the major events of the Revolutionary War rather than how the principles of the Revolution may or may not be acceptable in America today, what they learn will tend to be detached from their involvment as active citizens.

In social studies, the resemblance between what students are expected to learn, as expressed in the goals and objectives, and what is actually tested may be insufficient to measure whether the intended outcomes have been achieved. When content validity is judged inadequate, this means that the test does not cover a representative sample of the kinds of knowledge and skills that students are expected to learn. With the historical reversal of tests leading (instead of following) the content and purposes of a subject, it appears that the messiness of controversial issues, the uncertainty about historical facts and the myriad of potential interpretations for almost every topic related to exercising democratic citizenship would all be molded to the national testing requirements for comparability.

The Nature of Social Studies Content

Social studies is typically expected to prepare youngsters to be actively involved citizens of a democracy. This must necessarily mean preparing them with the skills and knowledge necessary to make intelligent decisions in the midst of uncertainty and compromise. In terms of content validity, can standardized testing, whether norm-referenced or criterion-referenced, typically based on multiple-choice items requiring mostly retrieval and recall, offer a reasonable measure of what needs to be learned for citizenship? The secondary question implicit in this discussion is whether citizenship can be developed through the study of history, geography, and civics as we currently implement these subjects in our schools. There is at least good reason to suspect that the current testing movement with all of its accountability baggage will lead us to adopt a *de facto* national curriculum that has little to do with developing citizenship.

The fact that we would undertake to develop citizenship means, by implication, developing "good" citizenship for we surely would not want to work toward any other kind. However, our collective interpretation of "good" remains full of such platitudinal ideas as "law-abiding," "patriotic," "reflective involvement," and so forth, any one of which could engage us in a far-reaching debate about what we, members of a democracy, most value in our behavior as citizens. Imagine the discussions that could occur not only among social studies professionals, but even the public-at-large regarding questions such as these: Are students who challenge authority less likely to become "good" citizens than those who accept and support the decisions of the elected leadership? Are they less likely to be patriotic? Does "good" refer to the citizen who has been well socialized into the operations of society and government or does it refer to the independent thinker capable of challenging and even interfering with those operations? Is it viable for "good" to refer to both? Should we teach our young about a singular model of citizenship, probably the democratic one pursued in our own nation, and involve students in learning the knowledge and skills most important for its continued practice, or should we seek to study different models of citizenship as they may be found around the world today? Would federal dominance via testing impede our numerous, disparate efforts to educate "good," citizens and possibly ignore the cultural diversity that has long been a significant component of our American brand of democracy? We need to be very clear about the risks posed by national testing before we embrace it as a means of raising our academic standards.

Beyond such uniquely American debates, the very conception of citizenship in our modern times is in a state of flux and uncertainty. Increasingly, we think of citizenship as a global affair with global responsibilities while our perceptions of the obligations imposed on us by national citizenship have hardly changed at all. The purposes of one's nation may well be in conflict with those of the world. How does a citizen decide from among competing citizenships? How do the characteristics of a global citizen differ from the characteristics of a national citizen, and what is the nature of the relationship that ought to exist between the two? What is the responsibility of schools everywhere toward each? Unfortunately, these problems have been entirely ignored in the NAEP test-development process. These problems go to the very heart of content validity.

The history framework completed in 1994 and based on *Lessons from History: Essential Understandings and Historical Perspectives Students Should Acquire* (Crabtree, 1990) has encountered opposition from a multitude of quarters. Congress voted 99 to 1 to withdraw support for the framework because it was not sufficiently favorable to our American role in history. Others interested in issue-oriented social studies education were also very disgruntled. Although the framework refers to citizenship from time to time, it hardly confronts the changing nature of citizenship or the continuing uncertainty and complexity that citizens face whenever they become involved in politics.

Recent curricular discussions concerning reform in social studies have revolved mostly around such questions as whether the time allocated to American history should be decreased in favor of studies in Western Civilization or World Civilization (Bradley Commission on History in the Schools, 1988; Curriculum Taskforce of the National Commission on Social Studies in the Schools, 1989.)[1] We have been paying little attention indeed to the nature of citizenship in a modern democracy and the kinds of actions and involvements that constitute the behaviors of "good" citizenship. Few have explored the nature of knowledge directly relevant to the achievement of effective citizen behavior in a modern democracy.[2] Under such circumstances, it is doubtful that testing can actually lead social studies curricular reform.

---

[1] The Bradley Commission Report and NCSS' *Charting a Course: Social Studies for the 21st Century* are representative of the kinds of proposals put forth for the revision of history studies.

See also: Thornton, S.T. (1990). "Should We Be Teaching More History?" *Theory and Research in Social Education* 18(1)53–60.

[2] Notable exceptions include the following:

Engle, Shirley H. and Anna Ochoa (1988). *Education for Democratic Citizenship: Decision-Making in the Social Studies.* New York: Teachers College Press.

Shaver, James P. (1989). "Lessons from the Past: The Future of an Issue-Centered Social Studies Curriculum." *The Social Studies* 80(5):192–196.

Thornton, S.T. (1990). "Should We Be Teaching More History?" *Theory and Research in Social Education* 18(1):53–60.

William Bennett (1988), while still Secretary of Education, professed shock that standardized tests had revealed ignorance among American students about the Monroe Doctrine and even about when the Civil War took place. According to Bennett, one-third of 17-year-olds could not identify Lincoln as the author of the Emancipation Proclamation, nearly half could not recognize Patrick Henry as the patriot who said, "Give me liberty or give me death," and 70 percent were unaware of the purposes of Jim Crow laws (p. A32). Indeed, many parents and teachers joined him in shock even though it is not at all clear how such knowledge would contribute to improved citizenship behavior.

What is it that we expect to achieve when we have students memorize the significant dates of American wars or the major steps in passing a bill or even what the Monroe Doctrine is about? In what ways does memorized knowledge of American history lead to increased knowledge about how to be a more active and effective citizen in a democracy? Do we believe that it is knowledge necessary to the functioning of a citizen or that it will help youngsters to become more enthusiatic about their participation in governance? Would Americans vote more frequently if their factual knowledge of American history were greater? Would they follow the ins and outs of Congressional debates more closely and make their views known more assiduously to their representatives if they could name all the states of the Union and their capitals or even all their senators?

The relationship of how and what we are testing and the practice of "good" citizenship is obscure indeed. Bennett talks extensively about the need to have students develop their thinking skills and study high-school subjects in greater depth (pp. A36–A37). He asserts the need to have tests that are not so "one-dimensional" that coaching in test-taking skills can improve the test scores (p. 37). However, nowhere does he discuss the kinds of knowledge and skills most relevant for effectively practicing citizenship in a democracy. He appears not to have thought about the appropriateness of using paper and pencil tests to determine how well students have mastered the knowledge and skills necessary for competent citizenship. It may well be that he views our traditional forms of history, geography, and civics as pivotal knowledge for social studies, but certainly the question of what knowledge is most valuable should be pursued as a curricular matter deserving of district, state, and national discussion, and not as a product of a federally-funded testing agency, no matter how wise and well-meaning it may be.

The issues related to testing and accountability in social studies are significant and largely ignored. In a democratic form of government, should the federal government have a central role in preparing the very young for "good" citizenship? Who is served by testing in social studies? Those seeking conformity? Historians? Civil libertarians? Citizens? Should such questions not be answered before the federal government is allowed to use testing in a stick-and-carrot approach that would essentially force American public schools to teach the same skills and content nationwide? Should a national social studies curriculum be established through a system of national testing? Indeed, should there be a national social studies curriculum?

THE AUTHENTIC ASSESSMENT MOVEMENT AND ALTERNATIVE TESTING

Considerable dissatisfaction with standardized, multiple-choice tests has come from a wide range of sources, not least of which is the former Secretary of Education, William Bennett. In January 1990, the Council for Basic Education, the American Association of Colleges for Teacher Education, the American Federation of Teachers, the National Association for the Education of Young Children, and the National Association of Elementary School Principals all joined a group of prominent researchers in requesting that alternative forms of assessment be used to measure progress toward attaining educational goals (Rothman, 1990b). They issued the *Statement of Genuine Accountability* in which they called for abandoning traditional testing instruments and for support to be given to more appropriate alternatives (Open Testing, *FairTest Examiner*, 1990). A. Graham Down, Executive Director of the Council for Basic Education expressed the group's dissatisfaction this way:

> The world we live in needs people who can think, write, evaluate, compare and weigh competing ideas. These abilities are the essence of education. But they cannot be assessed by multiple-choice tests. (*FairTest Examiner*, 1990, p. 6)

There is a growing awareness of the inadequacies in testing caused by the dominance of the multiple-choice item. The search for approaches to measurement that more clearly reflect the kinds of learning we say we would like to achieve, such as the ability to evaluate critically and to engage in creative problem solving, has gained momentum in what may be called the authentic-assessment movement of the 1990s.

Advocacy is growing for authentic assessments that would evaluate student performance in relationship to the real world reasons given for studying whatever may be included in the curriculum (Mitchell, 1990). For the study of citizenship, authentic assessment would establish the tasks that could be performed to demonstrate a student's readiness to serve as a citizen of a democracy (Parker, 1990, p. 16). These tasks, according to Walter Parker (1990), "must go to the heart of democratic citizenship," which means, "they would have to engage students in the use of already-developed knowledge in deliberations on the public's problems, especially its raging controversies" (p. 18). In sum, authentic assessment involves the effort to increase the content validity of evaluation. Citizens in a democracy must be engaged in the controversies of their times; they must be able to use the best available knowledge concerning the problems at hand so that they can participate intelligently in their governance.

The authentic-assessment movement is still in the early stages of development and its terminology is still in the making. Terms such as "alternative assessment," "performance assessment," and "authentic assessment" carry somewhat different and often ambiguous meanings, but they have in common an emphasis on the holistic evaluation of student performance as opposed to testing facts and skills isolated from each other as typically occurs in multiple-choice items.

There have been numerous efforts recently to pilot new approaches to assessment. For example, the New Standards Project, in collaboration with 17 states and 6 school districts, has been experimenting with ways of evaluating student performance by means of *portfolios* or collections of students' best performances and *projects* involving the students in challenging, reality-based tasks (Brewer, 1992, p. 28). An example of a mathematics project follows:

> The new Ninja Turtle cereal is offering a collector's set of four Teenage Mutant Ninja Turtle figures. Each specially marked box has only one figure: Donatello, Leonardo, Michelangelo, or Raphael. In order to get all four figures, you can collect one from each box of cereal, or you can send in one box top and $15.

> If each box of cereal costs $2.39, what would be the cheapest way to collect all four figures? A. Send one box top and $15, or B. Purchase boxes of cereal until you have a completed set.

> Design an experiment to determine how many boxes of cereal you must buy to get a complete set of four different figures. Did your test support your predictions (*Sample Tasks* in 1991, 16)?

In addition to projects, the written essay dealing with an assigned topic has become one of the most widely used instruments for alternative testing, in particular, for developing portfolios. The NAEP is planning a substantial increase in the number of open-ended items that require students to write their own responses. A special test, to be administered by the NAEP to some 2000 students, will attempt to assess oral fluency by having students read a text aloud to a teacher, after which they will orally respond to questions (Rothman, 1990b). Student portfolios of classroom work in reading will also be assembled and evaluated by teams of visiting experts. Students will be required to respond to open-ended questions in their own words. This emphasis on reflective fluency goes a long way toward the qualitative evaluation of student performance—how well students interpret and analyze situations, their ability to deal with problems, and their willingness and capacity to weigh the negatives of an outcome against the positives.

Most alternatives reflect an effort to move beyond test items requiring single, correct responses to tasks that require reflection and a series of complex activities. The contrast between the project example mentioned earlier and the typical multiple-choice item is considerable. For example, a typical item from the 'interpreting data' section of a Random House study guide (Hayes, 1991, p. 139) for fifth and sixth graders presents a chart showing the number of boxes of fruit ordered by a school on a monthly basis, and then asks:

> How many boxes of fruit does the school order each month?
>
> a) 75   b) 85   c) 120   d) 330

All twelve items included in the section are similar.

In social studies, if the achievement of good citizenship were to be accepted as a primary goal of study (as opposed to acquiring historical or geographical knowledge), then adult behaviors involved in the effective exercise of citizenship in a democracy would need to become the bases for assessing achievement. Fred M. Newmann and D.A. Archbald (1992) propose that the "quality and utility of assessment rest upon the extent to which the outcomes measured represent appropriate, meaningful, significant, and worthwhile forms of human accomplishment," attributes which they assign to the concept of *authenticity* (pp. 71–72). What are appropriate, meaningful, significant, and worthwhile forms of human accomplishment in terms of citizenship? Parker (1990) suggested among others the following tasks as suitable for the authentic assessment of democratic citizenship: (1) select a recent public controversy as described by newspapers and present the pros and cons of a position that might be taken with regard to the controversy; (2) compare and contrast the different ways societies have organized under the ideal of democracy; and (3) be capable of passing the United States citizenship test with 95 percent correct responses (p. 19). To the degree that tasks such as these are deemed representative of what the citizen meaningfully accomplishes in the real world of democracy, they can be considered a form of authentic assessment. In discussing academic achievement in general, Newmann and Archbald (1992) suggest the need to evaluate students' abilities to assemble and interpret information, to engage in disciplined inquiry and critical evaluation, and to conceive of new paradigms (pp. 72–73). These are certainly highly desirable behaviors for citizens in a democracy, but they are hardly sufficient. Other qualities are even more important for authentic achievement in social studies. Students studying for citizenship should become capable of engaging actively and reflectively in compromise; they should become capable of making decisions in the midst of uncertainty; and, most important, they should acquire the skills and patience necessary to continue inquiry in the face of burgeoning and unruly complexity. Their understanding of the real-world operations of political power at every level of governance from the global to the local should be greatly increased as should their willingness to become politically involved.

Certainly, as Newmann and Archbald (1992) emphasized, lists of "recommended knowledge or skills" (p. 76) would hardly describe authentic achievement nor would they be a sufficient basis for authentic testing. Newmann and Archbald suggest that substantive conversation (pp. 76–77), that is, conversation in which students express their points of view, attend to each other's inputs, and engage in solving problems they have not solved previously, could be used as an appropriate means of instruction. The school environment could support collaboration with others, the flexible use of time, access to a variety of tools and resources, and reasonable student discretion over the topics and projects pursued (pp. 78–79). Portfolios involving written solutions to new problem situations and projects engaging students in institutional and local governance structures reflect the study of democratic citizenship more fully and more accurately than any of the standardized, multiple-choice tests currently in use. Panels of experts could assess students' abilities to express ideas, to make use of the ideas of others, to employ the structures of governance effectively, to engage in inquiry, and so forth.

Reliability and the Alternative Testing Movement

Holistic, qualitative approaches to evaluating the accomplishment of citizenship goals in social studies are clearly more suitable to the nature of the social studies curriculum. The most challenging issue for the alternative testing movement concerns the intent to engage in national or statewide assessments that allow comparisons among the states and their schools. As Newmann and Archbald (1992) note, the feasibility of authentic assessment has not yet been demonstrated on a district or statewide basis (p. 82). For that matter, the feasibility of alternative assessment as it is currently being pursued by several states, as well as the NAEP in its effort to achieve a more satisfactory national test, remains to be demonstrated. The question is whether the diversity in responses possible with various authentic assessment techniques including portfolio collections and projects can be evaluated with a level of reliability sufficient to permit comparisons at any level beyond the individual classroom or school. Each portfolio should be reviewed by at least one evaluator and evaluators nationwide should apply the same standards to all work in ways that result in similar judgments. If their judgments are substantially dissimilar, then the reliability of the assessments is in doubt. Reliability in holistic, qualitative assessment is extremely difficult to accomplish within the same school system, let alone on a national basis. Even without the portfolios, open-ended questions would make scoring infinitely more complicated because a high degree of subjectivity would be introduced into the assessment process, and machine scoring would be rendered impractical.

The RAND Corporation (Rothman, 1992) has recently issued its findings concerning the state of Vermont's new assessment system involving portfolios. Interrater reliability in scoring portfolios was found to be very low, that is, there was little agreement among raters about the quality of students' work (p. 1). RAND proposes increased training for the evaluators as a possible remedy.

It is at best a doubtful remedy. Although there could be some improvement in interrater reliability based on increased training, authentic assessment using portfolios involves complex, qualitative determinations that are more in the humanistic rather than scientific vein. Under such circumstances, one can hardly expect a high interrater reliabilty. In essence, comparisons among schools based on alternative assessment scores would be highly suspect and unreliable. This might lead some to return to the multiple-choice, standardized test and its greater potential for reliability. But is what we gain from a high level of reliability worth our continuing with tests that are clearly inappropriate measures of such content as learning to be good citizens?

There is a fundamental incompatibility between concepts like independent thought or creativity and evaluation that is "standardized." The critical effects of such characteristics as the ethnicity of teachers and students, family and community expectations, socioeconomic conditions, and unique regional circumstances as well as differences in learning styles and personality (Massialas, 1991) are inevitably blurred by standardization and national control. Weighing the original performances of students, say, in Bangor, Maine, against those in Alexandria, Louisiana, or anywhere else yields nothing of value for the student, the schools, or the nation. Even if nationally based reliability for "standardized" alternative tests are proved to be feasible, what *rational* benefit could there be?

CONCLUSION

The current testing movement, linked to school accountability and multiple-choice tests, is an inadequate approach to assessing the social studies curriculum and its goals of developing effective citizenship for a democracy. In testing jargon, the content validity is weak. Efforts have been directed toward authentic assessment for it would evaluate school success in terms of real-world performance. However, good reliability among raters is exceedingly difficult to achieve and would certainly interfere with the effort to evaluate school performance according to some national scale that would permit comparisons among the states and their schools. The value of such comparisons for the progress of education in America is doubtful and the consumption of resources involved is certainly counterproductive.

The capacity of authentic assessment to reflect the real-world purposes of the curriculum is especially significant for social studies and certainly of greater value to student development than the standardized tests currently dominating educational assessment. The experience of authentic assessment by its very nature serves as an experience in citizenship and is therefore of instructional worth likely to benefit students as they move toward becoming effective citizens of a democracy.

Reflective Questions

1. *If the central goal of social studies is the development of citizenship, should knowledge directly related to the practice and understanding of citizenship play a central role in our evaluation of social studies? How important should history and geography be when the subject of social studies is evaluated? Explain your positions fully.*

2. *Who currently exercises control over the social studies curriculum? How would this change if a national evaluation comparing student performance state-by-state were successfully instituted? What advantages and disadvantages are likely to result from establishing a national system of assessment?*

3. *Do you agree that the schools should be held accountable? In what ways can we evaluate the schools without using student test results? How well spent are the resources, including time and effort, dedicated to evaluation? What is gained when we know the results?*

4. *What are the advantages of alternative testing for education in general and social studies in particular? What are the advantages of standardized testing? What is the liklihood that alternative forms of testing will become the dominant instruments of evaluation in American education? What are the reasons for your opinion?*

GLOSSARY

content validity   Refers to the degree of representativeness that a test has for the domain of content being measured.

criterion-referenced tests   Tests that measure an individual's achievement in a specific domain of knowledge. *Mastery and minimum competency tests* are widely-used examples.

norm-referenced tests   Tests that evaluate the performance of individuals relative to the performance of the group as a whole. The standard bell curve is often used as an instrument for making comparisons.

performance assessment   An holistic appraisal of student academic performance. *Authentic assessment* and *alternative assessment* are forms of performance assessment. Authentic assessment evaluates student behavior representative of meaningful and significant accomplishment in the area studied. Alternative assessment refers to non-standard assessments in general.

reliability   The extent to which a test demonstrates consistent measures across subjects and over time. *Interrater reliability* refers to the consistency of judgment among different raters.

ANNOTATED BIBLIOGRAPHY

Airasian, Peter W. (1987). "State Mandated Testing and Educational Reform: Contexts and Consequences." *American Journal of Education* 95:393–412.

An overview and analysis of state-mandated tests, the increased use of tests as instruments of policy, the "high stakes" pressure brought upon students, and the effects of the changed uses of tests on education.

Berlak, Harold, et al. (1992). *Toward a New Science of Educational Testing & Assessment*. Albany: State University of New York.

Questioning the assumptions of traditional standardized tests, the authors of this volume propose a model for evaluation based on the decision making of local schools and communities.

Beyer, L.E. (1988). *Knowing and Acting: Inquiry, Ideology and Educational Studies*. London: Falmer Press.

An analysis of the thinking skills composing inquiry, and how we can teach these skills to achieve mastery.

Cannell, J.J. (1987). *Nationally Normed Elementary Achievement Testing in America's Schools: How All 50 States are Above Average*, 2nd ed. Daniels, WV: Friends for Education.

An overview of the uses and misuses of standardized tests in America; particularly highlights the fact that the results of standardized tests from every state appear to indicate that the children of every state are above average.

Dorr-Bremme, D.W. and J.L. Herman (1986). *Assessing Student Achievement: A Profile of Classroom Practices (CSE Monograph Series in Evaluation No. 11)*. Los Angeles: UCLA Center for the Study for the Study of Evaluation.

An in-depth description of current evaluation practices in the classroom, including curriculum-embedded tests, teacher-made tests, norm-referenced tests, and criterion-referenced tests.

Houts, P., editor (1977). *The Myth of Measurability*. New York: Hart Publishing Co.

One of the earlier efforts debunking the assumptions and practices of testing in America.

Lybarger, M.B. (1991). "The Historiography of Social Studies: Retrospect, Circumspect, and Prospect." Pp. 1–15 in *Handbook of Research on Social Studies Teaching and Learning*, edited by J.P. Shaver. New York: Macmillan.

A discussion of the nature of the knowledge that has historically composed the social studies.

Messick, S. (1989). "Meaning and Values in Test Validation: The Science and Ethics of Assessment." *Educational Researcher* (March)18:2, 5–11.

The author takes the position that validity judgments are really value judgments, and social studies educators cannot meaningfully interpret the results of tests until the relationship of test scores to adult citizenship behavior is fully understood.

National Assessment for Educational Progress (1990). *The Nation's Writing Report Card.* Princeton: Educational Testing Service.

An influential report concerning the literary skills and literacy of American students.

Ovando, Carlos J. and Virginia P. Collier (1985). *Bilingual and ESL Clasrooms: Teaching in Multicultural Contexts.* New York: McGraw-Hill.

An extensive overview of bilingual and bicultural education in American schools, with particular emphasis on the traditional content areas.

Parsons, W.S. and M. Fairbairn, editors (1992). "African American History: Beyond Heroes." Special section in *Social Education* 56:6.

A collection of articles focusing on issues related to the development of the African American history curriculum, and its implementations in the schools.

Ravitch, Diane and C.E. Finn (1987). *What Do Our 17-Year-Olds Know? A Report on the First National Assessment of History and Literature.* New York: Harper & Row.

A report on the test performance of high-school seniors which is, on the whole, very poor, and, in the opinion of the authors, indicative of the need for radical school reform.

Wolf, D.P., P.G. LeMahieu, and J. Eresh (1992). "Good Measure: Assessment as a Tool for Educational Reform." *Educational Leadership* 50(6):8–13.

A practical proposal for instituting the use of performance tasks and portfolios, based on the collaboration of teachers and members of the community in general.

Zimmerman, B.J. and D.H. Shunk, editors (1989). *Self-Regulated Learning and Academic Achievement: Theory, Research and Practice.* NY: Springer-Verlag New York.

A collection of chapters dealing with the adaptation of a successful business approach based on self-regulating work teams to education; collaboration and formative feedback are essentials.

REFERENCES

Airasian, Peter W. (1987). "State Mandated Testing and Educational Reform: Contexts and Consequences." *American Journal of Education* 95:393–412.

Anrig, George R. (1992). "'A Very American Way:' Everybody's Getting Into the Act." *Education Week XI* 39:S7–S8.

Barr, R. and R. Dreeben (1983). *How Schools Work.* Chicago: University of Chicago Press.

Bennett, William (1988). "American Education: Making it Work" as reprinted in *The Chronicle of Higher Education* May 4, 1988. Pp. A29–A41.

Berlak, Harold (1992). "The Need for a New Science of Assessment." In *Toward a New Science of Educational Testing and Assessment*, edited by Harold Berlak, et al. Albany: State University of New York Press.

Bradley Commission on History in the Schools (1988). *Building a Curriculum: Guidelines for Teaching History in the Schools.* Washington, DC: The Educational Excellence Network.

Brewer, W.R. (1992). "Can Performance Assessment Survive Success?" *Education Week XI* 30:28.

Cattell, R.B. (1940). "A Culture-Free Intelligence Test, Part I." *Journal of Educational Psychology* 31:161–179.

"Coalition Calls for 'Genuine Accountability'" (1990). *FairTest Examiner* 4(1):1, +6.

Congressional Office of Technology Assessment (1992). *Testing in American Schools: Asking the Right Questions (Summary).* Washington, DC: Superintendent of Documents.

Corbett, H.D. and B. Wilson, (1990). *Testing, Reform, and Rebellion.* Norwood, NJ: Ablex Publishing.

Crabtree, Charlotte (1990). "Proposal of the National Center for History in the Schools: A Cooperative UCLA/NEH Research Program." Unpublished proposal submitted to the National Endowment for the Humanities.

Curriculum Task Force of the National Commission on Social Studies in the Schools (1989). *Charting a Course: Social Studies for the 21st Century.* Washington, DC: Issued by the National Council for the Social Studies.

Davis, Allison and Kenneth Eels (1953). *Davis-Eels Test of General Intelligence or Problem Solving Ability.* New York: World Book.

Dewey, John (1910). *How We Think.* Boston: D.C. Heath.

Dewey, John (1963). *Experience & Education.* New York: P.F. Collier (original publication 1938 by Kappa Delta Pi).

Eisner, Elliot W. (1985). *The Educational Imagination*, 2nd ed. New York: Macmillan.

Engle, Shirley H. and Anna Ochoa (1988). *Education for Democratic Citizenship: Decision-Making in the Social Studies.* New York: Teachers College Press.

Foster, J.D. (1991). "The Role of Accountability in Kentucky's Education Reform Act of 1990." *Educational Leadership.* 49(5):34–36.

Gardner, Howard (1983). *Frames of Mind: The Theory of Multiple Intelligences.* New York: Basic Books.

Gatto, John Taylor (1992). "Other Voices." *Education Week XI* 39:S14.

Glaser, Robert (1963). "Instructional Technology and the Measurement of Learning Outcomes." *American Psychologist* 39:93–104.

Goodlad, John I. (1992). "On Taking School Reform Seriously." *Phi Delta Kappan* 74(3):232–238.

Harris, Joan, and Joseph Sammons (1989). *How Standardized Tests Damage New York's Youngest Children*. New York: New York Public Interest Research Group.

Hayes, J., editor (1991). *How to Get Better Test Scores on Elementary School Standardized Tests*. New York: Random House.

Jennings, J.F. (1992). "Major Education Bills in Congress." *Phi Delta Kappa Legislative News* 2(1):1–4.

Lewis, A.C. (1992). "Preview of Chapter 1 Changes?" *Phi Delta Kappan* 73(10):740–41.

Linn, R. (1982). "Ability Testing: Individual Differences, Prediction and Differential Prediction." Part II, pp. 335–388, in *Ability Testing: Uses, Consequences, and Controversies*, edited by A.K. Wigdor and W.R. Garner. Washington DC: National Academy Press.

Marzano, R.J. and A.L. Costa (1988). "Question: Do Standardized Tests Measure General Cognitive Skills? Answer: No." *Educational Leadership* 45(8):66–71.

Massialas, Byron G. (1991). "Education for International Understanding." Pp. 448–458 in *Handbook of Research on Social Studies Teaching and Learning*, edited by J.P. Shaver. New York: Macmillan.

Mitchell, R. (1990). "Performance Assessment: An Emphasis on Activity." *Education Week* IX 18:25–36.

National Assessment Governing Board (1991). *The Levels of Mathematics Achievement: Initial Performance Standards for the 1990 NAEP Mathematics Assessment. National and State Summaries*. Washington, DC: National Assessment Governing Board.

National Education Goals Panel (1994). *The National Education Goals Report: Building a Nation of Learners*. Washington, DC: U.S. Government Printing Office.

Newmann, Fred M. and D.A. Archbald (1992). "The Nature of Authentic Academic Achievement." In *Toward a New Science of Educational Testing & Assessment*, edited by H. Berlak, *et al.* Albany: State University of New York Press.

"New York State Group Urges Ban on Testing in the Early Grades" (1989). *Education Week* IX 14:2.

Olson, L. (1991). "'Confusing' Array of Players Charts Course Toward National Standards." *Education Week* XI 8:1, 13–15.

Olson, L. (1995). "Students' Best Writing Needs Work, Study Shows." *Education Week* XIV 20:5.

Open Testing (1990). *FairTest Examiner* 4:1, 1–6. Cambridge, MA: National Center for Fair and Open Testing.

Ovando, Carlos J. and Virginia P. Collier (1985). *Bilingual and ESL Classrooms: Teaching in Multicultural Contexts*. New York: McGraw-Hill.

Parker, Walter C. (1990). "Assessing Citizenship." *Educational Leadership* 50(3):17–22.

Putka, G. (1990). "Educators Decry U.S. Push to Toughen School Testing." *Wall Street Journal* March 13, 1990. P. B–1.

Resnick, Lauren B. (1990). "Tests as Standards of Achievement in School." Pp. 63–80 in *The Uses of Standardized Tests in American Education*. Princeton: Educational Testing Service.

Rothman, R. (1990a). "Coalition Implores Bush, Governors to Avoid Use of Standardized Tests." *Education Week X* 19:1 + 12.

Rothman, R. (1990b). "Aiming for 'Definition of Literacy,' NAEP Considers 1992 Reading Test." *Education Week X* 21:22.

Rothman, R. (1990c). "In Protest, Pittsburgh Pulls Out of State-Level NAEP." *Education Week IX*, March 7, p. 5.

Rothman, R. (1992d). "RAND Study Finds Serious Problems in Vermount Portfolio Program." *Education Week XII* 15:1, + 20.

Salganik, L.H. (1985). "Why Testing Reforms are so Popular and How They are Changing Education." *Phi Delta Kappan* 66(9):607–10.

"Sample Tasks to Measure 'New Standards' in Math, Literacy" (1991). *Education Week XI* 1:16.

Shaver, James P. (1989). "Lessons From the Past: The Future of an Issue-Centered Social Studies Curriculum." *The Social Studies* 80(5):192–196.

Sizer, Theodore R. (1992). "8 Questions: On Cost, Impact, the Politics of Who Chooses." *Education Week XI* 39:S4–S5.

Skinner, B.F. (1953). *Science and Human Behavior.* New York: Macmillan.

Stufflebeam, D.L. and A.J. Shinkfield. (1985). *Systematic Evaluation.* Boston: Kluwer-Nijhoff Publishing.

Thornton, Stephen T. (1990). "Should We Be Teaching More History?" *Theory and Research in Social Education* 18(1):53–60.

Thorndike, Edward L. (1913). *Psychology of Learning,* (3 vols.). New York: Teachers College Press.

Tyler, Ralph W. (1949). *Basic Principles of Curriculum and Instruction.* Chicago: University of Chicago Press.

U.S. Department of Education (1990). *National Goals for Education.* Washington, DC: U.S. Department of Education.

Viadero, D. (1991). "Subject Specialists Decry Errors of Omission in Goals." *Education Week XI* 8:1, + 16–17.

Wiggins, Grant (1993). "Assessment: Authenticity, Context, and Validity." *Phi Delta Kappan* 75(3):200–214.

Willis, S. (June 1992). "Teaching Thinking." *ASCD Curriculum Update.* Alexandria, VA: Association for Supervision and Curriculum Development.

Wolk, R.A. (1992). "By All Measures: The Debate Over Standards and Measures." *Education Week XI* 39:S1–S2.

Chapter Nine

The Challenge of Multicultural Education: Prospects for Our Schools

Argy Araboglou
Broward County (Florida) Schools

EVENTS IN THE 1990s at the national and international levels brought, again, the importance of multiculturalism and its key instrument, multicultural education into focus. Events in Los Angeles that precipitated mob action and mass property destruction by minorities against other minorities in April 1992, while shocking, brought about the realization that Disneyland is not a substitute vehicle for tranquil intergroup and interethnic relations. Bloody ethnic strife in Yugoslavia since the spring of 1992 involving Croats, Serbs, Bosnians, and other ethnic and religious groups shocked the international community because the expression of hate and recrimination among the various ethnics manifested itself so suddenly and so forcefully. Obviously suppressed passions emerged to forge cataclysmic encounters. Indeed, the past decade or so is replete with expressions of physical violence by opposing groups, based on issues concerning ethnicity, race, religion, or social class. Cyprus, Lebanon, Palestine, South Africa, the former Soviet Union, Sri Lanka, Somalia, Turkey, and Iraq are some of the areas witnessing such tragic events. In many of these

253

areas the intergroup fight is carried on without any hope or visible solution. The fight of the Kurds in both Turkey and Iraq against an oppressive majority has been going on for years without any solution in sight. The fight of the majority, people of color, against the oppressive white minority in South Africa has also been carried out for years. Although apartheid was removed in 1994 when countrywide elections were held, unequal treatment of people based on race and ethnicity (for instance, the police force) still continues.

The cases above are perhaps extreme, but they are real. The events are happening, and people, adults and youth alike, are witnessing them or are part of them. In fact, it is virtually impossible in today's society to be only a spectator of these events. Interethnic strife is a fact of life and almost everyone is involved in such encounters. In the United States, a country that has been known as a "nation of immigrants," everyone, consciously or subconsciously, is a member of a group—a racial group, an ethnic group, or a group that has attributes based on gender or socioeconomic status. For example, one of every four people currently residing in the United States is a person of color. By the year 2020, nearly one-half of the school-age population will be persons of color (NCSS Task Force on Ethnic Studies, 1992). Massive immigration from Latin America in recent years has also contributed to the multicultural/multiethnic character of the United States and to changes in the population composition and possibly the historic dominance of certain groups, such as the WASP groups.

Given these conditions, there are at least two compelling reasons why multiculturalism should be systematically studied and universally experienced. First, the multicultural society at the local, national, regional, and global levels is a reality. It exists and it has both beneficial and detrimental effects on us. The beneficial effects have to do with change resulting from cross-cultural exchange. People from different cultures can all contribute to the advancement of a common civilization. Their contributions can be enormous. The detrimental effects have to do with violence and human destruction resulting from intergroup antagonisms and cross-cultural misunderstandings. If the phenomenon of multiculturalism is ignored, as it has obviously been ignored for several decades, we are left without intellectual power to make decisions on or anticipate such problems as the Los Angeles riots or the Yugoslavian genocidal fights that inescapably touch our lives. The problems of the world, the problems of the state and the nation are now in our living room, in our neighborhood streets and common areas, in our schools and other social institutions. Multiculturalism, both in its good and bad manifestations, has finally reached all of us; we can no longer ignore it, if self preservation still holds as an ultimate value.

The second compelling reason for attending cognitively and experientially to multiculturalism is because in every move we make in our community and in every encounter with other human beings we are faced with cultural traits which are different from ours. We are, indeed, constantly interacting with people and experiencing these differences. We are not simply observing cross cultural interactions on TV or reading about them—we live these interactions daily. If we are not in a position to cope with the differences in our daily encounters, we risk failure—we may develop physical and mental disorders, passivity in our work, isolationist attitudes, hate and anger, and the like. In a world of multiculturals, a monocultural is unlikely to survive!

This argument about the need to engage in and to study multiculturalism is basically a survival argument. Multiculturalism is the state of the real world, and for us to be real we must be consciously part of this reality. But there are other compelling arguments relating to democracy and the inalienable right that all humans have to participate on an equal basis in human pursuits. As the revised guidelines of the National Council for the Social Studies (1992) state, in a democracy "ethnic and cultural diversity should be recognized and respected at the individual, group, and societal levels" and "equality of opportunity should be afforded to all members of ethnic and cultural groups." (NCSS Task Force, *Social Education*, Sept. 92, pp. 277–278.)

Given the compelling reasons to attend to multiculturalism and multicultural education, what are some issues that need to be addressed in the field by social studies educators?

ISSUES IN MULTICULTURAL EDUCATION

 Issue 1: Is the philosophy of multicultural education antithetical to that of the "melting pot"?

The melting pot is the title of a play written by Israel Zangwill at the turn of the century (1908) in New York (Banks, 1994, 20). The play, which became an instant success, assumed that the various ethnic groups present in America at the time would mix together and form a new type of person, a person who would be superior to all other persons. Thus the "melting pot" idea was a process of transforming the ethnics into what the dominant culture at the time, the Anglo-Saxon culture, called for. The values and behavioral traits of the products of the melting pot would be the same as those who were born members of the dominant culture.

The melting pot idea was preceded by earlier movements such as the "nativist" movement, which was a response to immigrants coming to America during the latter part of the nineteenth century—especially those who were not members of the traditional Anglo-Saxon, Protestant group. For example, many new arrivals were Catholic. The quest of the dominant cultural group at the time was to "Americanize" and "assimilate" the newly arrived immigrants. These immigrants were looked down upon because they were considered to be inferior. Schools and colleges were used as instruments to carry out this quest for assimilation and amalgamation. A well-known educator of the period, Ellwood Patterson Cubberley, expressed the sentiment of the time about the immigrants as follows:

> Everywhere these people tend to settle in groups or settlements, and to set up here their national manners, customs, and observances. Our task is to break up these groups or settlements, to assimilate and amalgamate these people as part of our American race, and to implant in their children...the Anglo-Saxon conception of righteousness, law and order, and popular government....(Cubberley, 1909, 15–16).

In response to the movements mentioned, there were counter-movements that supported a philosophy of cultural pluralism. Horace Kallen, Randolph Bourne, and Julius Drachsler were some of the writers whose philosophy assumed that each ethnic or cultural group would make unique contributions to American society by bringing to the society their values, knowledge, and artifacts. In this context, American society would benefit by being thought of as a nation where cultural identities are retained, but they also contribute and enhance the whole. In more recent times, this argument is based on the "salad bowl" notion, that is, cultural uniqueness of different ethnic groups is carefully preserved, but within a national whole (Banks, 1994a, p. 21). Unfortunately, the arguments made by the defenders of the new immigrants were not convincing enough, and several pieces of legislation actually blocked entry of new immigrants from non–Anglo-Saxon countries. Needless to say, during this whole period the oppressive policies of "mainstream Americans" adversely affected Native Americans, African Americans, and Hispanic Americans. At this time African Americans sought to reduce racial and ethnic prejudice by promoting "intergroup education." This approach sought to clear intercultural misunderstandings. The assumption was that the intergroup education approach, which would be based on accurate knowledge and understanding of racial and ethnic minorities, would reduce racial conflict and tension. Intergroup education was not perceived to be a remedy for all schools—just schools where interracial problems existed. In fact most programs in intergroup education were federally funded and were rarely institutionalized (Banks, 1994, pp. 24–25). Although these efforts along with the Civil Rights movement brought about some reforms in the 1950s and 1960s in employment, in education, and in housing, the plight of African Americans and other minorities continued. Intergroup education, as a whole, did not produce long-run effects and quickly ended in the 1950s. It is claimed that U.S. education as well as American society, in general, failed to understand the goals of intergroup education and how the movement contributed to improved relations among diverse groups, in and out of school (Banks, 1994a, pp. 24–25).

Figure 9-1 clearly indicates how race, ethnicity, sex and age affect employment ("Florida Jobless," *Sun Sentinel* 1992, p. 12-B). It is obvious in studying the chart that Black teens are the most discriminated-against in employment (40.7% in July 1992). Hispanic youth was the second most discriminated-against group in employment (14.6% in July 1992).

Figure 9–1   Out of Work

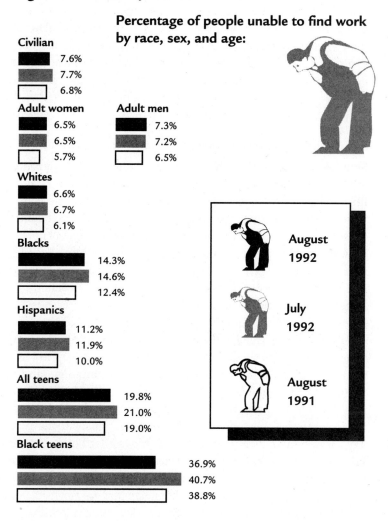

Percentage of people unable to find work by race, sex, and age:

Civilian
- 7.6%
- 7.7%
- 6.8%

Adult women
- 6.5%
- 6.5%
- 5.7%

Adult men
- 7.3%
- 7.2%
- 6.5%

Whites
- 6.6%
- 6.7%
- 6.1%

Blacks
- 14.3%
- 14.6%
- 12.4%

Hispanics
- 11.2%
- 11.9%
- 10.0%

All teens
- 19.8%
- 21.0%
- 19.0%

Black teens
- 36.9%
- 40.7%
- 38.8%

August 1992

July 1992

August 1991

Source: Sun Sentinel *Sept. 5, 1992. Reprinted with permission from the* Sun Sentinel, *Fort Lauderdale, Florida.*

Obviously intergroup education did not produce the desirable results. Prejudice still prevails and this prejudice is reflected in the schools as well.

The movements to homogenize the population have had varying success. Many ethnics did not melt and racial integration did not materialize. Multicultural education, which emphasizes ethnic and cultural diversity, is the approach used currently, and its philosophy is contrary to that of the "melting pot." Multicultural education is based on the idea of *e pluribus unum* (out of many, one). This position is based on the idea that out of cultural diversity a society is built with cohesion and is unified as a nation-state. In this society all ethnic and racial groups are recognized and respected; diversity provides for "societal enrichment, cohesiveness, and survival"; all cultural groups enjoy equal opportunity to succeed; and cultural identification is left to the choice of each individual (NCSS Task Force, 1992, p. 276). "Melting pot" approaches tried to force all groups to be one, that one being controlled by the dominant cultural group. Obviously the concepts of multiculturalism and melting pot contradict each other. In a democratic society, the melting pot argument has no validity; it is contradicted by the very essence of democracy.

Issue 2: *Should multicultural education be designed for minorities only?*

Some argue that multicultural education should be designed only for racial, ethnic, and linguistic minorities so that they can understand and gradually internalize the ideas, values, and ways of behaving of the mainstream culture. This assumption underlies the development and implementation of many programs developed at the national level, for example, Transitional Bilingual Education. This program, initiated and operated by the federal government, provides grants to school districts so that special classes of bilingual education or English as a Second Language (ESL) can accommodate the special needs of linguistic minorities. The underlying intent in this case is for the minority group (Hispanic, Korean, Chinese, Haitian, and so on) to learn the language and other cultural traits of the majority. Not surprising, there is no provision in most of the legislation—federal, state, or local—to provide programs that enable "mainstream" students to learn the language and culture of the minority. This example clearly shows how the "melting pot" ideology permeates much of the legislation enacted throughout the United States. Efforts to implement programs known as "two-way bilingualism" have yet to take root. Two-way bilingualism is based on the idea that both—the mainstream and minority language students—can learn from each other. For example, children whose home language is Spanish can learn English through their association and interaction with peers whose home language is English, and vice versa.

The authors of the new NCSS curriculum guidelines for multicultural education (NCSS Task Force, 1992) argue forcefully the need for multicultural education for all students. In a pluralistic society, operating under democratic principles, students need to know the special characteristics of different ethnic, social, and cultural groups. This knowledge and the skills that come with it will help erase or minimize cultural stereotypes and develop appropriate avenues for cross cultural communication. Multicultural education for all is based on the idea that all cultural groups can make positive contributions to society and that all students need the knowledge and experience of authors other than their own. The tragic experience of South Africa and *apartheid* is a living example of a country where multiculturalism and multicultural education were not accepted and practiced. Until recently, the result has been extreme civil strife and a virtual isolation of one racial group from the other.

To sum up, multicultural education is designed for all students representing all groups and subgroups in society. Through multicultural education, students "broaden their ethnic and cultural options, increase their frames of reference, develop greater appreciation for individual and ethnic differences, and deepen their own capacities as human beings" (NCSS Task Force, 1992, p. 285).

Issue 3: *Should multicultural education be defined as multiethnic, bilingual, or global education?*

The concept of multicultural education can be somewhat elusive if one defines it too broadly or too narrowly. In its broadest sense, multicultural education includes the study of people who are members of different ethnic, cultural, racial, religious, and regional groups. The study of gender and social-class differences of people, as individuals or members of the respective groups, for example, males-females, high-low SES groups, and physically disabled can also be part of multicultural education. In a more narrow sense, multicultural education focuses on the study of different cultures and deals with people whose ways of life are different from those of the dominant group.

If one were to accept the broad definitions of multicultural education, one would have to conclude that multicultural education is no different than global education or education that concentrates generally on the human species. In this case the argument would be that the application of the broader definition to school practice has resulted in a curriculum in which only Western, Anglo values dominate (the Anglocentric curriculum). Without special focus, the exclusion of the systematic study of racial and ethnic groups is the inevitable result. Study after study clearly documents the fact that the histories of ethnic and racial minority groups such as African Americans, American Indians, Hispanic Americans, and Asian Americans have been consistently ignored in school textbooks and other curriculum materials (Diaz, 1992). Thus, if multicultural education is defined very broadly, there is the danger that the study of various cultural groups other than mainstream groups will continue to be carried on in a cavalier fashion. Instruction would continue in the "business-as-usual" mode. Without any curriculum emphasis on ethnic and racial minority groups, distorted images of these groups that currently exist will never be removed from the schools and eventually from the larger society.

Given the need for focus, we agree with the NCSS Task Force that multicultural education should stress the study of all cultural groups including ethnic groups. The study of ethnicity is the focus. But ethnicity can also be studied in a global perspective. An ethnic group is a kind of a particular cultural group that has the following traits (NCSS Task Force, 1992, p. 276):

a. Its origins precede the creation of a nation-state or are external to the nation-state....

b. It is an involuntary group, although individual identification with the group may be optional.

c. It has an ancestral tradition and its members share a sense of peoplehood and an interdependence of fate.

d. It has distinguishing value orientations, behavioral patterns and interests.

e. Its existence has an influence, in many cases a substantial influence, on the lives of its members.

f. Membership in the group is influenced both by how members define themselves and by how they are defined by others.

Given the definition of an ethnic group provided earlier, multicultural education includes the study of the characteristics of the group to which the students belong. In this context, groups such as African Americans, Mexican Americans, Greek Americans, and American Indians are included in the deliberations of students in the classroom. These groups fit the definition of ethnic groups by virtue of race, national origins, home language, and so forth.

The definitional issues arising out of the NCSS's Ethnic Studies Guidelines concern some educators. For example, Judith Renyi and Dennis Lubeck (1994) question the meaning of multicultural education as presented by the task force. As currently presented, the term, they claim, is too broad, and the application of multicultural education is subject to current political and social influences, such as the influences of Western Traditionalists, the Afrocentrists, and the Multiculturalists. Multicultural education, they argue, should be an intellectual enterprise, teaching children "how to think, how to learn, how to make judgments, how to create knowledge, and how to participate actively in a transnational culture of the educated" (Renyi and Lubeck, 1994, p. 5). The best way to deliver multicultural education is through the arts and the humanities: "Humanities always put us in touch with other voices from our and other cultures, they are by their very nature multicultural" (p. 5). The school examples these educators present to illustrate how multicultural education can be infused in the curriculum are appropriate. As we know from experience, however, very few schools implement the study of all relevant cultures consistently and with due respect to the identity of the culture of the students involved. As mentioned by the Task Force, traditional coursework in both elementary and secondary schools excluded nonmainstream cultures altogether from consideration, and when they were studied, these cultures were studied superficially.

Issue 4: *Should multicultural education promote national isolation or world membership?*

The United States, considered by many to be the world's leading power, cannot endure and sustain itself in isolation. A financial crisis in Europe, for example, experienced in September 1992, had immediate repercussions in the financial conditions in the United States. Here is how one author described the potential fallout from this financial crisis:

> If you're planning a European trip in the next few weeks, you should benefit from the sudden upheaval in foreign currencies. The American dollar will probably rise in value. If you own a mutual fund that invests in European securities, its value is likely to go down and the prospects for improvement are not good. (Russell, 1992).

Another author reviewing the European financial crisis concluded as follows:

> The fallout of Europe's monetary crisis is of particular importance to South Florida, a hub of international trade, commerce and tourism.
>
> Most affected by the changes would be tourists from England, Italy and Spain, where currencies have come under severe pressure...(Birger, 1992).

Figure 9-2 shows diagrammatically how currency changes in one country have immediate global ramifications.

Just like the cases of financial crises, political crises and related political events have worldwide repercussions. For example, events in Bosnia-Herzegovina, Somalia, or China have immediate worldwide implications for humanitarian aid, international trade, commitment of troops, international human rights treaties, immigration, and so on. One does not go very far to realize how the world is interconnected—just read the headlines of the local paper or watch CNN. Through this means, the world unfolds in almost everyone's living room.

Given the reality of world interdependence, it is unimaginable that Americans can stay out of the global community. They are inescapably part of it, and because they are part of it, Americans need to be aware and participate in decisions with global ramifications and to do so reflectively and with empathy for other people. Multicultural education provides one of the best means of accomplishing this goal. Knowledge of the cultures of other people

Figure 9–2

THE RATE MANIPULATOR'S CHOICES

Interest rates can be used to manage the value of a nation's currency on world markets. Here's how:

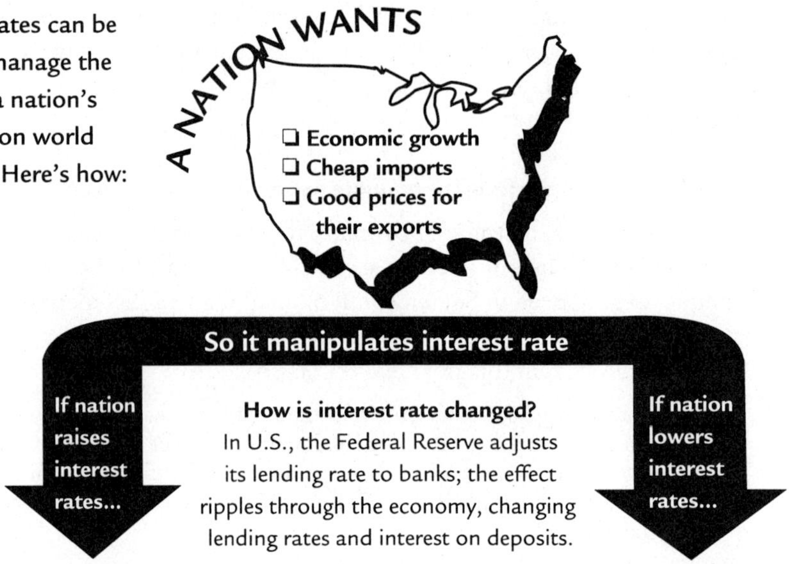

A NATION WANTS

❑ Economic growth
❑ Cheap imports
❑ Good prices for their exports

So it manipulates interest rate

If nation raises interest rates...

How is interest rate changed?
In U.S., the Federal Reserve adjusts its lending rate to banks; the effect ripples through the economy, changing lending rates and interest on deposits.

If nation lowers interest rates...

DESIRABLE EFFECTS

❑ More investors from abroad buy the nation's bonds and certificates of deposit

❑ That raises the value of nation's currency (investors must buy the nation's currency to make investments)

UNDESIRABLE EFFECTS

❑ Economic growth slows (harder for businesses to borrow for construction or inventory)

❑ Exports slow (country's products more expensive to buyers in other nations)

❑ Imported goods cost more (same reason as above)

DESIRABLE EFFECTS

❑ Encourages economic growth (U.S. is currently holding rates low in effort to stimulate business borrowing)

❑ Encourages exports (nation's goods are cheaper abroad)

UNDESIRABLE EFFECTS

❑ Fewer foreign investors buy the nation's bonds and CDs; instead, they invest in nations with higher interest rates

❑ Value of nation's currency drops (investors sell the currency to make investments eleswhere)

❑ Imported goods cost more

Some important exceptions

❑ Nation can directly raise value of currency by dipping into its reserves of foreign currency and buying back its own currency on world markets

❑ In times of crisis, investors rush to buy currencies of stable nations

Source: Miami Herald, Sept. 18, 1992. Reprinted with permission from Associated Press: News Reports

and the ability to look objectively at social developments of various cultural groups are the basic outcomes of multicultural instruction. The ultimate goal is for students to escape the narrow confines of their cultural or national group and to become bona fide members of the world community. Local and world conditions mandate the schools to promote a constant and unceasing movement from parochialism to cosmopolitanism. The study and experience of ethnicity can be done in a global perspective.

Issue 5: *Should there be multicultural education in the school curriculum?*

Some compelling reasons for multicultural education in the schools have already been presented. The current curriculum practice in U.S. schools is clearly centered on developments in the West. Significant contributions in the arts and the sciences by nonwestern cultures are persistently excluded from the curriculum. The NCSS Task Force (1992, p. 279) directly attends to this glaring gap in the curriculum of the schools as follows:

> Curriculum transformation is necessary for the nation's schools, colleges, and universities to describe accurately the Western roots of American civilization and to depict the diversity that characterizes the West. The debt that Western civilization owes to Africa, Asia, and indigenous America should be described in the curriculum....The West is conceptualized in a narrow way to include primarily the heritage of Western European upper-class males. Yet the ideas and writings of women and people of color in the United States are also Western. Zora Neale Hurston, Maxine Hong Kingston, Rudolfo A. Anaya, W.E.B. Du Bois, Carlos Bulosan, and N. Scott Momaday—like Milton, Shakespeare, Virgil, and Locke—are western writers....

Multicultural perspectives should permeate all areas of the curriculum. The content of the curriculum should be broadened to include the multicultural perspective—contributions as well as the struggles for survival of various ethnic and racial groups should be integrated not only into the social studies curriculum, but also in all areas—humanities, language-arts, math, science, business/vocational education, and physical education. Some of these curriculum areas are more prone to change to include the multicultural perspective, for example, social studies and language-arts. In these areas both knowledge content and instructional approaches can be changed. In other areas, that is, science and math, subjects that mostly use a universal language—such as symbols, numbers, and so forth—the content might not need as much change as does the method of instruction. In the latter areas of the curriculum, the ways students of different ethnic and racial groups learn play a pivotal role.

An example of how a multicultural perspective could influence a curricular change is the traditional rendering of the event of Columbus "discovering America." In 1992 when the quincentenary celebration of the event was announced many campuses in America experienced demonstrations against the celebration of this event which is usually expressed as praise for Columbus as a hero. The demonstrators basically sought to bring out the ill-effects of Columbus' arrival to the New World, involving the genocide of a whole people, that is, Native Americans. "The teaching of European imperialism to our children starts with the Columbus myth," said one opponent of the celebration. "Our view of the quincentenary is that we consider this an event that is absolutely pivotal in world history," retorted one of those responsible for staging an exhibit on the topic (Matus, 1991, p. 1). The question is, should our history textbooks and school-related activities continue to rely exclusively on narrations of significant historical events from a point of view that almost totally ignores other cultures? Shouldn't the curriculum reflect the fact that in a multicultural, democratic society the various cultural groups ought to be part of the country's history, even though the facts would be somewhat unpleasant to some when presented? Should historical events continue to be celebrated to glorify one ethnic or racial group at the expense of another?

Recently, there have been efforts by educators to counteract the mono-cultural emphasis still prevailing in our textbooks and ultimately effecting our classroom instruction. On the Columbian Quincentenary, for example, a statement endorsed by 31 educational and professional associations sought to correct some inaccurate and "romanticized" versions "of the encounter Columbus' voyages initiated between the Western and Eastern Hemispheres" (Wooster, 1992, p. 244). The statement, presented as a National Council for the Social Studies Position Statement (1992) can be summarized as follows:

1. Columbus did not discover a new world and, thus, initiate American history.
2. The real America Columbus encountered in 1492 was a different place from the precontact America often portrayed in folklore, textbooks, and the mass media.
3. Africa was very much a part of the social, economic, and political system of the Eastern Hemisphere in 1492.
4. The encounters of Native Americans, Africans, and Europeans following 1492 are not stories of vigorous white actors confronting passive red and black spectators and victims.
5. As a result of forces emanating from 1492, Native Americans suffered catastrophic mortality rates.
6. Columbus' voyages were not just a European phenomenon but, rather, were a facet of Europe's millenia-long history of interaction with Asia and Africa.
7. Although most examinations of the United States historical connections to the Eastern Hemisphere tend to focus on Northwestern Europe, Spain and Portugal also had extensive effects on the Americas.

This statement clearly aims at providing teachers the opportunity to initiate realistic interpretations of the Columbus period and to engage students in reflective thinking. A carefully selected annotated bibliography is also available to provide material teachers can use to introduce a larger, multicultural perspective in connection with the Columbian Quincentenary (*Social Education*, 1991, p. 347–348).

Contributions to North American civilization by various cultural groups have been largely omitted from textbooks and materials used in school. For example, the story of American Indians and their contributions are rarely mentioned in any of the current history textbooks. We may use pictures of famous leaders and Indian artifacts during "Indian Season" in schools (for one week or so), but Indian history is rarely integrated into the social history of the world, especially the history of North America. Yet, as one author puts it, "...the Indians 'Americanized' us" (Weatherford, 1991, p. 172). In fact, the Indians changed the life of the settlers in two major areas—in their diets and in the formation of a united government. As per Weatherford, the Indians were the world's greatest farmers: "Approximately 60 percent of all the food crops grown in the world today originated with the native farmers of North and South America" (Weatherford, 1991, p. 172). The Iroquois, during the period of the Constitutional Convention in Philadelphia, contributed significant ideas in the formation of the new government, for example, the principle of impeachment and aspects of federalism, the latter patterned after the Iroquois federalism (Weatherford, 1991, p. 174). Indian contributions to the American civilization went beyond foods and forms of government. They "influenced medicine by providing approximately two hundred important drugs...." They enriched the English language vocabulary with such words as "hurricane," "canoe," "barbecue," and "husky." "In the realm of technology, Indians first developed the vulcanization of rubber....In science, Indian astronomers in Mexico calculated a calendar more accurate than that of the Europeans..." (Weatherford, 1991, p. 175).

Given the contributions that American Indians made as part of social development, should we continue to allow their exclusion from standard textbooks? What can we do to assure that their place in history is valued and its importance recognized? The checklist in Box 9-A, initially prepared at the Newberry Library in Chicago, can provide the needed guidelines in examining materials and textbooks for use in schools. These guidelines can also be adopted for use in ascertaining whether or not standard textbooks include the histories and contributions of other racial or ethnic groups in America.

The multicultural curriculum as stated in the NCSS Task Force curriculum guidelines seeks to minimize or completely remove bias that has been built into the whole school environment over the years. Even though

---

Box 9–A   *Guidelines for Teaching about American Indian History Checklist*

A sample checklist for evaluating books about American Indian history continues in development. As a first approximation, the following questions are proposed, based on criteria provided by Center advisor, Cheryl Metoyer-Duran, Assistant Professor at the UCLA School of Library and Information Sciences. Discussions with Center staff and Fellows also added qualifications. As other questions occur to those using this checklist, the editor would appreciate suggestions and refinements. Rather than promote censorship, these questions are intended to specify the criteria used to judge a fair representation of Indian-related subjects and to assist readers in selecting materials for the classroom.

1. Is the image of Indians being presented that of real human beings with strengths and weaknesses, joys and sadness?

2. Do Indians initiate actions based on their own values and judgments, rather than react to outside factors?

3. Are stereotypes and cliches avoided or are references made to "obstacles to progress" or "noble savages" who are "blood thirsty" or "child like" or "spiritual" or "stoic"?

4. If fiction, are characters appropriate to situations and interactions rooted in a particular time and place?

5. Does the presentation avoid loaded words (savage, buck, chief, squaw) and tone that is offensive, insensitive, and inappropriate?

6. Do Indians appear to have coherent motivations of their own comparable to those attributed to non-Indians?

7. Are regional, cultural, and tribal differences recognized when appropriate?

8. Are communities presented as dynamic, evolving entities that can adapt to new conditions, migrate to new areas, and keep control of their own destinies? (Are traditions viewed as rigid, fixed, and fragile?)

9. Are gross generalizations avoided? (No reference to THE Indian, or THE Indian language, or THE Indian word for X.)

10. Are historical anachronisms present? (No prehistoric horses, glass beads, wheat, or wagons.)

11. Are encounters between Indians and others regarded as exchanges? (Are Indian sources of food, medicine, and technology acknowledged?)

12. Are captions and illustrations specific and appropriate for a time and place? (No wrapped skirts in the Arctic, or feather bonnets in the North Pacific, or totem poles in the Plains.) Are individuals identified by name when possible?

13. Are Indians viewed as heirs of a dynamic historical tradition extending back before contact with the Europeans?

14. Are Indian/Indian relations expressed as part of native life, both within and outside of individual communities?

15. Can this book contribute to an understanding and appreciation of American—and human—history?

These guidelines are reprinted with permission and first appeared in Meeting Ground, *No. 23, Summer 1990.* Meeting Ground *is published biannually as the Newsletter of the D'Arcy McNickle Center for the History of the American Indian. Reprinted with permission from the Newberry Library, 60 W. Walton, Chicago, IL 60610-3380; (312) 943-9090.*

---

authors and publishers have recently sought to make some revisions, contemporary historical interpretations of only mainstream culture persist. Thus, it is imperative for educators to sensitize teachers and students (especially new teachers completing degree requirements) to existing curriculum distortions and provide them the skills so that they are in a position to remedy these distortions. The key idea here is that the multicultural classroom cannot function without a multicultural curriculum. It goes without saying that a

---

Box 9–B   *Curriculum Guidelines for Multicultural Education*

- Ethnic and cultural diversity should permeate the total school environment.
- The curriculum should reflect the cultural learning styles and characteristics of the students within the school community.
- The multicultural curriculum should provide students with continuous opportunities to develop a better sense of self.
- The curriculum should help students understand the totality of the experiences of ethnic and cultural groups in the United States.
- The multicultural curriculum should help students understand that a conflict between ideals and realities always exists in human societies.
- The multicultural curriculum should explore and clarify ethnic and cultural alternatives and options in the United States.
- The multicultural curriculum should help students develop their decision-making abilities, social participation skills, and sense of politi-

cal efficacy as necessary bases for effective citizenship in a pluralistic, democratic nation.
- The multicultural curriculum should help students develop the skills necessary for effective interpersonal, interethnic, and intercultural group interactions.
- The multicultural curriculum should be comprehensive in scope and sequence, should present holistic views of ethnic and cultural groups, and should be an integral part of the total school curriculum.
- The multicultural curriculum should provide opportunities for students to study ethnic group languages as legitimate communication systems and help them develop full literacy in at least two languages.
- The multicultural curriculum should make maximum use of experiential learning, especially local community resources.

Excerpted from NCSS Task Force, "Curriculum Guidelines for Multicultural Education," Social Education, Vol. 56, No.5, September, 1992, pp. 279–287.

---

curriculum considered by the students to be irrelevant is bound to cause boredom, deviant behavior, increased drop-out rates, and underachievement.

Issue 6: *If there is a multicultural dimension in the school curriculum, should it be organized as separate units of study, as curriculum infusion into all content and activity areas, or as a full blown course?*

One major state university in the southeastern United States responded to the call to provide a multicultural curriculum by implementing a new requirement in the undergraduate component of the liberal arts courses. The requirement is expressed as follows: "Students can't earn a degree unless they take at least one course examining a culture other than their own, such as Asian literature, and at least one course examining diversity in the Western experience, such as Native American history" (Brooks, 1992, p. A9).

Although the faculty debated the new requirement for inclusion of multicultural courses into that university curriculum, it was relatively easy to change the policy. The same pattern did not hold, however, in efforts to change the curriculum of K to 12 from monocultural to multicultural. School boards, which for the most part are governed by members of the dominant culture (the WASP culture), are very reluctant to implement any drastic curriculum changes. The publishing industry supports them in that respect—a multicultural curriculum would require re-writing all the textbooks now in place. This would be a formidable job, and it would be costly. Thus the easiest way to respond to the outcry of the ethnic and racial groups that are chronically left out of the curriculum, is to add, here and there, in the textbooks, references to America as a multicultural society. This is, at best, a patch-up job, where no major restructuring of the curriculum and the materials related to it takes place. What is lacking in all cases is a commitment to multicultural education by school boards, teachers, administrators, students, and the general public. Will it take more traumatic incidents like those in Los Angeles and in Miami to demonstrate that a multicultural nation cannot survive without an actual multicultural practice in all institutional life, including the schools?

The prevailing practice now in schools is to include, intermittently, short units of study on ethnic or racial groups, usually in connection with the celebration of Black History or Hispanic History "month" or "week." While the occasion lasts, relevant inputs into the curriculum are provided by guest lecturers, pamphlets, posters, ethnic foods, costumes, artifacts, and so on. Once the special occasion terminates, however, references to multiculturalism terminate as well. Thus multiculturalism in the curriculum is coterminous with a special, short-lived occasion. Given this, we agree with the NCSS Task Force that short units of study connected with certain ethnic or racial observations can be helpful, but in no way do they form a bona fide multicultural curriculum.

A separate course in the school curriculum, as is the emerging trend in post-secondary institutions, is also unappealing for the following reasons: A separate course would by necessity be an elective one because the curriculum is already overcrowded with other subjects considered to be "basic," that is, math, science, social studies, language-arts. An elective course on the subject, however powerful, would not provide the opportunity to *all* students including mainstream culture students, to learn and experience multiculturalism. In fact, if such a course were offered, students of the dominant culture would be most unlikely to take it.

We consider the best way to provide a multicultural curriculum is to *integrate* multicultural content and experiences into the entire curriculum. In this sense the recommendation of the NCSS Task Force (1992) is quite appropriate.

> The curriculum should be reorganized so that ethnic and cultural diversity is an integral, natural, and normal component of educational experiences of *all* students, with ethnic and cultural content accepted and used in everyday instruction, and with various ethnic and cultural perspectives introduced. Multicultural content is as appropriate and important in teaching such fundamental skills and abilities as reading, thinking, and decision making as it is in teaching about social issues raised by racism, dehumanization, racial conflict, and alternative ethnic and cultural life-styles (NCSS Task Force, 1992, p. 285).

Only when multiculturalism is fully integrated into the K to 12 school curriculum will advancement in the field take place. Whether or not the subject is mathematics or social studies, the perspective of cultural pluralism must be introduced in a direct way. Teachers working with curriculum developers will have to take the initiative to demonstrate that such a curriculum is possible and that it can meet the imperative need of all citizens to learn about and develop empathy for all cultures in the United States and worldwide.

Issue 7: *Should instructors in multicultural education use special teaching methodologies?*

In a multicultural classroom setting, teachers will have to use special methods and procedures in the daily instructional tasks. Assuming that the content of instruction is multicultural, as described earlier, what are some things that teachers should keep in mind so that instruction can be effective? First of all, the learning styles of the students must be considered. Research, for example, indicates that both African Americans and students of Hispanic background respond better to teaching methods that emphasize cooperation rather than competition (NCSS Task Force, 1992, p. 281). Small-group work, peer tutoring, mentoring, cooperative learning, and the like are approaches that can be used effectively with multicultural groups. Also, all materials used in the classroom must be adapted for students with special needs. For example, students with limited English proficiency (LEP students) need to have their instruction and the materials related to it in the home language or in a specially designed program usually known as "English as a Second Language" (ESL). Needless to say, however, student groups with special needs, for example, linguistic and cultural, should not be held in isolation and be kept apart from other groups. While the special needs of these students are attended to, common instructional and co-curricular activities should also be scheduled so students from all cultural groups come together to pursue common educational goals.

One of the most important skills to be emphasized in the classroom is that of critical or reflective thinking. This skill, though complicated and multifaceted, is needed because its use will help students, members of both minority and mainstream cultures, identify and remove cultural stereotypes from their environment. This skill presumes that students are given all the other skills needed to investigate the matter before them critically, that is, skills in formulating testable hypotheses and in collecting relevant evidence. Take, for example, the cartoon in Figure 9-3 depicting the Arabs. How can we use cartoons like these to promote critical thinking about other cultures and thus diminish the influence of cultural stereotypes?

What is our role as teachers? Basically, the teacher's role is to be instrumental in getting the students to identify the hidden messages in the cartoons, and through the use of facts and evidence remove the inacurracies in the picture that are presumably representative of a culture and its people. The cartoon in question clearly represents the Arabs as terrorists or as mindless people who, while holding to traditional values, they talk about the return to democracy. Questions that should be asked here include these: What is the content of the cartoons? What is their intent? What cultural group is depicted in these cartoons? What do you know or what can you find out about this cultural group? Do the cartoons portray these cultural groups accurately? Why or why not? What action can you take, individually or as a group, to present to those who view these cartoons a clear picture of the character of those depicted in the cartoons? It should be noted here also that while students critically analyze the cartoons and uncover their hidden messages, they also gain insights into and understanding of cultures other than their own. But the process does not end there. There should be social action through social participation. Students should be able to devise strategies to remove cultural stereotypes from the larger society, not only from their school. For example, students can write to the newspapers who published the cartoons pointing out the inaccuracies and asking for an editorial apology. They might write an article that is more truly representative of the culture depicted in the cartoons. They can write

Figure 9–3

Reprinted with permission of The Miami Herald.

members of the culture in question to request presentations on their history and culture. In this way critical thinking and social participation activities are united to promote multiculturalism and multicultural thinking as a way of life.

All cartoons are not caricatures of other cultures. Some cartoons reveal built-in biases in the system and seek to sensitize the public to the underlying social injustices. The cartoon in Figure 9-4 on home loans for minorities is a case in point. The cartoon points to a system that does not treat minorities on an equal basis, as per the U.S. Constitution as well as legislation on the matter. The cartoon can form an excellent springboard for classroom use to initiate discussion of how and why minorities are subjected to this type of treatment. Once the analysis is performed, then it is important to develop a plan of action whereby students, individually or as a group, are involved in changing the system that discriminates against a substantial number of Americans.

It is certainly not difficult to find appropriate data in pursuing this matter. Newspapers and periodical literature provide abundant evidence. Table 9-1 for example, shows clearly the mortgage denial rate of minorities in Florida for 1990 and 1991.

As shown in the table, the rejection rate of African-Americans in 1991 was substantially larger than the total for the market, 47.6 percent compared with 29.6 percent. For whites only the rejection rate (not shown on the table) was 29 percent. Hispanics fared better than African-Americans because the

Figure 9–4

Reprinted with permission from the Tallahassee Democrat.

Table 9–1   Mortgage Denial Rates for Minorities

Market Segment	Applications 1990		Applications 1991		Originations 1990		Originations 1991		Denial Rate	
	Number	Dollars	Number	Dollars	Number	Dollars	Number	Dollars	1990	1991
Total	16,070	$910,630	19,118	$1,149,418	10,585	$659,703	12,161	$839,962	23.1%	29.6%
African-American	624	$24,407	699	$28,166	295	$13,674	327	$16,131	42.5%	47.6%
Hispanic	846	$40,093	956	$54,671	461	$26,927	573	$39,431	34.2%	32.0%
Other minority	325	$19,543	389	$25,547	196	$12,806	266	$19,320	27.1%	25.4%
Total minority	1,795	$84,043	2,044	$108,384	952	$53,407	1,166	$74,882	35.8%	36.2%
Total nonminority	14,275	$826,587	17,074	$1,041,034	9,633	$606,296	10,995	$765,080	21.5%	28.6%

Source: NationsBank, Charlotte, N.C.
Source: Miami Herald, Sept. 25, 1992, p. 1C

rejection rate decreased from 34.2 percent in 1990 to 32.0 percent in 1991. The questions to be asked here: Why are there significant differences in mortgage rejection rates among different cultural groups? How do these rejections affect each one of us? What can be done to remedy the situation? What can you do, specifically, to change this pattern? What action plan would you employ?

Newspaper articles can also be used as springboards for discussing multicultural issues. For example, negative remarks attributed to a university president on the abilities of a minority group and the protests that followed these remarks would constitute a bona fide basis to initiate in-depth discussions of intergroup relations (Castaneda, 1995, p. 3A) The questions to be asked here include these: Why are such remarks made by a university president? What values are subsumed under these remarks? What is the evidence for the claims made by this university president, if any? What are the consequences of such assertions? What do these remarks say about the feeling and attitudes of a member of one ethnic group toward another? Are these claims representative of a portion of the population? What can be done to bring out the truth about members of all ethnic groups? How does one go about combating prejudice and discrimination, as the statements by the university president described in the article suggest? What can you personally do to improve understanding and empathy between members of different ethnic groups?

Issue 8: *What should be the focus of multicultural education, for example, how "other" people live, removal of cultural stereotypes from school instruction, strengthening the self-concept of all students, or promoting self-awareness and pride?*

As we discussed, multicultural education has both a substantive dimension and a methodological dimension. The focus of the substantive dimension centers around the idea of culture. The key element here is how different cultures are reflected in the way the people who are part of the respective cultures think and behave. By definition, multicultural education is the study of cultures, that is, the study of a culture or cultures other than one's own. Practically speaking, multicultural education in the classroom applies to the study of such cultures as the Arabic-Islamic culture, the genesis of which can be traced to the Near East, or the culture of Native Americans, the genesis of which may be traced to the Americas.

How these cultures are to be studied is a methodological question. As the NCSS Task Force on Multicultural Education suggests, cultures should be studied through the application of critical-thinking skills. What types of problems have members of these cultures experienced over the years? How were these problems met? What were the similarities or differences in meeting these problems by members of different cultures? Why have certain cultures moved in certain directions? Students studying these cultures are asked to constantly develop and test hypotheses in the open forum of ideas. One key hypothesis emerging from the study of cultures is that when two or more cultures meet, then cultural change is inevitable. The examination of this hypothesis leads to other hypotheses that deal with the tempo, direction, and effects of cultural change and exchange. Many materials are available to the teacher that can be used as springboards or in testing these and related hypotheses (for example, Massialas and Zevin, 1970; Scourby, 1986).

The results of focusing on cultures other than our own and using critical thinking methods in studying them are many. Cultural stereotypes are removed, because cognitive understanding of cultural patterns is the main instructional goal. Students employing critical thinking skills can now examine their textbooks and other materials used in school from the point of view of accuracy and comprehensiveness. Are the claims made in these materials about the contributions of various cultures to American social development accurate? Are the issues about or conflicts among different ethnic or social groups presented in an unbiased way? Are these claims based on fact? Are the histories of the nations studied comprehensive, that is, do they include the histories and current social realities of all ethnic and racial groups or do they emphasize one only? If a monocultural interpretation of history is given, how can the other cultures be brought into the study?

The other results of multicultural education have to do with the self-concept of students who are involved in the process. Students who are outside the mainstream culture usually develop an inferiority complex because their own culture is either omitted from the school curriculum or it is presented in negative terms when it is included. As a result of this glaring omission, students drop out of the class, intellectually and psychologically. In many cases, students, in the absence of an alternative rational model (for example, their own historical accomplishments) express their feelings and warranted frustrations through what might be labeled nonconformist or deviant behavior. This behavior is the result of anger for being left out. When multicultural instruction is bona fide, that is, following along the lines presented in this paper, then the self-concept and sense of political and social efficacy of minority students will be strengthened. These students, deprived of the study of their own culture for years, will now begin to realize that their culture has contributed a great deal and that they can make contributions as well. Now they begin to better understand the world around them, and they gradually develop the skill and determination to change it. With an elevated sense of efficacy, students develop the feeling that they can control their environment and not be controlled by it.

For the mainstream students, multicultural education provides an important means for cross-cultural understanding. Through cognitive understanding, students also develop empathy toward other ethnic groups. They begin to value diversity as a way of life.

The cognitive study of cultures within a global prospective resulting in a "pluralistic perspective based on diversity" is salient in the NCSS *Curriculum Standards for Social Studies* (1994). As the Task Force indicates, "This perspective involves respect for differences of opinion and preference; of race, religion, and gender; of class and ethnicity; and of culture in general" (p. 6). The study of culture is the first topic of the 10 crucial thematic strands recommended by the task force to be included in the Social Studies program, grades K to 12.

Issue 9: *Should multicultural education be studied and practiced in conjunction with the hidden curriculum?*

The hidden curriculum refers to factors other than those included in the formal curriculum that influence student learning. Gender, social class, race, language background, and ethnicity are some factors that play a major role in the classroom. Schoolwide and classroom dynamics also play a major role in learning and instruction. We know, for example, that, traditionally, female students are less inclined than male students to pursue studies and eventually careers in science/technology and mathematics. Certain minority students are more likely than those in the mainstream to drop out of school. The hidden or unwritten curriculum also influences the type of civic education fostered in school. Students of low socioeconomic status are implicitly taught to accept the status quo and assume the role of follower in the social and political system. Students of high socioeconomic status, on the other hand, are constantly encouraged to question governmental policies and gradually begin to think of themselves as leaders (Boyd, 1979). As much as 90 percent of what is learned in school is estimated to be the result of the hidden curriculum (Massialas, 1989).

Students most adversely affected by the hidden curriculum obviously are those who are members of a racial, ethnic, or linguistic minority. These students are usually faced with numerous obstacles in carrying out their daily tasks. For example, many limited English proficiency (LEP) students face insurmountable problems as a result of the home language being different from the language used in school. Thus parental help, usually available to most mainstream students in connection with homework, relations with teachers, and so on, is not extended to these students. Minority students also receive more frequent and more severe punishment than mainstream students when an infraction of the school rules takes place. Infractions are more likely to take place among minority students because, as a rule, their culture is not recognized, and they are constantly made, directly and indirectly, to feel badly about themselves.

Given these conditions, it is only reasonable for schools and educators to directly connect multicultural education with the study of the hidden curriculum. The factors that alter the conditions of learning in the classroom (summed up in the concept of the hidden curriculum) are about the same as those that alter a person's status in society. The "fair treatment" and "equal opportunity" concepts of the American political tradition are drastically altered when applied to minorities. These concepts, and the opportunity to which they refer, are either denied to the minorities altogether or they are applied selectively. This condition holds on such matters as employment, health care, housing, education, and criminal justice. This condition, as we discussed, also extends into the classroom. Focusing on factors such as gender, race, ethnicity, linguistic background, SES, physical disabilities, and the like as they affect the life patterns of citizens is the essence of multicultural education. Thus the thoughtful examination of the hidden curriculum, which is considered to be crucial for the functioning of the schools (Goodlad, 1984), also becomes the focus of the formal school curriculum put in place as the *multicultural curriculum*. In this manner the study of the hidden curriculum and multicultural education are integrated into one, that is, the critical examination of social and cultural conditions as they impact the lives of citizens.

⬦ Issue 10: *Does research indicate that multicultural education benefits student learning?*

In reporting research findings on the matter, there are basically two avenues to pursue: (1) whether or not multicultural education programs benefit the mainstream, majority group students, and (2) whether these programs benefit the minority group students.

Research on the outcomes of multicultural education on mainstream students is limited. The bulk of the research has concentrated on the extent to which an intervention program, that is, a multicultural curriculum, reduces prejudice and increases positive feelings toward racial and ethnic minority groups. A review of research indicates that "students' racial attitudes can be affected by curriculum interventions, but the results of such interventions are inconsistent, complex, and probably influenced by many different factors..." (Banks, 1991, p. 460). Some studies, however, revealed that certain multicultural intervention programs (such as multicultural curriculum units, cooperative learning activities, and democratic teaching styles) resulted in positive racial attitudes among both white and black students. The research generally indicates that academic achievement of underrepresented groups can also be attained through certain classroom interventions (Banks, 1991; Pahl, 1990).

Research on cognitive styles of learning has significant implications for teaching and learning in the classroom. Minority students, in general, are more prone to respond well to teaching techniques and curricula that recognize that their cognitive learning tends to be "field-sensitive." These students learn better through cooperation, affection, and personalization, This approach contrasts sharply with students with "field independent" cognitive styles who thrive on highly analytical, sequential, and competitive approaches (Swisher, 1992). Although teachers should be careful to attend to the cognitive learning styles of their students, they need not stereotype minority students, thus preventing these students from receiving innovative instructional inputs. A prior determination that students are not capable of performing in certain ways often results in the self-fulfilling prophecy, thus certain students, through labeling, are never given the chance to excel. It should also be remembered that there is "great diversity within any culture...the learning-styles construct should be a tool for individualization, rather than a label for categorizing and evaluating" (Swisher, 1992, p. 70).

Research also indicates that linguistic minority students who are instructed in school in their native language do well academically. A reviewer summarizing the research on the subject concluded that "native-language maintenance seems to improve rather than jeopardize academic achievement" (Nieto, 1992, pp. 112–113) Bilingual education, which is generally the study of school subjects in two languages—the native language and English, as a rule helps minority students to meet academic expectations. Contrary to some popular beliefs, bilingual education is not a substitute for or detriment to learning English. Most research indicates that students learn another language (L2) better when their first language (L1) is recognized and fully developed. The controversy surrounding the effects of bilingual education, according to Nieto, is because the program has a low status among school personnel and parents. "Even their physical placement within schools is indicative of this. These programs are often found in large, windowless closets, in hallways, or in classrooms next to the boiler room. It is not surprising, then, that even the parents of children in those programs press for a quick exit for their children" (Nieto, 1992, p. 114). When students resist assimilation through the use of the native language and culture at school they meet with academic success. "The notion that assimilation is a necessary prerequisite for success in school and society is severely tested by current research" (Nieto, 1992, p. 116).

CONCLUSION

The theme of this paper is that multiculturalism is real and if schools are to deal with the real world, they are obligated to have multicultural education form the core of their instructional program. In a multicultural society evolving on democratic principles, the "melting pot" and assimilationist ideologies have no place. In this regard, we have argued that multicultural education should be designed for all students, not just ethnic, racial, or linguistic minorities. In an interdependent world, students and citizens depend on each other for their survival and well-being. To ignore other cultures is tantamount to reducing a person's intellectual power in the sense that ignorance will reduce life's choices. We have also argued that multicultural education is not centered on one country only, but rather its scope includes the world. Thus students are expected to think of themselves in a global perspective rather than a narrow nationalistic, at times chauvinistic, perspective. What is sought here is an understanding of people who are members of a cultural group other than "ours." When we understand other people, their thoughts, and actions, we begin to reduce or eliminate our phobias toward them, and eventually, we develop empathy for them. In a multicultural school setting and through multicultural education, cognitive understandings and empathetic feelings evolve in all groups—mainstream groups and minorities. In this manner intergroup relations improve and cultural obstacles in cross-cultural communication are reduced or eliminated altogether.

We have argued in this paper that a bona fide multicultural curriculum should be the basis for development in all content areas—social studies, math science, language-arts, vocational education, physical education, and art education. We know from experience and from research that unless the content and the method of presenting it address issues of relevance to the students, learning is unlikely to take place. What is more relevant than a matter that relates to the culture of each student? While students study the historic development of each group, they also understand and put in action the concept of *e pluribus unum*, that a stable democratic society is created on the basis of respect and recognition of all diverse cultures that contribute to it.

The paper explored ways in which the curriculum can be presented so that it is not an affront to the sensitivities of students. Different cultures exhibit different sensitivities, and these must be respected in the classroom. Students in different cultures learn differently, their cognitive styles differ, and unless these differences are recognized by the teacher, learning will be impaired.

One main goal of multicultural education is to remove cultural stereotypes in the students' environment. We have shown in this paper examples of these types of stereotypes (in the form of cartoons), and we suggested ways to deal with them in the classroom. We have also pointed to the need to change our textbooks so that historical events of significance (for example, the Columbus discoveries) are not presented from one point of view only. When textbooks present only the point of view of one group (the Anglocentric point of view), the teacher who truly believes in the goals of multicultural education should bring to class material that presents different viewpoints on each historic event.

The hidden curriculum plays a major role in educating citizens. The same factors that influence learning in schools—race, ethnicity, linguistic background, gender, social class—are also factors that govern a person's status in society. Thus the study of multiculturalism is in large measure the study of the hidden curriculum of the schools. In fact, the school can be studied as being a true microcosm of the larger society. When students learn about the culture of the school by focusing on the aforementioned factors impinging on the students, they also learn about conditions in the larger society. Along with the study of school culture, students are asked to take action and participate directly in matters that affect them. This comes mainly as a result of an increased sense of political and social efficacy among students of different cultural groups. In a democracy, these students learn how to exercise their rights and take an active part in formulating public policy. This action is consistent with the principles and ideals of American democracy.

Reflective Questions

1. *What arguments, pro and con, can you present to an audience of parents in discussing the introduction of multicultural education on schoolwide basis? What is your own position on the matter and why?*

2. *In your judgment, do schools with which you are familiar follow an assimilationist orientation or do they generally subscribe to cultural pluralism? Explain and give examples.*

3. *If you were visiting a school to establish whether or not multicultural education is practiced, what would you seek to observe once inside that school? What questions would you ask the administrators, teachers, students, and possibly parents?*

4. *Can you think of ways in which multicultural activities are integrated into the various fields of study or subject areas such as art education, music, science, math, language-arts, and social studies? Be specific and give examples.*

5. *If you were a curriculum specialist scheduling events for the school for a year-long period, how would you include multicultural themes and activities so that the students directly experience different cultures?*

6. *Is there a difference between global education and multicultural education? Explain.*

7. *How does the changing nature of the world society impact all of us, and what implications does it have for instruction in the schools?*

GLOSSARY

bilingual education   Refers to a curriculum and an instructional program that uses the native language of the student as well as English in fulfilling the objectives of the school. Transitional bilingual education seeks to provide LEP students with English language capability so that they can exit the program as soon as possible. Maintenance bilingual education seeks to teach LEP students English while preserving the native or home language. Two-way bilingualism refers to programs that provide the opportunity for two linguistic groups to learn the language of each group.

cultural assimilation   The process whereby immigrants are amalgamated into the dominant culture. Schools at the turn of the century were expected to perform this function.

cultural pluralism   Based on the idea that in a democracy all cultural groups should have the opportunity to function and to progress, including the right to maintain their own identity and cultural characteristics.

ESL   Refers to a program of studies in school (English as a second language) that seeks to provide the opportunity to learn English to children of limited English proficiency. In some cases, English is learned at the expense of the native or home language of the student.

global education   Seeks to enlarge the perspective of students so that a worldwide or cosmopolitan, rather than a narrow, parochial orientation guides them in the pursuit of learning at school.

LEP students   Applies to students with limited English proficiency enrolled in schools in the United States. Under federal legislation and Supreme Court rulings, schools are obligated to provide special programs to these students so that the opportunity to learn is not denied them.

mainstream culture   Refers to the culture of the dominant group in society. In the United States the mainstream culture has been identified traditionally as "the White Anglo-Saxon Protestant culture (WASP)."

melting pot   The idea that members of various ethnic groups in America would mix together and form a new type of person. The implicit goal here, advocated at the turn of the century when there were numerous immigrants entering the country, was to transform the ethnics into members of the dominant or mainstream culture.

multicultural education   The systematic study in school of cultures other than one's own. In its broadest context, multicultural education includes the study of members of different racial, ethnic, and linguistic groups as well as the study of groups that are different in gender, region, or personal exceptionalities.

multiethnic education   The systematic study in school of various ethnic groups.

WASP   Refers to White, Anglo-Saxon, Protestant Americans.

ANNOTATED BIBLIOGRAPHY

Baker, Gwendolyn C. (1994). *Planning and Organizing for Multicultural Instruction*, 2nd ed. Menlo Park, CA: Addison-Wesley.

Defines multicultural education as "a process through which individuals are exposed to the diversity that exists in the United States and the world." Helpful, appropriate multicultural strategies are recommended for classrooms other than social studies, such as language-arts, mathematics, music, science, and art.

Banks, James A. (1991). "Multicultural Education: Its Effects on Students' Racial and Gender Role Attitudes." Pp. 459–469 in *Handbook of Research on Social Studies Teaching and Learning*, edited by James P. Shaver. New York: Macmillan.

The chapter reviews current research on multicultural education, focusing on issues dealing with race and gender. Implications for practice are presented.

Banks, James A. and Cherry A. McGee Banks, editors (1989). *Multicultural Education: Issues and Perspectives*. Boston: Allyn & Bacon.

Contributors discuss multicultural education in terms of social class and religion, gender, ethnicity and language, and exceptionality. Provides good bibliography on these topics.

Banks, James A. (1994). *Multiethnic Education*. Boston: Allyn & Bacon.

A classic text on multiethnic and multicultural education. An excellent source for teachers who seek to introduce multicultural curricula in their social studies programs. Issues in the field are explored as well.

Banks, James A. (1994). *An Introduction to Multicultural Education*. Boston: Allyn & Bacon.

Tries to clarify the presumed confusion over the meaning of multicultural education. Makes the case that multicultural education is for everybody, not only cultural minority students. Describes the challenges to the "Anglocentric" curriculum.

Davidman, Leonard, with Patricia T. Davidman (1994). *Teaching with a Multicultural Perspective: A Practical Guide*. New York: Longman.

Identifies six factors that contribute to controversy over multicultural education (for example, the traditional vision of an American based on a "melted-down, assimilated, unidimensional Anglo-Saxon model" versus a "multidimensional, pluralist, rainbow image..." (in Chapter 5, p. 24). "Creating a Multicultural Curriculum with Content that Links Environmental, Global, Citizenship, and Multicultural Education" is of special interest.

Diaz, Carlos, editor (1992). *Multicultural Education for the 21st Century*. Washington, DC: National Education Association.

An excellent compendium of articles that review multicultural education research and theory in such areas as teaching practices, institutional climate, learning styles, evaluation practices, and teacher education.

Garcia, Eugene (1994). *Understanding and Meeting the Challenge of Student Cultural Diversity.* Boston: Houghton Mifflin.

Argues that "assimilation doesn't equal success." Discusses such practices as tracking and ability grouping, and their effects on student learning. "[S]tudy after study shows that children who do not perform well academically succeed best in heterogeneous groups" (p. 211).

Grant, Carl A. and Christine E. Sleeter (1989). *Turning on Learning.* Columbus, OH: Merrill Publishing.

Elaborates on five approaches for multicultural teaching plans for race, class, gender, and disability. Excellent examples of lesson plans and hands-on activities to promote multicultural education in the classroom.

Massialas, Byron G. (1991). "Education for International Understanding." Pp. 448–458 in *Handbook of Research on Social Studies Teaching and Learning*, edited by James P. Shaver. New York: Macmillan.

Analyzes the findings of current research on the effects of instructional programs dealing with global, international, or intercultural education. Extremely useful for educators who want to introduce multicultural education within a global perspective.

Nieto, Sonia (1992). *Affirming Diversity: The Sociopolitical Context of Multicultural Education.* New York: Longman.

An excellent resource for teachers, with suggestions about how to combat racism and discrimination in the school. The book, through case studies, identifies successful ways to build self-pride and confidence among minority students. Points out that multicultural education is also critical pedagogy, a pedagogy that seeks to "de-mythify" some of the truths that we have been taught to take for granted.

Scarcella, Robin (1990). *Teaching Language Minority Students in the Multicultural Classroom.* Englewood Cliffs, NJ: Prentice-Hall.

Focuses on problems encountered by language minority students in school. Provides suggestions about how to identify and deal with students who have different learning styles, such as field-sensitive versus field-independent cognitive styles. Provides research-based information about how to test in "culturally responsive ways."

Seelye, H. Ned (1984). *Teaching Culture*, Lincolnwood, IL: National Textbook Company.

The book discusses at length strategies for enhancing intercultural communication. The section on "culture assimilators," "culture capsules," and "culture clusters" is of particular interest to social studies teachers.

Weeks, William H., Paul B. Petersen, and Richard W. Brislin, editors (1985). *A Manual of Structured Experiences for Cross-Cultural Learning.* Yarmouth, ME: Intercultural Press.

This handbook presents a collection of exercises that focus on stimulating learning and instruction in multicultural groups. Useful manual for teachers who seek to capitalize on experiences brought to the classroom by different cultural groups. Many exercises are presented in a "pros" and "cons" structured format. Appendices provide checklists for evaluating the status of multicultural involvement in schools as well as for evaluating children's books.

REFERENCES

Banks, James A. (1991). "Multicultural Education: Its Effects on Students' Racial and Gender Role Attitudes." Pp. 459–469, in *Handbook of Research on Social Studies Teaching and Learning*, edited by James P. Shaver. New York: Macmillan.

Banks, James A. (1994). *Multiethnic Education*. Boston: Allyn & Bacon.

Birger, Larry (1992). "Europe's Crisis has Global Effects: Strong Dollar Mixed Blessing for South Florida." *Miami Herald* Sept. 18, 1992:C1.

Boyd, William Lowe (1979). "The Politics of Curriculum Change and Stability." *Educational Researcher* 79:12–18.

Brooks, Browning (1992). "Building the Bridge: Florida State's 30-Year Journey Into Racial Diversity." *Tallahassee Democrat* Sept. 22, 1992:1A, 9A.

Castaneda, Carol J. (1995). "Racial Remark Embroils Rutgers." *USA Today* Feb. 9, 1995:3A.

Cubberley, Ellwood P. (1909). *Changing Conceptions of Education*. Boston: Houghton Mifflin.

Diaz, Carlos, editor (1992). *Multicultural Education for the 21st Century*. Washington, DC: National Education Association.

"Florida Jobless Rate Hits 8.8%; U.S. Rate Drops." *Sun Sentinel* Sept. 9, 1992:12B.

Goodlad, John (1984). *A Place Called School: Prospects for the Future*. New York: McGraw-Hill.

Massialas, Byron G. and Jack Zevin (1970). *Cultural Exchange*. Chicago: Rand McNally.

Massialas, Byron G. (1989). "The Inevitability of Issue-Centered Discourse in the Classroom." *The Social Studies* 80(5):73–75.

Matus, Ron (1991). "Museum's Columbus Exhibit Sparks Protest." *Florida Flambeau* Sept. 9, 1991.

National Council for the Social Studies (NCSS) Task Force on Ethnic Studies Curriculum Guidelines (1992). "Curriculum Guidelines for Multicultural Education." *Social Education* 56:274–294.

National Council for the Social Studies (NCSS) Task Force (1994). *Curriculum Standards for Social Studies: Expectations for Excellence*. Washington, DC: NCSS, Bulletin 89.

NCSS Position Statement (1992). "The Columbian Quincentenary: An Educational Opportunity." *Social Education* 56(4):248–249.

Nieto, Sonia (1992). "We Speak in Many Tongues: Language Diversity and Multicultural Education." Pp. 103–126, in *Multicultural Education for the 21st Century*, edited by Carlos P. Diaz. Washington, DC: National Education Association.

Pahl, Ron H. (1992). "Review of 'Teaching for and Learning Social Studies Outcomes.'" *The Social Studies* 81(6):271–277.

"References" (1991). *Social Education* 55(6):347–348.

Renyi, Judith and Dennis R. Lubeck (1994). "A Response to the NCSS Guidelines on Multicultural Education." *Social Education* 58(1):4–6.

Russell, James (1992). "Europe's Crisis Has Global Effects: Self-Interest Undermining Drive for Unity." *Miami Herald* Sept. 18, 1992:C1.

Scourby, Alyce (1986). *The Greek Americans*. Boston: Twayne Publishers.

Swisher, Karen (1992). "Learning Styles: Implications for Teachers." Pp. 62–74 in *Multicultural Education for the 21st Century*, edited by Carlos F. Diaz. Washington, DC: National Education Association.

Weatherford, Jack (1991). "Indian Season in American Schools." *The Social Studies* 82(5):172–175.

Wooster, Judith S. (1992). "Choosing Materials for Teaching About the Columbian Quincentenary." *Social Education* 56(4):244–247.

Chapter Ten

SOCIAL STUDIES AND STUDENTS WITH DISABILITIES

James P. Shaver, Utah State University
Charles K. Curtis, The University of British Columbia

DISCRIMINATION AGAINST PERSONS WITH DISABILITIES has become a public policy target, and teaching students who have disabilities has become a classroom reality. Yet, there is little recognition in the social studies literature of the resulting curricular and instructional issues that ought to be addressed. When students with disabilities are mentioned in college methods textbooks or in journal articles, the focus is usually not on issues, but on general strategies for managing classrooms into which students with disabilities have been mainstreamed. For example, in a review of 21 social studies methods textbooks published since the passage of the Education of All Handicapped Children Act in 1975 (PL [Public Law] 94–142), we found only four (Jarolimek, 1990; Maxim, 1991; Michaelis, 1992; Savage and Armstrong, 1987) that contained some discussion of the issues posed by the teaching of students with disabilities in regular social studies classrooms.

The lack of attention in the literature does not mean, however, that no issues face social studies teachers who have children with disabilities in their classes. As a minimum, questions should be raised about the potential negative

285

impacts of disabilities on children's learning and on the ease and effectiveness with which the teacher can attain instructional goals for all students in the classroom.

What Do We Mean by "Disability"?

The discussion of such issues should begin with the definition and clarification of terms—always a crucial step in issue analysis (Oliver and Shaver, 1974; Shaver and Larkins, 1973). As used in this chapter, a *disability* is a physical or mental impairment. Whether a disability is a *handicap*—that is, a condition that has a detrimental affect on the person's performance—depends on context. A missing leg or arm is a disability that might not be a handicap (that is, create instructional problems) in a regular classroom—although a missing limb would be a handicap to a young person intent on participating in many sports.

As a matter of fact, consideration of the physical or mental characteristics that might constitute disabilities and the conditions under which they would be handicaps is a worthwhile and potentially interesting activity for teachers and students. The example of a missing leg or arm as a disability and sometimes a handicap is fairly obvious, as is severe mental developmental delay (mental retardation). Perhaps also so is cerebral palsy for a person who is bright intellectually, but has difficulty with motor control.

To what extent, however, is a handicap caused by the attitudes of others toward the disability, especially feelings of revulsion or fear? How about size as a disability or handicap: dwarfism, excessive height, or obesity? How about the very intelligent student who lacks social skills and so is an isolate? Is his or her intelligence a disability? A handicap? Does it pose instructional issues similar in any way to those raised by the presence in your classroom of a student with mild developmental delay?

As Larry A. Jones and Carrie Brown (1992) pointed out, "disability" and "handicap" are continua:

> Each of us is a mixed bag of abilities and disabilities...[although] some persons, such as those of very limited mental ability, are at a considerable, and so far biologically permanent, disadvantage..., [especially given] the ethic of competition....(p. 35).

This view of ability-disability and advantage-handicap invites each of us to look inward for a perspective, based on our own experiences, from which to consider and discuss issues having to do with teaching social studies to students with disabilities.

The "mixed bag" perspective on abilities and disabilities also suggests that related types of issues are not unique to disabilities. Rather, they are part of a general category of dilemmas that arise, or should be raised, whenever classrooms contain students who do not fit the "norm"—whether ethnically or culturally (as with Hispanic or African-American students; Shaver, 1988); economically (as with lower socioeconomic students; Anyon, 1980); somewhat different mentally or physically (as with "slow learners" or a missing hand); or strikingly different (as with blindness or cerebral palsy). Although the focus here is on children with physical and mental disabilities that are handicaps in regular classrooms and create special instructional challenges for teachers, setting the issues in the general context of diversity is an important conceptual move.

The Foci of This Chapter

Several instructional issues are raised in this chapter. The first is whether children with handicapping disabilities should be taught in regular classrooms. Discussion of this issue is often focused on factual questions about teachers' training and the support they receive. Are regular classroom teachers adequately trained to teach disabled students, and are they provided with the support services they need for managing and teaching these students in integrated classes? A second issue is whether the content of regular social studies curricula is appropriate for students with certain disabilities. A third issue is whether teachers should modify their classroom expectations and standards to accommodate students with disabilities.

In addition, an issue of curricular content is raised: Should *handicapism*— that is, the beliefs and attitudes that limit opportunities for persons with disabilities to participate in and enjoy the benefits of a democratic society—be of particular concern to social studies educators? Persons with disabilities have been, and continue to be, discriminated against. Should the social studies curriculum be designed to modify negative attitudes, as well as to involve students in the issues raised by such attitudes?

Should Children With Disabilities be Mainstreamed?

In a very crucial sense, the issue of whether children with disabilities that interfere with learning should be educated in regular classrooms was decided in 1975 with the passage of the Education for All Handicapped Children Act (PL 94–142). Education in the least restrictive environment was mandated, and most children with disabilities must now, by federal law, be integrated in regular classrooms in the United States. Such integration is dictated by provincial statutes or educational policies in Canada. Nevertheless, like many such issues, this one persists because of difficulties of policy implementation and because there is value conflict, leaving a residue of unease.

This issue is imbedded in a range of issues that involve, as Jones and Brown (1992) pointed out, a basic egalitarian ethic that implies that persons with disadvantages should be assisted to overcome them (see, for example, Veatch, 1986). The fundamental principle underlying that ethic—human worth and dignity—is at the heart of a democratic society. It drives continued concern with the status of women and of ethnic minorities in our society (for example, Simms and Contreras, 1980) and will be the context for continued controversy over PL 94–142 and over the implementation of the 1990 Americans with Disabilities Act (ADA), the main purpose of which is to overcome the handicapping effects of disabilities in the workplace and community.

Countering arguments, again made with reference to human worth and dignity, are based on such values as individual freedom, freedom of association, property rights (taxation for the costs of implementation), and the educational rights of those not disadvantaged.

The issue will persist. Laws (legislative acts or judicial decisions) rarely settle significant political-ethical issues immediately or in the long run at either the broad, societal or the personal-social level.

Public Law 94–142 was a response to the contention of advocacy groups, based on the equality principle, that services offered to disabled persons should be as "culturally normative" as possible (Wolfensberger, 1972). In that sense, the Education for All Handicapped Children Act was an extension of the civil rights movements of a decade earlier. Persons with disabilities are a minority, they are discriminated against based on identifiable but not relevant characteristics, and their educational opportunities in segregated settings cannot equal those of persons who have access to the mainline educational system. Demonstrating again the relevance of factual questions to political-ethical issues, special educators, parents, and other activists argued that the segregation of students on the basis of disability could not be justified because there was no evidence that separate programs for students with disabilities were more effective and because the educational and social needs of children with disabilities could best be met in regular classrooms (see, for example, Blatt, 1979; Dunn, 1968, 1973; Johnson, 1962).

Mainstreaming has been advocated in the special education literature (for example, Bookbinder, 1978; Johnson and Johnson, 1980; Pappanikou, 1981) on the ground that students with disabilities should be educated in an environment that resembles the real world more closely than a segregated program can. Such education, it is maintained, will provide the more normal life experiences that are necessary to prepare persons with disabilities for community living. Moreover, it is argued, educational mainstreaming will provide nondisabled students with opportunities to interact with individuals they would not likely otherwise encounter in a society where persons with disabilities are often shunned.

Authors (for example, Gearheart and Weishahn, 1980) have contended that experiences in mainstreamed classrooms will contribute to the intellectual and psychological growth of all students and lead to greater respect for human differences on the part of students without disabilities. There have, however, been very few studies of the impact of mainstreaming on the attitudes of other students toward those with disabilities. Shaver and his associates (1987, 1989) could locate reports for only seven studies. On the average, there was a small, positive shift toward more positive attitudes. The results were mixed, however: three studies yielded negative attitude outcomes. Carol Strong and Shaver (1991) noted the same phenomenon in a review of research on modifying attitudes toward persons with hearing impairment. They suggested that simply putting children with disabilities in a mainstreamed classroom without preparing the other students or planning for structuring interaction may well have a negative effect. If the attitudinal influence of mainstreaming is to be positive, Strong and Shaver concluded, the other students must be helped to understand disabilities and their impacts, and all of the students should be engaged in working together, cooperatively, toward shared goals (see Curtis, 1991).

Some arguments supporting the integration of children with disabilities in regular classes appeared in the social studies literature following the passage of PL 94–142. These arguments were often based on the values noted previously: the democratic commitment to human worth and dignity and the tenet that every individual deserves full opportunity to participate in the political, economic, and social life of their society. In this vein, Raman Rocha and Howard Sanford (1979) suggested that mainstreaming could provide a model of democracy through an educational environment in which the worth and dignity of each student is acknowledged and individual differences are recognized and accepted. John Herlihy and Myra Herlihy (1979) referred to judicial rulings that separate schooling inevitably results in educational inequalities, and suggested that the mainstreaming of students with disabilities was an affirmation of the basic right of all to equal treatment and opportunity. (Also see Herlihy and Herlihy, 1980.) According to Margo Sorgman, Sandra Sout-Henson, and Mary L. Perry (1979), a basic assumption underlying the integration of students with disabilities is that their interactions with nondisabled peers will lead to greater acceptance.

The authors of social studies methods textbooks have also discussed rationales for mainstreaming. G. Kelly (1979) maintained that mainstreaming approaches the "long sought goal of free and universal education for all who can benefit from it" (p. 186). John Michaelis (1992) suggested that children with disabilities in integrated classes benefit from acceptance by their nonhandicapped peers and that, moreover, the peers provide disabled children with role models of appropriate social behavior. Similarly, George Maxim (1991) proposed that disabled and nondisabled children who interact in mainstreamed settings would develop sensitivities and understandings about each other as a basis for positive interpersonal relationships. (Also see Walsh, 1980.)

In the social studies literature (and to some extent in the special education literature), then, rationales for mainstreaming students with disabilities have consisted for the most part of philosophical statements about the nature of democratic society; there have been few attempts to provide evidence for the assertions made. In fact, a search of the research literature revealed only two studies (Stoakes, 1964; Stroud, 1976), one reported before PL 94–142, that had direct relevance to a rationale for disabilities mainstreaming in social studies in particular. The findings suggested that students with mild retardation learned more social studies content and increased in self-esteem when placed in integrated classes (for a discussion of these studies, see Curtis, 1991, pp. 169–171).

With the limited research base, there is not sufficient empirical evidence in social studies to argue the pedagogical advantages of mainstreamed over segregated settings. The argument must rest largely on the commitment of social studies professionals to democratic values. Those who consider the issue should, however, address the countering factual and value claims: for example, that mainstreaming is often excessively expensive (for example, when an interpreter or special equipment and transportation must be provided); society has not provided regular teachers with adequate training or support services for teaching classes with disabled students in them; too much attention to disadvantaged/disabled students disadvantages "normal" students and hinders them in a competitive world; individuals should not be forced to associate with persons they find discomforting (whether disabled or different ethnically); property rights are denied when additional tax money is spent on the education of persons with disabilities.

Should Social Studies Curricula Be Modified or Different for Students with Disabilities?

The integration of students with disabilities in regular classes raises other important questions. One is whether the regular social studies program is appropriate for students with disabilities. One way to approach this question is to examine the results when social studies curricula are developed specifically for students with disabilities who are taught in special education classes.

Curtis (1978) reviewed social studies curricular materials published from 1950 through 1975 for special education programs in a number of cities, states, and provinces in the United States and Canada. The students for whom these curricula had been developed were described most frequently as mentally handicapped or slow learners, and the courses of studies often contained terms such as *adapted*, *practical*, and *basic* in their titles.

For the most part, the curricula were simplifications of traditional history and civics courses, often supplemented by lessons on patriotism, national symbols, holidays, traditions, and famous citizens. Frequently, the materials included lessons designed to inculcate a sense of duty toward the maintenance of one's self, family, and home; to provide information about making and keeping friends; and to encourage the acceptance of community responsibilities. A theme common to most of the programs was occupational preparation for gainful employment.

Other reviewers have reported similar findings. In his examination of social studies programs for educationable mentally retarded (EMR) students in Ohio, Marion B. Stroud (1976) identified corresponding patterns. Joav Gozali and James Gonwa (1973) conducted a content analysis of a social studies curriculum for EMR students in Wisconsin, entitled "Learning to be a Responsible Citizen." They found almost no mention of political participation but, instead, emphases on the "norms of civic duty" and on "descriptions of political events or institutions" (p. 51). E. Stevens (1958) perused a number of social studies curricula for mentally handicapped students and concluded that social living, rather than what is usually considered "social studies," was the focus in each.

There was a marked contrast between the curricula for students with mental disabilities and the social studies curricula developed during the 1960s and 1970s. The New Social Studies projects were focused on teaching the concepts and modes of inquiry of the academic disciplines and, in one case (Oliver and Shaver, 1974), on strategies for analyzing public controversy. Although those who published social studies curricula for special education students acknowledged citizenship as an important goal, the substantive differences in the special education and the New Social Studies curricula implied a marked difference in the way the authors viewed citizenship for the two populations.

In curricula for regular students, "good" citizenship consisted of effective participation in the democratic process. The citizen was to be open-minded, possess decision-making skills, and be firmly committed to the resolution of societal problems. In the curricula for special education students, on the other hand, "good" citizenship was defined as being gainfully employed and a nondisruptive member of the community. This citizen was to work at a job, respect and obey the law, maintain the family home and its furnishings in good repair, return borrowed articles, and help to keep the neighborhood clean, quiet, and orderly (Curtis, 1977).

Surveys conducted after PL 94–142 was enacted provide more recent information about social studies curricula for children with disabilities. Cynthia Sunal, Mary Paul, and John DeMary (1981) sought information about the curricula of public and private elementary and secondary programs for students with hearing impairments. They concluded that "a majority of programs provide minimal social studies education" (p. 71). According to their survey data, 40 percent of the day-school programs and 61 percent of the residential-school programs contained no, or only incidental, instruction in social studies. James R. Patton, Edward A. Polloway, and Mary E. Cronin (1987) surveyed teachers of mentally handicapped, physically handicapped, and learning disabled students in seven states. Large percentages of the teachers in resource-type programs (70 percent) and half-day programs (61 percent) reported that their students received no social studies instruction.

Clearly, presumed student differences have resulted in different social studies curricula for segregated students with mental developmental and other disabilities. Should the purpose of social studies education be dissimilar for those students? In a democratic society should some citizens be presumed, and structured by their schooling, to be less than full participants in political life? Is political participation a privilege that is dependent on some specified level of cognitive performance? Can our society afford to have decisions made by those without full intellectual development? If not, what types of intellectual development are relevant? And who is to set the acceptable levels? In the broader context of "disability," should not levels of empathy or of moral development also be of concern? Social studies educators who have argued that students with disabilities merit a social studies curriculum similar to that of other students include Curtis and Shaver (1980), Richard Luftig (1987), and Anna Ochoa and Susan Shuster (1980).

Should Standards in Mainstreamed Social Studies Classes Be Modified for Students with Disabilities?

Whether the content, and the implied or explicit objectives, of social studies curricula should be different for students with mental disabilities is a significant issue in a democratic society. A related issue is whether social studies teachers should be satisfied with lower levels of achievement by students with disabilities. Pertinent questions include whether the same tests should be administered to all students; whether it is fair to grade all disabled students with the same criteria used to judge the work of their nondisabled peers; whether students with disabilities should be evaluated on the basis of their personal educational growth, effort, or behavior, rather than against the usual normative standards for the subject area.

The responses to such questions should depend on a number of factors such as the type of disability and the degree to which the disability handicaps normal functioning in the classroom; the ability, age, and grade level of the student; and the skill and experience of the classroom teacher in working with students with disabilities. Also relevant are questions such as whether lowered expectations are disrespectful and likely to lead to or reinforce low self-expectations and performance. That concern is akin to the arguments heard when the high-school grade point average and ACT scores criteria for participation in college athletics were raised by the NCAA. Charges of ethnic discrimination were heard from one side. It was argued that young African-Americans would be kept out of collegiate athletic competition by standards that did not take into account their cultural-educational circumstances. A counter argument was that not to expect African-American athletes to perform up to the standards was discriminatory and degrading.

Interestingly, attitude–assessment developers Harold Yuker and J.R. Block (1986) have argued that people with acceptable attitudes toward people with disabilities hold them to the same performance expectations as those for normal functioning people. On Yuker's Attitude Toward Disabled Persons (ATDP) Scale, respondents are asked to agree or disagree with statements such as the following: "Disabled persons should not be expected to meet the same standards as nondisabled persons" (Form O, item 10); "You should not expect too much from disabled persons" (Form O, item 14); and, "Disabled children should not have to compete with nondisabled children" (Form B, item 21). Disagreement with these items contributes to a positive attitude score on the ATDP Scale.

The instructional standards issue might be posed as, how should the desirability of high expectations be balanced against the importance of providing realistic assistance to those with disadvantages, whether physical, mental, cultural, or economic? Should teachers' expectations for mainstreamed students with disabilities always be the same as for nondisabled students? Does the validity of an equal-expectations position rest on the assumption that the teacher will use appropriate teaching strategies and that students will be provided with the necessary learning materials and support services to minimize the handicapping effects of their particular disabilities?

The equal-expectations principle must be considered in a broader social context, too. Disabled students will leave school to participate in a community that consists largely of "normally functioning" individuals. Should these students not be held to the highest standards they can achieve in preparation for assuming adult roles in the community?

Specifically, how should the equal-expectations principle be applied as teachers, in conjunction with parents and others, prepare Individual Educational Programs (IEPs) and make decisions about how to present units of study to their mainstreamed students with disabilities? Usually included in an IEP are a needs assessment and statement of objectives, a list of instructional materials, descriptions of learning activities and teaching strategies, and evaluation procedures. Experienced teachers of mainstreamed classes know that even when IEPs are carefully planned and carried out, some mainstreamed students may neither learn at the same rate nor reach the same degree of understanding as many of their nondisabled peers. Should this realization result in the selection of different objectives and content or should it affect what the teacher accepts as a satisfactory level of achievement?

The following illustrates the dilemma: Suppose that for a unit on civil-rights legislation, a teacher of a high-school civics class with a mainstreamed mildly mentally disabled student provides her with simplified reading materials, gives concrete examples of civil rights drawn from real-life situations, and uses cooperative learning groups in instruction—approaches frequently recommended for teaching mildly mentally disabled students (see, for example, Curtis, 1982). The unit test consists of a series of descriptions of situations in which civil rights may have been denied. The student with the mild mental disability can identify the specific rights involved but, as Jones (1964) found, cannot, in contrast with most of the other students, state correctly whether a particular right was violated.

A bright young girl with severe cerebral palsy is also in the class. This student experiences great difficulty in forming intelligible speech and for the most part must rely on a language board to communicate. However, she readily comprehends the concept of civil rights and her understanding of the rights dilemmas, as assessed with a test individually administered by her full-time aide, exceeds that of most of the students in the class. Should IEP objectives and assessment for this girl be strikingly different from those prepared for the mildly mentally disabled student, although the basic content described in each is similar? Should the objectives or assessment for either differ from that for the class in general? Based on what are assumed to be reliable estimates of cognitive ability and on prior experience with comparable students, should the teacher decide that each mainstreamed student worked up to her ability level and, therefore, made satisfactory progress, earning a high grade, even though their achievement levels were dissimilar from each other and from those of other class members?

Are there sound pedagogical reasons for accepting different levels of achievement as satisfactory for students with disabilities? Should a teacher lower his or her expectations and accept lower performance simply because a student has a disability? What are the implications for the student's participation in society?

Should Handicapism Be Studied in Social Studies?

A persistent theme in the history of our country has been the struggle by minority groups to achieve full social, economic, and political participation. A commonly accepted purpose of social studies instruction is the examination of the value dilemmas inherent in the resulting conflicts. Underlying that goal is a concern for promoting the values, attitudes, and behaviors crucial to citizenship in a democratic society. Included have been efforts to increase the acceptance of cultural diversity and to diminish the effects of racism and sexism (Simms and Contreras, 1980).

In recent years, while members of ethnic groups and women continued their efforts to gain full participation and others weighed how far the society should go to ensure their rights, persons with disabilities have become a more vocal minority. Two interrelated social studies curricular concerns are similar for racism, sexism, and handicapism: how to enhance understanding of minority groups and how to promote the consideration of what policies should be established in response to minority demands (Shaver and Curtis, 1981b).

Racism and sexism have long been part of the American lexicon, but not *handicapism*—negative beliefs and attitudes toward persons with disabilities, based on unfounded perceptions and assumptions, that result in differential and unequal treatment (Bogdan and Biklen, 1977). Nevertheless, the concept is equally powerful. Indeed, after interviewing persons with disabilities throughout the United States, Sonny Kleinfield (1979) concluded that the negative attitudes central to handicapism are the single greatest barrier to full lives for persons with disabilities.

Although a variety of disabilities cut across ethnic and gender lines and economic, educational, and social strata, persons with disabilities tend to be perceived as members of a single, devalued group (Kleinfield, 1979). That oversimplified, undifferentiated (that is, stereotypical) conception and the accompanying prejudgments (prejudices) about the characteristics and capabilities of persons with disabilities are at the heart of handicapism, with negative effects similar to those of racism and sexism. Similarly, too, significant societal issues are posed by the status of persons with disabilities. For example, as a group, persons with disabilities have the lowest income and the highest level of unemployment of any segment of society.

Black studies and women's studies in social studies programs were a response to racism and sexism. Do studies designed to educate students about persons with disabilities and the negative effects of handicapism also have a place in social studies? Would appropriate goals be to encourage students to examine the debilitating effects of stereotyping, prejudice, and negative attitudes on persons with disabilities and to explicate and examine the political-ethical issues that are being, and will be, raised?

Some excellent books by special educators (for example, Barnes, Berrigan, and Biklen, 1978; Bookbinder, 1978; Ward, Arkell, Dahl, and Wise, 1979) contain descriptions of content and strategies for modifying children's attitudes toward persons with disabilities. The paucity of social studies publications in this area, however, suggests that, as a group, social studies educators have not had a great deal of interest in the problems of persons with disabilities, even though these problems could be readily included within the frameworks of existing courses. Our literature search disclosed only six such publications written by social studies educators (Curtis, 1984; Curtis and

Griffith, 1984; Maxim, 1991, p. 491; Shaver, 1983; Shaver and Curtis, 1981a; Watkinson and Peters, 1982).

The overall intent for this chapter has been to discuss issues, not to suggest teaching practices. However, given the scant attention to handicapism in the social studies literature, how to help students examine their own perceptions of persons with disabilities is a pertinent consideration. Student attitudes are relevant both to mainstreaming issues and to societal issues, to how persons with disabilities are treated in the classroom, and to societal policy deliberations.

Conceptual Frame

As with racism and sexism, helping students examine their own frames of reference is a crucial step. In fact, just as Charles Beard (1934) and John Dewey (1964) found it necessary to remind curriculum developers and teachers about the impact of their unexamined frames of knowledge and values on their instructional choices, students need to be made aware of the effects of their frames of reference. A starting point is recognition that each person has a *frame of reference*—composed of perceptual sets, feeling predispositions, beliefs, and values (Shaver and Larkins, 1973, p. 72)—based on his or her experiences. Different backgrounds lead to sometimes subtle, sometimes striking, differences in frames and in the often unconscious impacts on thought and behavior.

Our frames of reference contain *stereotypes*—"oversimplified, undifferentiated pictures of groups of persons" that often lead to unreflective prejudgments or *prejudices* (Shaver and Curtis, 1981a, p. 10). For example, persons with the motor skills disability that accompanies cerebral palsy are often judged, based on physical appearance, to be mentally deficient.

Our *attitudes*—"interrelated beliefs and feelings focused on some object or person...[that] predispose us to act in certain ways" (Shaver and Curtis, 1981a, p. 10)—are elements of our frames of reference that are crucial to handicapism. For example, because of a negative attitude, a person might avoid contact with persons with certain disabilities.

The above concepts should be introduced, defined, and discussed with students, illustrated with exemplars, and applied to handicapism and its effects on persons with disabilities. Examples of possible activities include the following, adapted from *Handicapism and Equal Opportunity* (Shaver and Curtis, 1981a, pp. 10–13, 17–23)*:

---

1. To illustrate the concept of frame of reference and the effects of differing backgrounds and situations, use responses to common events such as an early morning snowstorm that clogs roads and closes down traffic, or to other severe weather that might occur in your geographic area. Ask students to explore the reactions of different persons, such as a farmer in the middle of winter or in late spring, a student who is unprepared for a first-period history exam, the school superintendent, a businessman who needs to fly to another city to close an important deal. Or, use the possible responses to a school announcement of, for example, tryouts for cheerleading, the football team, or the class play to explore differences in frames of reference.

2. Help students apply the concept to disabilities and handicapism by considering situations such as these: A salesperson ignoring a person in a wheelchair who wants to make a purchase, talking instead to his or her companion (a common occurrence); a student who teases a developmentally delayed person about being a "retard"; an electronics manufacturer who hires disabled (for example, blind) assemblers; a coach who encourages a boy missing a hand to play basketball. What might each case suggest about individual frames of reference?

3. Introduce stereotypes and their prejudicial effects by asking students to react to class labels, such as "Republican," "Democrat," "professional athlete," "housewife," "teenager." What are typical stereotypes associated with the labels? Can the students identify exceptions to the stereotypes? The exploration of stereotypes about and prejudices toward adolescents—as exemplified, for example, by adults in hiring and social situations—can be provocative. Then, have the students list the terms often used to refer to persons with disabilities and ask whether they have positive or negative (good or bad) connotations. Have individual experiences with persons with disabilities influenced any students' reactions?

4. Moving to attitudes, have students examine their own attitudes towards persons with disabilities using questions such as the following (based on questions suggested by the Canadian Rehabilitation Council):
   a. Do you ever feel awkward in the presence of a person with a disability?
   b. Do you ever act toward persons with physical disabilities in such a way as to indicate that you think they are also mentally disabled (for example, talking to their companion rather than directly to them)?
   c. Would you like to have a person with a disability for a close friend?
   d. Can you list some of the problems individuals with disabilities have in using public transportation, gaining access to public buildings, and using public conveniences (such as restrooms)?
   e. Do you feel comfortable offering assistance to a person with a disability, such as a blind person?

      f.   If you were at a social gathering where a person with a disability was present, would you avoid that person? Or, would you pay special attention to him or her?

5. Explore with the students the reasons for the negative attitudes that many persons have toward those with disabilities, especially visible severe disabilities. Reasons might include the following (also see, for example, Kleinfield, 1979, pp. 182–183):

    a.   People who are different from ourselves can seem difficult to decipher and react to, as with a blind person's facial expressions.

    b.   We may feel fear, such as can be sensed visiting a hospital, because we are reminded that we, too, at any time could join the disabled group (a significant difference between handicapism, on the one hand, and racism and sexism, on the other).

    c.   The emphasis on physical beauty and prowess in our society makes physical or mental flaws discomforting.

    d.   Stereotypes are promoted by literature and television (for example, hunchbacks, eye patches, hooks for arms, and pegs for legs used as symbols of evil).

    e.   We may be uncertain about the extent of effects of disabilities and how to behave with a disabled person. (Should I offer to help a person in a wheelchair or a blind person through a door?)

    f.   Feelings of guilt for being able bodied can cause a reaction.

    g.   If the disability affects communication, it can be difficult to discern if there is mental impairment as well.

    h.   Disabled persons may not have positive attitudes toward themselves (a major handicap for many).

6. What it is like to have a disability can be explored using simulations and role playing. Simulations of visual, hearing, and physical impairments can usually be arranged easily with readily accessible props (for example, blindfolds, ear plugs, TVs without sound, talking with dental cotton in the mouth, or not allowing speech at all.) Intellectual disabilities are less accessible to simulation and role play, but with imagination, you and your students will think of ways—such as limiting the number of syllables in the words used to write a theme, use of over-technical language in a lecture, making over-rapid homework assignments, writing while rotating one's right foot in a clockwise direction on the floor (to simulate coordination problems of developmentally delayed persons).

    Give the students profiles of disabled students their age and have them examine what a day in the life of this student would be like. Include getting up in the morning, traveling to and from school, and functioning at school and at home in the evening.

Accessibility studies of local public buildings, shopping malls, and transportation systems are another way to help students understand what it is like to be disabled. Such studies will reveal the difficulties persons with disabilities encounter in moving about their communities. Disability surveys can be developed from criteria listed in American National Standards publications.

Instructional Strategies

Two strategies for organizing instruction have been suggested in the literature as means for improving attitudes toward students with disabilities, with some research evidence to support this claim. The first is peer tutoring, with a nondisabled student acting as a tutor to a disabled student. If the tutor is placed in a helping situation with a stake in the mainstreamed student's learning and, thus, in his or her welfare, a relationship of mutual respect will often develop. The result is more positive attitudes toward the mainstreamed student. In several studies in which peer tutoring resulted in more positive attitudes (see Curtis and Shaver, 1992), the tutors were first instructed in the characteristics of students with mental disabilities and then trained to tutor them. None of these studies, however, was conducted in a social studies classroom.

A second strategy with promise for improving attitudes toward those different from oneself (whether ethnically or disability-wise) is cooperative learning. In particular, David and Roger Johnson (for example, 1980) and their colleagues at the University of Minnesota have suggested that interpersonal attraction between students with disabilities and their nondisabled peers increases when cooperative groups are used in the classroom. Shaver, Curtis, Joseph Jesunathadas, and Carol Strong (1987, 1989) concluded that cooperative learning resulted in slightly more positive attitudes as compared with regular instruction. Curtis (1991) reviewed studies of cooperative learning in mainstreamed social studies classes and concluded that cooperative learning tends to promote positive interactions between mainstreamed and nondisabled students. Again, the likely outcome is enhanced attitudes toward students with disabilities.

Conclusion

Normalization—that is, living in the community, with life as ordinary as possible—has in recent years become a potent goal for persons with disabilities. Fewer persons with disabilities live in special institutions. Many now live in group homes in local neighborhoods, and others remain in their family homes. Concomitantly, education for students with disabilities in regular classrooms whenever possible is not only a mandate of the Education of All Handicapped Children Act, but also a deeply felt desire of parents whose children have disabilities.

Unlike even a few years ago, it is probable that, as a regular classroom teacher, you will at some time have one or more students with disabilities in a class. How you react in that situation has serious implications for the child with a disability and for society. The individual teacher is, after all, the key to what happens in the classroom. You can do much to determine whether the educational outcomes are positive for the child with the disability and for the other children in the classroom.

Whether and how you cope with issues such as those raised in this chapter will be a major determinant of the outcome. Should you accept having a child with a disability, even a severe disability, in your social studies classroom? If so, should you set different curricular goals and content for that student, and should you apply different standards for evaluating performance? Answering such questions can be complex and perplexing. Certainly, tenacious clarification of your own frame of reference will be crucial.

As with racism and sexism, handicapism is likely to be latent, even if not obvious, in each of us, teachers as well as students. Explication of your assumptions, beliefs, and perceptions, and examination of them for accuracy and consistency are crucial if, as John Dewey (1964) put it, your teaching is not to be "conducted blindly, under the control of customs or traditions that have not been examined or in response to immediate social pressures" (p. 164) or, as Charles Beard (1934) said, guided by "small, provincial, local, class, group, or personal prejudices" (p.182).

Without self-scrutiny, your unreflective perceptions and assumptions may well have negative consequences for a student with a disability in your class. It would, however, be a mistake to assume that such self-examination is essential only if you are teaching a student with a disability. As with racism and sexism, handicapism is a pervasive societal problem, one we have suggested in this chapter should also be a social studies topic. Clarity in regard to your own frame of reference—your conception of what is necessary, possible, and desirable (Beard, 1934)—is crucial, because, consciously or not, your curricular and instructional decisions will be shaped by reference to that frame.

The relevance to your decisions about how to treat handicapism in your curriculum may be evident. Equally important, however, are the implications of your frame of reference for the *hidden curriculum* of your classroom—the experiences you provide students that result in learning that is unintended and unplanned, often unsuspected, and frequently undesirable. Consider, for example, the comments you make about persons with disabilities; your reaction to jokes about such persons; whether you, intentionally or not, overlook the past and current contributions to society of persons with disabilities. An informal curriculum of acceptance and respect can be as important as consciously and openly addressing handicapism within the formal curriculum as an objectionable personal phenomenon and a serious societal problem.

The individual teacher is the primary determinant of events in his or her classroom. Your behavior should be based on careful consideration of issues such as raised in this chapter. Collectively, the actions of many individual teachers can diminish significantly the undesirable effects of handicapism and enhance the continued re-examination of the validity of social, economic, and educational distinctions based on disability.

Reflective Questions

1. *What are the similarities and differences in racism, sexism, and handicapism?*

2. *Does discrimination against persons with disabilities deserve the same attention in social studies as has been given to ethnic and gender-based discrimination?*

3. *What do you believe about the inclusion of students with disabilities in your social studies classes, especially if a student has a disability, such as cerebral palsy or hearing or sight impairment, that might be discomforting to other students and require extra teaching effort on your part?*

4. *If a student with a disability that affects learning is in your classroom, what criteria should you use to evaluate his or her achievements? Who should determine those standards?*

5. *Are you adequately prepared to teach students with disabilities such as mental retardation, blindness, cerebral palsy, and emotional disorders in your social studies classroom?*

6. *If you do not feel prepared to teach students with disabilities, do you need additional knowledge about disabilities and handicaps, assistance with developing an emotional-attitudinal base for dealing with students unlike yourself, greater familiarity with appropriate teaching techniques, and ways of organizing and presenting materials for students with various disabilities?*

7. *If you have a disability, or know someone who has, how will that influence your treatment of handicapism and your teaching of students with disabilities?*

GLOSSARY

ADA   The 1990 Americans with Disabilities Act that mandated that reasonable efforts must be made to accommodate persons with disabilities in the workplace.

attitude   A cluster of beliefs and feelings that influences how we act toward, for example, a person who belongs to an identifiable group such as those who are mentally retarded.

disability   A physical or mental impairment.

frame of reference   The perceptual sets, feeling predispositions, beliefs, and values through which each person views the world.

handicap   A disability that results in a detrimental effect on performance.

handicapism   Negative beliefs and attitudes, based on unfounded perceptions and assumptions, toward persons with disabilities that lead to inequities in treatment.

mainstream   To include children with disabilities in regular classrooms, rather than in special education classrooms.

PL 94–142   The 1975 Education for All Handicapped Children Act that mandated, among other things, that children with disabilities be educated in the least restrictive environment.

prejudice   Unreflective prejudgments.

stereotype   An oversimplified, undifferentiated view, for example, of a group of people.

ANNOTATED BIBLIOGRAPHY

Bowe, Frank (1978). *Handicapping America: Barriers to Disabled Persons*. New York: Harper & Row; Shirley Cohen (1977). *Special People: A Brighter Future for Everyone with Physical, Mental, and Emotional Disabilities*. Englewood Cliffs, NJ: Prentice-Hall; Sonny Kleinfield (1979). *The Hidden Minority: A Profile of Handicapped Americans*. Boston: Little, Brown.

These books review the historical treatment of people with disabilities; explore the social, economic, and political barriers faced by persons with handicaps; convey the human side of having a disability; and discuss legal developments and policy recommendations. Any or all are recommended for reading.

Gliedman, John and William Roth (1980). *The Unexpected Minority: Handicapped Children in America*. New York: Harcourt Brace Jovanovich.

Focused on the difficulties faced by disabled children and adults as a hidden minority, this report from the Carnegie Council on Children takes a civil rights approach to the social aspect of handicaps.

Herlihy, John G. and Myra T. Herlihy (1980). *Mainstreaming in the Social Studies*. Washington, DC: National Council for the Social Studies, Bulletin 62.

Ochoa, Anna S. and Susan K. Shuster (1980). *Social Studies in the Mainstreamed Classroom, K–6*. Boulder, CO: Social Science Education Consortium and ERIC Clearinghouse for Social Studies/Social Science Education.

These two works provide helpful suggestions for social studies teachers who have students with disabilities in their classrooms.

Pope, Andrew M. and Alvin R. Tarlov, editors (1991). *Disability in America: Toward a National Agenda for Prevention*. Washington, DC: National Academy Press.

This report by a national committee is a collection of up-to-date discussions of disabilities and possible actions to minimize their occurrence and their handicapping dysfunctions.

Shaver, James P. and Charles K. Curtis (1981). *Handicapism and Equal Opportunity: Teaching about the Disabled in Social Studies*. Reston, VA: Foundation for Exceptional Children.

Written for social studies teachers who wish to deal with handicapism, this booklet provides concrete suggestions for helping students comprehend the personal meaning of disabilities.

REFERENCES

Anyon, Jean (1980). "Social Class and the Hidden Curriculum of Work." *Journal of Education* 162:67–92.

Barnes, E., C. Berrigan, and D. Biklen (1978). *What's the Difference? Teaching Positive Attitudes Toward People with Disabilities.* Syracuse: Human Policy Press.

Beard, Charles A. (1934). *The Nature of the Social Sciences in Relation to Objectives of Instruction.* New York: Charles Scribner's.

Blatt, B. (1979). "A Drastically Different Analysis." *Mental Retardation* 17:303–306.

Bogdan, R. and D. Biklen (1977). "Handicapism." *Social Policy* 7(5):14–19.

Bookbinder, S.R. (1978). *Mainstreaming: What Every Child Needs to Know About Disabilities.* Boston: The Exceptional Parent Press.

Curtis, Charles K. (1977). "Citizenship Education and the Slow Learner." Pp. 74–95 in *Building Rationales for Citizenship Education*, edited by J.P. Shaver. Washington, DC: National Council for the Social Studies, Bulletin 52.

Curtis, Charles K. (1978). *Contemporary Community Problems in Citizenship Education for Slow-Learning Secondary Students.* Unpublished doctoral dissertation. Logan: Utah State University.

Curtis, Charles K. (1982). "Teaching Disabled Students in the Regular Social Studies Classroom." *The History and Social Science Teacher* 18:9–16.

Curtis, Charles K. (1984). "Teaching About the Rights of the Disabled." *The Social Studies* 75:260–264.

Curtis, Charles K. (1991). "Social Studies for Students At-Risk and With Disabilities." Pp. 157–174 in *Handbook of Research on Social Studies Teaching and Learning*, edited by J.P. Shaver. New York: Macmillan.

Curtis, Charles K. and J. Griffith (1984). *Handicapism.* Vancouver, BC: Canada Studies Foundation.

Curtis, Charles K. and James P. Shaver (1980). "Slow Learners and the Study of Contemporary Problems." *Social Education* 44:302–309.

Curtis, Charles K. and James P. Shaver (1992). "Changing Attitudes Toward Persons with Mental Retardation: A Review of Research." *International Journal of Special Education* 7:201–218.

Dewey, John (1964). "The Relation of Science and Philosophy as a Basis for Education." Pp. 15–19 in *John Dewey on Education: Selected Writings*, edited by R.D. Archambault. New York: Random House.

Dunn, L. (1968). "Special Education for the Mentally Retarded—Is Much of it Justified?" *Exceptional Children* 35:5–22.

Dunn, L. (November, 1973). *The Normalization of Special Education.* Laycock Memorial Lecture. Saskatoon: University of Saskatchewan.

Gearheart, W.R. and M.W. Weishahn (1980). *The Handicapped Student in the Regular Classroom*, 2nd ed. St. Louis: Mosby.

Gozali, Joav and James Gonwa (1973). "Citizenship Training for the EMR: A Case of Educational Neglect." *Mental Retardation* 11(1):49–50.

Herlihy, John G. and Myra T. Herlihy (1979). "Introduction." *Social Education* 43:58.

Herlihy, John G. and Myra T. Herlihy (1980). *Mainstreaming in the Social Studies.* Washington, DC: National Council for the Social Studies, Bulletin 62.

Jarolimek, John (1990). *Social Studies in Elementary Education*, 8th ed. New York: Macmillan.

Johnson, David and Roger Johnson (1980). "Integrating Handicapped Students into the Mainstream." *Exceptional Children* 47:90–98.

Johnson, G. (1962). "Special Education for the Mentally Handicapped—A Paradox." *Exceptional Children* 29:62–69.

Jones, Larry A. and Carrie Brown (1992). "Toward an Ethic of Assistive Technology for Persons with Mental Retardation." *Disability Studies Quarterly* 12(4):34–38.

Jones, W.E. (1964). *An Investigation of the Case Method of Instruction in Selected Eighth Grade Civics Classes.* Unpublished doctoral dissertation. Berkeley: University of California.

Kelly, G. (1979). *Elementary School Social Studies Instruction: A Basic Approach.* Denver: Love Publishing.

Kleinfield, Sonny (1979). *The Hidden Minority: A Profile of Handicapped Americans.* Boston: Little, Brown.

Luftig, Richard L. (1987). *Teaching the Mentally Retarded Student: Curriculum, Methods, and Strategies.* Boston: Allyn & Bacon.

Maxim, George W. (1991). *Social Studies and the Elementary School Child*, 4th ed. New York: Merrill Publishing.

Michaelis, John U. (1992). *Social Studies for Children*, 10th ed. Boston: Allyn & Bacon.

Ochoa, Anna S. and Susan K. Shuster (1980). *Social Studies in the Mainstreamed Classroom, K-6.* Boulder, CO: Social Science Education Consortium and ERIC Clearinghouse for Social Studies/Social Science Education.

Oliver, Donald W. and James P. Shaver (1974). *Teaching Public Issues in the High School.* Logan: Utah State University Press. (Original work published 1966).

Pappanikou, A. (1981). "Introduction." Pp. xi–xv in *Mainstreaming Emotionally Disturbed Children*, edited by A. Pappanikou and J. Paul. Syracuse: Syracuse University Press.

Patton, J.R., E.A. Polloway, and M.E. Cronin (1987). "Social Studies Instruction for Handicapped Students: A Review of Current Practices." *The Social Studies* 78:131–135.

Rocha, Raman and Howard Sanford (1979). "Mainstreaming: Democracy in Action." *Social Education* 43:59–62.

Savage, Thomas V. and David G. Armstrong (1987). *Effective Teaching in Elementary Social Studies.* New York: Macmillan.

Shaver, James P. (1983). "Teaching about the Handicapped in Social Studies: Attitudes Toward Disabilities." *The History and Social Science Teacher* 18:129–134, 140.

Shaver, James P. (1988). "Cultural Pluralism and a Democratic Society." *Education and Society* 1(1):11–17.

Shaver, James P. and Charles K. Curtis (1981a). *Handicapism and Equal Opportunity: Teaching About the Disabled in Social Studies.* Reston, VA: Foundation for Exceptional Children.

Shaver, James P. and Charles K. Curtis (1981b). "Handicapism: Another Challenge for Social Studies." *Social Education* 45:208–211.

Shaver, James P., Charles K. Curtis, J. Jesunathadas, and C.J. Strong (1987). *The Modification of Attitudes toward Persons with Handicaps: A Comprehensive Integrative Review of Research.* Final report to the U.S. Department of Education, Office of Special Education and Rehabilitative Services. Logan: Utah State University, Bureau of Research Services. (ERIC Document Reproduction Service No. ED 285 345).

Shaver, James P., Charles K. Curtis, J. Jesunathadas, and C.J. Strong (1989). "The Modification of Attitudes toward Persons with Disabilities: Is There a Best Way?" *International Journal of Special Education* 4(1):33–57.

Shaver, James P. and A.G. Larkins (1973). *The Analysis of Public Issues Program.* Boston: Houghton Mifflin.

Simms, R.L. and Gloria Contreras, editors (1980). *Racism and Sexism: Responding to the Challenge.* Washington, DC: National Council for the Social Studies.

Sorgman, Margo, Sandra Sout-Henson, and Mary L. Perry (1979). "The Least Restrictive Environment: Social Studies Goals and Practices." *The Social Studies* 70:108–111.

Stevens, E. (1958). "Analysis of Objectives for the Education of Children with Retarded Mental Development." *American Journal of Mental Deficiency* 63:225–235.

Stoakes, D.W. (1964). *An Educational Experiment with the Homogeneous Grouping of Mentally Advanced and Slow Learning Students in Junior High School.* Unpublished doctoral dissertation. Boulder: University of Colorado.

Strong, Chet J. and James P. Shaver (1991). "Modifying Attitudes toward Persons with Hearing Impairments: A Comprehensive Review of the Research." *American Annals of the Deaf* 136(3):252–260.

Stroud, M.E. (1976). *The Achievement of Social Studies Objectives of a Persisting Life Problems Curriculum by Educable Mentally Retarded Pupils in Four Alternative Mainstreaming Settings in Ohio.* Unpublished doctoral dissertation. Canton: Kent State University.

Sunal, Cynthia, Mary Paul, and John DeMary (1981). "Social Studies for the Hearing Impaired: The State of the Art." *Theory and Research in Social Education* 9(3):61–72.

Veatch, Robert (1986). *The Foundations of Justice: Why the Retarded and the Rest of Us Have Claims to Equality.* New York: Oxford University Press.

Walsh, Huber (1980). *Social World.* New York: Macmillan.

Ward, M., R. Arkell, H. Dahl, and J. Wise (1979). *Everybody Counts: A Workshop Manual to Increase Awareness of Handicapped People.* Reston, VA: Council for Exceptional Children.

Watkinson, A. and Y. Peters (1982). "Teaching About the Rights of Disabled Canadians." *The History and Social Science Teacher* 18:17–21.

Wolfensberger, W. (1972). *The Principle of Normalization in Human Services.* Toronto, Canada: National Institute on Mental Retardation.

Yuker, Harold and J.R. Block (1986). *Research with the Attitude Toward Disabled Persons Scales (ATDP), 1960–1985.* Hempstead, NY: Center for Study of Attitudes Toward Persons with Disabilities.

Chapter Eleven

RESPONDING TO GENDER EQUITY IN THE SOCIAL STUDIES CURRICULUM

Leslie Rebecca Bloom, Iowa State University
Anna S. Ochoa, Indiana University

> "Men, their rights and nothing more; women, their rights and nothing less."
>
> *S.B. Anthony, 1820–1906*

INTRODUCTION

We are writing this chapter during a time that limits and denies, rather than nourishes, the promise and potential of women. For example:

- Affirmative action programs are being de-emphasized and even eliminated.
- The right to abortion has not only been challenged, but also has resulted in murders of health-care professionals.
- Equal pay for equal work is still beyond the reach of most women.

These examples demonstrate a pattern of holding women in line or diminishing their rights. They make ever more urgent the need for educators at all levels to be responsive to women's concerns. Although the above events

309

illustrate the depth of gender discrimination in our society, the statements that follow reflect this discrimination in the context of school and family.

Statement by a parent: "We must find a way to send our son John to college, but Dorothy, our daughter, may have to settle for business school." Many of us have heard similar statements that reflect the norm that males will be family breadwinners—consequently their education is more important than that of females. Statements like this are still prevalent today even though women are the single bread winners in many families.

By an education professor to a female student who is an experienced teacher and who is having trouble phrasing a response: "Well, don't worry your pretty little head about it. Let's go on." Not only does this statement denigrate this student's capability, it is not supportive of her ideas or verbal development. The professor concludes that being pretty will be more important for this woman than being able to converse about educational topics and ideas.

By a male college English professor to a graduate seminar after the women students, 50 percent of the class, requested that women poets be included in the syllabus: "O.K. We can add Marianne Moore. She writes like a man." This professor makes it abundantly clear that he has little respect for the intellectual requests of the women in his class, that he has contempt for poetry that represents the voices and experiences of women, and that the only legitimate sources of study are those works produced by men.

By a classroom teacher to a female fourth grader who comes in from the playground covered with dust on her clothes from playing baseball: "Little girls shouldn't get dirty like that. You should wait till after school when you change into your play clothes to play baseball." The message is clear. Staying clean and pretty is more important than being active and sports-minded.

> Although women's names and faces appear more often in today's social studies textbooks than in earlier ones, their genuine contributions to social life are still generally omitted.
>
> *Nel Noddings, 1992.*

Each of these statements reinforce such social norms as women don't need as much education as men, they don't need to be as articulate, they don't need to give much consideration to intellectual ideas, they don't need to be represented in the curriculum, and they don't need to be as physically active as their male counterparts.

Additional illustrations could be generated. But those included affirm the entrenchment of attitudes that have limited and continue to limit the quality of educational opportunities in today's educational environment. These examples illustrate the compelling need for classroom practices that do not reproduce gender discrimination. Social studies teachers, classes, and programs must necessarily attend to these matters if the values of freedom and equality are to be honored.

Gender and Academic Achievement

As we begin this discussion, we think it is useful to compare male and female academic achievement across the several subject areas and place social studies achievement in the context of achievement in such school subjects as reading, math, and science. Although we recognize that these national tests scores are limited and problematic, they do represent an indicator that permits comparison of male and female achievement.

Reading and Writing

Recent reports comparing achievement scores for females and males in reading and writing are mixed. Although the U.S. Department of Education (1992) reports that females have higher scores than males in reading and writing, a recent document issued by the American Association of University Women (AAUW, 1992) claims that gender differences in verbal ability have virtually disappeared and males have caught up with females, at least in how verbal ability has been measured. In other words, the common belief that females outperform males in verbal ability is not emphatically supported. All of us need to recognize that verbal ability, including reading and writing skills, is strongly connected to academic performance in social studies as well as other subjects. Moreover, it is essential to the exercise of democratic citizenship.

Mathematics and Science

In overall mathematics performance, the long-standing advantage held by males is declining. However, it has not been eliminated. Recent results from NAEP, the National Assessment of Educational Progress (Mullis, 1991), reveal that at grades four and eight, differences in achievement across gender were at a minimum. However, grade twelve males showed a small advantage in all parts of the mathematics test except in algebra.

In science, gender differences are still very visible, and the National Center for Educational Statistics'(1990) *Science Report Card* reports that the size of the gender gap has remained large since 1978. Indeed, this gap may be increasing.

Social Studies

In social studies, it is critical to recognize that attitudinal achievement is as important as academic achievement. Student attitudes may well be more significant and long-lasting than academic knowledge gains. Research by

Annie Rogers and Carol Gilligan (1988) has made it clear that white, upper and middle-class females, whose privileged backgrounds might be expected to give them advantage over their working-class counterparts, feel ambivalent about themselves and their opportunities. In addition, the AAUW report (1992) and Myrna Sadker and David Sadker (1994) found steady declines in the self-esteem and self-confidence of young women as they move from childhood to early adolescence. The American Association of University Women (AAUW) (1992) report stated that 69 percent of elementary school boys revealed that they were "happy the way I am," while only 60 percent of elementary girls so indicated. Among high-school students this gap increased considerably. Forty-six percent of the boys were "happy the way they were," while only 29 percent of the girls were satisfied with themselves (AAUW, 1992, p. 12). Such findings send a clear signal that the world in which girls grow up increasingly drains them of their self-esteem, especially during their middle and high-school years.

Not only is the lack of self-esteem for girls problematic, but as the National Center for Educational Statistics (1990) reports in *The U.S. History Report Card*, girls' academic achievement is behind that of boys in civics, history, and geography. These findings are troubling, given that the National Council for the Social Studies has placed considerable emphasis on both curriculum and teaching practices related to women and women's issues. As early as 1976, the council issued a bulletin edited by Jean Dresden Grambs titled *Teaching About Women in the Social Studies*. Since that time, conferences and articles of the Council have persistently reinforced this message; however, even before teachers have had the opportunity to develop new curriculum and girls have had the opportunity to benefit from this proactive stance, we see a retrenchment taking place as evidenced by the lack of attention to gender in the recent National Council of Social Studies Standards (1994).

Spurred by the Education 2000 effort and promoted by both Presidents Bush and Clinton, a spate of standards have been issued by several academic and professional groups that have substantial implications for social studies teachers and students alike (see, for example, The National Council for the Social Studies [NCSS], 1994; The National Center for History in the Schools, 1994). A review of both documents is disappointing because of their lack of attention to women's concerns. Although nothing in these documents suggests that women's curricula should be de-emphasized, neither is there explicit and affirmative attention to this matter. Consequently, the documents seem to be neutral and noncommitted on the topic of gender.

The *National Standards for U.S. History: Exploring the American Experience, Grades 5–12* (1994) in particular, has been subject to considerable controversy. To some, the standards appear too critical of practices and policies of the United States.[1] These standards have spurred state and local discussions about the need to abandon multicultural requirements because they conflict with "true" American education. Unfortunately, the controversy awakened by these standards has been settled by accommodating the critics with revisions. A proposed revised publication is likely to reflect a more Western, Eurocentric, and masculinist view.

Given this social climate, active work toward creating gender equity both in girls' academic achievements and in attitudinal gains must be seen as central concerns of social studies educators, if women are to assume the responsibility of leadership in a democratic society.

The Gender Equity Approach

The Gender Equity Approach embraces two important principles: (1) *The principle of inclusiveness* that recognizes the need for the curriculum and particularly, the social studies curriculum, to represent all groups in terms of race, ethnicity, religion, gender, social class, sexual orientation, and ability; and (2) *the principle of equity* that recognizes that the goals of equality cannot be reached without fostering both the academic and self-esteem achievements of girls and young women, especially those who are also oppressed by discrimination based on race, ethnicity, religion, ability, or social class.[2] The Gender Equity Approach is characterized by a curriculum where the history, issues, and perspectives of

---

[1] On January 18, 1995, the U.S. Senate enacted, by a vote of 99–1, a resolution to disapprove the National History Standards. The resolution indicated that any agency funded by the federal government, such as the Department of Education and the National Endowment for the Humanities, should have a decent respect for the contributions of Western Civilization and U.S. history, ideas, and concepts they found lacking in the perspectives of the standards.

[2] It should be noted that throughout this chapter, we use gender as the central category of analysis. However, we recognize that gender discrimination or sexism represents a very incomplete view of women's oppressive experiences. Discrimination based on race, ethnicity, religion, social class, ability, and sexual orientation must also be seen as essential aspects of women's social and material conditions. According to Bell Hooks (1989), using gender as the sole category of analysis can be misleading because it masks the way "that women can and do participate in politics of domination" (p. 20). In addition to practicing racism, especially in the form of white supremacy, and class elitism, some women practice domination by their "lesbophobia" (Tallen, 1990). Additionally, Jewish and "Third-World" women respectively describe ways that Christian and "First-World" women treat them as invisible or colonize them. These critiques suggest that numerous factors determine the social construction of femaleness and the diverse experiences of oppression (Hooks, 1989).

These critiques, however, neither mean that gender cannot be used as a central analytic category for social studies or that sexism should not be of central concern to educators. On the contrary, Bell Hooks asserts that because sexism is so prevalent in girls' and women's daily lives, and because it takes place in the home, ending patriarchal domination *should* be of primary

diverse women are fully integrated into the ongoing curriculum and where the pedagogical approach is responsive to the interests and needs of young women so that ultimately, they will enjoy a condition of full equality.

The rationale for a gender equity approach is a strong one. First of all, from a moral perspective, gender equity is the means by which teachers can authentically facilitate a strong level of achievement for girls and young women. Simply put, it is the right thing to do. It maximizes the chances that girls and young women will not be discriminated against and will, therefore, have the equal opportunities they deserve. Even more powerfully, a gender equity approach, with its ultimate goal of gender equality, brings the Fourteenth Amendment's emphasis on equality to life in the classroom and addresses the ultimate value of expanding human dignity that ideally undergirds all democratic practices and institutions.

Democratic citizenship, gender equity, and social studies serve as a triad of concepts that share high moral ground. In particular, the compatibility of the goals of social studies and effective *democratic citizenship*, along with *equity for women* are mutually supportive. Each is inextricably tied to democratic values, and each enhances the other.

Secondly, from economic and political perspectives, it is to the distinct advantage of society to tap the voices, talents, and energies of all its citizens, and to include women in the workplace, in public forums, in decision-making settings, and in creative activities. Society suffers to the extent that any group is systematically excluded or marginalized. A democracy suffers when its principles of inclusiveness and equality are violated. Further, both the economy and the body politic suffer because they do not benefit from the ideas, perspectives, and creativity of discriminated groups. For women, the costs of exclusion are both economic (Will we ever reach a time when women earn a dollar for every dollar earned by a male?) and political (Will women ever represent 50 percent of the U.S. Senate or occupy the Presidency?). For many women, a discriminatory job market means that hopes and dreams go unfulfilled and that many women never reach their goals and aspirations.

Progress in the political world has been very limited for women at the local, state, and national levels. Men outnumber women by far in legislative bodies, in leadership roles, in executive agencies, and in the judicial arena even though women constitute 52 percent of the U.S. population. Clearly,

---

concern. Her point is that if women do not learn to resist sexism in the home and with family, we will never have the strength to resist prejudices such as racism, class elitism, anti-Semitism, ethnocentricism, and lesbophobia/homophobia in the world. Therefore, with Hooks, we see the need to eradicate patriarchal oppression as a component of ending all forms of prejudice. Further, and we recognize that this is problematic, when we discuss girls and women, we use these terms to include the racial, ethnic, religious, economic, and sexual orientation diversity of women.

political participation extends beyond formal positions in government. Political participation also takes place in grass-roots settings such as community special interest groups, school board meetings, or on the editorial pages of local newspapers. All such political activities, big or small, require a strong level of self-esteem. It is impossible to imagine anyone asserting her own viewpoint without it.

In contrast with the *gender equity approach*, some educators advocate what we call a *gender fairness perspective*. This view sees the necessity to treat all students alike, or as much so as possible. It seems obvious to us, however, that if the academic achievement of girls and young women lags behind that of males or if their self-esteem level is consistently lower, then treating both males and females equally in classrooms is likely to do nothing more than maintain the discrepancy between them, rather than improve the relative position of girls and young women. Consequently, we vigorously advocate a Gender Equity Approach, which implies that females need to receive both encouragement regarding self-esteem and special attention in the curriculum and in classrooms.

We wish to emphasize that our advocacy for gender equity does not mean that boys and young men should be shortchanged. But though males—particularly white males from middle and upper-class backgrounds—as all students, deserve opportunities to learn and be supported in achieving academic outcomes, the education of females calls for a nonconventional approach if schools are to serve as settings where females can attain their educational potential.

Educational responsiveness to girls' needs calls for both formal and informal curricula and teaching practices that integrate women into the ongoing agenda of the classroom, bring significant women figures to the classroom as role models, validate the social experiences of females, and encourage the voices of all students in the curriculum. In a democracy, it is critical that young girls and women come to believe their voices count.

In the remainder of this chapter, we will apply the Gender Equity Approach to help social studies teachers reconceptualize their curricula; specifically, we will identify the strengths and weaknesses of alternative approaches for integrating women into the curriculum.

Integrating Women into the Social Studies

What then should a women's history of the world do? It must fill the gaps left by conventional history's preoccupation with male doings, and give attention and dignity to women's lives in their own right. Women's exclusion from the annals of history represents a million million stifled voices. To recover the female part of what we have called history is no mean achievement. Any women's history therefore has to be alert to the blanks, the omissions and the half-truths. It must listen to the silences and make them cry out. (Miles, 1989, p. xii.)

When, in 1929, Virginia Woolf despaired over the omission of women from the history books and called for young women scholars to supplement the existing lop-sided accounts of history, she recommended that this women-centered rewriting of history be given "some inconspicuous name so that women might figure there without impropriety" (Woolf, 1929, p. 47). If Woolf were to return today and examine library shelves, she would find not only that the fear of impropriety has faded, but that women's scholarship constitutes the rewriting of history she desired (Kerber and De Hart, 1995; Kerber, Kessler-Harris, and Sklar, 1995; Scott, 1988). Despite the abundance of trade books, biographies, novels, journals, anthologies, videos, and teaching materials available to teachers and curriculum planners, many social studies curricula still pay but cursory attention to women in history, or present the same "famous women" over and over, or omit them altogether, or create a separate course on Women's History. The implication of such practices is that "real" social studies does not include the history and scholarship of women.

Three questions deserve the attention of serious social studies educators: (1) How can teachers compensate for social studies textbooks, curricula, and tests that fail to include women as subjects? (2) How can teachers convey to female students that social studies is not another male field from which they are denied access (Hahn and Bernard-Powers, 1985)? (3) How can teachers employ teaching strategies that best ensure equitable and active learning opportunities for all students, especially girls and young women? These three questions frame the major issues that the remainder of this chapter will address.

We have drawn from a broad range of literature to identify diverse ways to integrate women into social studies curriculum and to create gender equitable classrooms. Major Issue 1, Curriculum Models for Integrating Women into the Curriculum, discusses three models of the larger issues of curriculum design, and Major Issue 2, Content Models for Integrating Women into the Curriculum, describes five methods for organizing the content of social studies curricula. We conclude the Major Issues sections with a brief discussion of feminist pedagogy that we consider interwoven with and integral to gender equity curriculum and content restructuring.

MAJOR ISSUE 1: CURRICULUM MODELS FOR INTEGRATING WOMEN INTO THE CURRICULUM

A number of creative and effective models for integrating women into diverse educational curricula have been described by educators such as Theresa McCormick, 1994; Johnella Butler and John Walter, 1991; Mary Kay Tetrault, 1987; Esther Chow, 1985; Betty Schmitz, 1985; and Bonnie B. Spanier,

Alexander Bloom, and Darlene Boroviak, 1984. In this section, we will focus on three models that are most compatible with conventional public school schedules and curricula: the comparison model, the segregated model, and the integrated model. Each of these models, at different degrees of complexity, is appropriate for both elementary and secondary levels. Their application, however, will vary according to the learners' intellectual and critical thinking abilities.

The Comparison Model

Using the comparison model, teachers incorporate materials about and by women into existing class materials for the purpose of comparison. These comparisons take a variety of forms, such as comparisons between men and women, comparisons among women, and comparisons across race, gender, ethnic, and social-class differences. For example, to study the Depression, men's and women's accounts of their experiences are compared to demonstrate the different ways they endured and responded to economic hardships. To study the Civil War, comparisons are made of the diaries, biographies, autobiographies, or oral histories of diverse groups of women including white women slave owners, African-born women slaves, free-born black women, white women abolitionists, black women abolitionists, northern women, and southern women. These accounts are then compared with similar accounts by men. Having an assortment of comparisons communicates the complexity and multiplicity of diverse voices and the ways in which gender, race, and economic class are meaningful categories for social studies examination. As a pedagogical strategy, making diverse comparisons allows students to learn that the study of social issues is not the study of a unified view of events.

The comparison model stresses both differences and similarities among multiple voices. Often, students reduce and simplify the task of making comparisons to polarizing points of view. Therefore, if the comparison model is to be effective, students must learn to find similarities among diverse voices and to examine how two people can hold similar and disparate opinions on one issue at the same time. Students must also learn to appreciate that individuals themselves can hold conflicting views of complex issues.

Strengths of the Comparison Model

For young children, the comparison model has pedagogical strength not only because children are well versed in verbalizing "what is the same and what is different" about things, but also because the comparison model can dramatically highlight similarities and differences. For example, an elementary teacher might show videos depicting children in three countries. The students could be instructed to look for some differences and similarities among boys' and girls' roles and interactions. Following the videos, teachers would ask the students to compare and contrast cultural differences. Additional lessons and stories on each country might follow. Teachers would then help students locate similarities and articulate differences in positive and thoughtful ways. Thus, the children learn, not only about world cultures and the ways that gender relations are constructed in childhood, but also about treating differences as positive.

Another benefit of the comparison model is that it would compel the use of teaching materials not usually integrated into the curriculum. Generating materials on women to use for comparisons will serve as a heuristic for locating new, diverse readings or videos. The comparison model is especially beneficial because it has the potential to challenge the unified, simplified, or coherent picture of women and ethnic groups that many textbooks tend to sustain.

Weaknesses of the Comparison Model

One argument against this model is that high-school students who have been socialized and educated with the dominant male perspective may view the inclusion of women at this point in their studies as "tokenism." By tokenism, we mean that the sudden visibility of women into the curriculum for comparison can appear to be gratuitous, as if the teacher was caving into pressures by the dreaded women's liberation or cultural diversity movements! Like all the other approaches to integrating other perspectives into the curriculum, the attitude of the teacher has a great impact on how the inclusion of women, ethnic minorities, and Third World cultures will be received by students who may not have seriously studied them as part of social studies before.

For elementary as well as high-school students, the approach could backfire if students are not informed about the women they are studying. For example, if Sojourner Truth's antislavery speeches (circa 1843–1883) are studied in comparison with John Greenleaf Whittier's antislavery tracts (circa 1833–1860), the social, educational, geographic, and biographical differences between them must be fully explored. That Truth was born into slavery, spoke Dutch as her first language, and was illiterate, therefore necessitating transcription of her speeches, must be discussed so that the substantive content and lyrical quality of her speeches is not undermined by the roughness of the transcribed words, which results in denigration by students.

For any comparisons of men's and women's oral or written words, students need to be aware of the historic, social, and cultural specificity of the text; that is, they must understand the cultural expectations and educational attainments of the women they are studying. This knowledge may reduce the tendency to judge women unfairly. Describing the political and social settings in which the words of women were produced allows students to make comparisons based on the merits and experiences of each woman and staves off the tendency to conclude that gender differences are simply the result of biological factors, rather than social and cultural differences.

The comparison model could also fail if it leads to the perpetuation of women's marginality by only stressing stereotypical differences from the dominant white and/or male culture (Collins, 1991). For example, if the women chosen for comparison demonstrate only a narrow range of women's experiences—nurses, teachers, and mothers—then the essentialist stereotype that women are naturally nurturing is perpetuated. If the women chosen for comparison only demonstrate women's oppression, then again, the comparison can only claim to perpetuate stereotypes. Therefore, it is critical to the comparison model that a wide range of women's experiences across race and class are portrayed so that women, as a category for study, are not falsely stabilized into one or two types of women. In other words, the comparison model must not ignore differences among women in an attempt to compare women with men. Comparisons of diverse women must be encouraged so that the intersections of gender, race, and class are *always* present.

Segregated Model

The segregated model sets aside a period of time to focus on women as a "special topic" separate from the regular curriculum. This can take the form of a separate unit on selected women in U.S. history. Or, during African-American History Month or Women's History Month, a social studies teacher may set aside one hour each week during those months to study "exceptional" women in history. Social studies textbooks frequently employ this model, as represented by the use of graphic boxes to place information on famous women or African-Americans outside the narrative text.

Strengths of the Segregated Model

One of the greatest benefits of the segregated model is that it offers a concentrated study of women. This model, if handled well, can demonstrate that women and ethnic minorities are deserving of special attention in academic studies. This proactive approach spurs teachers and students to openly discuss ways that certain groups have traditionally been omitted from the curriculum. The segregated model can also be a strong pedagogical tool for encouraging students to pursue a specific topic of interest pertaining to women in social studies.

Weaknesses of the Segregated Model

The segregated model shares many problems with the comparison model. For both models, there is a danger of marginalizing women, either by not addressing the cultural, biographical, and educational differences between women and men, or by approaching the subject half-heartedly and peripherally. For example, if Susan B. Anthony were only mentioned during Women's History Month, and was not also given the serious attention she deserves as part of U.S. history, then her achievements are rendered peripheral and unimportant. Often, the women who are included in curricula and textbooks have had the range and complexity of their achievements reduced by historians and curriculum makers who select for publication only that which *they* deem relevant. Such superficial treatment and lack of commitment does more harm than good, and teachers must compensate for this. The segregated model can also lead to teachers deciding that it is easier to omit the study of women altogether because they lack sufficient time to cover the main curriculum.

Integrated Model

The integrated model incorporates the study of women into the existing elementary or secondary social studies curriculum. Women in their ethnic and economic diversity are conceptualized as an integral part of the curriculum, rather than as a subject matter for special consideration or comparison. Therefore, classroom materials and homework assignments about women are integrated into the conventional social studies teaching materials and are treated as "normal" to the topics of study. For example, while studying the "expansion" or colonization of the West in the 1800s, the experiences and contributions of white and Native American women are woven naturally into the fabric of the unit and issues of expansion are historically situated and problematized (Bigelow, Miner, and Peterson, 1991).

Strengths of the Integrated Model

The integrated model assures women a central place in the curriculum and avoids their marginal and superficial treatment. By making the "exceptional" ordinary, the integrated model socializes children and young adults to the equal importance of women and men. Begun in early grades, the integrated model is likely to increase self-esteem for girls and children's respect for women, countering some of the misogyny children encounter every day.

Weaknesses of the Integrated Model

Implementing the integrated model requires a great deal of institutional support and teacher preparation. For many teachers whose own education was traditional, there may be a need to do independent research, and to gather, reproduce, or create materials on their own, possibly at their own expense. Ideally, school systems would provide teachers with "paid-to-attend" workshops or would compensate them for their curriculum development. Another problem that teachers may encounter is resistance from colleagues, principals, parents, or students who consider the study of women peripheral to the traditional curriculum. Further, standardized tests do not usually include questions on women's history. As a result, teachers may encounter especially substantial criticism for teaching content that is not tested.

MAJOR ISSUE 2: CONTENT MODELS FOR INTEGRATING WOMEN INTO THE CURRICULUM

> We are learning that the writing of women into history necessarily involved redefining and enlarging traditional notions of historical significance, to encompass personal, subjective experiences as well as public and political activities. It is not too much to suggest that however hesitant the actual beginnings, such a methodology implies not only a new history of women, but also a new history. (Gordon, Buhle, and Dye, 1976, p. 89)

When women are studied in many social-science and liberal-arts classes, they are usually only included as suffragettes and reformers, leaving out their participation in national and international politics, the arts, the work force including domestic work, peace movements, and the military. Further, their experiences as homemakers, wives, sisters, daughters, and mothers are diminished or ignored by male-centered curricula that fail to recognize and value the many different ways that women contribute to creating the cultures of their countries.

One reason women are not included in the curriculum is because they do not fit the norm of the "ideal citizen." The ideal citizen for study in many social studies curricula is a U.S. born white, upper-or middle-class, educated male. This ideal citizen, as traditionally conceived, is one who separates his public life from his private life, emphasizes individualism over community, and glorifies rational thought over emotional engagement (Nicholson, 1986). Therefore, women, ethnic minorities, families in poverty, and those who cannot afford or who are denied adequate education, can never fit this narrowly defined, elitist norm of ideal citizenship. To achieve greater diversity in our conception of citizenry, especially in the U.S., social studies curricula must be reconceptualized not only to include the study of women, but also to critique and diminish the reverence traditionally paid to wars and colonization in the study of history.

Social studies teachers can incorporate the study of women and citizenship into a wide range of topics and bring students into social studies classrooms as active participants in many ways. Historian Virginia Leonard (1981) recommends four approaches for organizing course content to achieve these goals, and we suggest a fifth. Leonard's (1981) models include the biographical approach, the political approach, the historical era approach, and the family and community approach. The fifth approach that we have identified is the critical gender issues approach.

The Biographical Approach

In the biographical approach, biographies, autobiographies, interviews, journals, diaries, and photographs are used as the focus of study. When classes focus on the biographies or autobiographies of great men, students learn that only men create culture and history. The biographical approach includes biographies and autobiographies of women along with those of men. Because, until recently, there were fewer published autobiographies and biographies of women, the biographical approach includes the study of diaries, journals, and letters of women within the overall genre of auto/biography.[3]

Strengths of the Biographical Approach

Having students read women's auto/biographies makes legitimate the significant role women have had in social and cultural production (Barry, 1990). Women's auto/biographies can be used to give girls and young women positive role models and to engender boys' and young men's respect for women. Because they present authentic life stories, which are typically more interesting than textbook presentations of history, auto/biographies such as *Lakota Woman* by Mary Crow Dog, *Dust Tracks on the Road* by Zora Neale Hurston, or for younger children, *Walking the Road to Freedom: A Story about Sojourner Truth* by Jeri Ferris for example, can generate a higher level of student interest in a particular time period, social phenomena, or geographic location. Auto/biographical writings can also take the emphasis off history as so many facts and dates to be memorized and demonstrate instead that history comprises multiple stories about which individuals hold subjective views that can be diversely interpreted.

> With regard to the sexual connotations of words, can we all not think of what a dream would be realized for the race when the noun 'soldier,' for example, ceases to conjure up romantic notions of masculinity, but will instead have been unsexed and (at long last) put in its true place in history by the more accurate associations it recalls: 'tragedy…the organized waste of human life and potential'?
> *Lorraine Hansberry, "In Defense of the Equality of Men," 1961.*

Recent scholarship on the genre of biography and autobiography demonstrates that the stories of famous men's lives are limited (Smith, 1987; Jelinek, 1980). They typically focus on the man's linear progress toward his intellectual and career goals, on the ways in which he is connected to and shapes society, and on his inevitable successes in the world. They rarely include reflections on his family or other aspects of his personal life. The majority of men's auto/biographies emerged from periods of war and therefore

---

[3] The term auto/biography is used to include both autobiographies and biographies.

tend to maintain masculinist values of the hero and the need for war. In comparison, women's autobiographies flourished during times when women were needed for public service or social reform, such as from 1890 to the first World War and then again during the late 1960s to 1970s. Rather than only focusing on the public aspects of their lives, women also include stories about domestic life and the people who were important to them. The integration of auto/biographies of women is therefore imperative to counter the male-centeredness of recorded history and to problematize what it means to be a citizen, to create culture, and to actively advance social change.

Auto/biographies can also be a catalyst for student writing assignments. Students might be encouraged to write a biography of someone from their own family or of someone from the community, collecting information either from interviews or local archives. In this type of assignment, students make connections between their families, their community, and the larger social and historical issues; they become active history-makers.

Weaknesses of the Biographical Approach

If the auto/biographies focus solely on famous people, the biographical approach tends to glorify only those who are considered exceptional. Therefore, auto/biographies of famous men and women must be balanced with stories about the lives of ordinary people from diverse backgrounds so that the students come to see acts of greatness in the struggles and achievements of a variety of people. Another danger of focusing only on famous individuals is that individualism is aggrandized, and the collective nature of social change may not be explored.

An excellent example of an autobiography that could be used in a high-school social studies classroom is James Comer's (1988) book, *Maggie's American Dream: The Life and Times of a Black Family*. The book begins with the narratives of Comer's mother's life history, detailing her childhood in poverty during the 1910 to 1920s, her desires for a better life, and, despite the racism and segregation they faced, the success she and her husband had creating a loving and economically secure family. Comer's own story follows, in which he recalls events of his childhood, the Civil Rights Movement, the racism he faced at college, and reflections on his commitment to using his degree in child psychology to educate African-American children. Books by authors such as Comer, as well as anthologies, journals, diaries, and letters (see, for example, Bell-Scott, 1994; Hine, 1993; Merriam, 1971), should be used in social studies classrooms because they offer alternative perspectives on social phenomena, controversial issues, and historical events that many students would not otherwise encounter. These materials release formerly hidden voices into the curricula.

The Political Approach

The political approach calls for a complete reconceptualization of the foundations of social studies curricula, using the study of women's activism as a lens through which to critique societies, social values, cultures, and histories. The political approach focuses on women as suffragettes (see, for example, O'Hare, 1995; Wheeler, 1995), feminists, unionists, abolitionists, civil rights protesters and activists in peace and environmental movements.

That women have long used public forums such as strikes, speeches, and marches for achieving social change is an important component of this approach—one that links women of the past to the present. Also critical to this approach is that it highlights how women's roles in these activities were instrumental in transforming the world. Further, it is an approach that allows us to shift the focus of social studies away from men's political investments and emphasize the politics of peace and negotiation, a topic all too often overlooked (Noddings, 1992; Brock-Utne, 1988). Most important, the political approach asks us to reconceptualize the definitions of political activism so that activism will encompass a wider range of women's activities. As Patricia Hill Collins (1991) notes, "white male conceptualizations of the political process produce definitions of power, activism, and resistance that fail to capture the meaning of these concepts in Black women's lives" (1991, p. 140). In particular, Collins notes that because "survival" is not defined as political activism, Black women's struggles to maintain community survival in the face of institutional racism is omitted as political activism, thus contributing further to Black women's erasure from history.

To incorporate this political approach, teachers might want to organize the curriculum thematically, using topics such as labor, education, health care, peace movements, international trade, and human rights to organize the materials. For example, in a unit on labor, students could study the changes over time of women's participation in the work force, examining labor laws, types of jobs made available to women, and attitudes toward women at work. Major figures such as "Mother" Mary Jones, the union activist; Charlotte Perkins Gilman, who wrote a treatise to abolish housework; Madame Walker, America's first black woman millionaire, and Frances Gilman, Secretary of Labor in the F.D. Roosevelt administration could also be studied. Further, oral histories of ordinary women who worked in war industries during World War II, such as those told in the book, *Rosie the Riveter Revisited* (Gluck, 1988) would also be included in the unit to examine how women's contributions influenced the labor market, the politics of the sexual division of labor, and the influence of these work experiences on the women themselves. Closer to home, students could explore women's activism in their own communities.

Strengths of the Political Approach

A more complex and authentic view of historical, social, international, and political events would be portrayed by the political approach and would demonstrate that women worldwide have used the public forum for some time to achieve equality. It would also confirm that they have long participated as active citizens in the public debate about major questions that touch the lives of U.S. citizens. This approach will not only contribute to dispelling the myth that women care only about home and family and do not engage in political or potentially dangerous public actions, but most important, this approach can heighten the complexity of the very concept of political activism.

Weaknesses of the Political Approach

The political activism of women is an important dimension of women's history and social activity. It is just one dimension, however. Therefore, the concept of women's activism would be weakened if it did not also include women's community organization work, volunteer work, their involvement in school governance, and local politics. Without the inclusion of these less recognized forms of political activism, the political approach runs the risk of repeating the male fallacy of only sanctioning as meaningful that which is at a state or national level.

The Historical Era Approach

The historical era approach is especially suited to classrooms in which social studies is taught in the conventional, chronological manner as recommended by The National Center for History in the Schools (1994). In this approach, women are included in standard periodizations, such as the era of the American Revolution or the era of the Great Depression and World War II. Women's social and economic status and their diverse roles during these time periods are examined along with men's roles.

Strengths of the Historical Era Approach

The historical era approach is the least controversial of the approaches. The focus on standard categories of eras allows teachers to help students understand that although social, cultural, economic, and political constraints on women, particularly women-of-color and women in poverty, have been great over time, many of these women have strenuously resisted oppression. The historical approach can be structured to generate an analysis of how women's increasing presence in historical time periods as scholars, scientists, politicians, activists, wage earners, and so on, influenced institutions and the social relations between men and women.

Weaknesses of the Historical Era Approach

One reason that the historical era approach is often rejected by those committed to including women in the curriculum is that it does not allow sufficiently deep coverage. Another reason some feminists disparage this approach, calling it the "add women and stir" method, is that it rarely questions the role that gender has played in the lives of women. By leaving in place the conventional curriculum, the historical era approach maintains the limited view of social studies as the study of wars, colonization, and technological advances, and therefore narrows the range of who or what constitutes meaningful areas of study. Further, as Sandra Harding (1987) notes, adding women to existing curricula "does not encourage us to ask what have been the *meanings* of women's contributions to public life *for women*" (pp. 4–5, original emphasis). Harding provides the following example to illustrate this limitation.

When studying the Civil War, to add women, teachers may focus on how both white and black women worked courageously in the antislavery, black suffrage, and anti-lynching movements. In this example, the diverse portrayals of women is laudable. However, these diverse portrayals may not, Harding suggests, lead to an understanding of what it meant for these women to work in these movements *as women*. What may go unanalyzed, she argues, is that these shared activities taught women "public speaking, political organizing, and the virulence of white men's *hostility* to women learning how to speak and organize" (1987, p. 5, original emphasis). Her point, which is similarly argued by Linda Nicholson (1986) and Patricia Hill Collins (1991), is that in the traditional study of history, adding women does not ensure that the gendered meanings of women's experiences would be explored.

The Family and Community History Approach

We argue that social studies all too often focuses only on men and their heroic public lives. An emphasis on the family's role in society offers a balance that affirms that social studies is indeed about social issues that effect us all (Engle and Ochoa, 1988). Implementing this approach requires that the changing role of the family, the changing status of women, and the changing nature of relationships such as marriage or parenting become the focus of analyses in social studies. This approach also includes the study of local and community events, politics, civic organizations, and demographics.

Nel Noddings (1992), advocating a similar approach to rethinking social studies curriculum, suggests that emphasis on the private life, including love and caring, must be made central topics in primary and secondary classes. She envisions students studying a topic such as the history of love, from homosexual love in classical Greece to our current multiple and contested understandings of love and sexuality to examine both how love and politics are related and to help students plan for their own future family lives and careers.

Strengths of the Family and Community History Approach

There are numerous strengths to this approach. First of all, it encourages students to collect data about their families and local community. Data collection might include conducting interviews with family and community members, retrieving archival information such as old letters, newspapers, and artifacts, and visiting the local historical society. In other words, the students themselves become historians and history-makers. Furthermore, as history-makers, students would learn to make connections among family, local, national, and even international history and events.

Another positive aspect of this approach is that the focus on communities, families, and relationships between and among men and women challenges the concept of what "social studies" means. It asserts that the personal is political and that students' own lives are integral to culture and society and are connected to the past. This is a particularly important message for young children to learn, for it helps socialize them to participatory democracy.

Weaknesses of the Family and Community History Approach

One major drawback of this approach is that locating information on changing family norms may not be readily available in textbooks traditionally used in social studies education. Therefore, teachers and students will probably need to research information on particular time periods, geographic locations, or subtopics—thus turning a weakness into a strength. For example, teachers and students can together become inquirers, seeking out information on marriage and divorce practices and laws, norms of parenting, and statistics on women in the work force, to demonstrate how the family changed over a particular time period. For some historical time periods or geographic locations however, gaps in available information may make the research difficult. Photographs, if available, could also be used to supplement written materials. On the positive side, this approach encourages collaboration among students and teachers and students.

Critical Gender Issues Approach

Social studies, like many other subjects, is often taught as if there are simple answers to the questions we have about the nature of society, or worse, it is taught without asking those questions for which there are no answers. The critical gender issues approach asks teachers to focus their classes on the questions that are unresolvable and that, because of their controversial nature, are frequently absent from classroom discourse. Complex, but critical issues, such as reproductive rights and abortion choice; women in the military and clergy; institutional racism, sexism, and heterosexism; women in poverty; gendered patterns of immigration and unemployment; gender biases in health care and social services; and the selling of condoms and birth control pills in high schools must be legitimate issues for classroom research and discussion.

One example of this approach for secondary school is a unit on violence against women. This unit could address rape and hate crimes, the increasing frequency of battered women, the escalating numbers of homeless women and children, and the laws and law enforcement practices and social regulations regarding these problems. One forceful way to organize such a unit would be to focus on guiding questions that defy simple answers. By posing an open-ended question such as *what needs to be done to create a safer world for women?*, students would be encouraged to examine the sexism of current laws, to consider more effective legal possibilities, and to search out the historical roots of how current violence is grounded in the traditional view of women as property.

Students would also be encouraged to see how violence against women is cultural; that is, they should examine this phenomena in other countries. After students evaluate data, they would be encouraged to discuss the issue and formulate a stand that they would like to take, recognizing that their stand should be informed by their classmates' diverse perspectives and information. This process could lead to community action that might take the form of writing letters to the editor, volunteering at a women's shelter, making a presentation to a school assembly as a way to widen awareness about these issues, participating in a "take back the night" march, or asking law enforcement personnel to participate in an open forum regarding their policies in the community. Whatever the topic, the focus should always be on examining the ways in which gender is constructed in particular historical, social, and cultural ways.

Strengths of the Critical Gender Issues Approach

This approach involves students in making decisions about how the unit would be studied. It also encourages students to make connections between their own beliefs and their understandings of world events, cultural biases, and the meaning of gender. Because this focus requires that students be able to articulate *informed* views on the issues, they must become active inquirers into their own learning, seeking out information via the various research methods discussed above. Further, this approach involves students in facing crucial issues; it creates a much needed opportunity for them to have a discourse on meaningful citizenship issues.

Weaknesses of the Critical Gender Issues Approach

The critical gender issues approach is not for the timid! Several problems could arise. First, the issues that must be raised to make this approach work are issues about which students and teachers alike will feel very deeply and strongly. Therefore, the classroom will likely become emotionally charged. Students whose former opinions are displaced by their research and class discussions may also feel vulnerable; the ambiguity of complex issues has the potential to engender discomfort. The teacher will necessarily face something of a challenge as he or she attempts to integrate emotion, reason, and ambiguity in classroom discussions.

Another problem with this approach is that academic rigor is lost if student discussions take place solely on the basis of opinion, and not on evidence they have accumulated from their reading assignments and research. If they are unable to draw from their readings to support their opinions, the learning potential of this approach is diminished. Therefore, teachers will need to structure the discussions and written assignments so that students learn to make thoughtful and reasoned arguments, listen to and respect others' opinions, analyze evidence and the sources of their evidence, and bring these to bear on classroom dialogue.

Another problem might be student resistance. High-school students' expectations of what the classroom is "supposed" to be like may be firmly ingrained as are their opinions on controversial issues. Therefore, though some students might enjoy the approach and it may spark their interest in current and past events that shape their lives, others will need additional support and encouragement to openly discuss issues that are controversial. With this in mind, we suggest that teachers provide assistance to students who are reticent to speak by teaching them discussion skills, give them safe opportunities to verbalize their research and opinions, and both accept and challenge their ideas with enthusiasm, kindness, and interest.

Some school districts will find certain issues unfit for classroom discussion for a variety of reasons, not least of which is that they challenge the prevailing concept of what education is. Therefore, teachers who wish to use this approach may need to be prepared with a well-developed rationale for examining controversial issues as part of the curriculum when their teaching is questioned by administrators, parents, or students.

CURRICULAR DECISIONS: CHOOSING MODELS AND CONTENT FOR SOCIAL STUDIES

In summary, each of these models and approaches described can make contributions to the study of women and their inclusion in the social studies curriculum. All have drawbacks. However, each one of them advances the salience of women in the curriculum. Teachers may want to use a combination of models and approaches, or select just one or two. Auto/biographical writings especially could be used in combination with any of the models and in combination with other approaches. The list of resources and suggested readings at the end of this chapter, although representing but a small percentage of available resources on women, will facilitate this endeavor.

As the reader might have noted, throughout the descriptions of the methods and approaches to incorporate women into the social studies curriculum, we described pedagogical techniques, such as having students become history-makers or effective discussants. It is difficult, if not impossible, to separate curriculum and content from pedagogy. Therefore, we would like to conclude with a few words about feminist pedagogy, a philosophy of teaching that will not only facilitate the inclusion of women in the curriculum, but which also addresses gender equity in the classroom environment.

Feminist pedagogical[4] models base their understanding of teaching and learning processes on the idea that gender is a critical component of teaching and learning (see, for example, Belenky, Clinchy, Goldberger, and Tarule, 1986; Bunch and Pollock, 1983; Culley and Portuges, 1985; Maher, 1985, 1987; Tetrault, 1987; Weiler, 1988). Frances Maher further defines feminist or gender pedagogy as "a combination of teaching practices and curriculum content that explicitly relates students' viewpoints and experiences to the subject matter, yielding for each topic a sense of personal involvement and multiple, mutually illuminating perspective taking" (1987, p. 186). This different model of what it means to know and to learn allows classroom interactions between teachers and students, and among students to be conceptualized differently than in the traditional classroom where texts and teachers transmit knowledge to students, the empty vessels who are passively filled.

One major concern of feminist pedagogy is the way that teachers interact with their students. May Belenky and her coauthors (1986) explain that a feminist teacher is like a midwife, helping students to give birth to their ideas. Frances Maher (1987) and Maher and Mary Tetrault (1994) describe feminist teachers as democratic facilitators, using their questioning skills to help students ask critical questions, examine multiple perspectives, and challenge justifications to simple solutions to conflicts. Although feminist educators give up some content authority in the classroom to allow students to gain theirs, their role is not to abolish their authority altogether; rather, feminist educators

---

4 Because so much has been written on feminist pedagogy since the late 1970s, it would be impossible to fairly represent the multitude of ideas that exist. Therefore, we have selected one major aspect of feminist pedagogy to share, classroom interactions, simply as an introduction to those for whom feminist pedagogy is a new concept.

envision themselves as participants in the learning process and refrain from transmitting authoritative solutions.

When presenting new subject matter, for example, feminist educators would not begin with a lecture or quiz on textbook readings; rather, they would begin by having students share their own prior knowledge of the topic, explore their familiarity with or misconceptions of new terms, and relate the new topic to their personal histories. In this way, a new topic is begun with a common understanding of terms, a recognition of multiple perspective, and a personally grounded understanding of what is to be studied. Such a beginning permits students to pose questions about their interests, and in this way, they become part of the curricular process. The classroom becomes theirs, in a sense, and the knowledge is owned by them.

Student-student interactions are also significant in the feminist classroom. Most important, students themselves need to be viewed as inquirers, deeply and personally responsible for and active in their learning. Students in a feminist classroom cannot be passive recipients of knowledge; knowledge is not deposited in them, like money in a bank, as Paulo Freire says (1970). To encourage students to become active and involved, they must learn how to question, discuss, conduct research, and work in groups. Further, they must develop the self-esteem necessary to participate in rigorous discussion and recognize that their voices count, that personal knowledge is a form of knowledge, and that their interpretations of texts and media are valid if informed and thoughtful.

Many feminist educators use discussion groups and collaborative learning groups as means through which students develop the skills and self-esteem described above. Having students become inquirers and work in groups suggests that teachers will work less hard. What actually results, however, is that feminist teachers often work even harder than ever before! What is deceptive is that much of the work is accomplished in preparation for classroom groups, in facilitating the groups, and in being ready for anything!

Although the term "feminist classroom" implies that the teacher must be a woman, feminist pedagogical strategies can be successfully adopted by both feminist and nonfeminist, male and female teachers alike if they accept the epistemological and pedagogical assumptions upon which the pedagogy is based. Further, we believe that feminist pedagogy encourages the best possible classroom environment and will be a benefit for all students, both female and male.

CONCLUSION

In this chapter we have focused on issues that are fundamental to gender equity in social studies. At the same time, we fully recognize that, in this relatively new field, others may define the issues in different ways. Our issues emerge from our own perspectives and have been informed by our selections from the growing literature in the field.

Critical to the accomplishment of gender equity classrooms are teachers who care and care deeply about the conditions girls and women face. Education, and in particular equitable education, is based on commitments—to a better future, to a more just world, to equity for the oppressed. We sincerely hope that among those teachers who read this chapter, we will find those who care enough to examine these issues seriously and carry their commitment to their students.

What we have written is not without bias. One cannot be, and we think should not be, unbiased about gender equity. Even those who ignore the topic are in effect taking a stand. In our construction of this chapter, we have made our own commitments clear. We believe our efforts in writing this chapter will be a success if it helps teachers clarify and implement their commitments on gender equity.

Reflective Questions

1. *Select one or two teachers who taught your social studies classes at either the elementary, middle, or high-school levels and examine the assumptions they may have made regarding gender, achievement, and women in history and society. What examples would support your points of view? Were their teaching styles responsive to both males and females? Give examples to support your answers.*

2. *What meaning do you make of the following quotation, based on your personal and professional experiences: "The aim [of social studies] is to have students relate subject matter to aspects of their own lives, so that courses and issues have personal meaning at various stages of their growth and development" (Maher, 1987, p. 192)?*

3. *If the gender equity approach is based on the assumptions that women are socialized in oppressive relations to men and schools participate in this oppression, how might male teachers contribute to social change?*

4. *If the gender equity approach also is concerned with ways that schools reproduce white racism, how might white teachers contribute to anti-racist teaching?*

5. *If you were designing a unit on a particular issue or area of social studies, how would you go about integrating women of diverse ethnic histories into your unit? What teaching strategies would you use?*

6. *What would you do in your classroom to increase the chances that your students, and especially your female students, will become active democratic citizens?*

GLOSSARY

equality   In a school setting, equality means treating all students in the classroom the same, regardless of their individual differences and needs.

equity   Equity signifies an attempt, especially by educators, to ensure that all students can achieve their fullest potential. Therefore, equity entails providing benefits for some social groups or individuals to offset the effects of discrimination. For example, if the desired outcome is democratic participation, young girls and women may need additional encouragement to nurture the self-esteem necessary for full participation.

gender   The term gender is used to refer to the social construction of sex, and it implies a rejection of the biological determinism of the term "sex." That is, when children are born, they are first designated as a sexed body, male or female. Following this, males and females are socialized according to the cultural and historical norms of a gender corresponding to their sex. Boys are expected to take on masculine gender roles, and girls are expected to take on feminine gender roles. Children receive messages about what it means to be gendered from parents, peers, media, schools, and religious organizations. In our society, there is a great deal of pressure to conform to the gender role that fits the biological sex.

In this chapter, we use the term gender to fit the above description; however, we also use it to connote that the discussion of social studies includes the examination of the *relationship* between males and females, not only to redress the omission of women in history, but also to examine the way that knowledge about social studies, as it is traditionally taught, maintains the marginalized status of women and the unequal distribution of power based on sex that has prevailed throughout history. In a sense, we are using the term gender to assert that the study of women in social studies is necessarily also about the study of men—and that the study of relations between the two sexes within the context of the social studies curriculum is critical.

ANNOTATED BIBLIOGRAPHY

Books

The American Association of University Women (1992). *How Schools Shortchange Girls.* Washington, DC: AAUW and the NEA.

> The only study of its kind, this book examines not only the formal, but also the informal curriculum, and how they disadvantage girls' education, K–12. The authors compile and analyze an impressive quantity and variety of data to make sense of girls' experiences in school. In addition, a video entitled "Shortchanging Girls, Shortchanging America" is available from the AAUW. (For more information, call 1-800-225-9998, extension 91.)

Bunch, Carolyn and Sandra Pollack (1983). *Learning Our Way: Essays in Feminist Education.* Trumansburg, NY: Crossing Press.

> This is one of the earliest and most important books on feminist education. It contains a series of thoughtful essays that examine feminist education in various institutions.

Contreras, Gloria (1989). "A Gender Balancing Resource List." *Social Education.* 51(3):200–205.

> Contains an extensive list of audiovisual resources, teaching materials, and journals pertaining to the study of women. The article describes the types of resources available from diverse sources and gives addresses and phone numbers for obtaining these materials.

Culley, Margo and Catherine Portuges (1985). *Gendered Subjects: The Dynamics of Feminist Teaching.* London: Routledge & Kegan Paul.

> Addressed primarily to teachers and students at the college level, secondary teachers will clearly see the implications for their classrooms. Contains critical chapters on feminist pedagogy and feminist authority in the classroom. Includes serious discussions on the role of authority in the feminist classroom and working with racial differences from a feminist approach.

Klein, Susan, editor (1985). *Handbook for Achieving Sex Equity through Education.* Baltimore: The Johns Hopkins University Press.

> Twenty-five chapters that present solid treatments of a comprehensive range of topics in the area of sex equity, plus an especially strong topic relating sex equity to the social studies curriculum.

Spanier, Bonnie, Alexander Bloom, and Darlene Boroviak, editors (1984). *Toward a Balanced Curriculum: A Sourcebook for Initiating Gender Integration Projects.* Cambridge: Schenkman Publishing.

> As the title suggests, this book would be useful for teachers and administrators who are attempting to reform the curriculum in many subject areas. This book contains lists of resources and suggestions for assessment.

Spender, Dale (1982). *Invisible Women: The Schooling Scandal.* London: The Women's Press.

> An excellent introduction to the issue of sexism in society. Spender examines how sexism is related to both the curriculum and classroom pedagogy.

Stone, Linda, editor (1994). *The Education Feminism Reader.* New York and London: Routledge & Kegan Paul.

> The twenty-two essays in this volume represent a diversity of voices about feminism and education. They discuss issues such as multiculturalism, female identity, curriculum and educational reform, postmodernism, feminist pedagogy, and the history of women and schooling.

Tetrault, Mary Kay, editor (1987). *Social Education* 51(3).

> This issue of *Social Education*, edited by Mary Kay Tetrault, contains a number of excellent articles that examine the role of gender in the social studies. Of special interest is Tetrault's phase theory as it applies to teaching history and Frances Maher's comparison between inquiry teaching and feminist pedagogy.

Weiler, Kathleen (1988). *Women Teaching for Change: Gender, Class and Power*. South Hadley, MA: Bergin and Garvey.

> Based on ethnographic and life history studies of teachers who have committed themselves to feminist teaching, Weiler examines the impact of their teaching both on their students and on themselves.

The Wellesley College Center for Research on Women. *The Women's Review of Books*. Wellesley, MA 02181, telephone: 617-283-2500.

> *The Women's Review of Books*, published monthly, is an excellent source for teachers who want to know about new books about the scholarship of women. They publish reviews and articles on numerous sources that social studies teachers will find quite helpful in developing their own understandings of the diverse histories of women.

Journals

Although space does not permit us to present annotations on the following journals, we would like to list them as being particularly responsive to gender equity in education. Many of them publish articles that suggest teaching materials and strategies for including women and discuss theoretical issues of gender, race, and class. They should be available in college libraries; phone numbers are listed for additional information.

Feminist Teacher
Editorial Collective
Wheaton College
Norton, MA 02766
Telephone: 508-285-7722

History and Social Science Teacher
16 Overlea Blvd.
Toronto, Ontario
Canada M4H 1A6
Telephone: 416-425-1924

History Teacher
Society for History Education, Inc.
California State University
1250 Bellflower Blvd.
Long Beach, CA 90840
Telephone: 310-985-1653
Fax: 310-985-5431

OAH Magazine of History
112 N. Bryan Street
Bloomington, IN 47408

Radical Teacher
Boston Women's Teachers' Group
Box 102
Cambridge, MA 02142

Rethinking Schools
1001 E. Keefe Avenue
Milwaukee, WI 53212
Telephone: 414-964-9646

Social Education
National Council for the Social Studies
3501 Newark Street, N.W.
Washington, D.C. 20016
Telephone: 202-966-7840

The Social Studies
Heldref Publications
1319 Eighteenth Street, N.W.
Washington, D.C. 20036-1802
Telephone: 202-296-6267
Fax: 202-296-5149

REFERENCES

American Association of University Women (1992). *How Schools Shortchange Girls*. Washington, DC: AAUW/NEA.

Barry, Kathleen (1990). "The New Historical Syntheses: Women's Biography." *Journal of Women's History*. 1(3):75–105.

Belenky, Mary F., Blyth M. Clinchy, Nancy R. Goldberger, and Jill M. Tarule (1986). *Women's Ways of Knowing: The Development of Self, Voice, and Mind*. New York: Basic Books.

Bigelow, B., B. Miner, and B. Peterson (1991). *Rethinking Columbus: Teaching about the 500th Anniversary of Columbus's Arrival in America*. Milwaukee: Rethinking Schools, Ltd.

Bell-Scott, Patrick (1994). *Life Notes: Personal Writings by Contemporary Black Women*. NY: W.W. Norton.

Brock-Utne, Birait (1988). *Feminist Perspectives on Peace and Peace Education*. New York: Pergamon Press.

Bunch, Charlotte and Sandra Pollack (1983). *Learning our Way: Essays in Feminist Education*. Trumansburg, NY: Crossing Press.

Butler, Johnella E. and John C. Walter, editors (1991). *Transforming the Curriculum: Ethnic Studies and Women's Studies*. Albany: State University of New York Press.

Chow, Esther N-L. (1985). "Teaching Sex and Gender in Sociology: Incorporating the Perspective of Women of Color." *Teaching Sociology*. 12(3):299–311.

Collins, Patricia Hill (1991). *Black Feminist Thought: Knowledge, Consciousness, and the Politics of Empowerment*. New York: Routledge & Kegan Paul.

Comer, James (1988). *Maggie's American Dream: The Life and Times of a Black Family*. New York: Plume Books.

Crow Dog, Mary (1990). *Lakota Woman*. San Diego: G. Weidenfeld.

Culley, Margo and Catherine Portuges (1985). *Gendered Subjects: The Dynamics of Feminist Teaching*. London: Routledge & Kegan Paul.

Engle, Shirley H. and Anna S. Ochoa (1988). *Education for Democratic Citizenship: Decision-Making in the Social Studies*. New York: Teachers College, Columbia University.

Ferris, Jeri (1988). *Walking the Road to Freedom: A Story about Sojourner Truth*. Minneapolis: Carolrhoda Books, Inc.

Freire, Paulo (1970). *Pedagogy of the Oppressed*. New York: Continuum Publishing Group.

Gluck, Sherma B. (1988). *Rosie the Riveter Revisited*. New York: New American Library.

Gordon, A.D., M.J. Buhle, and N.S. Dye (1976). "The Problem of Women's History." Pp. 75–92 in *Liberating Women's History*, edited by Berenice Caroll. Champaign-Urbana: University of Illinois Press.

Grambs, Jean Dresden (1976). *Teaching about Women in the Social Studies*. Washington, DC: National Council for the Social Studies.

Hahn, Carole L. and Jane Bernard-Powers (1985). "Sex Equity in Social Studies." Pp. 280–297 in *Handbook for Achieving Sex Equity Through Education*. Baltimore: The Johns Hopkins University Press.

Hansberry, Lorraine (1961). "In Defense of the Equality of Men." Pp. 2058–2067 in *The Norton Anthology of Literature by Women*, edited by S. Gilbert and Susan Gubar. New York: W.W. Norton.

Harding, Sandra (1987). *Feminism & Methodology*. Bloomington: Indiana University Press.

Hine, Darlene C., editor (1993). *Black Women in America: An Historical Encyclopedia.* Brooklyn: Carlson Publishing.

Hooks, Bell. (1989). *Talking Back: Thinking Feminist, Thinking Black.* Boston: South End Press.

Hurston, Zora Neale (1991). *Dust Tracks on a Road.* NY: Harper Perennial. (Originally published in 1942).

Jelinek, Esther, editor (1980). *Women's Autobiography.* Bloomington: Indiana University Press.

Kerber, Linda K. and Jane S. De Hart, editors (1995). *Women's America: Refocusing the Past.* New York: Oxford University Press.

Kerber, Linda K., A. Kessler-Harris, and K.K. Sklar, editors (1995). *U.S. History as Women's History.* Chapel Hill: University of North Carolina Press.

Klein, Susan, editor (1985). *Handbook for Achieving Sex Equity through Education.* Baltimore: The Johns Hopkins University Press.

Leonard, Virginia (1981). "Integrating Women's History into the Secondary and College Curriculum." *The Social Studies.* Nov/Dec:265–270.

McCormick, Theresa M. (1994). *Creating the Nonsexist Classroom: A Multicultural Approach.* New York: Teachers College Press.

Maher, Frances (1985). "Pedagogies for the Gender-Balanced Classroom." *Journal of Thought* 20(3):48–64.

Maher, Frances (1987). "Inquiry Teaching and Feminist Pedagogy." *Social Education* 51(30):186–192.

Maher, Frances A. and Mary Kay Tetreault (1994). *The Feminist Classroom: An Inside Look at How Professors and Students are Transforming Higher Education for a Diverse Society.* NY: Basic Books.

Merriam, Eve, editor (1971). *Growing Up Female in America: Ten Lives.* Boston: Beacon Press.

Miles, Rosalind (1989). *The Women's History of the World.* Topsfield, MA: Salem House Press.

Mullis, Ina, et al. (1991). *The State of Mathematics Achievement: NEAP's 1990 Assessment of the Nation and the Trial Assessment of the States.* Princeton, NJ: Educational Testing Service.

The National Council for the Social Studies (1994). *Curriculum Standards for the Social Studies: Expectations of Excellence.* Washington, DC: NCSS, Bulletin 89.

The National Center for History in the Schools (1994). *National Standards for U.S. History: Exploring the American Experience, Grades 5–12.* Los Angeles: The National Center.

National Center for Educational Statistics (1990). *The 1990 Science Report Card: National Assessment of Fourth, Eight, and Twelfth Graders.* Princeton, NJ: Educational Testing Service.

National Center for Educational Statistics (1990). *The U.S. History Report Card.* Princeton, NJ: Educational Testing Service.

Nicholson, Linda (1986). *Gender and History: The Limits of Social Theory in the Age of the Family.* New York: Columbia University Press.

Noddings, Nel (1992) "Social Studies and Feminism." *Theory and Research in Social Education.* XX(3):230–241.

O'Hare, Carol (1995). *Jailed for Freedom: American Women Win the Vote.* Troutdale, OR: New Sage Press.

Rogers, Annie and Carol Gilligan (1988). *Translating Girls' Voices: Two Languages of Development.* Cambridge: Harvard Graduate School of Education. Harvard project on the Psychology of Women and the Development of Girls.

Sadker, Myra and David Sadker (1994). *Failing at Fairness: How America's Schools Cheat Girls*. New York: Charles Scribner's.

Schmitz, Betty (1985). *Integrating Women's Studies into the Curriculum: A Guide and Bibliography*. Old Westbury, NY: The Feminist Press.

Scott, Joan W. (1988). "Gender: A Useful Category of Historical Analysis." Pp. 81–100 in *Coming to Terms*, edited by E. Weed. New York: Routledge & Kegan Paul.

Smith, Sidonie (1987). *A Poetics of Women's Autobiography: Marginality and the Fictions of Self-Representation*. Bloomington: University of Indiana Press.

Spanier, Bonnie, Alexander Bloom, and Darlene Boroviak, editors (1984). *Toward a Balanced Curriculum: A Sourcebook for Initiating Gender Integration Projects*. Cambridge: Schenkman Publishing.

Tallen, B.S. (1990). "How Inclusive is Feminist Political Theory?: Questions for Lesbians." Pp. 241–257 in *Lesbian Philosophies and Cultures*, edited by J. Allen. Albany: State University of New York Press.

Tetrault, Mary Kay (1987). "Rethinking Women, Gender and the Social Studies." *Social Education* 51(30):172–178.

U.S. Department of Education. *USA Today*, Section D, Page 1, July 8, 1992.

Weiler, Kathleen (1988). *Women Teaching for Change: Gender, Class and Power*. South Hadley, MA: Bergin and Garvey.

Wheeler, M.S., editor (1995). *One Woman One Vote: Woman's Suffrage in America*. Troutdale, OR: NewSage Press.

Woolf, Virginia (1929). *A Room of One's Own*. New York and London: Harcourt Brace Jovanovich.

Chapter Twelve

DIGITAL TECHNOLOGY AND SOCIAL STUDIES

Ronald H. Pahl
California State University

BACKGROUND

All information—as we know it in text, voice, and image—is now digitized or is being digitized, says David Thornburg in his book *Education in the Communication Age* (Thornburg, 1995). As a result, says Thornburg, the current paradigm shift is away from a focus on information and toward more comprehensive and faster digitized communication of this information as we emerge into the twenty-first century. Computers have already passed televisions in total sales per year—$8 billion to $7.5 billion (Levy, 1994). United States presidents now receive more e-mail—at president@white-house.gov—in three months than past presidents received letters during their whole term in office (Schwartz, 1994). Our economic communication in paper money and ATM machines is rapidly becoming E-Money transferred by our computers at home (Levy,1994). Word processors for the past two decades have transferred digitized information into paper. As we enter the twenty-first century, however, DataGlyphs by Xerox now reverse this process by codifying small cards of ordinary paper with micro-bursts of information that can be directly read into a computer. With DataGlyphs in 2003 A.D., a student can turn in her social studies term paper on a small piece of paper the size of a business card (Levy, 1994).

To paraphrase an 'ancient' cartoon sage named Pogo, "We have met the revolution and the revolution is us." The digital revolution is ours. We can not ignore it. It surrounds us. It engulfs us. We are part of it. But we need to slow down for a moment.... As social studies teachers carefully nurtured in the textbooks and chalk boards of another era, we need to stop and carefully examine the implications of this revolution in digital technology. What is the place of digital technology in our social studies classrooms? This multifaceted question has technological, pedagogical, social, and economic implications. The multifaceted nature of this question is the center of this chapter.

THE ISSUE

What is the place of Digital Technology (DT) in the social studies classroom? Ten major problem areas associated with digital technology and social studies are examined in this chapter. First, the definitions of DT (Problem 1) and social studies (Problem 2) are reviewed followed by a brief description of the relationship between the two (Problem 3). Then, the advantages and disadvantages of using DT in the social studies classroom are examined (Problem 4). The levels of understanding of DT by social studies teachers (Problem 5) and the appropriate DT hardware and programs (Problem 6) for each are then discussed. Then, some major cultural problems caused by the introduction of DT in the classroom are examined (Problem 7). The analysis then looks at teacher training (Problem 8) and financing (Problem 9) of DT, and how teachers can keep up to date in digital technology (Problem 10). The conclusion calls for a careful, systematic, and instructionally integrated plan of action before DT is implemented into the social studies classroom. The chapter end material includes a glossary of some DT terms, a suggested reading list, and further questions that need to be examined to increase our understanding of the role of DT in the social studies classroom.

Problem 1: What is digital technology?

At its most fundamental level, electronic digital technology (DT) is easy to understand. Very small electronic on and off switches—called transistors—were invented by the Bell Laboratories in 1947 (Myers et al., 1986). These switches, serially linked, could produce "instant" commands or information as the letter "S"—off, on, off, on, off, off, on, on—or 01010011 in machine language.

"Digital" on-off commands to activate the series of transistors could be input, stored, and recovered in incredibly small spaces on magnetic cards, tape, disks, and optical discs.

This digital process—at the root of DT—has created an electronic revolution that has gained speed since 1947. On-off switches once the size of a hand are now the width of a hair, hour-long mathematical calculations when done by hand now take a nanosecond—a billionth of a second. As small things take less space and fast things take less time, the manufacturing costs of this new digital equipment are much cheaper. The result is almost a perfect product for any capitalist system—a smaller, faster, cheaper product.

The impact of this digital or "computer technology" revolution has effected us all. Hand-held calculators now replace slide rules, digital watches replace wind-up ones, digitized CDs (optical compact discs) replace long-play records; and ROM (Read-Only Memory) cards replace CDs. And the revolution continues to expand and pick up speed. Typewriters are already "ancient" machines, having been replaced by word processors. Card catalogs, books and even "old" magnetic computer disks have been replaced by CD-ROMs (CDs with text, images, and sound) and CDIs (interactive optical CDs that can record information). With all these changes, the smaller, faster, cheaper revolution of DT is now at the door of the social studies classroom—waiting to come in.

The most visible manifestation of this revolution is the central processing unit (CPU)—commonly called a "computer"—consisting of thousands of small electronic transistors linked together in fingernail-sized microchips. With the CPU/computer coordinating instructions, the traditional attachments are natural—a keyboard to enter instructions, a monitor to see what is happening, a printer puts the results on paper. Some of the more exotic DT applications that are linked to the CPU and hold potential for use in the social studies classroom—as LCDs (liquid crystal displays)—will be examined later.

Although mathematical at its digital base—the name "computer" is an anachronism. From word processing and drawing pictures to writing and playing musical scores and many other applications, DT has extended far past just being a "computer." This misnamed CPU has added to some of the computer's mystique and this mystique has continued to play havoc with some very reluctant social studies teachers who really do not want to become "computer" users. This mystique certainly started when the first non-transistor computer called ENIAC arrived in 1946, weighing in at 30 tons and occupying a 15,000-square-foot crib. With the same memory—64K (64,000 pieces of information)—as a classic Apple (7 pound) microcomputer, the ENIAC was quite boring by computer standards of 50 years later. But the sheer size of ENIAC added to the mystique along with the media hype about how complex it was to operate.

During the late 1970s, Madison Avenue's advertising minds attempted to soften this fearful image with soft, pastel-colored computers with the down-home wholesome name of "Apple." The mystique, however, of the gargantuan ENIAC still lingered, and the media hype of the day stressed its immense power and the complexity of computers that could only be tamed by brilliant mathematical minds. The cartoons of the day also played on this mythology and tied it to Mary Shelley's classic Frankenstein—mad scientists creating technological nightmares. This fearful myth played itself out in an endless line of films—the best being *Forbidden Planet, 2001,* and *Wargames*—that were also accompanied by a much weaker ilk of sci-fi productions.

The early programs of the first "microcomputers" did not help dispel the fearful computer myth. These early programs were often quite unforgiving if you pushed a wrong key on the computer and required fluency in a mathematics-based programming code such as BASIC. For most nonmathematical social studies teachers of the 1980s and 1990s, computers were something to be avoided at all costs. They were too complex and demanded too much time to learn.

During the Industrial Revolution of the early nineteenth century in England, groups of "Luddites"—unemployed farm workers—tried to physically destroy the new factories that were eliminating their agrarian livelihoods. Such a strong political and religious reaction against the all powerful computer has yet to take place, but the beginnings of such a movement are evident. One "Neo-Luddite" named Kirkpatrick Sale (Katz, 1995 and Kelly, 1995) has demonstrated his opposition to the dominance of technology in society by smashing a computer with a sledge hammer. The popularity of "dumb" programs and movies as "Beavis and Butthead" and "Dumb and Dumber" also express a more subtle social anti-technology sentiment. It remains to be seen, however, whether or not political and religious reactionaries will also take up the cause and become "Neo-Luddites" against DT as the twenty-first century begins.

The myth of the all-powerful computer also invaded the opposite end of the spectrum. The promoters of computers in the classroom—as William Gibson (1984) in his award-winning sci-fi novel, *Necromancer*—talked of "cyberspace" in which young computer jockeys of the future whiz their machines through invisible worlds of computer data in a cyberspace classroom of the future. Such computer education promoters saw, and still see, DT as capable of almost everything. It is without limits, possibly even to the point of eliminating the need for a teacher. Such threats, real or imagined, have obviously frightened many noncomputer-using social studies teachers even more.

We have seen a change, however, during these transition years to the twenty-first century. The mythical fear of the great ENIAC beast appears to have subsided, and small, pastel-colored microcomputers appear to be proliferating everywhere. There is also a profusion of programs on the market that do not demand a high degree of mathematical programming skills and that are applicable for the average social studies teachers in the classroom. Many new social studies teachers entering the field grew up with microcomputers at home and in their classrooms. Many other new teachers have been exposed to computers in teacher education programs required by their states. This combination of factors will certainly lead to a greater use of DT in the social studies classrooms of the future. How much and what form this entry of DT takes into the social studies classroom will be explored later.

Problem 2: What is social studies?

From its origins in the early twentieth century, social studies has emerged as the major part of the K to 12 curriculum concerned with the maturation of young citizens in our nation and the world. Following the classic James Barth and Samuel Shermis article (1970) and Robert Barr's (1970) often overlooked reaction to Barth and Shermis, at least three basic traditions of instruction exist in the social studies. Briefly these three traditions are the transmission of basic citizenship values and beliefs; the acquisition of social science and history knowledge; and analysis and making decisions about major social problems. Rather than three separate entities in the classroom, Barr (1970) sees social studies as composed of all three. With citizenship in the middle and the goal of social studies, the knowledge and content base of history and social science rests on one wing with the problem orientation and decision making on the other wing. There are few disagreements with the citizenship center of social studies. The century-old arguments over the definition of social studies rests in Barr's two wings. Which is more important: the content of history and the social sciences or the process of problem solving and decision making in the classroom? The differences between these two traditional wings of social studies are critical in examining the implementation of DT in the social studies classroom, as will be seen in the analysis of the following problems.

Problem 3: How should digital technology fit into the social studies classroom?

With a raging current of DT innovations threatening to flood the social studies classroom, more than a few educators are concerned. The fear is more than just new innovations teachers do not know how to use. A basic tenet of almost every textbook on education is that instructional activities must be driven by curriculum. Following this tenet, any DT-based instructional activities added to the classroom should be directed by the social studies curriculum of the course. Following Barr's (1970) interpretation of Barth and Shermis (1970), supporters of the knowledge and content wing of social studies would be interested in DT that augments students' knowledge of history and the social sciences. Supporters of the problems and decision-making wing would be interested in DT that assists students in analyzing and making decisions regarding major social problems.

Of more importance, however, is the central citizenship tradition of social studies. How does introducing DT into the classroom affect the transition of societal values and attitudes?

If students are left to themselves to learn from DT programs without the teacher's intervention, what values and attitudes are being transmitted? Are the values and biases of a "human" teacher required to shape the attitudes and opinions being formed by students in the social studies classroom (Bowers, 1988)? Or is it better to give students the freedom to use computer programs and other DT, as maintained by David Thornburg (1995), and shape their own attitudes and opinions? This issue will be reviewed in more detail under the later discussion of cultural problems associated with DT.

In recent years, however, the issue of digital technology in the classroom has moved abruptly in a new direction. Brain research of the 1980s (Hart, 1983; Samples, 1987; and Caine and Caine, 1991) has demonstrated the need to go beyond the curriculum to the mental development of each child. Central in this new research is that cognition cannot take place in isolation from emotion. They are directly connected together. The classroom implications of this may be immense. Teachers may not be able to teach a lesson without taking the motivation of each child into consideration. Electron microscope photographs (Samples, 1987) show that the billions of neurons with their pattern-seeking dendrites need stimulation to reason. Without stimulation these dendrites shrink and fail to connect, fail to recognize any pattern, and thereby fail in cognition. Failing to take interest and motivation into account when planing instruction is to risk not achieving the cognition needed. Summarized, this brain research calls on us to, yes, design instruction according to the curriculum of the course, but also to stimulate the child's interest. Do DT-based instructional programs hold a greater interest for the child in the social studies classroom than a traditional "human" teacher-led classroom—and thereby a stronger interest in learning?

⬦ Problem 4: What are the possible advantages and disadvantages of using digital technology in the social studies classroom?

This problem will be examined in three steps: learning theory, curriculum and instruction, and classroom culture.

1. Digital Technology and Learning Theory

Jean Jacques Rousseau, two hundred years ago in *Emily* (1979 translation), proposed that education should nurture a child's natural capabilities. Ironically, both the critics and the supporters of DT in the social studies classroom use Rousseau's argument to defend their positions.

C.A. Bowers (1988) and Theodore Roszak (1986) criticize DT by noting that human minds think with ideas, not information. Major ideas are formulated with insight and imagination, not by data alone. Both fear that the mass of information now available to any student in the classroom may simply crowd out ideas. Rozak's central theme is that ideas should not be confused with information. Bowers continues this same theme by insisting that a child not be required to learn and manipulate predigested pieces of information. Rather, says Bowers, the child would grow up naturally by developing ideas and then testing them out in the surrounding environment. Bowers believes DT takes away the "natural" learning relationship between the teacher and the student and replaces this relationship with a machine.

Tom Snyder and Jane Palmer (1986) take just the opposite view, but for the same reasons. They see DT as a "mind-tool" with which students can invent their own structures for best solving the problems that confront them. Renate Nummela Caine and Geoffrey Caine (1991) more recently make a similar argument in seeing DT as a means of developing a brain-based education in which students are "immersed" in meaningful knowledge and situations. In such an education, students must grapple on their own with real issues, make mistakes without fear of reprimand by a teacher, and use their own creative mental images to develop their own solutions to problems. Judi Harris (1994) supports this position also when she has her students gathering real-world information on-line using the Internet. Different perspectives of recent news events can be obtained and compared. Different geographical and climatic conditions across the country can be described from first-hand experiences. Problems can be presented on-line for comparative solutions to be presented (Harris, 1994).

Which is more natural for the child—the teacher or the computer as a guide? Too bad Rousseau is not alive to help us solve this basic intellectual dilemma.

2. Digital Technology and Curriculum and Instruction

The textbook is without question the center of the curriculum and instruction for most social studies classrooms. It is also the center of controversy in discussing the entry of DT into the classroom. R.P. Taylor and N. Cunniff (1988) and Robert McClintoch (1988) find that the textual orientation of teachers is a major factor limiting the adoption of DT in the social studies classroom.

Bowers (1988) takes the opposite view by seeing reading and writing as lost arts and directly blames their decline on the increasingly visual and oral culture created by television and DT. Taylor and Cunniff (1988) counter by claiming Bowers overreacts. Graphic computerized instruction, they insist, will never replace textual representation. They point out, however, that DT graphic instructions reach many more students in the classroom who are more visually and spatially oriented.

But Taylor and Cunniff also carry the argument one more level. Do textual evaluations fully measure learning, they ask? Does a student's written description of a concept mean that the student can apply that concept? How often, they ask, is a concept transformed for the sole purpose of rendering it into text rather than fully understanding it. The old saying—a picture may be worth a thousand words—illustrates this point. A more lyrical illustration, however, comes from Ron and Suzanne Scollon (1985), who quote a Navajo sage: "Separate the word from the body. That's death." Following this line of thinking Taylor and Cunniff continue, "When the word becomes an object—in print—it falsifies our most basic relationships. The word comes to take precedence over the situation, analysis takes precedent over participation, isolated thought takes precedence over conversation and story telling, and the individual takes precedence over the community."

For any who have experienced traditional nonliterate cultures the immense power of oral memory is an enlightenment. It is something that "literate" peoples lost when they began to rely on the written word as the truth. Though Bowers fears the possible loss of the text as the most important means of study, perhaps it is also important to take a careful look at gains that can be obtained from using digital visual and oral sources.

3. Classroom Culture—Motivation, Discipline and Cooperation

As any teacher who has spent 10 minutes in a computer-based classroom can verify, the climate of this classroom is quite different from a traditional chalk-and-talk U.S. history classroom.

The focal points are the computer monitors. The teacher is suddenly an assistant—not the focal point—to improve the use of the DT. There is also a constant level of noise—communication—between students assisting one another. The problem of discipline is rare, even during the last period of the day. Student motivation also appears high, even among at-risk students. At traditional parent nights, weaker students who would never bring their parents to a traditional teacher and classroom, can be often found proudly showing off their work to their parents in a computer-based classroom. Are DT-based classrooms better for learning than traditional teacher-centered classrooms? In motivation, discipline, and cooperation, the computer-based classroom wins hands down. In overall learning, more research is still needed.

In perhaps the largest computer study to date, the *Vision: Technologically Enriched Schools of Tomorrow* (TEST) study commissioned by the International Society for Technology in Education (ISTE), came to four major conclusions regarding the use of computers in the classroom (Braun, 1990):

1. "Students improve problem-solving skills, outscore classmates, and learn more rapidly in a variety of subject areas when using technology as compared with conventual methods of study."
2. "Students find computer-based instruction to be more motivational, less intimidating, and easier to persist with than traditional instruction."
3. "In many cases, students' self esteem was increased when they used computers. This change has been most dramatic in cases of at-risk and handicapped youngsters."
4. "Using technology encourages cooperative learning, turn taking among young children, peer tutoring, and other valuable social skills."

The advantages and disadvantages of DT use in the classroom can be covered in much greater depth. Central to this issue, however, is the radical nature of change that DT brings to the social studies classroom. The strangeness of such a new learning environment is certainly a disadvantage to the traditional teacher. The major advantages are the readiness with which students quickly adopt and become comfortable with a computer-based classroom. What we need to know, however, is what is learned and how it is learned when a wide variety of DT is applied in the social studies classroom.

Problem 5: What levels of understanding do social studies teachers have about digital technology?

Although no official list of levels of teacher computer knowledge exists, this author has successfully used five levels of understanding about DT in various workshops and surveys of social studies teachers. In our later discussion of hardware, software, and training these same levels will be used for convenience—and levity's—sake:

Level 1: *I don't wanna, but I gotta attend this lousy computer workshop. How can I cope?*
The teacher at Level 1 has little or no computer experience and has little apparent interest in utilizing DT in the classroom.

Level 2: *I wanna learn about computers, what do I need to do?*
The teacher at Level 2 is at a critical stage. The interest is there, but there is little, if any, skill or knowledge about computers. In computer circles Level 2 teachers are called cyberplebes.

Level 3: *I write letters to my ma and do my grades on a computer, but how do I use it in a classroom?*
The teacher at Level 3 has some beginning experience at personally using a computer and is interested in expanding this use to the classroom.

Level 4:   *The computer lab is free fifth period, what can I do?*
   The teacher at Level 4 is very comfortable with computers for personal use and limited classroom use and is ready to learn more.

Level 5:   *You name the computer program, I have it. What can we do for fun in my class now?*
   This teacher at Level 5 is on the bridge of the Starship Voyager ready to trek outward at warp speed to use the latest technology in and out of the social studies classroom.

These levels of social studies teacher understanding and use are essential in planning, establishing, and effectively implementing a cost-effective DT program in K to 12 schools. As we will see in the following problem areas, all DT equipment and programs are not appropriate for all social studies teachers.

⟨⟩ Problem 6: What types of digital technology are appropriate for different levels of social studies teachers and their classrooms?

Problem 6 will be examined in seven steps: computer hardware, instructional applications, multimedia, optical storage devices, distant learning devices, traditional computer applications, and future classroom applications.

1. Computer Hardware

Level 1 and Level 2 teachers have no computer or DT experience. More than a few innovative school districts have attempted to introduce DT to Level 1 and Level 2 teachers by osmosis—put a computer in their classrooms, and they will use them. Sometimes it worked, but often it did not. DT training designed specifically for teachers at each level of DT use might be a possible alternative to a computer-introduction-by-osmosis program.

For Level 3 and 4, during the 1980s and early 1990s, the major question for teachers was what kind of computer to buy—an Apple MacIntosh (Mac) or MS-DOS/IBM? The two were very different kinds of computers. The Mac was designed for new users with graphic icons, rodents (mice) to click, and basically a friendly design to help teachers and students through complex programs. Although the Macs were more expensive than the MS-DOS machines, their friendly demeanor made them a great success in schools. The MS-DOS was more the workhorse of the two, with a standard Selectric keyboard for people who could type. All computer commands on the MS-DOS were either keyed in code words as < autoexec > or key combinations < Alt-Ctrl-Del >, but the advantage of the MS-DOS was more power—faster, more storage capacity, more bells and whistles—and it was cheaper than the Macintosh. The MS-DOS style computers dominated and continue to dominate school front offices and the business industry.

During the last decade of the twentieth century, Apple Computer has continued its traditional near monopoly on computers in the elementary school, but has failed to gain in any other market share of education or business. MS-DOS style computers, on the other side of the microchip, have made significant inroads into the secondary schools and now split that market with Macs. The MS-DOS style computers have been steadily able to offer more power and more software applications for social studies teachers at cheaper prices.

What computer should a Level 3 or 4 teacher buy for the twenty-first century? There is likely no correct answer. Both Macs and MS-DOS styles of computers are very similar (Collis and De Diana, 1990 a and b) and will become more similar as Apple and IBM develop more joint computer products such as the Power Mac, which can run both Mac and MS-DOS programs. MS-DOS style computers now have rodent-run programs with friendly easy-to-use graphic display for beginning computer users, very similar to the Macs. The Macs now have the MS-DOS Selectric style keyboards to make it easier for experienced typers to use. Several kinds of programs such as Mac In DOS also translate programs back and forth between Mac and MS-DOS computers. In the heavily competitive computer industry, we can fully expect major changes, mergers, and joint ventures as we emerge into the new century, and they will create a whole new range of choices for us.

Elementary school teachers, as a group today, likely prefer Macs because their fellow teachers also have Macs or other older Apple IIe computers and can share software programs. Secondary school teachers have a tougher decision—an easier and more expensive Mac or a more power and less expense MS-DOS style computer. Among computer users, a common saying used to be "Pick the software you want to use, then buy the computer that runs that software!" The saying has less validity as software companies now have common protocols, as EASI (Education Application Software Interface) for program development in layers. With these protocols, most top computer programs are now written for both Mac and MS-DOS style computers. In the end, it might be good educational sense for schools to buy both computers—if the money is available—and train teachers and students to be familiar with both.

2. *Instructional Applications*

The early 1980s saw an infinite number of simple Drill and Practice (pronounced "drill and kill") programs available for social studies teachers on the Apple IIe computer. The themes covered every low-level application in the social studies curriculum: the names of the states, the names of the presidents, the amendments to the Constitution. Drill and kill till learned. Is there a purpose for drill and practice programs in social studies? What things do we definitely want our young citizens to memorize—states, capitals, amendments, countries? These are boring repetitive items to learn in a regular classroom, but not if individualized in a game format. If these are things to be memorized for Barr's content wing of social studies, then there is a purpose for drill and practice computer programs.

During the 1990s games—such as *Where in the World/USA/History is Carmen Sandiego?* (Brøderbund)* and its many variants such as *Mario Is Missing!* (Software Toolworks)—have largely replaced many of the old drill-and-kill programs of the 1980s. They are easy do use and fun. Students from third grade to college can play them. In fact, these educational programs are so much fun, a new term has been coined for them—"edutainment." They also teach such mundane social studies knowledge items as states, capitals, and countries. Will these computer edutainment games replace the social studies teacher? No, these games should be treated as any other learning activity with formal objectives and debriefing. These games also give the teacher the opportunity to engage the students in depth experience with a given social studies topic—something rarely available with textbooks alone. This in-depth experience also lends itself to a deeper level of analysis in the debriefing following the game.

Simulations have been an early staple of digital technology in the social studies classroom since the early 1980s. MECC's classic *Oregon Trail* has long been a staple with several upgrades for the Apple IIe computer and is now even available on CD-ROM for both MS-DOS and Mac style computers. These simulations attempt to place the students in the shoes of people participating in an event and have them act out different roles. In *Oregon Trail*, students role-play an individual on the wagon train moving west. Great old programs as *Oregon Trail* refuse to die. The *Trail* now has 40 reading, writing, and problem-solving activities entitled *Writing Along the Trail*. In another classic simulation entitled *SimCity* (Maxis) and many new variations as *SimCity 2000*, students are the mayor and city council of a city—small town USA, San Francisco during the 1906 quake, or many other alternative cities. How do they run their cities? Where should new roads go, railways, schools, houses, football stadiums, airports, industry, and how high should taxes be raised to pay for this? The SimCity program reacts to the "city council's" plans with such delightful results as pollution, crime, traffic congestion, and even tax revolts. Suddenly the message of the game is very clear—we are the products of our own decisions. Obviously, *SimCity* is designed with the

---

* Note: Digital technology sources, addresses, and telephone numbers appear near the end of the chapter, starting on page 381.

analysis and decision-making wing of social studies teachers in mind. It is not very complex; Level 2 and Level 3 teachers can learn to use it in their classrooms with very little effort. By projecting the computer screen on the wall with an LCD (liquid crystal display), a Level 3 teacher could involve a whole class in making citywide decisions and analyzing the consequences. Computer simulations, like the ones mentioned and others such as *President Elect* (Strategic Simulations), and *Castles* (Interplay), offer alternative fun activities to lesson mixes in a school's regular curriculum. They are participatory, they contain a great deal of information about an event, and students must analyze this information and decide on actions to take. The consequences of their actions become immediately apparent and often demand follow-up corrective decisions. Should computer simulations be a part of a Level 2 to Level 5 social studies teacher's repertoire of lessons? The answer should be an unqualified yes!

3. Multimedia

A newer genre of DT emerged during the 1990s called Multimedia. For Level 2 and Level 3 teachers every computer company in the world has been manufacturing low-cost and easy-to-use MPCs (multimedia personal computers) with high-resolution color monitors, sound boards, speakers, CD-ROMs and microphones. Software companies are now producing an amazing variety of social studies edutainment CD-ROMs for MPCs for all grade levels. A few examples of these include the following:

- *From Alice to Ocean: Alone Across the Outback* (Claris). For a color Mac MPC and grades 4 and above. Robin Davidson narrates her 1,700 mile, six-month trek across Australia's outback chronicled by *National Geographic*.
- *Who Built America: 1876–1914* (Voyager). This contains the voices and images of ordinary Americans and new immigrants at the turn of the century with thousands of primary documents for research and personal exploration.
- *OneWorld Atlas* and *OneTribe* CD-ROMs (Virgin Sound and Vision). These are examples of fully interactive tours of our physical and cultural planet that include a wealth of maps, information, and cultural sound tracks. From the origin myths of Maori islanders to the chanting rituals of Tibetan monks, BBC video footage and soundtracks from Peter Gabriel's *RealWorld* provide an atlas for the twenty-first century.

Such outstanding multimedia as Virgin's *OneTribe* can provide an easy enticement for Level 1 to Level 3 social studies teachers to acquire an MPC and try it out in their classroom, but multimedia goes much further than just edutainment extravaganzas. Full scale multimedia productions, however, are the sole domain of Level 5 social studies teachers. Such full scale multimedia productions are based on authoring programs with which a Level 5 teacher can digitize his or her own videos, images, sound, animation and text to create personalized programs for the classroom. Several popular authoring programs include *Digital Chisel* (Pierian Spring Software) for Macs and *Elastic Reality* (Avid Technology) for MS-DOS and Power Macintosh machines to make movie-quality productions. In fact, *Elastic Reality* has been used extensively to produce the great graphic effects in many recent science fiction and fantasy motion pictures.

Almost all multimedia programs have hypertext at their root. Hypertext links any kind of information no matter how divergent—written messages, graphs, photos, or sound—from the details of a complicated legal trial to tracing the origins of the AIDS disease. *HyperCard* (made by Apple for the Macintosh) is a simple version of hypertext in which users place information desired into common "stacks" for easy retrieval using "buttons" on a text or picture to access the stack. The advantage of HyperCard is that Level 4 teachers and students can build and use "stacks" for their classroom presentations with a relatively little training.

Full hypertext programs, as *HyGlos* and *Houdini* (MaxThink), however, are more sophisticated and have a potential to make a much greater impact on social studies education. Using hypertext any given document can have a "jump" or a "button" (using HyperCard vocabulary) to reference every major name or word in the document to other indexes and documents using or explaining the same word. The U.S. Constitution, for instance, on hypertext would link every key word or phrase, such as < electors > in Article 2 to an index listing all major references and writings on electors in the Electoral College. The result is a gigantic cross-referenced matrix of documents, writings, photos, and graphs that are all linked and cross-linked in virtually a limitless number of ways. A student or teacher using hypertext to follow a personal line of questions about a topic will find out in a matter of moments exactly what is known about a topic. For a pure social studies hypertext application, see Ron Pahl's *Who Killed King Tut?*, an ancient hypertext murder mystery (Pahl Education Consortium).

Such advanced levels of multimedia may be impractical for a Level 2 or Level 3 teacher, but a Level 4 or Level 5 teacher can create a self-contained multimedia interactive program for classroom use on virtually any topic in social studies. With the proper equipment and enough training time, teams of Level 5 high-school students could produce their own multimedia productions for use in class. Such student-centered multimedia productions could well be the ultimate goal of digital technology in the social studies classroom. Very close to William Gibson's (1984) *Necromancer*, young computer jockeys can whiz their cyberspace machines through invisible worlds of computer data with current multimedia equipment. Such a goal is not too far fetched. Several students in this writer's experience are true cyberspace jockeys capable of very sophisticated multimedia work. Given the proper equipment and training, they produce fascinating multimedia reports. For teachers interested in such advanced Level 5 multimedia, American Expositions, Inc. also holds annual "Multimedia Expos" across the nation to bring together teachers and other specialists who are interested in this exciting area of DT.

For Level 3 and Level 4 teachers, not ready for such exotic DT, but wanting to expand the use of computers in the classroom, desktop publishing may be the answer. Handing students plain typed handouts are OK for starters, but how about having student teams produce their own "historical" newspapers to report on a specific era of the past. Major word-processing programs, such as WordPerfect or Microsoft Word, can be used with different font sizes, newspaper columns, and inexpensive clip art to develop great recreations of a different era such as the French Revolution. Many other word processors have such similar features for a wide variety of prices. For Level 5 teachers and students, the Adobe PageMaker program can take these same word processor produced pages and turn them into very realistic reports and newspapers.

A simple program entitled BannerMania (available from Brøderbund) will allow Level 1 and Level 2 teachers to make flashy banners to liven up their classrooms quickly. Two major disadvantages to this program: (1) make sure enough paper is in stock as banners can be quite long; and (2) keep a good hold on the disk—other teachers will want to borrow it.

4. Optical Storage Devices

Laserdiscs are digitized laser imprints of as many as 650,000 images on a disc of aluminum foil encased in plastic. Several formats of these discs existed during the 1970s and 1980s, but did not have the capacity to re-record old discs. Although laser discs were superior in quality of image and storage, VHS video tape recorders—with the re-record feature—became and remain the major visual media used by social studies teachers. In the 1990s all laser discs were standardized into the CAV (constant angular velocity) format that allows access to still digitized images; the images can be controlled through computer programs in MPCs and other authoring programs.

Where laser discs shine is in the high quality of the digital imagery combined with the teacher's ability to pick different images and film clips very quickly and then return, just as quickly to show them again if there is a question. This ability to pick and move around the "image database" of the laser disc has been greatly enhanced by the addition of the bar code reader (available from Pioneer) to instantly scan the frame number of the images desired. Laser discs such as ABC News Interactive's *In the Holy Land* (available from the Optical Data Corporation) on the Jewish/Palestinian problem also have computer programs included that allow teachers to develop their own interactive program sequence in the classroom. The same laser disc, however, can still be accessed with a bar code reader to do the same sequences as on the computer, but without the hassle of programming.

The combination of the laser disc with the bar code reader will likely be very appealing to Level 1 and Level 2 teachers and newer social studies teachers without the vested base of a large VCR tape collection. A Level 1 teacher can use a barcode scanner to bring to the screen exactly the images he or she wishes without a moment's pause in the presentation. This can be an easy way to introduce Level 1 and Level 2 teachers to DT use in the classroom for virtually every social studies subject. Most laserdisc players and bar code readers on the market are produced by Pioneer.

Needless to say the laser disc, bar code reader, and interactive computer programs are already appealing to the Level 4 and Level 5 social studies teacher. These are parts of an important visual database that can be used in building a "brain-oriented" classroom in which groups of students can pursue their own research on social studies topics in "cyberspace."

Are laser discs, laser disc players, and bar code readers worth the money for the social studies classroom? Have a Level 1 and a Level 5 teacher look together at any of the following laser discs (available from Educational Resources):

- *The Blue Planet* (IMAX) in which we see ourselves and how we are changing this fragile and beautiful planet. Grades K to 12.
- *Here I Have Lived—Abraham Lincoln* (MediaTECH) with more than 1,300 still and video pictures of Lincoln before he became President—with documents, music, lesson plans, and barcodes. Grades 3 to 12.
- *Seven Days in August* (EduFAX) which captures the events and emotions surrounding the building of the Berlin Wall in 1961 during the height of the Cold War. Contains three hours of photos, four different games, teacher's guide, and barcodes. Grades 7 to 12.

Both levels of social studies teachers will want to use them in their classrooms. The major problem with laser discs is financial—how many can you afford to buy?

CD-ROMs, or small laser disc players, are a recent addition to DT in the classroom. Identical to popular CDs for music, CD-ROMs store mostly the visual and written information that larger laser discs do. The advantage of CD-ROMs is that they can be directly loaded into a computer and accessed as a regular disk drive, but they can store much more information—a full encyclopedia, the complete papers of the Constitutional Convention, a near complete photo documentary of the Civil War. David Thornburg (1995) states that we are currently entering a Communication Age—he could well have said a CD-ROM age for virtually all forms of information—text, visual and sound—are being stored on this medium. Several CD-ROM catalogs exist with more than 10,000 titles available from sources around the world on virtually any subject. CD-ROMs are easy to use and relatively inexpensive. A few interesting CD-ROM titles are the following:

- *Touring Indian Country* (MPI Multimedia). This Windows/MS-DOS CD-ROM for grades 4 to 12 tours Native American communities with Eagle Walking Turtle. Music, video, photos, and text are from 150 Native American nations.
- *CNN Newsroom: Global View*. (Softkey International). This Windows/MS-DOS CD-ROM allows students to examine international issues and world geography with maps, charts, speeches, radio broadcast transmissions, and video clips.
- *Crosscountry USA*. (Datatech Software). This CD-ROM for Mac, Apple IIe, and MS-DOS lets students take control of an 18-wheeler to cross the country and learn U.S. geography along the way. Students compete to find the shortest route after eating at Cool Cathy's Cafe and gassing up at Perky Pete's. This program for all "roads scholars" in grades 4 to 8.

Such CD-ROMs can be used just as library research tools for the content wing of social studies for Level 1 through Level 3 teachers and students, or as great vehicles for the cyberspace jockeys at Level 4 and Level 5 to explore the known universe. For the highest quality CD-ROMs and laser discs available, Voyager has been the consistent front runner in this field.

CD/Is (Compact Disc/Interactive)—also called flopticals—are the newest optical medium. The advantage of CD/Is is that they are erasable laser discs. Created by Phillips in Europe in 1992, CD/Is combine the best features of CD-ROMs and video tapes, and they may eventually replace both. For those interested, annual CD/I conferences are sponsored by Knowledge Industry Publications, Inc.

As we proceed into the twenty-first century, such optical storage devices as CD-ROMs and CD/Is will be replaced by ROM Cards, small "credit card" sized storage devices that can be entered into a nearby computer. These ROM cards will contain all of the programs and information we need for business and pleasure.

5. *Distant Learning Devices*

Modems have long been attached to computers for long-distance learning and communication. Students can communicate between rooms or across town or across the nation to compare opinions on world events, or research specific historical or current events. Rose Reissman (1992) is a sixth-grade teacher who uses the modem to have her students share their experiences in Reader's Circles with students in other classes and other schools. M.D. Roblyer (1992) in Florida presents another example in which social studies classrooms contact fellow students in England in a program called Campus 2000 to share opinions and improve international understanding. Social studies departments who want to link up with schools around the world on a modem, but at a minimum cost can contact the *Global Schoolhouse Project* (formerly *FrEdMail*).

Are modems for all social studies teachers? Obviously not. A survey by the National Education Association (NEA) in 1993 found that only 4 percent of all K to 12 teachers had access and knew how to use the Internet and e-mail (Honey, 1994). With so few teachers "on the Net," especially social studies teachers, efforts must be made to provide access for Level 4 and Level 5 teachers to on-line communications and to provide time and training to enable them to integrate such activities into formal social studies lessons.

On-line databases and newslinks have, perhaps, the greatest potential for impacting social studies in the near future. *Dialog*, although relatively expensive, has the greatest potential for immediate application when linked to a school library and then used to research topics on almost any subject. *Prodigy* and similar commercial on-line services as *Compuserve* provide an immediate access to news of the world as well as such up-to-the-minute current events as the latest polls for an upcoming election. Several major newspapers and weekly news magazines, such as *Newsweek* (see Newsweek Interactive) are also available on line with photos, graphics, sound, games, and reader interaction.

Noncommercial on-line services may also be the textbooks of the near future. In this scenario, publishers would provide and continually update information needed on a given course for a set fee paid by a school district. Students in a classroom could then access the on-line text whenever they needed. Publishers would love this—no more expensive books to print. Students would love it—no more huge texts to lug from class to class. The Sierra Club would love it—no more trees to cut down. The lumber and paper companies, however, would likely have strong objections to on-line texts.

Fax machines may be the digital technology answer in distance learning for Level 1 and Level 2 teachers. Lobbying a state senator by fax on upcoming legislation and conducting a written debate between two classes in neighboring cities on bias in TV news are two easy uses of fax machines by social studies teachers. Two teachers across town sharing lessons may be a third example. We are just beginning to see the possible uses that fax technology can play in social studies education.

6. Traditional Computer Applications

Word Processors What are the advantages of a word processor over a typewriter? This question is for senior teachers because many young word processing veterans might not know what a typewriter is. Ease of use, ease of correction, ease of reuse, ease of storage are some of the responses the questioner may receive. Any disadvantages? Learning how to use a word processor is usually the first answer, sloppy handwriting from lack of practice is the second, then the list becomes very short.

Typical findings of word processor studies, like that of K. Robinson-Stavely and J. Cooper (1990), is that computer-using students are significantly better with fewer punctuation errors, greater number of words, longer sentence length, and greater use of complex sentences than their noncomputer using peers. Linda Polin (1991) reports similar findings, including increased student interest in revising papers once they are written. Following such findings, schools like Hesperia High School in California instituted a writing program for all sophomores at the school and report similar personal writing mechanics improvements for a large majority of their students.

Bowers (1988, p. 23), however, is fearful that keyboarding skills will replace cursive writing in the elementary school. Teachers in favor of keyboarding note that cursive writing is a very difficult task for young people. Locating and typing words and sentences is much easier on a computer. This results, they say, in students who learn how to write more rapidly, enjoy writing better, and write more than their noncomputer using peers. Will word processors replace handwriting in the elementary school curriculum? They might, but in the distant future.

During the 1980s and early 1990s, it was easy to define a word processor—they were used to enter, store, and print documents. More recently, however, the dominant word processors, such as *WordPerfect* (Novell/WordPerfect Corporation) and *Word* (Microsoft Corporation) also do numerous other functions such as labeling, tabling, graphic layout, and even mathematical functions. Word processors are evolving along with the rest of computer technology. Many computer supporters see word processing as the first step in any computer training program if only to improve a teacher's efficiency in lesson preparation and correspondence. Word-processing programs will likely be a stable center of any computerized social studies program for some time to come.

Databases Making sense out of long lists of cross-referenced data was among the first purposes of computers, and this will remain a major purpose for some time to come. Databases are incredibly useful at diagnosing unseen relationships, trends, or just simply listing world leaders chronologically and then alphabetically. Available commercial databases cover an incredible number of topics. Two interesting examples are

- *Vital Signs* (World Watch Institute). This is the famous database—updated yearly— that forms the basis of the influential *State of the World*.
- *CIABASE* (Ralph McGehee). Eight megabytes of CIA deeds, duds, and dirty works culled from 850 public sources with 100 categories such as "assassinations," "blackmail," "media," and "psywar."

Using social studies databases in the classroom—though very good for developing inductive reasoning—are often very complex and time consuming. As Lee Ehman, Allen Glenn, V. Johnson, and Charles White (1992) well illustrate, database programs—especially older ones in such programs as *AppleWorks* and Microsoft *Works*—can have complex command structures and lead to confusion in the classroom unless proper instruction is provided. These programs should be used by experienced Level 4 and Level 5 teachers only. Databases—with huge pages of seemingly "meaningless" data—are also a new experience for most students, and care should be taken to not intimidate new users. Instruction in database use needs to be done slowly, carefully and systematically before full database studies are conducted. Ehman, Glenn, Johnson, and White, in their study of database use in social studies, concur: "Keeping track of the overall picture of problem solving, especially when it involves computer databases, is often difficult. Clear structure assists students to find that picture and keep it in focus" (p. 196).

A clear trend for computer databases is increased simplicity of use as well as their integration with graphing and mapping functions. These simplified databases use hypertext jumps instead of complex charts and tables to move easily from topic to topic. *PC Globe*, *PC USA*, *MacGlobe* and their sister CD-ROM entitled *Maps N Facts* (made by PC Globe and all available from Brøderbund) are fine examples of this new trend—basically computerized atlases, they also incorporate gigantic global databases with easy graphing functions. Although containing a very complex CIA database on the nations of the world, they are still simple enough for Level 1 and Level 2 teachers and a fifth or sixth grader to operate and convert into visual data with less than 15 minutes of practice time.

Spreadsheets   Any social studies lesson that involves large numbers of calculations could certainly use a spreadsheet to speed and ease the drudgery of endless mathematical calculations. But most social studies teachers do not use spreadsheets for their lessons. Personal surveys conducted yearly by this author indicate that the sole computer use of many social studies teachers is for keeping class records and grades on a spreadsheet—Level 3 teachers. These dreary tasks for any teacher are an easy way to entice a Level 2 teacher to become a Level 3 teacher. Numerous grading programs are on the market. Highly recommended is *Grade Machine* (Misty City Software) or *ClassMaster* (Techbyte International). For those wishing to design their own grading system—Level 4 or 5 teachers—any *spreadsheet* program such as *Lotus 1-2-3* (IBM/Lotus) or *QuattroPro* (Novell/WordPerfect) for MS-DOS style computers and Excel (Microsoft) for Macs would be appropriate.

Before using the spreadsheet in the classroom, several days of initial instruction can be expected. Once mastered, however, students can then accomplish such impressive tasks as making their own simplified national budget and comparing it with the one presented to Congress each year; comparing popular and electoral votes by state in a national election; buying and selling stock in a simulated classroom stock market. Spreadsheets take patience and time to learn properly, but once mastered, they become very useful tools for both teacher and student in high school. For a creative example of using a spreadsheet in social studies, see "So Ya Wanna Be Rich?" (Pahl, 1995), which teaches spreadsheet use while creating a stockmarket simulation game.

7. Future Classroom Applications of Digital Technology

Integration and portability are the two key words of DT as technology becomes smaller, faster, cheaper, and more powerful. Cellular telephone technology became popular in the early 1990s and is available for computers. This same technology is currently being linked with television to produce an integration of telephone-computer-television called *interactive television*. Two-pound computers that can be worn around the waist are already available (Infogrip) as are translucent computer monitors that are worn as a pair of glasses (Virtual I/O). All these items are already available for classroom use. Will any of these items catch on and revolutionize the way we teach? And what can we expect in the next few years? Do not limit your imagination!

At the very outer limit of our imagination today is *Virtual Reality* (VR). Wraparound goggles, data gloves studded with digitized sensors, a full simulated 3-D image surrounding the student—we are now entering the zone of Virtual Reality. Right now VR is strictly for the Level 5 computer "trekkie," with visions of cyberspace running in his or her head—and lots of money. Perhaps a VR version of MECC's classic *Oregon Trail* will be available in four or five years or a very realistic and personal debate with the makers of the Declaration of Independence in Philadelphia of 1776? VR is still on the future horizon, and not in the classroom,…yet!

⇄ Problem 7: What social and cultural issues are involved when DT is introduced into the classroom?

Are computers our salvation for the social studies classroom, or our damnation? Serious critics of computer technology use such as Bowers (1988, p. 44)and neo-Luddites as Kirkpatrick Sale (Kevin Kelly,1995), see an ultimate danger in computer technology of a "Machina sapiens" capable of reproducing itself and replacing Homo sapiens. If the bimolecular computer (reported on NPR Radio, June 4, 1992) at Wayne State University ever becomes a reality—based on pattern recognition of protein chains and enzymes—we can expect more such primeval fears to be expressed both in scholarly print and supermarket tabloids.

Though perhaps not as lurid as some mad-scientist horror thrillers, several very profound social and cultural issues must be discussed regarding social studies education and computer technology. Cultural change, ideology, digital and analog thinking patterns, privacy, equity, and the cross-cultural transfer of technology are a few major issues that need to be discussed.

Cultural Change and Technology

In language well understood by social studies teachers, Bowers (1988, p. 6) and Kirkpatrick Sale (Kevin Kelly,1995) ask, what cultural manifest destiny do computers bring to the classroom that cuts across class and ethnic distinctions? How blindly are we rushing toward a technological future without looking at the changes computers are making to our classrooms, schools, and society? McClintoch (1988, p. 351) questions whether we understand the changes inherent when we change "the stuff of culture into binary code."

Bowers fearfully looks at the impact of computer technology on language. What if language mediates the transmission of culture and computers radically modify language? What impact do computers have on our culture? In a purely computer-oriented classroom environment, what happens to language selection patterns, handwriting, verbal interaction, writing composition, and paragraph formation skills?

Despite the critics, like Bowers, it is equally as difficult to imagine a people becoming computerized and then willfully rejecting computers to return to longhand messages, typewriters, and slide rules. The trend towards the binary world of computer technology is clearly a manifest destiny. We will not be able to reverse it; hopefully, however, we will be able to continue to critique it and guide it in directions that are beneficial to humankind.

Computers as Ideology

Bowers (1988), the ever-present computer critic, argues that the ever-efficient computer, like all human scientific endeavors, is never free of bias. The danger in school is that students—and teachers—hold just the opposite view and often accept computer generated information as "the truth." We need to be aware, says Bowers, that computer generated data forever reflects the programmer's cultural, gender, and ethnic bias—even in things that often appear to be neutral programs. Certainly this blind faith in technology is an inherent danger of using computer products in the classroom.

Bowers argues for the teacher's continued presence in the classroom as the mediator of the student's understanding of culture—aware of the tools of technology, but also of their inherent bias and weaknesses. The major bias of the computer, says Bowers, is that the computer terminal is seen as an extension of the individual, who is rational and able to make decisions on his own in the tradition of John Locke, Thomas Hobbes, and Jeremy Bentham— the ultimate capitalist. The computer promotes the Cartesian model of the individual as the detached observer who acquires objective information from a database. What this model does not view is the relationship of the individual and the information to the past, to cultures, and political ideology. What is lost in this computerized model of society, says Bowers, is social thinking in groups that bond with a common identity such as a strong traditional culture, which values group identity over individual identity.

Can we recapture culture and community and still have technological progress? If so, then technology must be directed toward benefiting humankind rather than being developed for its own sake. More than 100 years ago Auguste Comte separated science from its philosophical base and promoted scientific research for its own sake. Perhaps it is time to rein in science and technology and retie them to philosophy for the benefit of humankind.

Mark Clayton (1987, p. 22) holds a similar view: "Schools need to teach their engineers how to design machines that work with human interaction built in—not cut out." To do this DT needs to be carefully considered and planned to enhance and promote the well-being of each individual and the community and not just the makers of a new piece of hardware or software. The existence of on-line communities can, however, rapidly change any concern about this problem. Though much criticism has been leveled at computers for not being personal, thousands of virtual on-line communities have sprung up on their own. Discussion groups on almost any subject can be found on the Internet. These communities also give voice to many who do not normally have the capacity to participate in discussions, especially the handicapped (Honey, 1995).

In recent years, much concern has been raised about how much violence on television affects our children at home. What has often been ignored is the brutal interactive violence on computer "shooting" games. Children physically pull the trigger on their computer "games" as often as several hundred times a minute to eliminate the "bad guys." The action is hot and heavy, and the children are fully engaged and off the street. But how much are such DT programs training children to readily accept violence as part of their lives? And how much are the computer displays of combat missions training our youth to become the fighter pilots of the future? This issue needs to become a central question of discussion in our classrooms.

Digital and Analog Thinking Patterns

Computer technology uses *digital* thinking processes of discrete binary bits of information that are given an equal weighing. Normal human thought uses *analog* thinking, which incorporates relationships, context, redundancies, memory, and pattern recognition. The problem for teachers, says Bowers (1988, p. 64), is that metaphoric language of analog thinking in humans when placed in a computer could well be taken superficially as fact and the point of the metaphor missed. To be fair to computer programmers, however, mistaking a metaphor for a superficial fact is a common mistake of humans throughout history. Jesus, for example, was a frequent user of metaphoric language, but is often today still interpreted literally.

Bowers (1988, p. 75) is also concerned that the teacher and the student using computers only are out of touch historically when they consider the past only as isolated raw bits of information from the past—literally digital readouts of history. According to Bowers, such computer users lack a sense of continuity with the past. Bowers obviously does not recognize that the computerized history he criticizes is very close to the history practiced by the French historian Fernand Braudel (1979) who sees history as a series of very complex isolated events rarely, if ever, connected with each other. To Braudel the large sweeping generalizations and syntheses of civilizations are largely figments of vivid imaginations. But Bowers' point is well taken. History composed of data generated from computer databases does express biases and is not neutral information. It is up to individual teachers and students to analyze this data, to recognize its sources, and to make appropriate decisions based on these analyses.

Privacy

"Quis custodiet ipsos custodes?" (Who will guard the guardians?) asked Juvenal almost two thousand years ago. In our age of digital technology, this problem is as strong as ever. Where and what kind of line do we draw as to what is private and what is not. The issue certainly comes from the computerized mailing lists generated by commercial companies, and how much they know about us. More of an issue, however, are attempts by the FBI and National Security Agency (NSA) to push legislation through Congress to simplify the way they conduct electronic surveillance of new digital technology such as e-mail. This governmental effort at wider use of wire taps may be politically popular "to cut crime." This FBI and NSA effort, however, is clearly is a violation of our fourth amendment rights to privacy according to EPIC (Electronic Privacy Information Center), which is a project of the Fund for Constitutional Government and the Computer Professionals for Social Responsibility.

Also concerned with this same constitutional issue of privacy is the Progress & Freedom Foundation, which has drafted a Magna Carta for the Knowledge Age to ensure that the freedoms of speech and privacy are maintained in the future. Write by snail mail to the Foundation at 1250 H. St. NW, Suite 550, Washington, D.C., 20005, fax a request to 1-202-484-9326, or e-mail a request to PFF@aol.com.

Equity—Gender

Do social studies teachers need to fight a gender bias in computer technology? Carole Hahn and Jane Bernard-Powers (1985) note extensively documented gender inequities in four major areas of social studies education: under-representing and stereotyping of females in textbooks; gender differences in political knowledge and attitudes; student attitudes toward women in politics; and the "hidden" curriculum of male-dominated groups: teachers, student body leaders, and school administrators.

Jane Schubert's (1986) study of gender equity in computer learning found that in a scientific context, computers as an object of study were not interesting to females. Females, however, were more interested than males in using computers to improve their work in other areas, for example, word processing and data management. Schubert's findings verify this writer's own survey which found very few females taking the Advanced Placement Computer course in high school and yet a large number of female students enrolled in regular computer courses teaching word processing, spreadsheet, and database technology. The same parallel can be seen in the job market. Very few computer technicians, in this writer's experience, are female, but a large number of females are computer trainers and specialists in school systems and industry.

Much as the gender biases found by Hahn and Bernard-Powers (1985) in the 1980s are rapidly changing in politics, the same may be true in computer technology. Jane Schubert's (1986) review of computer literature in the 1980s found very few articles written by females, whereas this writer, when surveying articles written for *The Computer Teacher* for 1991 to 1994, found a virtual tie in the number of articles written by males and females. Kate Mackowiak (1991) came to the same conclusion in a sample of 118 university faculty members when she found no differences between sexes or ages of those who were using computers in their courses.

Concerning the obvious gender differences that still exist in computer-related education, social linguists such as Deborah Tannen (1986) may give us a few clues as to why such differences continue to exist. Women, says Tannen, are more concerned with relationships in communications in an analogic thinking of pattern and meaning from the past. Men tend to view communication as a conduit for sending and receiving information and are more comfortable in a Cartesian world of observation, measurement, and objective facts.

Given this evidence, we must realize that computer technology is not gender-neutral. Gender bias still exists. One of the more popular computer programs of the last decade, *The Oregon Trail* (MECC) is a good example of gender bias that still exists in context—the males on the Trail are doing all the action. Gender bias appears to be softening, but it still remains and work needs to be done to remedy the inequalities that still exist. Two programs that specifically address this issue in computer technology are these: *The Neuter Computer: Computers for Girls and Boys*, consisting of 56 school-based, gender neutral activities developed by the Computer Equity Training Project and *EQUALS in Computer Technology*.

Equity—The At-Risk Student

Perhaps the most damning indictments of education in the United States is that at-risk students in America number 4.5 million; two-thirds of these students are from families at or below the poverty line, and the 45 largest urban school districts contain 30 percent to 50 percent of all at-risk students in the U.S. Equally disturbing is the clashing, but unquestionable evidence that "...wealthier communities possess more computers in their homes and schools..." (Jane Schubert, 1986). More disturbing is evidence that the gap between rich and poor is increasing and that access to computer technology in our schools may be one major factor that is increasing that gap. These sad statistics record our nation's educational failings, yet some politicians have the gall to state that money has nothing to do with good education.

According to the Colorado Model, the cost to the state of 500,000 dropouts over four years is one billion dollars. By the most conservative estimates the cost of dropouts to the nation is $500 per year per dropout. By dropping the dropout rate in half, the model estimates a savings of $11 billion per year nationwide. U.S. industry also spends an estimated $25 billion annually in developing basic skills among their employees. Together with the $11 billion, we can estimate the United States is spending $35 billion per year to compensate for inadequacies in our educational system (Braun, 1990).

Where does computer technology fit into this frightful picture of our disadvantaged youth? Under present conditions, students from wealthier communities with more computers and computer training will obtain the computer-oriented jobs of the future. The future under these conditions looks bleak and the inner-city poverty-fed rebellions may well be an increasing phenomena arising from the desperation brought on by such conditions. These desperate conditions, however, are not irreversible.

Technology-rich classrooms have been shown by Ludwig Braun (1990) and others to be effective in enticing potential dropouts to stay in school and to become more productive members of society. The International Society for Technology in Education's (ISTE) previously mentioned impressive Technologically Enriched Schools of Tomorrow (TEST) survey of computer education (Braun, 1990) concludes that "Technology, combined with properly trained teachers, offers a dramatic solution to the dropout problem. The success of numerous technology-enriched programs suggests that we could possibly cut dropout rates at least in half and increase the basic-skills levels of our students overall if we provide schools with adequate amounts of technology and with teachers trained in its uses" (p. 4).

Research evidence is clear (Braun, 1990): at-risk students of all ethnic backgrounds can perform and even excel at the tasks required of them by our schools and society. So why do we spend so much money making larger prisons to house the drop-outs of our schools? The evidence presented earlier indicates that computer technology can dramatically assist these at-risk youngsters. How can we get our society to make a commitment, even if on a relatively short, experimental basis, to immerse a large number of at-risk youth in computer technology? (We will discuss finance later in the chapter) It could become a very small step toward ameliorating the very large problem of inequities in our society.

Equity—Special Needs Students

Reports on using computer technology for special-needs students, though not as compelling as for disadvantaged youngsters, show distinct signs of promise. William Shennum and Marcella Nino (1992) studied what worked and what did not work for educating various levels of disturbed children using available computer technology. They also report that the computer lab was a setting where behavioral difficulties were neutralized to a degree. They found that even with seriously emotionally disturbed, especially disruptive children, the computer proves to be an equalizer. Children who do not succeed in school generally (as defined by achievement test scores) may find success in a computer environment.

Lynne Anderson-Inmann (1990–91) summarized research on using computers with learning disabled students. She reports that reading programs that give immediate verbal feedback to vocabulary problems are an effective way to increase word recognition. She finds that disabled students, as most other students, perform better at writing in personally meaningful contexts rather than unfamiliar situations. Can social studies teachers in special-education resource classes effectively use computers and digital technology? Although more study is needed, it appears that such technology for students with individual learning needs is an important learning tool.

Exporting Computer Technology to Other Cultures and Languages?

The transfer of computer technology to other cultures, languages, and countries is a major stumbling block for establishing international understanding. The problem can be well illustrated in even a simple transfer using British software in U.S. classrooms. Laura Perez and Macey Taylor (1987, p. 7), after reviewing a British Council Software game for classroom use, commented "London Adventure would have to be completely redone for students in the United States because it is an adventure game set in London, with British English and units of measure…" and therefore unusable in most U.S. schools.

Certainly in a state of frustration at the inability to successfully transfer computer technology to other cultures, B. Wombi (1988) states that "technology is like genetic material—it is encoded with the characteristics of the society which developed it, and it tries to reproduce that society." Despite this frustration, Third World nations have readily seen computer technology as a possible means of competing with the United States, Europe, and Japan on a level playing field and are working to rapidly increase computer use in their schools. The hurdles, however, on the track of computer technology are immense even for a "developed" nation such as Mexico. For U.S. readers, it might be well to realize that Mexico, in the 1990s, is listed in the top 20 percent of the developed countries of the world according to Gross National Product (GNP).

Marco Murray-Lasso (1988, p. 3), from the National University of Mexico, gives a detailed description of some major problems of transferring U.S. computer technology into Mexico. "The first constraint," he says, "is cultural. Mexico will not accept culture-dependent computerized educational materials that were developed for other cultures." A fine software program for Mexican schools that is not blatantly culture-dependent is Brøderbund's popular *Carmen Sandiego*. OK, let's introduce it into Mexican social studies courses—what problems will we encounter?

J. Nielsen's (1986) seven-level virtual protocol model of human-computer interaction is of great assistance. Murray-Lasso (1990), based on Nielsen, sees 12 cultural constraints on introducing educational technology products as *Carmen Sandiego* (CSD) into his country—five of these constraints are listed here:

- *Language:* The vast majority of schools, more than 90 percent teaching Spanish only, could not use the program, nor could they consult *The World Almanac* or the *Book of Facts*.
- *Curriculum:* The curriculum and social organization of learning is controlled by the Ministry of Education in Mexico City, so there is little opportunity in the curriculum to use CSD even if it were language-appropriate and a computer were available.
- *Values:* The program would also clash with the traditional classroom valued by the Mexican Ministry of Education in which the authoritative teacher transmits information to students. CSD promotes individual initiative and imagination, which is contrary to Ministry dictates and would likely not be approved if a formal adoption question was presented.
- *Teachers:* The education level of the teachers would be an issue in some rural areas where the education level is low and in-serving opportunities rare.
- *Economics:* Only about 6,000 primary and secondary schools in Mexico, out of 100,000, have at least one 16K to 64K computer. Most of these computers are also not compatible with CSD because they do not have disk drives (too difficult to repair in rural areas). Although $49 in U.S. terms is inexpensive for a piece of software, in Mexican terms the same amount of money could buy all the books and tools needed by three public schools for a school term.

Conclusions: *Carmen Sandiego*, though widely regarded as an inexpensive and attractive item of DT in the United States, will not be used extensively in Mexico.

What can be done to remedy such cultural constraints of technology transfer? Many of these factors are just too great to be handled by a small number of educators. Teachers and educators can, however, build the infrastructures essential to support future changes by promoting software exchanges and adaptation training through talks, newsletters, demonstrations, and other activities based at the school. Researchers and professional societies need to initiate projects to study cultural and social implementation problems. Schools and organizations need to develop collaboration projects between countries to develop CD-ROMs, laser discs, and other computer products that can be easily adopted by more than one country. International standards committees also must be formed to discuss simple items such as the use of commas and decimal points (this differs greatly even between the United States and England), the writing of dates (most countries place the month after the date), the fluctuating values between different currencies of the world, and more complex issues such as universal nomenclatures and symbols for computer technology (Murray-Lasso, 1990). Cross- cultural issues in social studies and computer technology clearly are in need of much research, patience, and empathy.

⧓ Problem 8: What organizational and training issues impact the infusion of DT into the the social studies classroom?

Organizational Issues

"Form and function are one thing," stated the master of American architecture—Frank Lloyd Wright (Doris Ray, 1991). Are the *forms* of our current social studies classrooms meeting the citizenship *functions* for which they are intended?

For learning the knowledge and content of history and the social sciences, the current classroom *forms* are likely sufficient. But if the aim is to develop problem-solving, decision-making citizens, social studies classrooms need to focus more on creating a "brain-based" problem-solving environment for each individual student. Such a unified form and the function of "brain-based" learning can be seen in Seymour Papert's (1980) now-classic vision of a fully computerized classroom as a very private one free of institutionalized learning. The image of a "cyberspace" social studies classroom, with student teams freely exploring the digitized universe around them to come up with solutions to problems faced by society, fully fits this vision. For most schools, however, Doris Ray (1991, p. 12) sees this image of a "cyberspace" education as unrealistic. "In the majority of…schools, technology is being ignored or overlooked. Most educators use technology very little. This is perhaps due more to the educational and organizational barriers inherent within the schools than it is to a lack of interest or desire."

Ray (1991) sees that such brain-based schools need to be constantly reflective and experimental to constantly improve the education they offer. Ray's description comes very close to the quality based educational program envisioned by Edwards Deming (see Pahl, 1992). In Deming's view the quality of the team, rather than the individual, is important. Constant mutual assistance and monitoring are needed to ensure that all skills and learnings are mastered. The administration, teachers, and students form teams to work for quality. There is no constant standard of judgment or bell curve of success and failure—only constant striving for improvement. No automatic promotions or failing one third of the class. Skills are measured and charted. Problems are corrected in process, not afterwards by a cleanup crew, probation officer, or unemployment clerk.

In support of linking form and function together, Ray (1991) noted six strategies to enhance school-technology relationships:

1. "Respect the fundamental importance of human beings and their social systems." Innovations throughout history have failed because they did not consider the attitudes, values and beliefs of the people involved. "You have to start with people." "The investment made in the development of human resources are the most important ones a school can make."
2. "Develop and nourish creativity and vision."
3. "Improve and enlarge the notion of leadership." "Enlarging leadership also means expanding the cast of players in schooling, forging better collaborative relationships with parents, communities, and business and industry."
4. "Increase everyone's access to technology."
5. "Support research and development." Schools that actively foster organizational climates for research also create a climate of tolerance and openness.
6. "Build a technological infrastructure." Rather than add an overflowing plate of technology, schools need to seek ways to identify technology that support the directions of change desired by the school community. It should be a process of gradual development and one in which technology becomes the essential platform of communication within the school.

Training

Fred D'Ignazio (1990) sees the nineteenth-century "trickle-down" means of dissemination of information through "textbooks" revised by publishers every five years as insufficient for the twenty-first century. He stresses the need to see training and inservice not as an occasional activity by school districts, but as an ongoing and constant process of keeping up-to-date with the rapid changes around us.

Kate Mackowiak (1991), in a sample of 118 university faculty members, found that the nonavailability of computers, the lack of appropriate software, and, above all, the lack of training are the major barriers to computer usage. Ray (1991) agreed by noting that the majority of educators generally seem to understand little about the capacities of technology available to them. They often cite, she says, a desire to learn about it, but cite lack of time, financial resources, and the lack of support for training in technology.

In a sample survey of social studies educators and computer technology coordinators from across the country, the writer of this chapter found that everyone sampled listed "training" as one of the most important issues concerning the introduction of computer technology into social studies classrooms. It is also clear that this training needs to be geared to the specific level of DT knowledge and skills of each teacher.

Now which wing of social studies should this training emphasize: the acquisition of knowledge or problem solving and decision making? If computer education specialists such as Janice Woodrow (1991) have any say, DT training should focus problem-solving and decision-making programs so teachers see computers as tools and not just sources of information. The educational advantages of DT, say Janice Woodrow and others, are not in the acquisition of knowledge for its own sake, but rather for developing student skills in the acquisition and analysis of knowledge needed for specific decisions.

Not forgotten in this concentrated discussion of computer technology and social studies is the need to develop curricula that use computer technology effectively and implement state and local guidelines. Perhaps the best example of such an effort is the work of Montgomery County Public Schools in Maryland. Under the guidance of Richard Wilson, county social studies teachers come together for two weeks each year to develop and revise existing curriculum. In recent years computer technology has been an integral part of this effort with a focus on developing innovative HyperCard stacks for use in social studies courses at each of the different grade levels. A successful by-product of this effort is a cadre of computer-trained social studies teachers who are developing their own curriculum and then in turn training others by developing more curriculum. Certainly it is a win-win situation for everybody and social studies teachers in particular.

D'Ignazio (1990) described the Teacher Explorer Center at East Lansing (Michigan) High School: The Teacher Explorer Center is a pilot site in the state to train teachers as "teacher explorers" who as knowledge navigators can pilot their classrooms as far as human knowledge will allow. Each classroom consists of five "inquiry centers"—one for the teacher and four student centers—that are self-contained modules linked to local computer networks, telephone lines, and cable TV. Each center focuses on a specific aspect of a given assignment to eventually come together in a large multimedia report. Following a model similar to that of the Teacher Explorer Center, California Technology Project (CTP) and its regional organizations throughout the state have been conducting Technology Leadership Academies (TLAs) focused on specific curricular areas.

How should DT workshops for social studies teachers be conducted? The answer may be in conducting them exactly the way classes should be organized to take advantage of the power of DT and the natural learning abilities of students.

⋙ Problem 9: What financial issues constrain the introduction of DT into the social studies classroom?

"We must, as a nation, recognize that the short-term costs of improving our schools and incorporating technology into the curricula are much less than the long-term costs resulting from an undereducated or inappropriately educated population." (Braun, 1990). Ray (1991, p. 11) was blunt and to the point: Any discussion of school improving technology in our schools must involve financing. "Schools spend much less on technology than other organizations, and they use the technology longer." "Clearly...technology is not yet an educational priority. Until it is, schools can hardly hope to use technology to its potential."

L. Perelman (1989) was also direct in pointing out the clashing dichotomy of the computer literate workforce needed by U.S. companies and the lack of public financial support given to provide a technology-rich education in our schools. He noted that 80 percent of current U.S. jobs require the use of computers, but the national student to computer ratio in schools is still about 30 to 1. The decade of the 1990s has shown some improvement in this area, but it has not been significant—especially in the poorer communities. Perelman also noted the disparity between industry and schools in their support of technology: business and industry currently spent between $7,000 to $300,000 to support each position; schools spend less than $1,000 on technology to support each teacher. And, he noted the computers and technology used by the schools are archaic by industrial standards.

In pure economic terms, computers are good investments for companies, noted Joao Batista Oliveira (1990 p. 318), because computer technologies are basically one-time costs with only low maintenance costs added over time. Computer technology has initial high fixed costs and extremely low variable costs, which, in normal economic markets, makes such products attractive to users. In financially strapped school systems, however, such economic thinking is ignored in favor of cutting any expenditure outside of essential personnel and services.

Despite this negative financial news, some schools are continuing to purchase computers in large numbers. How are they paying for this?

To make any wide impact, clearly public support at the local and state level is essential. One of the more promising plans is from Indiana. Arthur Hansen (1992) reported that Indiana's "Buddy" system envisions personal computers in the home of every student in grades 4 through 6. Implementing the system would cost the state between $110 and $144 million (3 percent of the K to 12 education budget of $4 billion). The proposal is for the state to provide one-third of the cost, while parents and local school districts pay for the rest. This model would reduce the costs to the state to $100 per student, or 1 percent of the total education expenditure. Participating parents would also receive a tax credit for the cost of the "Buddy" computer. Low-income families would receive a computer from the state. Middle-income families would also have the option of leasing a computer. Though not fully implemented, the Indiana plan does show promise of what innovative financing teamwork can do at the state and local levels.

From another angle, Martha Hancock and Ivan Baugh (1991) reported that Jefferson County Public Schools in Louisville, Kentucky, launched a multimillion dollar project in the late 1980s to place computer labs in county schools. The program did not cost the tax payers any additional tax levies. The program was jointly funded by the business community, which provided a significant percentage of the funds through a local educational foundation, local parent teacher organizations, and the school district. Poorer schools were directly paired with business partners to assist each school in raising sufficient funds. Over a five-year period, 1984 to 1989, the county installed more than 9,000 computer workstations in their schools through this project.

Often overlooked in financing technology are indirect support from public and private institutions for such activities as training, in-kind incentives, licensing agreements, and compatibility coordination. Also particularly useful for implementing technology are clearinghouses for exchanging information, research and development roundtables, and feedback on new products for producers.

Mary Jane Mitchell (1990) presented a short description of how schools and school districts can apply for corporate grants: Groups to contact are parent groups, local alumni associations, service organizations, businesses, private foundations, and charitable trusts. Mitchell noted two major sources exist for corporate grants:

- Corporate 500: The Directory of Corporate Philanthropy (Public Management Institute)
- National Directory for Corporate Giving (Foundation Center Cooperating Collections Network)

Apple Computer, Inc., has sponsored a very useful package entitled *A Guide to Alternative Funding* (see Innovative Technology Solutions), which is a rich 81-page document of guidelines on how to write grants and possible government and nongovernment sources along with actual phone numbers of grant-oriented agencies.

Problem 10: How can social studies teachers keep up-to-date with digital technology?

Keeping up with a fast moving train is not easy, especially when the train is continually changing its shape, its direction, and even the track itself. The changes in the digital technology locomotive are rapid and diverse, far beyond the ability of an individual teacher or even department to keep up. The need is great for the National Council for the Social Studies (NCSS), state councils, and local councils to pool their expertise to systematically and yearly review changes in DT and recommend what might augment and strengthen existing instructional programs. Local school departments can contribute to this effort by conducting their own yearly reviews. To assist these local school efforts, NCSS has a detailed, but dated, "Software evaluation guidelines" (NCSS, 1984). Easier to use and a little more recent is Terry Northup's NOSES (Northup Objective Software Evaluation System). Local departments can use these two sources to make their own evaluation guides for all of DT, not just computer software. For such use, Northup's NOSES is presented in Table 12–1 (from Gene Rooze and Terry Northup, 1989).

Table 12–1

Identification Information:

    Program Name: _____

    Source: _____

    Subject Matter Area(s): _____

    Type: _____

    Computer System Requirements: _____

    Price: _____

    Brief Description: _____

Content:

    Grade Level of Subject Content: _____

    Description of Goals or Topics Covered: __

    Approximate Reading Level: _____

    Accuracy of Information Presented: _____

Usability:

    Clarity and Simplicity of Directions: _____

    Amount of typing required: _____

Documentation:

    Adequacy of Printed Instructions: _____

    Support Materials: _____

    Suggestions for Follow-up: _____

Educational Techniques:

    Variety of Reinforcements: _____

    Wrong Answer Response: _____

    Hint: _____

    Explanation: _____

    Branching: _____

    Screen Report of Final Results: _____

Management of Student Records:

    Passwords/Protection: _____

    Handling of Successive Scores: _____

    Ease of Updating: _____

    Retrieval: _____

    Report of Time Taken: _____

Graphics:

    Variety: _____

    Clarity: _____

Other Comments:

    _____

    _____

    _____

Name of Evaluator: _____

Date: _____

Other Useful Organizations and Magazines for "Keeping Up-to-Date"

- Computer Using Educators (CUE): CUE has two excellent conferences each year, one in the fall in northern California (Santa Clara) and a second in the spring in southern California (Palm Springs) as well as a fine newsletter for Level 2 to Level 4 teachers.
- *The Computing Teacher:* This journal is for the nontechnical Level 2 to Level 4 K to 12 teacher and has easy-to-read and easy-to-use implementation strategies for computer technology. Contact: The International Society for Technology in Education (ISTE).
- *Electronic Learning:* The magazine for "technology and school change" is a good Level 3 to Level 4, inexpensive (free!) way to keep up with the changes and ideas of using technology in education. Contact Scholastic for a subscription.
- *Journal of Research on Computing in Education:* This publication is the best available on current research on computer education for Level 4 and Level 5 educators. Contact ISTE.
- *Learning Services:* LS is perhaps the best overall DT educational catalog for both elementary and secondary school teachers. If there is a one stop shop for DT—from laser disc players, CD-ROMs and bar code readers to the latest software for Macs, MS-DOSs, and the Apple IIe computers for all grades K to 12, LS may be the place.
- *New Media:* If you are Level 4 and aspiring to be Level 5, this magazine is full of 3-D graphic boards, morfing techniques, video accelerators, and hot multimedia authoring programs. This is a true Level 5 magazine for those who plan to develop the hot social studies multimedia edutainment for the twenty-first century. Contact *New Media* for a free subscription.
- Social Studies School Service: Although many social studies teachers have used their large orange social studies catalog for years, SSSS also produces a fine computer catalog. Thumbing through this catalog alone should generate ideas on how DT can be effectively used in the classroom.
- Tom Snyder Productions: This company has produced consistently good social studies software for many years for all three types of computers: Mac, MS-DOS, and the old Apple IIe. Their catalog is always a joy to read for new ideas and has many products designed specifically for the one-computer classroom. They also stage many local workshops around the nation.
- *WIRED:* Nothing is dull about this magazine—in either its print or on-line interactive format. The graphics are hot. The articles are cutting edge. It is a slick, high profile, highly charged glimpse of the digital revolution. If you are Level 1, forget it. Level 2s may become overwhelmed. Level 3s will experience techno-shock. Level 4 or Level 5s will not be disappointed by *WIRED.*

CONCLUSION

Much as the stone tool did for Homo Habilis, agriculture did for Neolithic humans, and the industrial revolution did for humankind, digital technology is undeniably changing the very nature of our existence both as humans and as social studies educators. Digital technology brings many advantages to the social studies classroom—more student interest and involvement, less teacher direction and more student-directed learning, and more involvement of at-risk and special students. But there are also dangers along the way: the unconscious acceptance of a digitized manifest destiny, the possibility of greater social and economic inequities, the inability of much DT to transfer to other cultures without the wholesale destruction of these cultures. From curriculum development and teacher training to hardware and software selection, social studies educators must be proactive if the central citizenship goal is to remain intact. At the national, state, and local levels, social studies educators must consciously and systematically monitor major changes in digital technology and recommend how and which of these changes meet this central goal.

Reflective Questions

To facilitate this proactive position that social studies educators need to take with digital technology, 10 questions reflecting on the issues presented in this chapter are presented here:

1. *Do students make better learning gains in computer-oriented social studies classrooms in cooperative groups or when using computers alone?*

2. *Why is it easier for teachers to maintain discipline in a computer-oriented classroom compared with a traditional teacher-centered classroom?*

3. *How do we measure the effectiveness of "brain-based" cooperative and self-directed activities in the computer-oriented classroom?*

4. *Is the use of nontextual, visual, and graphic imagery a more powerful way to teach social studies concepts compared with traditional text and lecture methods?*

5. *What are the costs and benefits of using hypertext-building as a means of developing student higher-order thinking skills?*

6. *What are the costs and benefits of using laser disc databases in place of student textbooks?*

7. *What is the best means of training teachers to use computer-based instruction?*

8. *How can we systematically select the best hardware and software for our social studies classrooms?*

9. *What is the best means of transferring DT between different cultures without the more technological culture destroying the other?*

10. *How can we systematically plan and finance computer technology for our classrooms?*

GLOSSARY

CAI   Computer Assisted Instruction.

CAV   Constant Angular Velocity, the acceptable format for all laser discs and laser disc players, especially for multimedia purposes.

CD/I   Compact Discs/Interactive, also called flopticals, are erasable and rerecordable CD-ROMs.

CD-ROM   Compact Discs-Read Only Memory are identical to the small laser-driven CDs used for music, but can also be used to store written and visual data along with sound. New MPC computers and edutainment centers have the capability of playing all three—CDs, CD-ROMs, and CD/Is—as television, sound entertainment centers, and computers merge together.

CPU   Central Processing Unit, the correct name of the central part of any "computer" that contains the microprocessors, silicon boards, and disk drives that form the working hub or "brains" of the computer.

cyberspace   William Gibson's (1984) sci-fi image of computer generated worlds created out of raw data, digitized and transformed into instantly available sights, sounds, voices, and smells of a virtual world upon request.

desktop fusion   The merging together of long-distance sources of information, interactive communication, visual images, sound, analysis systems (database, spreadsheets, and hypertext), and textual composition (word processing) into a small portable laptop computer.

DT   Digital Technology: the whole world of miniature electronic on-off switching technology that resulted from the 1947 invention of the transistor—from bar codes and computers to remastered phonograph records and digital images transmitted from the moons of Saturn.

edutainment   Computer learning programs in which the line between playing and learning is hard to distinguish. This will increasingly become the norm for educational software as we proceed into the twenty-first century.

gigabyte (GB)   One billion bytes of digital information stored in the computers memory or on disk. In 1980 computers were measured in thousands of bytes (B), by 1990 the measure was millions of bytes (MB), by 1995 the measure was gigabytes (GB) or billions of bytes of information.

Internet (the Net)   The open on-line system of digital communication by computer which has thousands of databases and talk groups that discuss every conceivable topic. The Internet is the rapidly growing "information highway" of the future and has already become its own world within DT with its own vocabulary, books, and magazines. Within the Net sub-culture "gophers" look for specific topics, "browsers" look to see what is available, and such entities as the World Wide Web connect the user to anything available within the DT world.

LAN   Local Area Networks are systems that link groups of computers together to share work and resources.

LCD   Liquid Crystal Displays are the flat screens that are the key technology in all the small laptop computers. Translucent LCDs are also placed on *cool* overhead projectors and work done on a computer can then be projected onto a screen or wall for viewing in a regular classroom.

MPC   Multimedia Personal Computers are computers that have the capacity of integrating sound, visuals, and text into a single presentation.

multimedia   The combining of video, voice, graphics, and text into a full edutainment presentation on MPCs.

nanoseconds   Billionths of a second, the speed of our fastest computers now, but likely the speed of an average computer in the year 2000 A.D.

ROM cards   Portable "credit card" sized computer storage devices that will replace current disk drives, CD-ROMs, and CD/Is in the future.

VR   Virtual Reality is the emerging technology in which the DT program looks, sounds, and *feels* like the real thing.

virtual workplace   In a physical workspace, we work and interact with the people and products around us to make society function. In the virtual workplace of the twenty-first century, computers, fax machines, video monitors, and telephones link us "virtually"—with the effect of being real—with the real world around us.

MAJOR SOURCES OF DIGITAL TECHNOLOGY

Adobe Corporation, 411 First Avenue South, Seattle, WA 98104, 1-206-622-5500

American Expositions, Inc., 110 Greene Street, Suite 703, New York, NY, 10012, 1-212-226-4141

Apple Computer Inc., 20525 Mariani Avenue, Cupertino, CA 95014, 1-800-538-9696

Avid Technology Inc., 1 Park West, Tewksbury, MA 01876, 1-800-642-4122

Borland, 1800 Green Hills Road, P.O. Box 660001, Scotts Valley, CA 95067, 1-408-438-5300

Brøderbund, 17 Paul Drive, San Rafael, CA 94903, 1-415-492-3500

Campus 2000, Helen Milner, P.O. Box 7, 214 Grays Inn Road, London, England, WCIX 8EZ

Claris Corporation, 5201 Patrick Henry Drive, Santa Clara, CA 95052, 1-800-735-7393

Compuserve, P.O. Box 20212, Columbus, OH 43220, 1-800-368-3343

Computer Equity Training Project, *The Neuter Computer: Computers for Girls and Boys.* Women's Action Alliance, 370 Lexington Avenue, New York, NY 10017

Computer Using Educators (CUE), Inc., 4655 Old Ironsides Drive, Suite 200, Santa Clara, CA 95054, 1-408-492-9197

Datatech Software, 4250 Dawson Street, Suite 200, Burnaby, BC, Canada VSC 4B1, 1-800-665-0667.

Dialog Information Services, 3460 Hillview Avenue, Palo Alto, CA 94304, 1-800-3DIALOG

Educational Resources, 1550 Executive Drive, Elgin, IL 60123, 1-800-624-2926

EduFAX (available through Educational Resources)

Electronic Privacy Information Center (EPIC), 666 Pennsylvania Avenue, SE, Washington, DC 20003, 1-202-544-9240 or e-mail info@epic.org

EQUALS in Computer Technology, Lawrence Hall of Science, University of California, Berkeley, CA 94302

Foundation Center Cooperating Collections Network, 79 5th Avenue, New York, NY 10003, 1-800-424-9836

Global School Project (formerly FrEdMail Foundation), Bonita, CA, 1-619-475-4852

IBM/Lotus, EduQuest, P.O. Box 2160, Atlanta, GA 30055, 1-800-426-4338 or on the World Wide Web: http://www.ibm.com

IMAX (Available through Educational Resources)

Infogrip, 1141 E. Main Street, Ventura, CA 93001, 1-800-397-0921

Innovative Technology Solutions, Inc., 103 Springfield Center Drive, Suite 204, Woodstock, GA 30188, 1-404-924-3317

International Society for Technology in Education (ISTE), 1787 Agate Street, Eugene, OR 97403, 1-800-336-5191

Interplay Productions, 3710 South Susan, Suite 100, Santa Ana, CA 92704, 1-800-969-GAME

Knowledge Industry Publications, Inc., 701 Westchester Avenue, White Plains, NY 10604, 1-800-800-5474

Learning Services, P.O. Box 10636, Eugene, OR 97440, 1-800-877-9378

Lotus (see IBM/Lotus)

Maxis Software (available from Brøderbund)

MaxThink, 2437 Durant Avenue #208, Berkeley, CA 94704, 1-415-428-0104

MECC, 3490 Lexington Avenue North, St. Paul, MN 55126, 1-800-228-3504

MediaTECH (available through Educational Resources)

Microsoft Corporation, 16011 NE 36th Way, P.O. Box 97017, Redmond, WA 98073, 1-206-882-8080

Misty City Software, 10921 129th Place, N.E., Kirkland, WA 98033, 1-206-828-3107

MPI Multimedia, 16101 S. 108th Street, Orland Park, IL 60462, 1-800-777-2223

New Media, P.O. Box 10638, Riverton, NJ 08076, 1-609-786-4430

Newsweek Interactive, 333 Route 46 West, Mountain Lake, NJ 07046, 1-800-634-6848

Novell/WordPerfect Corporation, 270 W. Center Street, Orem, UT 84057, 1-800-541-5096

Optical Data Corporation, 30 Technology Drive, Box 4919, Warren, NJ 07060, 1-800-LASER-ON

Pahl Education Consortium, 1411 North Joyce Avenue, Rialto, CA 92376, 1-714-773-3808

PC Globe, Inc. (available though Brøderbund)

Pierian Spring Software, 5200 S.W. Madison Avenue, Portland, OR 97201, 1-800-472-8578

Pioneer Electronic Corporation, Sherbrooke Plaza 600 East Crescent Avenue, Upper Saddle River, NJ 07458

Prodigy, Prodigy Services Company, 445 Hamilton Avenue, White Plains, NY 10601, 1-914-993-8000

Progress and Freedom Foundation, 1250 H. St. NW, Suite 550, Washington, DC, 20005, fax: 1-202-484-9326, or e-mail: PFF@aol.com

Public Management Institute, 358 Brannan Street, San Francisco, CA 94107, 1-415-896-1900

Ralph McGehee, P.O. Box 5022, Herndon, VA 22070, 1-703-437-8487

Scholastic, 555 Broadway, New York, NY 10012, 1-800-544-2917

Social Studies School Service, 10200 Jefferson Boulevard, Culiver City, CA, 1-800-421-4246

SoftKey International, 1 Athenaeum Street, Cambridge, MA 02142, 1-800-227-5609.

Software Toolworks (available through Educational Resources)

Strategic Simulations. 1046 N. Rengstorff Avenue, Mountain View, CA 94043, 1-415-964-1353

Tandy Corporation, 700 One Tandy Center, Fort Worth, TX 76102, 1-800-243-2015

Techbyte International, 908 Niagara Falls Blvd., N. Towawanda, NY 14120, 1-800-535-3487

Tom Snyder Productions, 80 Coolidge Hill Road, Watertown, MA 02172, 1-800-342-0217

Virgin Sound and Visions (available from Learning Services)

Virtual I/O, 1-800-646-3759 or e-mail: i.glasses@vio.com

Voyager Company, One Bridge Street, Irvington, NY 10533, 1-800-446-2001

WIRED, P.O. Box 191826, San Francisco, CA 94119, 1-800-769-4733; e-mail: subscriptions@wired.com

WordPerfect (see Novell)

World Watch Institute, 1776 Massachusetts Avenue, NW, Washington, DC 20036, 1-202-452-1999; e-mail: wwpub@igc.apc.org

REFERENCES

Anderson-Inman, Lynne (1990–1991). "Enabling Students with Learning Disabilities: Insights from Research." *The Computing Teacher* 18(4):26–29.

Anonymous (1988). "Technology and the At-Risk Student." *Electronic Learning* 8(3):36–49.

Barr, Robert D. (1970). "The Question of Our Professional Identity: Reactions to the Barth/Shermis Article." *Social Education* 34(2):751–754, 759.

Barth, James L. and S. Samuel Shermis (1970). Defining the Social Studies: An Exploration of Three Traditions." *Social Education* 34(2):743–751.

Bowers, C.A. (1988). *The Cultural Dimensions of Educational Computing: Understanding the Non-Neutrality of Technology*. New York: Teachers College Press.

Braudel, Fernand (1979). *The Wheels of Commerce*. New York: Harper & Row.

Braun, Ludwig (1990). "Executive Summary of the Final Report, Vision: TEST (Technological Enriched Schools of Tomorrow)." *The Computing Teacher* 18:4.

Braun, Ludwig (1990). "School Dropouts, Economics, and Technology." *The Computing Teacher* 18(6):24–25.

Brody, Robert and Glenn Deutsch (1992). "Virtual Reality: What a Concept!" *USA Weekend* March 20:8.

Caine, Renate Nummela, and Geoffrey Caine (1991). *Making Connections: Teaching and the Human Brain*. Alexandria, VA: Association for Supervision and Curriculum Development.

Carland, Jo Ann C. and James W. Carland (1990). "Cognitive Styles and the Education of Computer Information Systems Students." *Journal of Research on Computing in Education* (Fall) 23(1):114–126.

Clayton, Mark (1987). "A Technology of Big Outlays, Modest Returns." *The Christian Science Monitor* Sept. 26:18–19.

Collis, Betty A. and Italio De Diana (1990a). "The Portability of Computer-Related Educational Resources: An Overview of Issues and Directions." *Journal of Research on Computing in Education* 23(2):147–172.

Collis, Betty A., and Italio De Diana (1990b). "The Impact of Different Portability Factors During the Life Cycle of an Educational Software Adaptation Project." *Journal of Research on Computing in Education* 23(2)306–317.

D'Ignazio, Fred (1990). "Electronic Highways and the Classroom of the Future." *The Computing Teacher* 17(8):20–24.

Ehman, Lee, Allen Glenn, V. Johnson, and Charles White (1992). "Using Computer Databases in Student Problem Solving: A Study of Eight Social Studies Teachers' Classrooms." *Theory and Research in Social Education* 22(2)179–206.

Ferrington, Gary and Kenneth Loge (1992). "Virtual Reality: A New Learning Environment." *The Computing Teacher* 19(7)16–20.

Gardner, Howard (1983). *Frames of Mind: Theory of Multiple Intelligences*. New York: Basic Books.

Gibson, William (1984). *Necromancer*. New York: Ace.

Habermas, Jurgen (1971). *Towards a Rational Society*. Boston: Beacon Press.

Hahn, Carole L. and Jane Bernard-Powers (1985). "Sex Equity in Social Studies." Pp. 280–297 in *Handbook for Achieving Sex Equity Through Education*, edited by Susan S. Klein. Baltimore: The Johns Hopkins University Press.

Hancock, Martha K., and Ivan W. Baugh (1991). "The New Kid Graduates." *The Computing Teacher* 18(7):17–21.

Hansen, Arthur G. (1992). "A Buddy Computer in the Home: Five-Year Progress Report." *T.H.E. Journal* 19(2):61–65.

Harris, Judi (1994). *The Computing Teacher* March:32–36.

Hart, Leslie (1983). *Human Brain and Human Learning*. Village of Oak Creek, AZ: Books for Education.

Honey, Margaret (1994). "NII Roadblocks—Why Do So Few Educators Use the Internet?" *Electronic Learning* October:14–15.

Honey, Margaret (1995). "Online Communities." *Electronic Learning* January:12–13.

Katz, Jon (1995). "Return of the Luddites." *WIRED* June:162–165, 210.

Kelly, Kevin (1995). "Interview with the Luddite." *WIRED* June:166–168, 211–216.

Levy, Steve (1994). "E-Money—That's What I Want." *WIRED* December:174–179.

Mackowiak, Kate (1991). "The Effects of Faculty Characteristics on Computer Applications in Instruction." *Journal of Research on Computing in Education* 23(3):396–410.

McClintoch, Robert O. (1988). *Computing and Education: The Second Frontier*. New York: Teachers College Press.

Myers, David L., Valarie A. Elswick, Patrick W. Hopfensperger, and Joseph P. Paviovich (1986). *Computer Programming in BASIC*. Boston: Houghton Mifflin.

Mitchell, Mary Jane (1990). "Private Funding for Educational Technology Projects." *The Computing Teacher* 18(3):38–39.

Murray-Lasso, Marco (1988). "Problems Confronting the Implementation of Computers in Latin American Educational Systems: The Case of Mexico." Paper presented at the annual meeting of the American Educational Research Association, New Orleans.

Murray-Lasso, Marco (1990) "Cultural and Social Constraints on Portability." *Journal of Research on Computing in Education* 23(2):252–271.

NCSS (1984). "Software Evaluation Guidelines." *Social Education* 48(7):573–576.

Nielson, J. (1986). "A Virtual Protocol Model for Computer-Human Interaction." *International Journal of Man-Machine Studies* 24:301–312.

Oliveira, Joao Batista (1990). "The Economics of Educational Software Portability." *Journal of Research on Computing in Education* 23(2):318–333.

Pahl, Ronald H. (1992). "Quality Management and Teacher Education." Unpublished paper.

Pahl, Ronald H. (1994). "Who Killed King Tut?—An Ancient Hypertext Murder Mystery." Rialto, CA: Pahl Education Consortium.

Pahl, Ronald H. (1995). "So Ya Wanna Be Rich?—A Spreadsheet Stock Market Simulation Game." Pp. 261–270 in *Computers in the Curriculum*, edited by Everett Murdock and Peter Desberg. Dubuque, IA: Wm. C. Brown.

Papert, Seymour (1980). *Mind Storms: Children, Computers and Powerful Ideas*. New York: Basic Books.

Perelman, L. (1989). "Schools: America's $500 Billion Flop." *Washington Post* (3 Dec.):C3.

Perez, Laura M. and Macey B. Taylor (1987). "Program Evaluation: British Council Software Series." *C.A.L.L. (Computers and Language Learning) Digest* 3(7):7–9.

Polin, Linda (1992). "Computers for Student Writing: The Relationship between Writer, Machine and Text." *The Computing Teacher* 18(7)6–7.

Polin, Linda (1991). "Vygotsky at the Computer: A Soviet View of 'Tools' for Learning." *The Computing Teacher* 19(1):25–27.

Ramsey, Sheila (1984). "Double Vision: Non-Verbal Behavior East and West." Pp. 139–167 in *Nonverbal Behavior: Perspectives, Applications, Intercultural Insights*, edited by Aaron Wolfgang. Toronto: C.J. Hogrefe.

Ray, Doris (1991). "Technology and Restructuring—Part I: New Educational Directions." *The Computing Teacher* 18(6):9–20.

Ray, Doris (1991). "Technology and Restructuring—Part II: New Organizational Directions." *The Computing Teacher* 18(7):8–12.

Reissman, Rose (1992). "Creating a Readers' Circle Online." *The Computing Teacher* 19(5):35–36.

Richman, Ellen (1988). "Equity in Technology." *The Computing Teacher* 15(5):35–37.

Robinson-Stavely, K. and J. Cooper (1990). "The Use of Computers for Writing: Effects on an English Composition Class." *Journal of Educational Computing Research* 6(1):41-48.

Roblyer, M.D. (1992). "Electronic Hands-Across the Ocean: The Florida-England Connection." *The Computing Teacher* 19(5)16–19.

Rooze, Gene E. and Terry Northrup (1989). *Computers, Thinking, and Social Studies*. Englewood, CO: Teacher Ideas Press.

Roszak, Theodore (1986). *The Cult of Information: The Folklore of Computers and the True Art of Thinking*. New York: Pantheon.

Rousseau, Jean Jacques (translated by Alan Bloom) (1979). *Emile.* New York: Basic Books.

Samples, Bob (1987). *Open Mind Whole Mind*. Rolling Hills Estates, CA: Jalmar Press.

Schipper, Diane (1991). "Practical Ideas: Literature, Computers, and Students with Special Needs." *The Computing Teacher* 19(2):33–37.

Schneidewind, John (1992). "Technology Gains Drive Prices Lower." *USA Today* (July 9):B1–B2.

Schubert, Jane G. (1986). "Gender Equity in Computer Learning." *Theory into Practice* 25(4):267–275.

Schwartz, Evan I. (1994). "Power to the People." *WIRED* December:88–92.

Scollon, Ron and Suzanne Scollon (1985). *The Problem of Power*. Haines, AK: Guttenberg Dump.

Shennum, William A. and Marcella C. Nino (1992). "The Five Acres Computer Learning Project." *The Computing Teacher* 19(5):41–43.

Snyder, Tom and Jane Palmer (1986). *In Search of the Most Amazing Thing: Children, Education and Computers*. Reading, MA: Addison-Wesley.

Tannen, Deborah (1986). *That's Not What I Meant!* New York: William.

Taylor, R.P. and N. Cunniff (1988). "Moving Computing and Education Beyond Rhetoric." In *Computing and Education: The Second Frontier*, edited by R. McClintock. New York: Teachers College Press.

Thornburg, David D. (1990). "Preparing Our Children for Their Future, Not Our Past." *CUE Newsletter* 12(4):8–9.

Thornburg, David D. (1995). *Electronic Learning.* January:20–21. Thornburg's book, *Education in the Communication Age*, can be obtained by calling 1-415-508-0314 or e-mailing dthornburg@aol.com.

Watson, Jim (1990–1991). "Cooperative Learning and Computers: One Way to Address Student Differences." *The Computing Teacher* 18(4):9–12.

Wombi, B. (1988). "Domination by Cooperation." *IDRC Reports* 17(1):24–25.

Woodrow, Janice E.J. (1991). "Teacher Perceptions of Computer Needs." *Journal of Research on Computing in Education* 23(4):475–493.

Chapter Thirteen

ACADEMIC FREEDOM

Jack L. Nelson
Rutgers University

IT IS APPROPRIATE TO END A BOOK on critical issues in social studies with a chapter on academic freedom. This topic transcends the traditional educational focus on teaching practice and the school curriculum. It ties together the fundamental grounds for social studies instruction in American schools with the most significant aspect of teaching. It includes the essential rationale for social education in grades K to 12 and through higher education, a philosophic set of ideals for the field, curricular expectations drawn from the nature of social studies knowledge, and an expression of the necessity for freedom for teachers and students to ensure that the rationale is upheld.

Academic freedom can be defined as essentially the same as excellent teaching: the right and responsibility to search for and express knowledge. To expand one point in the definition, the right of teachers and students to academic freedom carries a collateral responsibility to the interests of knowledge. The National Council for the Social Studies Position Statement on The Freedom to Teach and the Freedom to Learn notes:

> Basic to a democratic society are the freedoms of teachers to teach and of students to learn.... A teacher's freedom to teach involves both the right and the responsibility to use the highest intellectual standards in studying, investigating, presenting, interpreting, and discussing facts and ideas relevant to his or her field of professional competence. (1974)

Academic freedom is an especially significant concern for social studies teachers because 1) social studies is the subject most directly connected with the basic ideas of democratic society, and 2) social studies is the subject most vulnerable to political restraint and censorship. This duality, an educational responsibility to the core of a democratic society and a vulnerability that results from the proper exercise of that responsibility, underscores the importance of academic freedom for teachers and students in social studies.

Academic freedom exists within social and educational contexts and is limited or amplified by those contexts. An understanding of those settings, in their diversity, assists in understanding the concept of academic freedom and the various threats to it. In differing time periods, and in divergent communities in the same time period, threats to academic freedom increase or subside. There has never been a time or a community where there was not some threat, but there are periods and communities where such threats are minimal and freedom is more assured. In the American democracy at the end of the twentieth century, there is still a need for vigilance to protect and further develop the ideal of academic freedom.

This chapter makes several claims and examines counter arguments against those claims. One claim is that democratic civic education is a special responsibility of social studies. A second claim is that the basis of good social studies instruction is controversies—controversy is the vital element in the field. The third claim is that censorship in a variety of forms arises because of controversies that should be examined in social studies classes. Fourth, this chapter claims that academic freedom is the single most important aspect of teaching—academic freedom is what makes teaching a profession. And the fifth claim is that the previous three claims are not well understood in social studies education or in teacher-education programs where social studies teachers are prepared.

These are intertwined ideas: a democracy depends upon an enlightened public and opportunity for dissent; enlightenment and divergent views are the stuff of controversy; and if controversy is basic to social studies and censorship is one of the responses to controversy, a strong and reasoned sense of academic freedom is key to excellent social studies instruction. This chapter will, first, consider the democratic root of social education; second, examine controversial social studies topics; third, discuss the nature and forms of censorship; and, fourth, pursue the claim about academic freedom.

Democracy and Schooling

Democracy, as a succession of political theorists have argued, requires an knowledgeable public. A knowledgeable public is, itself, dependent on education. Bertrand Russell identified this point in his statement that without universal education, "democracy cannot exist except as an empty form" (1928, p. 128). Universal education, however, can also occur in a dictatorship. It is not simply the fact that schools are readily available to the populace that democracy is supported; rather, the nature and form of that schooling determines the quality of democratic education.

Without access to information and ideas, and the development of critical thinking necessary for a knowledgeable public, universal education can be detrimental to democracy. Russell recognized this potential defect in noting that universal schooling under governmental supervision runs the risk of teaching docility, undue respect for existing institutions and authority, and the avoidance of criticism. There are many examples of this problem in the schools of various nations, including the United States. Some of these are explored later in the discussion of problems in democratic schooling and on the topic of censorship.

The key point here is that simply requiring school-age students to be in school does not a democracy make. Some key factors in democratic schooling separate it from the mere mandate for universal schooling. Democracy is furthered through critical thinking, access to information and ideas, providing credible divergent views, and active participation in public life. American schools have an immense responsibility to educate in these areas.

Historically, U.S. schools have undertaken democratic education as a social studies focus. In curriculums dating back to the 1600s, the secondary-school social studies subjects of moral philosophy, civics, and history provided basic ideas related to democratic life. From his tours of the United States in the middle 1800s, Alexis de Tocqueville found that social education contributed significantly to democracy, "It cannot be doubted that in the United States the instruction of the people powerfully contributes to support the democratic republic" (de Tocqueville, 1850, edited by Mayer, 1969, p. 304).

Later, courses in such fields as sociology, economics, psychology, global studies, and law-related education also featured the development of such democratic concepts as equality, justice, and human rights. Social studies instruction in elementary schools has long involved consideration of personal, family, and community development within a democratic setting. Aside from the sometimes excessive indoctrination to simplisitic patriotism found in some elementary schools, most elementary-school social studies programs emphasize developing attitudes and behaviors consistent with democratic citizenship. And modern progressive schools of all levels encourage democratic values, critical thinking, and student participation in social life.

Although the whole school is involved in education for democracy, social studies takes central academic responsibility for it. Other subjects (for example, English, math, science, the arts, physical education, and vocations) often include democratic ideas and classroom practices, but none has this as a central focus. English is closest because the study of literature assists in understanding personal, political, and social values. Social studies, however, is the core subject for democratic education. It is the field that takes on the primary task of civic education and its democratic ideals.

This history of democratic education shows considerable success over the long haul. Henry Steele Commager noted,

> No other people ever demanded so much of schools and of education as have the American. No other was ever so well served by its schools and its educators.... From the very beginning of our national existence, education has had very special tasks to perform in America. Democracy could not work without an enlightened electorate....To the schools went the momentous responsibility of inculcating democracy, nationalism, and equalitarianism. (1964, p. 546).

There are, however, some continuing and current strains in the provision and improvement of democratic education.

Some Problems in Democratic Education

The link between school and democracy is widely understood in the United States, but it may have become so common that it has lost its vitality. We make the statement that democracy depends upon schooling without examining its meaning and its practice in modern society. Many school-district curriculum guides include strong statements about teaching democratic values and student participation in society, but the school itself may convey an undemocratic hidden curriculum (Apple, 1990; Giroux, 1988). Schools in which student and faculty views are not given serious consideration, where authoritarian edicts and rigid rules constitute school governance, where there are no activities that foster student participation in the life of the school, and where restrictions limit student and faculty freedom to study social issues are hardly able to exemplify democratic values. Students learn the hidden curriculum, that democracy is something to which we give lip service only.

In addition, the vast majority of social studies curriculum documents include as an objective developing student critical thinking as preparation for knowledgeable life in a democracy, but the actual curriculum is often devoid of critical-thinking content or process. Students are expected to accept platitudes about democracy and slogans for critical thinking, but are not expected to actually engage in democratic decision making on real issues or the critical thinking that should precede it. There is an unwritten assumption that students should hear that the United States is a democracy and that thinking citizens are necessary to its survival, but that it is too risky to actually expect students to engage in critical thinking on community and personal issues or participate in school governance.

Another problem in democratic education exists in the nationalistic emphasis that permeates some school curricula, textbooks, and other features of the social studies program. Nationalistic education consists of deliberate efforts to use the schools to require students to have simplistic, positive views of the nation-state and its government and negative views of any ideas considered to be counter-national (Naylor, 1973; Nelson, 1976).

In fact, every nation provides forms of nationalistic education in its schools. Where nationalistic education undermines democratic education is where the emphasis on patriotic chauvinism requires contorting knowledge to hide the defects that each nation has, or to give an unnecessarily negative portrayal of counter-national ideas. These efforts deny critical thinking, a basic condition in an open democracy. Examples of this in the United States include unscholarly curriculum and textbook treatments of U.S. history that suggest that we are a chosen people, superior to others (Gellerman, 1938; Billington, 1966). Many patriotic groups in the United States have a history of pursuing political restraint or censorship to ensure that nationalistic education occurs, despite the loss to democratic education (Pierce, 1933; Beale, 1936). Such attempts to restrain or censor social studies instruction are an obvious attack on academic freedom (Ochoa, 1991; Daly, 1991).

Clearly many issues remain in developing an enlightened electorate for a democracy. It is not self-evident that schools and teachers consistently and continuously have the requisite freedoms to fulfill their democratic obligation. Self-governance necessitates freedom of thought; schooling for self-governance must be consistent by providing academic freedom for teachers and students. To do otherwise limits democracy because a lack of academic freedom cripples the mind, restricts expression, and distorts the search for truth.

Academic Freedom and Democracy

Academic freedom is important to the whole of education in that a free society cannot thrive without the freedom of students and teachers to inquire. John Dewey put it succinctly but powerfully, saying, "Since freedom of mind and freedom of expression are the root of all freedom, to deny freedom in education is a crime against democracy" (1936, p. 136). All of education suffers when the academic freedom of teachers of any subject is restricted, but social studies education in the United States has a special obligation to democracy and to the freedom that it entails. Teachers, in fulfilling this obligation, often run into problems generated by the second claim of this chapter—that the center of social studies is controversy.

Controversy and Social Studies

Controversy is at the heart of social studies instruction. Carole Hahn, in discussing the substantial scholarly work on the relation between social studies instruction and controversy, stated: "The rationale for including controversial issues in social studies instruction rests on the necessity of preparing citizens to participate in the democratic decision-making processes within a pluralistic society" (1990, p. 470). She further noted that research over the past quarter-century consistently shows positive citizenship results from having students explore controversial issues in an "open, supportive classroom atmosphere" (1990). Other scholars have agreed that controversies are basic to social studies instruction (Engle and Ochoa, 1988; Oliver and Shaver, 1974; Hunt and Metcalf, 1968).

The essential content of the field is controversies in

the past, present, and future in local and global settings; the social sciences, humanities, and organization of knowledge; the personal and the social.

No one seriously argues that the historical and contemporary material selected for instruction in social studies is everything that has occurred or is occurring; there would be simply too much to cover. Social studies, instead, consists primarily of those events considered important. And important events are almost always those surrounded by controversies.

The American Revolution is among the most taught topics in social studies. It was a very controversial war, and some historical interpretations of the war are very controversial. Tories and rebels were in active and serious opposition, and few escaped the turmoil of the war. Although the Revolution can be taught as though it is merely an archival artifact of history, that approach destroys the sense of its actual controversiality and the historical disputes over the causes and effects of it. Teaching this basic social studies information as though it involved no conflict takes away from its social studies value. That value rests on the idea that the American Revolution represents an important conflict in human and national history, something worth teaching every American student.

Every war is the result of controversy and the subject of historical controversy. In addition to wars, other examples of controversial and commonly taught historical content include politics, intrigue, social turmoil, mass movements, and intellectual ferment. Historical and current events important enough for social studies instruction are controversies. And futuristic study is, by its nature, controversial.

Similarly, local-to-global settings in which these historic events occurred provide a richer context for their study, necessary to better understanding. As with historical material of worth, the most valuable geographic ideas for social studies instruction are also based on or enveloped by controversy. It is true that physical geography mainly provides map or globe information to understand location, and is not especially controversial except in theoretic terms. But cultural geography, political geography, and economic geography constitute the main substance of geographic learning in social studies. These areas are controversial. Examining current ethnic and economic issues in Eastern Europe, Africa, or South America requires understanding of more than physical location. Significantly divergent interpretations given to territoriality claims by diverse groups, climatological effects of pollution, alterations in trade routes, and strategic considerations of political locations illustrate the kinds of conflicts inherent in geographic study. Cultural, economic, and political considerations are controversial and should be examined in social studies courses. Other examples of local-to-global controversies for social studies instruction include various environmental issues, disparate global economics, and nationalistic terrorism.

Knowledge derived from other social science and humanities fields and used to inform social studies is also based upon controversial events and explanations. Sociology, economics, political science, anthropology, psychology, urban study, policy studies, gerontology, women's studies, ethnic studies, philosophy, ethics, and literature each provide substantial controversial material for social studies courses (Nelson and Michaelis, 1980). The subject of knowledge itself is controversial (Young, 1971; Popkewitz, 1987; Cherryholmes, 1988; Stanley, 1992). What knowledge, who decides, and what interests are served by the organization of knowledge are fundamental questions of the critical literature (Nelson, Carlson, and Palonsky, 1993). They are primary questions for schools, and for the social studies.

Personal and social controversies are the third main element of social studies. Ideas about self-concept, self-respect, and self-development often conflict with societal norms. Individualism and individuality can be understood as competing concepts, one emphasizing egotistic elements and selfishness and the other independence and creativity. Both can be situated in conflict with social roles, expectations, and responsibilities. In addition, personal and social controversies surround such significant concepts as the relative weight of individual rights and social order, justice and equality, affirmative action and discrimination, and personal development and social responsibility. Disputes over child rearing, provisions for health care, racism and sexism, employment policies, crime, pornography, and the influence of social class illustrate these social studies controversies.

A Counter-Argument: Social Studies Is Traditional History

Some consider social studies to be historical and social-scientific information to be transmitted to youth (Ravitch and Finn, 1989; National Commission for the Social Studies in the Schools, 1989; Whelan, 1992). This position does not deny that controversies exist in social studies material, but it claims that such controversies are not the core of the field; rather, proponents argue that a specific body of traditional history and geography needs to be transmitted and should be the center of social studies instruction.

The idea of transmitting information drawn from the work of historians and certain social scientists implies that it can be done without controversy. Transmission suggests that the material is not altered by critical thinking or diverse views. By shifting curricular emphasis from current or pervasive social issues to traditionally well-known information distilled by generations of historians, schools provide less likelihood that diverse views and controversy will arise. This view of social studies content assumes that information on the founding of the nation, its wars, and its political development has been extensively examined by historians and that there are generally accepted versions that should be transmitted by teachers. Those teachers are not expected to be scholars, to express skepticism, or to inject controversy into the transmission.

The primary purpose for social studies instruction in this mode is to ensure that students learn factual material that has been approved by scholars in the field. History taught under the rubric of transmission of cultural heritage is the accumulation of necessary data widely recognized as appropriate (Ravitch and Finn, 1989; Hirsch, 1987). If there is such general agreement by scholars on accuracy, and general agreement that the information is important, there is likely to be little that is controversial.

One principal problem with this approach was noted by John Dewey:

> Since the subject matter as well as standards of proper conduct are handed down from the past, the attitude of pupils must, upon the whole, be one of docility, receptivity, and obedience" (1936, p. 18).

This comment is strikingly similar to the defect noted by Bertrand Russell, and cited earlier in this chapter, for universal schooling that is not democratic. Transmission of history and social-science information can be accomplished without getting students or their parents upset. The socially acceptable information to be transmitted is likely to be objectionable only to a small fringe of people who have more radical views. A further assumption is that the information approved by scholars and the mainstream public is important enough to be transmitted to younger generations.

It is true that one tradition of social studies is presenting chronological American history in a manner that sterilizes all controversy. As Robert

Barr, James Barth, and Samuel Shermis (1977) found in their studies, transmission of the cultural heritage is the most popular approach to social studies instruction.

It is possible to be exceptionally boring while teaching about history, the social sciences, and social issues. The fascinating subjects identified previously can be taught as sterile facts without dispute. However, as Alfred North Whitehead identified this problem:

> In the history of education, the most striking phenomenon is that schools of learning, which at one epoch are alive with a ferment of genius, in a succeeding generation exhibit merely pedantry and routine. The reason is, that they are overladen with inert ideas. Education with inert ideas is not only useless, it is, above all things, harmful (1929, p.13).

Social studies teachers who recognize their special obligation to education for democracy and who understand the controversial nature of social education, realize the second fundamental reason that academic freedom is of such importance to social studies: the vulnerability of the field.

Social Studies as the Most Vulnerable Subject: Censorship

Social studies is the subject field most concerned with human behavior, moral ideas, politics, economics, interpretations of history, and the wide variety of other social issues about which people feel very strongly. As a result, there is a long history of efforts by various groups and individuals to censor, restrict, control, and influence social studies teaching (Sinclair, 1924; Beale, 1936; Pierce, 1933; Gellerman, 1938; Nelson, 1976; Palonsky and Nelson, 1986; Nelson and Stanley, 1985). Each effort is an attempt by that person or group to "put their spin" on what is taught to youth about life and society. And some of these efforts are very serious and threatening attacks on teachers.

Consider these examples:

- A high school teacher of economics in Grand Island, Nebraska, was ordered by her principal to stop teaching politics in her economics class, as though politics and economics have no relationship with each other (Strope and Broadwell, 1990).
- A teacher using a simulation game to teach about the Civil War was called in by the principal who told her to avoid discussion of blacks in American history and indicated that controversial material should not be discussed in the classroom (Kingsville Independent School District v. Cooper, 1980). The court upheld the teacher's rights in this case, but the chilling effect from such administrative threats frightens many teachers into submission.
- In California, a local school board passed a resolution that no material with "Russia" in it could be used until the Board had approved it.

- A teacher in a middle school in New Jersey marked out all the swear words in classroom copies of *A Day in the Life of Ivan Denisovich* before students could read the books.
- An elementary school teacher from Colorado, who later won the NCSS Academic Freedom Award for her courage, was prevented by the school board from showing a feature movie film about a man who runs for major political office because "it was too controversial and showed politics in a bad light." She got the NCSS award by resisting and fighting the censorship—and she won.

Edward Jenkinson (1990), professor of English education, recently identified a group of right-wing critics of the public schools and their efforts to censor and restrict what is taught. He cited, for example, the work of the Reverend Tim LaHaye, a founder of the Moral Majority, who is quoted as writing:

> Secular educators no longer make learning their primary objective. Instead our public schools have become conduits to the minds of our youth, training them to be anti-God, anti-family, anti-free enterprise and anti-American (LaHaye, 1983, cited in Jenkinson, 1990, p. 10).

Jenkinson, from his 17 years studying the many attempts to censor school materials, identified the following as under attack by these right-wing critics: sociology, future studies, global education, sex education, drug and alcohol education, humanism, critical thinking, decision making, values education, world geography, and American history where the term democracy rather than republic is used to define the nation and which includes positive views of the United Nations or international studies. Obviously, this list is part of the content of social studies.

Some may naively think that censorship is an historic problem, occurring in the past during the morally strict Victorian age, the nation-threatening world wars, and the politically volatile McCarthy period, but not now in our more sophisticated age. Certainly, there was much overt censorship in those times, restricting sexual material, military information, and political and economic ideas. But censorship is not a problem that has been solved. Sexual material, such as the debate over what to tell students about AIDS, is still subject to severe efforts to restrict information and discussion. Military information—as the "pool news media coverage" of the Gulf War showed so clearly—is restricted in some ways more than the formal censorship of World War II. And political and economic ideas are still restricted in schools and textbooks.

Increasing Censorship: A New McCarthyism?

Indeed, there is evidence that the incidence of censorship has actually increased in the current period. People for the American Way have been tracking, state by state, incidents of censorship in and around schools for about a decade. Their most recent analysis of educational censorship shows that the number of attacks on academic freedom more than doubled between 1982 and now. They identify a contemporary resurgence of right-wing censorship activities (*Attacks on the Freedom to Learn*, 1985–86, 1991, 1994). The most popular topics of censorship included satanism, sex, creationism, and so-called anti-American material. Certain authors have been among the most censored in schools; they include John Steinbeck, Judy Blume, Stephen King, and J.D. Salinger.

Other current evidence confirms the extensive nature of censoring activities and the fragility of academic freedom in the schools. The American Library Association regularly produces the *Intellectual Freedom Newsletter*, which cites examples of censorship of books and materials in schools and libraries across the United States. Each issue is filled with examples of efforts to restrict knowledge. Literature censorship has not abated during the past decades ("Censorship: a Continuing Problem," 1990; Simmons, 1991). School boards and administrators in many districts still exhibit censorious interests, limiting teacher and student freedom (Mesibov, 1991; Daly, 1991). Recent court decisions permit school officials to censor some school materials and allow extra latitude for administrators to censor student newspapers before they are printed (Pico, 1990; "Censorship," 1990).

Overt, Covert, and Self-Censorship

Overt censorship, where officials take formal action to ban, restrict, or limit material, appears to be on the increase. Covert censorship is often hidden, but appears to constitute the majority of censorious efforts. Covert censorship can include such practices as a parent complaint to a school principal, who surreptitiously takes a book out of circulation to avoid controversy. It can also include changes by publishers during textbook development to avoid potential conflict. Covert forms of censorship are not easily detected by teachers because the potentially controversial material is simply not available easily.

One type of covert censorship can be called teacher self-censorship. It is covert because the action is only known to the teacher, but the result on learning is the same. Teacher self-censorship differs from professional judgment about what to include in a class. The primary difference lies in the reasons for selecting or rejecting ideas for students to examine. All teachers must limit what they cover, simply because there is not enough time or the students are not yet ready or there are academic reasons to exempt certain information. Teachers who make a professional judgment based on the best academic interests of the class are not engaging in self-censorship. Teacher self-censorship occurs when the reasons for not including some material are that they might be controversial, or the administration or board might object, or some parents or community group might complain. When these political reasons are the basic grounds for limiting material, the action is self-censorship. Unfortunately, it is not easy to see teacher self-censorship, but it may be the most frequent type of censorship in schools.

Despite the obvious evidence of censorship and attempts at censorship in schools, there are mixed opinions about the legal rights of censors and of teachers (O'Neil, 1981; Mawdsley and Mawdsley, 1988; Turner-Egner, 1989). In the main, teachers have considerable rights regarding academic decisions about teaching materials and teaching methods. School boards, in some states, have considerable power over the curriculum and library materials. There is much uncharted law on censorship in society and in schools, but many cases. However, a high proportion of censoring efforts do not become legal issues; teachers accommodate and do not resist or they do resist and the censors withdraw. Much school censorship occurs because of fear of controversy by boards, administrators, and teachers—not because the censors have the right to restrict ideas.

The extensive evidence of censorship in and around schools may mislead teachers into the idea that they should avoid controversy so they don't get into trouble. As suggested earlier, that would be a disservice to the field of social studies, based as it is on human controversy. Avoiding controversy, and the potential of censorship, may be safe, but it may not be high quality teaching. The suffering is borne by students who are restricted in their intellectual development by teachers who are excessively fearful. Teachers should be knowledgeable about legal, social, and historic conditions related to controversy and censorship. They should recognize the various rights involved in compulsory education: students, parents, administrators, boards. And teachers should be sensitive to community interests, student capacities, and to their professional responsibilities. A solid grounding in the relationship of democracy to social studies, and the resulting necessity for academic freedom, is essential for the good social studies teacher.

Academic Freedom and the Teaching Profession

One claim of this chapter is that academic freedom is the core of the teaching profession. The point here is that every profession has some defining characteristic, some ideal toward which it continues to strive. For people in law, it is justice; for medical practitioners, it is health. For the profession of teaching, the defining characteristic is education—the enlightenment of society. Education and enlightenment require freedom of intellect and of expression. That required freedom is academic freedom for teachers to ensure academic freedom for students (Nelson, 1990; Nelson, Carlson, Palonsky, 1993).

The National Council for the Social Studies has developed a well-reasoned statement of principles on academic freedom that encompasses this idea of centering the profession on that freedom and indicates some of the problems. The NCSS statement, part of which was noted earlier in this essay, includes the following:

> Basic to a democratic society are the freedoms of teachers to teach and of students to learn. Especially as they apply to pre-collegiate public education, court decisions, unfortunately, have not consistently supported these rights throughout the nation....The present lack of judicial clarity places a heavy burden of responsibility on pre-collegiate educators....A teacher's freedom to teach involves both the right *and* the responsibility to use the highest intellectual standards in studying, investigating, presenting, interpreting, and discussing facts and ideas relevant to his or her field of professional competence. As professionals, teachers must be free to examine controversial issues openly in the classroom (NCSS, 1974).

The one element that unites teachers of all levels and subject fields in a profession is academic freedom. We may differ significantly in our approaches to the classroom, in our academic specializations, or in our understanding of the learning process. But we have a common commitment to the liberating qualities of education. A few teachers may not share this view, just as in law or medicine, there are a few practitioners who do not have an interest in justice or improving health, but that does not destroy the essential core of the profession. Without a commitment to freedom, teachers are no more than mechanistic functionaries who can be manipulated by power.

Social Studies Teachers and Critical Competence

For teachers, the pursuit of academic freedom requires one fundamental condition: competence. Competence is a combination of critical knowledge and wisdom. For teachers, this condition mandates that they know their subject and their students and that they exercise wise judgment in determining what is taught, when, and how. Further, as William Stanley points out, social studies teacher competence must go beyond technical descriptions of subject knowledge and teaching skills to include critical examination of each (Stanley, 1991; Whitson and Stanley, 1988). This critical competence assumes that the teacher has intellectual interests and is more than a mechanical transmitter of information. It also assumes that such competence involves providing active participation by students in considering and challenging ideas. This is the essence of real critical thinking, seeing traditional knowledge as open to criticism and recognizing conflicts in interpretations of knowledge. It is also consistent with the idea that social studies is made up of controversial content.

Teacher competence is a necessary condition for academic freedom; otherwise freedom is merely license for a teacher to do whatever she or he wishes. Teachers who flagrantly abuse their status in classrooms do not deserve academic freedom; they have not shown competence, and they have abused the academic freedom of students. The basis on which tenure should rest is that a teacher has demonstrated competence and deserves the protection to academic freedom afforded by tenure. Pre-tenure teachers also have academic freedom, but it is not as well protected. Pre-tenured teachers are partly protected by laws and partly by the organizational strength of tenured teachers who should stand up for academic freedom. Tenure should be seen primarily as a protection for academic freedom, such that tenured teachers cannot be fired for searching for and presenting their views of truth. Among the responsibilities of tenure for tenured teachers is to support nontenured teachers in protecting their academic freedom.

A Counter-Argument: Academic Freedom Is for Professors Only

Because of the history of American education and the compulsory nature of pre-collegiate schooling, some argue that academic freedom is reserved only for scholars in universities and is improperly suited to classroom teachers (Kirk, 1955; Hook, 1953). This argument follows from the idea that academic freedom is intended to protect the search for truth by professors and is limited to findings in the scholar's field. This approach to academic freedom would not protect professors who make political statements in public, except when those professors are doing research on that political topic. Thus, the professor of English who speaks out about politics or the running of the university can lose his or her teaching position. But if that professor presents a controversial statement on the topic in English in which he or she is an expert, he or she would not risk loss of employment.

From that reasoning, this position holds that academic freedom is too fragile to make it available for pre-college-level teachers who are not academic scholars. By broadening its protection to include all teachers, it loses its special protection for scholars in their fields. This position accepts the idea that teachers are employed mainly to transmit information to youth, not to seek truth. From this view, the schoolteacher's role is to learn what scholars have found and to present it to students. For that, goes the argument, teachers do not require academic freedom.

A second rationale for not extending academic freedom to school teachers is that most of them work in publicly financed schools that students are compelled to attend. The compulsory nature of schooling does not allow students to avoid teachers. That puts a special burden on teachers to not attempt to impose their views on a captive audience. Parental rights to determine what their children learn are paramount, and teachers are perceived essentially as civil servants employed to fulfill the expectations of the community and the state. As state and community employees, teachers have an obligation to teach that which the government deems appropriate. This would mean that any material considered objectionable to the community or the state would not be taught. For this kind of work, academic freedom is not necessary.

These arguments against academic freedom for teachers are serious and thoughtful, although this chapter takes the position that they are incorrect. There is something to be said for the special protection of scholars and for the fact that students are a captive audience. But teachers, in the contemporary society, should be intellectual scholars and should be capable of making professional judgments of the needs and capacities of their students. These are necessary conditions of the teaching competence identified earlier.

In early America, many teachers were ill-educated. Ichabod Crane, in Washington Irving's story, *The Legend of Sleepy Hollow*, may be an example of this. However, current state requirements for teacher credentials, academic standards to complete them, the period of student teaching to judge pedagogical talents, and the two or three year full-time probationary period of teaching before tenure provide much more evidence of the competence of teachers and their scholarly quality. Nearly all teachers now have bachelor's degrees, and most have or are working on master's degrees. Teachers have a right to expect professional treatment and an obligation to provide professional service. Professional service for teachers means opening ideas and expanding horizons for students while providing academic freedom for those students to consider controversial ideas. For social studies teachers, this is a very significant matter, basic to the field.

Although some in higher education might argue that they alone deserve academic freedom, there is general recognition in higher education of the need for teachers at all levels to be protected. The history of academic freedom in the United States shows that college professors were the first to claim academic freedom and have been especially active in its defense. The American Association of University Professors (AAUP) was formed in 1915 primarily to defend the academic freedom of professors. The AAUP developed the most prominent document on higher education freedom, *The 1940 Statement on Academic Freedom and Tenure*, and has been in the forefront of groups who support academic freedom. The AAUP investigates colleges when a complaint about academic freedom has occurred. If the investigation shows an infraction, the AAUP tries to resolve the matter; if the college administration won't correct the problem, the AAUP can vote to censure the administration and publishes those censured colleges in the AAUP journal, *Academe*. Professors are, thus, notified about the lack of protection at that college and many will not take positions there. The AAUP, however, does not claim that academic freedom is limited only to college-level teachers. Although their focus, naturally, is on colleges, they have been active in supporting academic freedom for pre-collegiate teachers. These actions include providing legal assistance, submitting amicus briefs on behalf of teacher freedom in teacher court cases, and developing a document indicating the link between college and pre-college teaching (*Liberty and Learning in the Schools*, 1986).

Academic Freedom and Teacher Education in Social Studies

Academic freedom is crucial to defending competent social studies teachers from attacks for doing what they should be doing. Yet, academic freedom is a topic often overlooked in teacher education and seldom covered during the probationary period in school districts. It is somewhat understandable why school administrators would not be eager to stimulate an interest in academic freedom during the probationary teaching period. It is not always in the administrators' interest to have an active and creative teaching force. But it is not clear why most standard textbooks used in teacher education provide much material on the history, philosophy, psychology, and practice of teaching—but little on academic freedom. It could be that the authors assume that academic freedom is already well accepted and need not be addressed, that it is too complicated and variant to be easily examined, or that it is not in their specialized knowledge. None of these reasons is sufficient, however. As argued previously, academic freedom is under continuous attack and is the core of the profession. Teachers-in-preparation need to discuss questions of academic freedom and examine the status of it in the schools.

Academic freedom is not a simple and obvious concept. Several divergent definitions and interpretations, and not all teacher activities, fall under its umbrella. First, academic freedom is not a license to do whatever any teacher desires to do. Its exercise requires competence and thought. Second, academic freedom is a freedom that has a very tenuous constitutional base and a variant court-case history in the United States. Third, differences of opinion exist among scholars about the extent to which academic freedom should be applied to teachers of all levels of school. And fourth, situations differ significantly, and academic freedom is one of those concepts, such as democracy and justice, that can be highly situation-specific. There is general support among educators for academic freedom, but wide disparities about what that means in practice.

Social studies education depends upon academic freedom to properly fulfill its obligations to improvements in student knowledge and in the civic culture. A democratic society demands it. Social studies teachers, as the most vulnerable of all teachers, should develop a well-reasoned code of professional conduct based on the concept of academic freedom for themselves and their students. There may be no better way to summarize a book on critical issues in social studies than to emphasize the necessary relationships among democracy, social studies, controversy, and academic freedom.

Reflective Questions

1. *Which teachers deserve the protection of academic freedom?*

2. *In what situations should parental rights supercede teacher freedoms?*

3. *How far should academic freedom protect teachers?*

4. *Why are social studies teachers more vulnerable than other teachers?*

5. *What kinds of teacher preparation should be available for dealing with academic freedom issues?*

6. *Should academic freedom include freedom for students to study whatever they wish?*

7. *What determines the limits of academic freedom for teachers and students?*

8. *What rights does the community have in educating young people?*

9. *How should censorship efforts be handled in schools?*

10. *Are there any sound reasons for censoring what is taught in social studies?*

11. *Who should determine, and through what process, how controversial topics are examined in social studies classes?*

12. *What are the current threats to academic freedom for social studies teachers and students, and how can they be addressed?*

GLOSSARY

academic freedom The liberty of thought claimed by teachers and students, including the right to "enjoy the freedom to study, to inquire, to speak..., to communicate... ideas" (*Dictionary of the History of Ideas*, 1973).

censorship Efforts to ban terms, ideas, books, topics, or other materials from use by schools, libraries, or other institutions.

political restraint Efforts to limit what is taught or how something is taught by putting pressure on school officials.

teacher self-censorship Avoiding potentially controversial material because some element in the community of the schools might object.

ANNOTATED BIBLIOGRAPHY

Attacks on the Freedom to Learn. (1982 to current). Washington, DC: People for the American Way.

This is an annual review of censorship efforts across the United States. It includes comparative data, by state, type of censor, and type of material censored. It is valuable information to keep track of threats to academic freedom.

Beale, Howard K. (1936). *Are American Teachers Free?* New York: Charles Scribner's.

This book is one in the series from the 1930s National Commission on Social Studies in the Schools. It reports on a major study of censorship and academic freedom conducted in the 1930s, but the problems it identifies are still relevant today.

Gellerman, William (1938). *The American Legion as Educator.* New York: Teachers College Press.

This book traces how one political organization tried to influence social studies teaching by censorship, coordinated attacks, nationwide and local political action, and developing its own American history textbook and trying to get it adopted in schools. It indicates the kinds of pressure that can be problematic for social studies teachers.

Hofstadter, Richard and Walter Metzger (1955). *The Development of Academic Freedom in the United States.* New York: Columbia University Press.

This historical treatment of the subject provides a useful perspective on why academic freedom is so fragile in American society.

Ochoa, Anna S., editor (1990). *Academic Freedom to Teach and to Learn.* Washington, DC: National Education Association.

This is a collection of articles on the topic of academic freedom, including a statement of rationale and many examples of problems as well as practical suggestions for school district policies and practices.

O'Neil, Robert S. (1981). *Classrooms in the Crossfire.* Bloomington: Indiana University Press.

This is a clearly written summary of court cases about academic freedom matters. It shows the mixed character of legal opinion on these matters.

The Rights of Students (1988). Washington, DC: American Civil Liberties Union.

This summarizes the legal basis for student rights and presents practical assistance. It is very useful as a guide and as class material for social studies classes on rights and responsibilities. Students need to know their legal rights.

The Rights of Teachers (1988). Washington, DC: American Civil Liberties Union.

This is a summary of teacher rights as determined by court cases and legal interpretations of laws. It is a very useful guide for teachers, and new editions include current information.

REFERENCES

American Association of University Professors (1986). *Liberty and Learning in the Schools*. Washington, DC: AAUP.

Apple, Michael (1990). *Ideology and Curriculum*. New York: Routledge & Kegan Paul.

Attacks on the Freedom to Learn (1991, 1990, 1985–86). Washington, DC: People for the American Way.

Barr, Robert, James Barth, and S. Samuel Shermis (1977). *Defending the Social Studies*. Washington, DC: National Council for the Social Studies, Bulletin 51.

Beale, Howard K. (1936). *Are American Teachers Free?* New York: Charles Scribner's.

Billington, Ray Allen (1966). *The Historian's Contribution to Anglo-American Misunderstanding*. New York: Hobbs, Dorman.

Bosmajian, H.A., editor (1987). *The First Amendment in the Classroom*. New York: Neal-Schuman.

Burress, L. and Edward B. Jenkinson (1982). *The Students' Right to Know*. Washington, DC: National Council of Teachers of English.

Carlson, Kenneth (1987). "Academic Freedom in Hard Times." *Social Education* 51:429–30.

"Censorship, A Continuing Problem" (1990). *English Journal Roundtable*, 79:87–89.

Cherryholmes, Cleo (1988). *Power and Criticism: Poststructural Investigations in Education*. New York: Teachers College Press.

Commager, Henry Steele (1964). *Living Ideas in America*. New York: Harper & Row.

Daly, James K. (1991). "The Influence of Administrators on the Teaching of Social Studies." *Theory and Research in Social Education* 14:267–282.

Dewey, John (1938). *Experience and Education*. New York: Macmillan.

Dewey, John (1936). "The Social Significance of Academic Freedom." *Social Frontier* 2:136.

Engle, Shirley and Anna Ochoa (1988). *Education for Democratic Citizenship: Decision-Making in the Social Studies*. New York: Teachers College Press.

Forum (Bulletin). Washington, DC: People for the American Way.

Gellerman, W. (1938). *The American Legion as Educator*. New York: Teachers College Press.

Giroux, Henry (1988). *Schooling and the Struggle for Public Life: Critical Pedagogy in the Modern Age*. Minneapolis: University of Minnesota Press.

Hahn, Carole (1990). "Controversial Issues in Social Studies." Pp. 470–480 in *Handbook of Research on Social Studies Teaching and Learning*, edited by James P. Shaver. New York: Macmillan.

Hentoff, Nat (1980). *The First Freedom: The Tumultuous History of Free Speech in America*. New York: Delacorte.

Hirsch, E.D., Jr. (1987). *Cultural Literacy: What Every American Needs to Know*. Boston: Houghton Mifflin.

Hook, Sydney (1953). *Heresy, Yes—Conspiracy, No*. New York: John Day.

Hunt, Maurice P. and Lawrence E. Metcalf (1955, 1968). *Teaching High School Social Studies*. New York: Harper & Brothers.

Jenkinson, Edward B. (1990). "Child Abuse in the Hate Factory." In *Academic Freedom to Teach and to Learn*, edited by Anna Ochoa. Washington, DC: National Education Association.

Kirk, Russell (1955). *Academic Freedom*. Chicago: Regnery.

Kingsville Independent School District v. Cooper (1980). 611 F.2d 1109 (5th Cir).

Liberty and Learning in the Schools (1986). Washington, DC: American Association of University Professors.

Mawdsley, R.D. and A.L. Mawdsley (1988). *Free Expression and Censorship: Public Policy and the Law*. Topeka: National Organization on Legal Problems of Education.

Mesibov, L.L. (1991). "Teacher-Board of Education Conflicts over Instructional Material." *School Law Bulletin* 22:10–15.

National Commission on Social Studies in the Schools (1989). *Charting a Course*. Washington, DC: The National Commission.

National Council for the Social Studies (1974). *The Freedom to Teach and the Freedom to Learn*. Position Statement. Washington, DC: National Council for the Social Studies.

Naylor, David T. (1973). "A Study of the Perceptions of New Jersey Educators Regarding Nationalistic Education." *Theory and Research in Social Education* 1:49–73.

Nelson, Jack L. (1976). "Nationalistic versus Global Education." *Theory and Research in Social Education* 4:33–50.

Nelson, Jack L. (1990). "The Significance of and Rationale for Academic Freedom." Pp. 10–21 in *Academic Freedom to Teach and Learn*, edited by Anna S. Ochoa. Washington, DC: National Education Association.

Nelson, Jack and John Michaelis (1980). *Secondary Social Studies*. Englewood Cliffs: Prentice Hall.

Nelson, Jack L. and Anna S. Ochoa (1987). "Academic Freedom, Censorship, and the Social Studies." *Social Education* 51:424–27.

Nelson, Jack L. and William Stanley (1985). "Academic Freedom in Social Education: Fifty Years Standing Still." *Social Education* 49:662–64.

Nelson, Jack L., Kenneth Carlson, and Stuart Palonsky (1993). *Critical Issues in Education: A Dialectic Approach*, 2nd ed. New York: McGraw-Hill.

Ochoa, Anna S., editor (1990). *Academic Freedom to Teach and Learn*. Washington, DC: National Education Association.

Oliver, Donald W. and James P. Shaver (1966, 1974). *Teaching Public Issues in the High School*. Logan: Utah State University Press.

O'Neil, Robert S. (1981). *Classrooms in the Crossfire*. Bloomington: Indiana University Press.

Palonsky, Stuart and J. Nelson (1986). "Political Restraint in the Socialization of Student Teachers." *Theory and Research in Social Education* 7:19–34.

Pico, S. (1990). "An Introduction to Censorship." *School Media Quarterly*. 18:84–87.

Pierce, Bessie (1933). *Citizens' Organizations and the Civic Training of Youth*. New York: Charles Scribner's.

Popkewitz, Thomas (1987). *The Formation of the School Subjects*. Philadelphia: Falmer.

Ravitch, Diane and Chester Finn (1987). *What Do our 17-Year-Olds Know?* A Report on the First National Assessment of History and Literature. New York: Harper & Row.

Russell, Bertrand (1928). *Sceptical Essays*. London: G. Allen.

Simmons, John S. (1991). "Censorship in the Schools: No End in Sight." *ALAN Review* 18:6–8.

Sinclair, Upton (1924). *The Goslings*. Pasadena: Sinclair.

Stanley, William B. (1991). "Teacher Competence for Social Studies." Pp. 249–262 in *Handbook of Research on Social Studies Teaching and Learning*, edited by James P. Shaver. New York: Macmillan.

Stanley, William B. (1992). *Curriculum for Utopia: Social Reconstructionism and Critical Pedagogy in the Postmodern Era.* Albany: State University of New York Press.

Strope, J.L. and C. Broadwell (1990). "Academic Freedom: What the Courts Have Said." In *Academic Freedom to Teach and to Learn*, edited by Anna S. Ochoa. Washington, DC: National Education Association.

de Tocqueville, Alexis (1850, 1969). *Democracy in America*, edited by J.P. Mayer. New York: Doubleday.

Turner-Egner, J. (1989). "Teachers' Discretion in Selecting Instructional Materials and Methods." *West's Education Law Reporter* 53:365–379.

Whelan, Michael (1992). "History and the Social Studies: A Response to the Critics." *Theory and Research in Social Education* 20:2–16.

Whitehead, Alfred North (1929). *The Aims of Education and Other Essays.* New York: Macmillan.

Whitson, James Anthony and William Stanley (1988). *Practical Competence: A Rationale for Social Education.* Paper presented at National Council for Social Studies, Orlando, FL.

Young, M.F.D. (1971). *Knowledge and Control.* London: Collier-Macmillan.